ULTIMATE

JAPANESE

BEGINNER–INTERMEDIATE

ULTIMATE

JAPANESE

BEGINNER–INTERMEDIATE

HIROKO STORM, PH.D.,

TEIKYO LORETTO HEIGHTS UNIVERSITY,
DENVER, COLORADO

Previously published as *Living Language® Japanese All the Way™*

ACKNOWLEDGMENTS

Thanks to the Living Language team: Tom Russell, Elizabeth Bennett, Christopher Warnasch, Zviezdana Verzich, Suzanne McQuade, Amelia Muqaddam, Denise De Gennaro, Linda Schmidt, John Whitman, Alison Skrabek, Helen Kilcullen, Heather Lanigan, Fabrizio La Rocca, Guido Caroti, and Sophie Chin. Special thanks to everyone who assisted in the writing and development of this book: Fuhito Shimoyama, Ken-ichi Miura, Yuki Matsuda, Mutsuko Endo Hudson, Noriko Mizuno, and Ichiro Kishimoto.

CONTENTS

INTRODUCTION

Living Language® Ultimate Japanese is a practical and enjoyable way to learn Japanese. The complete course consists of this text and eight hours of recordings. You can, however, use the text on its own if you already know how to pronounce Japanese.

With *Ultimate Japanese*, you'll speak Japanese from the very beginning. Each lesson starts with a dialogue about common situations that you are likely to experience at home or abroad. You'll learn the most common and useful expressions for everyday conversation.

Key grammatical structures introduced in the dialogue are clearly explained in a separate section. The lessons build on one another. The material you've already studied is "recycled," or used again, in later lessons as you learn new words, phrases, and grammatical forms. This method helps you gradually increase your language skills while reinforcing and perfecting material learned previously. Separate reading and writing sections will gradually teach you how to read and write Japanese characters.

In addition, brief notes on cultural topics will add to your understanding of Japan, its language, and its people.

COURSE MATERIALS

THE MANUAL

Living Language® Ultimate Japanese consists of forty lessons, eight review sections, and four reading sections. The review sections appear after every five lessons, and the reading sections after every ten lessons. Read and study each lesson before listening to it on the recordings.

DAIAROOGU (Dialogue): Each lesson begins with a dialogue presenting a realistic situation in a Japanese locale. The dialogue is followed by a translation in colloquial English. Note that while there are many regional dialects and accents, we will be using standard Japanese grammar and vocabulary throughout the course.

HATSUON (Pronunciation): In lessons 1 through 10, you will learn the correct pronunciation of syllables and individual sounds.

BUNPOO TO YOOHOO (Grammar and Usage): This section explains the major grammatical points covered in the lesson. The heading of each topic corresponds to its listing in the table of contents.

MOJI (Characters): This reading and writing section will gradually teach you how to recognize, read, and write Japanese characters.

TANGO TO HYOOGEN (Vocabulary and Expressions): In this section you can review the words and expressions from the dialogue and learn additional vocabulary.

RENSHUU (Exercises): These exercises test your mastery of the lesson's essential vocabulary, structures, and Japanese characters. You can check your answers in the *KOTAE* (Answers) section.

KARUCHAA NOOTO (Cultural Note): These brief notes about Japanese customs put the language in its cultural context. Cultural awareness will enrich your understanding of Japanese and your ability to communicate effectively.

FUKUSHUU (Review): Review sections appear after every five lessons. These sections are similar to the exercises in format but integrate material from all the lessons you have studied to that point.

YOMU RENSHUU (Reading Practice): The four reading passages are written in Japanese characters and not translated. However, the material covered in the preceding lessons, along with the vocabulary notes that accompany the reading, will enable you to infer the meaning, just as you would when reading a newspaper abroad.

APPENDICES: There are two appendices—a summary of accents and a list of particles.

GLOSSARY: Be sure to make use of the two-way glossary in the back of the manual to check the meanings and connotations of new words.

INDEX: The manual ends with an index of all the grammar points covered in the lessons.

The appendices, glossary, and index make this manual an excellent source for future reference and study.

RECORDINGS (SETS A & B)

This course provides you with eight hours of audio practice. There are two sets of complementary recordings: The first is designed for use with the manual, while the second may be used without it. By listening to and imitating the native speakers, you will be able to improve your pronunciation and comprehension while learning to use new phrases and structures.

RECORDINGS FOR USE WITH THE MANUAL (SET A)

This set of recordings gives you four hours of audio practice in Japanese only, with translations in the manual. The dialogue of each lesson, the pronunciation sections of lessons 1 through 10, and the vocabulary section are featured on these recordings. All the words and expressions that are recorded appear in **boldfaced type** in your manual.

First, you will hear native Japanese speakers read the complete dialogue at a normal conversational pace without interruption; then you'll have a chance to listen to the dialogue a second time and repeat each phrase in the pauses provided.

Next, listen carefully to learn the sounds from the pronunciation sections. By repeating after the native speakers, you will gradually master the sounds.

Finally, the most important and commonly used vocabulary will also be modeled by the native speakers for you to repeat in the pauses provided.

After studying each lesson and practicing with Set A, go on to the second set of recordings (Set B), which you can use on the go—while driving, jogging, or doing housework.

RECORDINGS FOR USE ON THE GO (SET B)

The "On the Go" recordings give you four hours of audio practice in Japanese and English. Because they are bilingual, Set B recordings may be used without the manual, anywhere it's convenient to learn.

The forty lessons on Set B correspond to those in the manual. A bilingual narrator leads you through the four sections of each lesson.

The first section presents the most important phrases from the original dialogue. You will first hear the abridged dialogue at normal conversational speed. You'll then hear it again, phrase by phrase, with English translations and pauses for you to repeat after the native Japanese speakers.

The second section reviews and expands upon the vocabulary in the dialogue. Additional expressions show how the words may be used in other contexts. Again, you are given time to repeat the Japanese phrases.

In the third section, you'll explore the lesson's most important grammatical structures. After a quick review of the rules, you can practice with illustrative phrases and sentences.

The exercises in the last section integrate what you've learned and help you generate sentences in Japanese on your own. You'll take part in brief conversations, respond to questions, transform sentences, and occasionally translate. After you respond, you'll hear the correct answer from a native speaker.

The interactive approach on this set of recordings will teach you to speak, understand, and *think* in Japanese.

SYLLABLE TABLES

Japanese is spoken in distinct beats. Each beat has approximately the same duration and is referred to as a "mora." A mora is similar to a syllable, so this book uses the term "syllable" instead of "mora."

The Japanese syllables can be classified into six kinds:

NUMBER OF SYLLABLES

(1)	a vowel by itself	5	*a, i, u, e, o*
(2)	a consonant + a vowel	58	*ka, te,* etc.
(3)	a syllabic consonant	4	*p, t, k, s*
(4)	the nasal syllabic consonant	1	*n'* (sometimes *m'* or *ng'*)
(5)	a semi-vowel + a vowel	4	*ya, yu, yo, wa*
(6)	a consonant + *y* + a vowel	33	*kya, myo,* etc.

total 105

These 105 syllables are represented by *kana* characters. They are divided into two groups, shown in Tables I and II, respectively. The syllables in Table I are represented by the basic *kana* characters and the ones in Table II by variations of the basic characters. When you learn *kana* characters starting in Lesson 1, refer back to these tables.

TABLE I

LINE

1 (vowel syllables)	*a*	*i*	*u*	*e*	*o*
2 (*k*-line)	*ka*	*ki*	*ku*	*ke*	*ko*
3 (*s*-line)	*sa*	*si* (*shi*)	*su*	*se*	*so*
4 (*t*-line)	*ta*	*ti* (*chi*)	*tu* (*tsu*)	*te*	*to*
5 (*n*-line)	*na*	*ni*	*nu*	*ne*	*no*
6 (*h*-line)	*ha*	*hi*	*hu* (*fu*)	*he*	*ho*
7 (*m*-line)	*ma*	*mi*	*mu*	*me*	*mo*
8 (*y*-line)	*ya*		*yu*		*yo*
9 (*r*-line)	*ra*	*ri*	*ru*	*re*	*ro*
10 (*w*-line)	*wa*				
11 (nasal syllabic consonant)	*n'*				

total 45

TABLE II

LINE

1 (*g*-line)	*ga*	*gi*	*gu*	*ge*	*go*
2 (*z*-line)	*za*	*zi*	*zu*	*ze*	*zo*
		(ji)			
3 (*d*-line)	*da*			*de*	*do*
4 (*b*-line)	*ba*	*bi*	*bu*	*be*	*bo*
5 (*p*-line)	*pa*	*pi*	*pu*	*pe*	*po*

consonant + *y* + vowel

6	*kya*		*kyu*	*kyo*
7	*sya*		*syu*	*syo*
	(sha)		*(shu)*	*(sho)*
8	*tya*		*tyu*	*tyo*
	(cha)		*(chu)*	*(cho)*
9	*nya*		*nyu*	*nyo*
10	*hya*		*hyu*	*hyo*
11	*mya*		*myu*	*myo*
12	*rya*		*ryu*	*ryo*
13	*gya*		*gyu*	*gyo*
14	*zya*		*zyu*	*zyo*
	(ja)		*(ju)*	*(jo)*
15	*bya*		*byu*	*byo*
16	*pya*		*pyu*	*pyo*

syllabic consonants

17	*p*	*t*	*k*	*s*

total 60

The syllables in parentheses are closer to the actual pronunciations and are the spellings used in this text. For example, on line 3 (*s*-line) in Table I, the slot where one would expect to find *si* is instead filled by *shi*.

The syllable *n'* on line 11 in Table I is different from the *n* on line 5 in Table I and the *n* on line 9 in Table II. *N'* is a full syllable by itself, and it occurs only after another syllable. If it is followed by a vowel or *y,* it does not "run into" that vowel or *y* but is pronounced separately. In this book, the apostrophe that distinguishes between *n'* and *n* is omitted except in cases when ambiguity occurs. Compare:

ta-n'-i unit	or	*ta-ni* valley
(3 syllables)		(2 syllables)

In the following examples, the apostrophe is unnecessary, as there is no danger of ambiguity.

hon	book	*ho-n*	*ringo*	apple	*ri-n-go*
		(2 syllables)			(3 syllables)

DAI IKKA
Lesson 1
SHOOKAI.   Introductions.

A. DAIAROOGU (Dialogue)

GAKUENSAI DE.

Mr. Yamada and Ms. Tanaka run into each other at the university.

TANAKA: **A, Yamada san, konnichi wá.***

YAMADA: **Konnichi wá. Shibáraku desu née.**

TANAKA: **Ogenki desu ka.**

YAMADA: **Ée, máa maa.**

TANAKA: **Kochira wa watashi no tomodachi désu. Suzuki san désu.**

YAMADA: **Yamada désu. Hajimemáshite.**

SUZUKI: **Hajimemáshite.**

YAMADA: **Suzuki san mo gakusei désu ka.**

SUZUKI: **Iie, watashi wa gakusei ja arimasén. Sotsugyóosei desu.**

YAMADA: **Áa, sóo desu ka.**

SUZUKI: **Yamada san wa?**

YAMADA: **Watashi wa gakuchoo no hísho desu.**

TANAKA: **Watashítachi wa kore kara shokudoo e ikimásu. Issho ni ikimasén ka.**

YAMADA: **Ée, ikimashóo.**

———————

AT THE SCHOOL FESTIVAL.

TANAKA: Oh, Mr. Yamada, hello.

YAMADA: Hello, I haven't seen you for a long time.

TANAKA: How are you? [Are you fine?]†

* (´) is an accent mark. See Appendix A for accents.
† The English translations in brackets are more literal.

YAMADA: Fine. [Yes,] not too bad.

TANAKA: This is Ms. Suzuki, a friend of mine. [This is a friend of mine. This is Ms. Suzuki.]

YAMADA: I am Yamada. How do you do?

SUZUKI: How do you do?

YAMADA: Are you a student, too, Ms. Suzuki?

SUZUKI: No, I'm not [a student]. I'm an alumna.

YAMADA: Is that so?

SUZUKI: How about you, Mr. Yamada?

YAMADA: I'm the university president's secretary.

TANAKA: We're going to the cafeteria [from] now. Won't you come [go] with us?

YAMADA: Yes, let's go.

B. HATSUON (Pronunciation)

1. SYLLABLES

Note that the following words are divided into syllables as shown in the third column.

neko	cat	*ne-ko*
hooki	broom	*ho-o-ki*
aoi	blue	*a-o-i*
ippoo	one side	*i-p-po-o*
gakkoo	school	*ga-k-ko-o*
chairo	brown	*cha-i-ro*
kin'yuu	finance	*ki-n'-yu-u*
kinyuu	entry	*ki-nyu-u*
zen'in	everybody	*ze-n'-i-n*
zenin	approval	*ze-ni-n*
hantai	opposition	*ha-n-ta-i*

2. VOWELS *A, I, U, E, O*

a	like the <u>a</u> in f<u>a</u>ther, but short and crisp	**a** ah, oh; **ashita** tomorrow **aki** autumn; **asa** morning
i	like the <u>ee</u> in keep, but short and crisp	**isu** chair; **inu** dog **ai** love; **ike** pond

8

u	like the <u>u</u> in <u>l</u>ute, but without rounding the lips	**umi** sea; **uchi** house
		usagi rabbit; **kau** to buy
e	like <u>e</u> in pr<u>e</u>y	**e** to; **ehon** picture book
		koe voice; **ue** top, up, above
o	like the *o* in c<u>o</u>rn, but shorter	**obi** sash; **kao** face
		aoi blue; **to** and

C. BUNPOO TO YOOHOO
(Grammar and Usage)

1. NOUNS

Japanese nouns have no gender distinctions, no singular or plural distinctions, and no articles. Thus *shokudoo* "cafeteria" can be "a cafeteria," "the cafeteria," "cafeterias" or "the cafeterias." Usually the context determines the particular meaning of a word.

2. THE COPULA *DESU* WITH NOUNS

In the English sentence "A is B," "is" is an inflected form of the copula (linking verb) "to be." The English copula "to be" conjugates as "am," "are," or "is," depending on the subject.

The Japanese copula *desu*, unlike the English "to be," does not change its form according to the subject.

*Watashi wa * gakusei <u>desu</u>.*
    I <u>am</u> a student.

Kochira wa Suzuki san <u>desu</u>.
    This <u>is</u> Ms. Suzuki.

Watashitachi wa sotsugyoosei <u>desu</u>.
    We <u>are</u> alumnae/alumni.

Note that *desu* is always at the end of the sentence.

3. NEGATION OF THE COPULA WITH NOUNS

The negative of *desu* "to be" is *ja arimasen* "not to be" or *de wa arimasen* "not to be." *De wa arimasen* is more formal, and *ja arimasen* is more common in casual conversation.

---

* *Wa* is a particle indicating the topic of a sentence: "as for." For a detailed explanation, refer to Lesson 1, C8.

Watashi wa gakusei ja/de wa arimasen.
　　I am not a student.

Kore wa shokudoo ja/de wa arimasen.
　　This is not a cafeteria.

Watashitachi wa sensei ja/de wa arimasen.
　　We are not teachers.

4. VERBS

The Japanese tense system, which has only a present and a past, is formed with suffixes. Verb forms* are not affected by person or number.

a. The present affirmative suffix *-masu*

The suffix *-masu* indicates that the verb is in the present tense in the affirmative. Please note that Japanese uses the present tense to express future actions, too.

ikimasu	go (am going, will go)
kimasu	come (am coming, will come)
oyogimasu	swim (am swimming, will swim)

Watashitachi wa ashita ikimasu.
　　We are going [there] tomorrow.

Abe san wa kyoo kimasu.
　　Ms. Abe will come today.

Watashi wa mainichi oyogimasu.
　　I swim every day.

Note that Japanese verbs, like the copula *desu* "to be," stand at the end of the sentence.

b. The present negative suffix *-masen*

-masen is the negative form of *-masu*.

ikimasen	do not go (am not going, will not go)
kimasen	do not come (am not coming, will not come)
oyogimasen	do not swim (am not swimming, will not swim)

---

* There are two kinds of forms, normal forms and plain forms. We will first deal with the normal forms. The plain forms will be dealt with in Lesson 12.

Watashi wa ikimasen.
I am not going [there].

Yamada san wa kyoo kimasen.
Mr. Yamada will not come today.

Watashitachi wa ashita oyogimasen.
We will not swim tomorrow.

    c. *-mashoo* "let's"

-mashoo indicates a suggestion.

Ikimashoo.
Let's go.

Tabemashoo.
Let's eat.

Oyogimashoo.
Let's swim.

5. PERSONAL PRONOUNS

Japanese personal pronouns are not used as often as their English counterparts. If the context is clear, they can be omitted.

wata(ku)shi	I	*wata(ku)shitachi*	we
anata	you	*anatagata *, anatatachi*	you (plural)
kare	he	*karera *, karetachi*	he and (an)other person(s)/they
kanojo	she	*kanojotachi*	she and (an)other person(s)/they

While there are various words for "I" and "you," *watashi* and *anata* are the most common. For plurals, *-tachi* is attached to the singular. *Watakushi* and *watakushitachi* are more formal than *watashi* and *watashitachi*.

Often *anata* "you," *kare* "he," and *kanojo* "she" are not appropriate, especially when the person referred to is superior or not close to you. In these cases, use the person's name instead.

Suzuki san mo gakusei desu ka.
Are you [Ms. Suzuki] a student, too?

---

* Although *-tachi* can be used with *anata* and *kare*, *-gata* and *-ra* are more common, respectively.

If Ms. Suzuki is not the addressee, the same sentence can mean:

Suzuki san mo gakusei desu ka.
Is she [Ms. Suzuki] a student, too?

6. DELETION OF THE SUBJECT

In Japanese, the subject of a sentence, whether a noun or a pronoun, can be deleted as long as the context makes it clear.

Suzuki san desu.
(This) is Ms. Suzuki.

Sotsugyoosei desu.
(I) am an alumna/alumnus.

Mainichi shokudoo e ikimasu.
(I) go to the cafeteria every day.

7. QUESTIONS

Japanese forms questions by adding a particle at the end of the sentence. Japanese uses many particles to show how the words of a sentence relate to each other. Often these particles cannot be translated. The particle *ka* at the end of a sentence indicates a question. Compare:

Tanaka san wa gakusei desu.
Ms. Tanaka is a student.

Tanaka san wa gakusei desu ka. *
Is Ms. Tanaka a student?

Kore wa shokudoo desu ka.
Is this a cafeteria?

Yamada san wa kimasu ka.
Is Mr. Yamada coming?

Note that the word order does not change. *Ka* is simply added to the end of the statement to form a question.
When *-masen* is used with *ka*, it can be either a negative question, an invitation, or a suggestion.

Ikimasen ka.
Don't/won't you go?
Why don't you/we go?

* No question mark is used except when the sentence would otherwise be ambiguous.

Tookyoo e kaerimasen ka.
    Don't/won't you go back to Tokyo?
    Why don't you/we go back to Tokyo?

8. PARTICLES

Particles such as *ka*, which is used at the end of a sentence, are called "sentence particles." The particles *wa*, *e*, *no* and *mo*, which are usually used after nouns, are called "phrase particles."

a. *Wa* (topic)

Wa shows that the noun it follows is the topic of the sentence. In many cases, *wa* is used after the subject. Literally, *wa* means "as for."

Watashi wa gakusei desu.
    I am a student. [As for me, I am a student.]

Yamada san wa?
    How about you, Mr. Yamada? [As for you, Mr. Yamada?]

Abe san wa mainichi kimasu.
    Ms. Abe comes every day. [As for Ms. Abe, she comes every day.]

Watashi wa ashita ikimasen.
    I will not go tomorrow. [As for me, I will not go tomorrow.]

b. *E* "to"

E "to," "toward" indicates that the noun it follows is the destination toward which the motion is directed.

Shokudoo e ikimasu.
    We are going to the cafeteria.

Gakkoo e kimasu.
    I will come to school.

Uchi e kaerimasu.
    I will go back to my house.

c. *No* (possession, relation, location)

No, when connecting nouns, can indicate possession, relation, or location. The meanings vary according to the connected nouns and context.

POSSESSION: *Yamada san no uchi*
                                     Mr. Yamada's house

RELATION:	*Kochira wa watashi no tomodachi desu.*
	This is my friend [lit. I's friend].
RELATION:	*Watashi wa gakuchoo no hisho desu.*
	I am the university president's secretary.
LOCATION:	*Tookyoo no daigaku*
	A university in Tokyo
LOCATION AND RELATION:	*Tookyoo no daigaku no gakusei desu.*
	I am a student at a university in Tokyo.

d. *Mo* "also"

Mo can be translated as "also," "too," "as well," or "either" (in a negative sentence). Compare:

Watashi wa gakusei desu.
    I am a student.

Watashi mo gakusei desu.
    I am a student, too.

Suzuki san wa Tookyoo e ikimasen.
    Ms. Suzuki will not go to Tokyo.

Suzuki san mo Tookyoo e ikimasen.
    Ms. Suzuki will not go to Tokyo, either.

e. No particles with time nouns

Usually time nouns such as *kyoo* "today" are used adverbially * without particles.

Kyoo ikimasen.
    I am not going today.

Ashita oyogimasu.
    I am going to swim tomorrow.

9. THE HONORIFIC *SAN*

Japanese has several terms of respect used when addressing people or talking about them. *San*, the most common one, can be added to the family name, the given name, or the full name. To use a person's name without *san* or other equivalents is impolite, except in special cases. The English equivalent would be "Mr." or "Ms." Do not, however, use *san* in combination with your own name. Compare:

* For an explanation of adverbs, see Lesson 5, C4.

Suzuki san desu.
   This is Ms. Suzuki.

Yamada desu.
   I am Yamada.

Tanaka san desu ka.
   Are you Ms. Tanaka?

Ee, Tanaka desu.
   Yes, I am Tanaka.

D. MOJI (Characters)

There are two kinds of Japanese characters—*kana* and *kanji. Kana* include two sub-types, *hiragana* and *katakana. Hiragana, katakana,* and *kanji* are mixed in Japanese writing. Each of the *hiragana* and *katakana* characters represents one syllable and has no meaning other than the representation of sound. Each *kanji* character, on the other hand, is an ideographic symbol (a character representing a thing or an idea). You will gradually learn how the three kinds of characters are mixed in writing.

HIRAGANA

Let's first deal with *hiragana*. There are forty-six basic *hiragana* characters plus their variations. The forty-six basic *hiragana* characters represent the syllables in Table I on page 5. Although there are only forty-five syllables in Table I, there are two *hiragana* characters for the syllable *o*, making forty-six *hiragana* characters altogether. Here is the first line.

LINE 1	*a*	*i*	*u*	*e*	*o*
	あ	い	う	え	お

STROKE ORDER

a	‐	ナ	あ	
i	ヽ	い		
u	‐	う		
e	‐	ラ	え	
o	‐	お	お	

Read the following:

ええ	*ee*	yes
いいえ	*iie*	no

15

E. TANGO TO HYOOGEN
(Vocabulary and Expressions)

tomodachi	friend
gakusei	student
sotsugyoosei	alumnus, alumna
gakuchoo	university president
sensei	teacher
hisho	secretary
gakkoo	school
daigaku	university, college
shokudoo	cafeteria
uchi	house
kore	this
kochira	this person (used when introducing someone)
wata(ku)shi	I
wata(ku)shitachi	we
anata	you (singular)
anatagata/anatatachi	you (plural)
kare	he
karera/karetachi	they
kanojo	she
kanojotachi/kanojora	they
kyoo	today
ashita	tomorrow
mainichi	every day
ikimasu	to go
kimasu	to come
kaerimasu	to go back, come back
oyogimasu	to swim
tabemasu	to eat
desu	to be
maa maa	not too bad, so-so
kore kara	(starting from) now
issho ni	together
ee	yes
iie	no
(a)a	ah, oh
(Aa) soo desu ka.	Is that so?/I see./Really?
Ohayoo gozaimasu.	Good morning.
Konnichi wa.	Hello.
Shibaraku desu ne(e).	I haven't seen you for a long time.

16

Ogenki desu ka.	How are you?
Hajimemashite.	How do you do?
Konban wa.*	Good evening.
Oyasumi nasai.	Good night.
Sayoonara.	Good bye.
Arigatoo gozaimasu.	Thank you very much.
Sumimasen.	I am sorry./Excuse me./Thank you.
Doo itashimashite.	You're welcome./Don't mention it.
san	suffix attached to a person's name
-tachi	suffix to show plurality

RENSHUU (EXERCISES)

A. Indicate whether the sentence is affirmative (+) or negative (−) and translate.

1. *Kore wa watashi no uchi desu.*
2. *Tanaka san wa gakusei ja arimasen.*
3. *Ashita Yamada san mo kimasu.*
4. *Kore kara uchi e kaerimasu.*
5. *Watashi wa sensei de wa arimasen.*

B. Choose the correct answer.

1. What do you say when you meet someone for the first time?
   a. *Sayoonara.* b. *Hajimemashite.* c. *Doo itashimashite.*
2. What do you say when you meet someone in the evening?
   a. *Konban wa.* b. *Ohayoo gozaimasu.* c. *Arigatoo gozaimasu.*
3. What do you say when you meet someone you have not seen for a long time?
   a. *Sayonara.* b. *Oyasumi nasai.* c. *Shibaraku desu nee.*
4. What do you say when you understand what someone has said?
   a. *Konnichi wa.* b. *Aa soo desu ka.* c. *Shibaraku desu nee.*
5. What do you say before you go to bed?
   a. *Konban wa.* b. *Doo itashimashite.* c. *Oyasumi nasai.*

C. Fill in the blanks with the correct particles.

1. *Tanaka san wa watashi _____ tomodachi desu.*
   Ms. Tanaka is a friend of mine.
2. *Watashi _____ gakusei desu.*
   I am a student, too.
3. *Suzuki san _____ sotsugyoosei desu _____ .*
   Is Ms. Suzuki an alumna?

* The first *n* in *Konban* is an example of a syllabic *n* (see syllable tables on page 5). Although it's always written as *n*, it is sometimes pronounced *m* (before *m, b,* or *p*) or even *ng*. You'll learn more on page 100, but for now, pay close attention to the recordings.

17

4. *Ashita gakkoo* _____ *ikimasu* _____ .
   Will you go to school tomorrow?
5. *Yamada san* _____ *gakuchoo* _____ *hisho desu.*
   Mr. Yamada is the university president's secretary.

KARUCHAA NOOTO
(Cultural Note)

The Japanese mention the family name first when using full names. For example, with the name *Yamada Hajime, Hajime* is the given name, and *Yamada* the family name. In this book, even the English translations will follow the Japanese custom. The Japanese usually do not have middle names.

It is customary to call a person by his or her family name plus *san* if he or she is not related to you. In many cases, family names are used even among close friends. Your colleagues or classmates may not even know your given name. Usually the Japanese use given names among relatives. However, some men are called by their family names by their in-laws. For example, a man whose family name is *Yamada* may be called *Yamada san* by his wife's mother. She may even say *Yamada san* when she just refers to him, as well. His wife may even use her husband's family name without *san* when referring to him, although she will use his given name when calling him or when talking to his relatives about him. For example, a wife may say to her relatives or nonrelatives, *Yamada wa ashita Tookyoo e ikimasu.* "Yamada is going to Tokyo tomorrow [My husband is going to Tokyo tomorrow]." However, when expressing the same idea to his relatives, she may say, *Hajime san wa ashita Tookyoo e ikimasu.* "Hajime is going to Tokyo tomorrow." On the other hand, a husband may use his wife's given name without *san* when addressing her and when referring to her.

KOTAE (ANSWERS)

A. 1. + This is my house. 2. − Ms. Tanaka is not a student.
3. + Tomorrow Mr. Yamada is coming, too. 4. + I am going home now. 5. − I am not a teacher.
B. 1. b 2. a 3. c 4. b 5. c
C. 1. *no* 2. *mo* 3. *wa, ka* 4. *e, ka* 5. *wa, no*

DAI NIKA
Lesson 2
KOKUSEKI.   Nationalities.

A. DAIAROOGU (Dialogue)

TOOKYOO NO KAISHA DE.

Ms. Morita and Mr. Kawamura are expecting Mr. Smith, an American businessman, at their office.

MORITA: **Súmisu san wa kyóo kimásu ka.**

KAWAMURA: **Ée. Kinoo Oosaka no hónsha e ikimáshita. Dákara, kyóo koko e kimásu. Súmisu san no tomodachi mo issho ni kimásu.**

MORITA: **Súmisu san no tomodachi mo amerikájin desu ka.**

KAWAMURA: **Iie, amerikájin ja arimasén. Furansújin desu. Namae wa Móroo san desu.**

MORITA: **Áa sóo desu ka. Móroo san no ryokoo mo shutchoo ryókoo desu ka.**

KAWAMURA: **Iie, tábun kankoo ryókoo desu. Kyóo minná de bangóhan o tabemasén ka.**

MORITA: **Íi desu ne. Ginza de nihonryóori o tabemashóo ka.**

KAWAMURA: **Sóo desu ne.**

Nokku no oto.

KAWAMURA: **Hái, dóozo. A, Súmisu san to Móroo san, irasshái!**

AT A COMPANY OFFICE IN TOKYO.

MORITA: Is Mr. Smith coming today?

KAWAMURA: Yes. He went to the main office in Osaka yesterday. Therefore, he's coming here [to this place] today. Mr. Smith's friend is coming along with him [as well].

MORITA: Is Mr. Smith's friend American, too?

KAWAMURA: No, he isn't American. He's French. His name is Mr. Moreau.

MORITA: I see. Is he on a business trip, too?

KAWAMURA: No, he's probably on a sightseeing trip. Why don't we all have dinner together today?

MORITA: That sounds nice. Should we have Japanese food in Ginza? *

KAWAMURA: Good idea.

There is a knock at the door.

KAWAMURA: Yes, come in, please.

KAWAMURA: Oh, Mr. Smith and Mr. Moreau, welcome!

B. HATSUON (Pronunciation)

BORROWED WORDS

Many foreign words have been adopted into Japanese with some modification to meet the Japanese pronunciation system.

Smith	**Sumisu**	France	**Furansu**
Moreau	**Moroo**	New York	**Nyuuyooku**
America	**Amerika**	juice	**juusu**

C. BUNPOO TO YOOHOO (Grammar and Usage)

1. VERBS IN THE PAST AFFIRMATIVE

The suffix -*mashita* indicates that the verb is in the past tense in the affirmative.

	PRESENT	PAST	
go (am going, will go)	*ikimasu*	*ikimashita*	went
eat (am eating, will eat)	*tabemasu*	*tabemashita*	ate

* Ginza is a shopping district in Tokyo.

20

Kinoo Oosaka e ikimashita.
    Yesterday he went to Osaka.

Moo tabemashita.
    I ate already.

Ototoi koko e kimashita ka.
    Did she come here the day before yesterday?

2. *-MASHOO KA*

The sentence particle *ka*, which indicates questions, used with *-mashoo* "Let's . . ." turns the suggestion into its corresponding question, "Should (shall) I/we—?"

Tabemashoo ka.
    Should I/we eat?

Asatte ikimashoo ka.
    Should I/we go the day after tomorrow?

Uchi e kaerimashoo ka.
    Should I/we go home?

3. PARTICLES

a. *O*

O indicates that the noun it follows receives the action of a sentence. The English equivalent is the direct object.

Bangohan o tabemashoo ka.
    Should we eat dinner?

Ocha o nomimashoo.
    Let's have [drink] tea.

Sumisu san wa yoku nihonryoori o tabemasu.
    Mr. Smith often eats Japanese cuisine.

b. *De* "at"/"in"

De "at" /"in" is used after a noun denoting a location where an action takes place.

gakkoo de   at school
Nihon de   in Japan

Ginza de nihonryoori o tabemasen ka.
    Why don't we eat Japanese in Ginza?

Oosaka no resutoran de gohan o tabemashita.
    I had a meal at a restaurant in Osaka.

Kissaten de juusu o nomimashita.
    I drank juice at the coffee shop.

    c. *To* "and"

To connects nouns. The English equivalent is "and." *

Sumisu san to Moroo san
    Mr. Smith and Mr. Moreau

Udon to gyooza o tabemashita.
    I ate noodles and *gyooza* (dumplings).

It is possible to connect more than two nouns with *to* in a list.

Hon to enpitsu to keshigomu o kaimashita.
    I bought a book, a pencil, and an eraser.

4. WORD ORDER

The Japanese word order is quite different from English. Statements and questions follow the same word order. Verbs and the copula "to be" are always at the end of a sentence, unless a sentence particle such as *ka* follows.

Yamada san wa Oosaka e ikimashita.
    Mr. Yamada went to Osaka.

In a sentence "A is B," the copula should immediately follow B.

A   B
Moroo san wa Furansujin desu.
    Mr. Moreau is French. [Mr. Moreau French.]

Phrase particles follow the words they modify.

Nihon e
    to Japan [Japan to]

Amerikaryoori o tabemashoo ka.
    Should we eat American cuisine?

Furansu de tokei o kaimashita.
    I bought a watch in France.

* Unlike "and" in English, *to* can be used only to connect nouns. For other equivalents of "and" (to connect verbs, adjectives, or the copula), see Lessons 17 and 18.

With *no*, the two nouns are strictly ordered. *No* stands after the noun that modifies the other.

Morita san no uchi
   Ms. Morita's house

Although the above-mentioned restrictions apply, the Japanese word order is usually rather flexible.

Sumisu san wa kyoo koko e kimasu.
Kyoo Sumisu san wa koko e kimasu.
Sumisu san wa koko e kyoo kimasu.
   Mr. Smith is coming here today.

5. THE USES OF *HAI* AND *EE*

Both *hai* and *ee* correspond to "yes." While *ee* is more natural in daily casual conversation, *hai* is preferred in more formal settings.
   There are other differences between *ee* and *hai*. In the following situations, *ee* cannot be used.
   Use *hai* to answer your door.

Hai doozo.
   Yes, (come in) please.

Use *hai* in response when your name is called.

Yamada san.
   Mr. Yamada!
Hai.
   Yes, present! (when taking attendance)

When you give something to someone, use *hai*.

Hai doozo.
   Here you are.

When you respond to someone's request, use *hai*.

Hai.
   Yes, (I will do it).

When you answer the phone, use *hai*.

Hai, Yamada desu.
   Yes (hello), this is Yamada.

D. MOJI (Characters)

The following *hiragana* characters represent the syllables in the second through the fifth lines of Table I (page 5).

HIRAGANA

	ka	ki	ku	ke	ko
LINE 2	か	き	く	け	こ
LINE 3	sa	shi	su	se	so
	さ	し	す	せ	そ
LINE 4	ta	chi	tsu	te	to
	た	ち	つ	て	と
LINE 5	na	ni	nu	ne	no
	な	に	ぬ	ね	の

STROKE ORDER

ka	つ か か
ki	ー ニ き き
ku	く
ke	۱ ⸌ け
ko	⁻ こ

sa	ー ナ さ
shi	し
su	ー す
se	ー ナ せ
so	⸌ ⸍ そ

ta	⁻ ナ た た
chi	⁻ ち
tsu	つ
te	て
to	⸌ と

na	⁻ ナ た な
ni	۱ ۱⸌ に
nu	⸌ ぬ
ne	۱ ね
no	の

Read the following:

うち	*uchi*	house
あした	*ashita*	tomorrow
ここ	*koko*	here
とけい	*tokei*	watch

E. TANGO TO HYOOGEN
(Vocabulary and Expressions)

kuni	nations
Nihon	Japan
Amerika	America
Furansu	France
Doitsu	Germany
Chuugoku	China
kokuseki	nationalities
nihonjin	Japanese
amerikajin	American
furansujin	French
doitsujin	German
chuugokujin	Chinese
ryoori	cuisine, cooking, food
nihonryoori	Japanese cuisine
amerikaryoori	American cuisine
furansuryoori	French cuisine
doitsuryoori	German cuisine
chuugokuryoori	Chinese cuisine
or chuukaryoori	
ocha	tea (but not black tea)
juusu	juice
udon	noodles
gyooza	a kind of dumpling
gohan	meal, cooked rice
bangohan	dinner, supper
resutoran	restaurant
kissaten	coffee shop
namae	name
honsha	headquarters (of a company)
ryokoo	trip
shutchoo (ryokoo)	business trip
kankoo ryokoo	sightseeing trip
hon	book
enpitsu	pencil
keshigomu	eraser
tokei	watch, clock
nokku	knock
oto	sound
koko	this place, here
kinoo	yesterday

ototoi	the day before yesterday
asatte	the day after tomorrow
nomimasu	to drink
kaimasu	to buy
dakara	therefore, so
tabun	probably
minna de	all together
moo	already
yoku	often
hai	yes
doozo	please
Ii desu ne.	That is a good idea./That sounds nice.
Irasshai(mase).	Welcome. Can I help you?
Soo desu ne.	I agree./That will be fine.

RENSHUU (EXERCISES)

A. Indicate whether the sentences are true or false based on the dialogue.

1. *Moroo san wa doitsujin desu.*
2. *Moroo san wa Sumisu san no tomodachi desu.*
3. *Sumisu san wa kinoo Oosaka e ikimashita.*

B. Choose the correct verb.

1. *Ocha o* (a. *nomimashita.* b. *tabemashita.*)
2. *Udon o* (a. *nomimashita.* b. *tabemashita.*)
3. *Koko de* (a. *kimashita.* b. *oyogimashita.*)
4. *Ginza e* (a. *ikimashita.* b. *kaimashita.*)

C. Translate the following into English.

1. *Doitsuryoori o tabemashoo ka.*
2. *Tanaka san to Abe san wa moo kaerimashita.*
3. *Ototoi enpitsu o kaimashita.*
4. *Ginza no kissaten de ocha o nomimashita.*

D. Transform each sentence as indicated in parentheses.

1. *Yamada san wa uchi e kaerimashita.* (question)
2. *Kankoo ryokoo desu.* (negative)
3. *Juusu o nomimasu.* (past tense)
4. *Tanaka san wa ashita kimasu.* (negative)

E. Complete the sentences using the given words, and then suggest an action. Change the verb to *"~mashoo ka."*

Example: *nihonryoori, tabemasu → nihonryoori o tabemashoo ka.*

1. *eiga, mimasu*
2. *Shinjuku, ikimasu*
3. *kissaten, ocha, nomimasu*

KARUCHAA NOOTO
(Cultural Note)

In Japanese cities, especially in big cities, you will find various kinds of ethnic restaurants, ranging from fast food to fancy gourmet establishments. In Western-style restaurants, you can eat delicious but extremely expensive steaks. The variety of beef known as "Kobe beef" is notoriously high priced, but recently, less expensive beef imported from the United States has been marketed more and more. Chinese restaurants are popular, too. *Gyooza*, a kind of dumpling, originally came from China, but since it is so popular in Japan, the Japanese feel almost as if it is their own. *Gyooza* are eaten with a dip commonly made of soy sauce, vinegar, hot spices, and sesame oil. American fast food and family restaurants have extended their franchises to Japan, and these restaurants have been well-received, especially among young people. In many cities there are several McDonald's as well as Japanese versions of popular American fast-food chains.

At home, people cook Western food, Chinese food, and, of course, Japanese food for themselves and for guests. The evening meal is usually the main meal in Japan, but some people have a large breakfast, too. The traditional Japanese breakfast includes cooked rice, *miso* (soy bean paste) soup, and pickled seasonal vegetables, and sometimes a piece of salty (cured) fish such as salmon. Occasionally, people like to mix a raw egg with soy sauce and pour it over rice.

KOTAE (ANSWERS)

A. 1. F 2. T 3. T
B. 1. a 2. b 3. b 4. a
C. 1. Should we eat German cuisine? 2. Ms. Tanaka and Ms. Abe went back already. 3. I bought a pencil the day before yesterday. 4. I drank tea at a coffee shop in Ginza.
D. 1. *Yamada san wa uchi e kaerimashita ka.* 2. *Kankoo ryokoo ja arimasen.* 3. *Juusu o nomimashita.* 4. *Tanaka san wa ashita kimasen.*
E. 1. *Eiga o mimashoo ka.* 2. *Shinjuku e ikimashoo ka.* 3. *Kissaten de ocha o nomimashoo ka.*

DAI SANKA
Lesson 3

KAIMONO.   Shopping.

A. DAIAROOGU (Dialogue)

DEPAATO.

Ms. Miki and Ms. Abe, who are neighbors, are having an afternoon chat.

MIKI: **Kinoo Shinjuku e ikimáshita ka.**

ABE: **Ée, depáato de kutsú o kaimáshita.**

MIKI: **Dóno depáato de.**

ABE: **Shimadaya de kaimáshita.**

MIKI: **Áa, Shimadaya wa íi desu ka.**

ABE: **Ée, Shimadaya no kutsú wa yasúi desu yo. Watashi no kutsú wa tatta nisen'en déshita kedo, kookyuuhin désu yo.**

MIKI: **Watashi wa tokidoki Hanábishi e ikimásu kedo, Hanábishi no kutsú wa takái n desu. Démo, yoofuku wa totemo yasúi desu yo.**

ABE: **Sóo desu ka. Ítsu ka issho ni Hanábishi e ikimasén ka.**

MIKI: **Ée, ikimashóo. Tokoró de, kore kara náni o shimashóo ka.**

ABE: **Áa, kore kara Hanábishi e ikimasén ka.**

MIKI: **Ée, íi desu ne. Ikimashóo.**

DEPARTMENT STORES.

MIKI: Did you go to Shinjuku yesterday?

ABE: Yes, I bought shoes at a department store.

MIKI: At which department store did you buy them?

ABE: I bought them at Shimadaya.

MIKI: Oh, is Shimadaya a good department store?

ABE: Yes, shoes at Shimadaya are inexpensive. My shoes were only two thousand yen, but they're high-quality shoes.

MIKI: I sometimes go to Hanabishi. Their shoes are expensive, but their clothes are very reasonable.

ABE: Is that right? Why don't we go to Hanabishi sometime?

MIKI: Yes, let's go. By the way, what should we do now?

ABE: Oh, why don't we go to Hanabishi?

MIKI: Okay, let's go.

B. HATSUON (Pronunciation)

VOWEL CLUSTERS

When two identical vowels such as *aa, ii, uu, ee* or *oo* appear together, they are held twice as long as the single vowel. Compare:

kado	corner	**kaado**	card
chizu	map	**chiizu**	cheese
su	nest	**suu**	number
beru	bell	**beeru**	veil
hoshi	star	**hooshi**	service

When two or more different vowels appear in succession, each vowel is pronounced clearly and distinctly and is articulated for the same length of time.

ue	top, up, above	**akai**	red	**aoi**	blue
baiu	rainy season			**koe**	voice

The combination *ei* is an exception to this rule, for in everyday speech, it is often pronounced like *ee*.

keiko	practice	**eiga**	movie

C. BUNPOO TO YOOHOO
(Grammar and Usage)

1. NUMBERS *

0	zero, rei	6	roku	
1	ichi	7	shichi, nana	
2	ni	8	hachi	
3	san	9	ku, kyuu	
4	shi, yon	10	juu	
5	go			

The numbers 11 through 19 are formed by adding 1 through 9 to 10.

11   **juuichi** (10 *juu* + 1 *ichi*)   12   **juuni** (10 *juu* + 2 *ni*)

For tens, the numbers 1 through 9 are multiplied by 10; for hundreds, by 100; and for thousands, by 1000.

20	**nijuu** (2 *ni* × 10 *juu*)	1000	**sen, issen**
100	**hyaku**	2000	**nisen** (2 *ni* × 1000 *sen*)
200	**nihyaku** (2 *ni* × 100 *hyaku*)		

2. JAPANESE CURRENCY

The English name for Japan's official monetary unit is "yen," but in Japanese, it is pronounced *en*. The symbol for it is "¥."

ichien	one yen
juuen	ten yen
hyakuen	one hundred yen
Hyakuen desu.	It is one hundred yen.
Kore wa sen'en desu.	This is one thousand yen.
Kore wa nisen'en desu ka.	Is this two thousand yen?

---

* In this lesson only a few easy numbers are introduced. For more about numbers, see Lesson 9.

3. NOUNS PLUS COPULA IN THE PAST AFFIRMATIVE

The past tense of the copula *desu* "to be" in the affirmative is *deshita*.

Watashi no kutsu wa tatta nisen'en deshita.
My shoes were only two thousand yen.

Kasa wa sen'en deshita.
The umbrella was one thousand yen.

Compare the different forms of the copula: *desu* (present affirmative), *ja arimasen* (present negative), and *deshita* (past affirmative).

Watashi wa gakusei desu.
I am a student.

Watashi wa gakusei ja arimasen.
I am not a student.

Watashi wa gakusei deshita.
I was a student.

4. *I*-ADJECTIVES

There are two types of adjectives in Japanese: *i*-adjectives and *na*-adjectives.* *I*-adjectives all end in *i*.

takai	expensive	*yasui*	inexpensive
ii or *yoi*†	good, nice, fine, okay	*warui*	bad

The final *i* of an *i*-adjective is always preceded by *a, i, u,* or *o*. It is never preceded by the vowel *e*.

    I-adjectives change their forms depending on the tense or whether they are affirmative or negative.‡ In the present affirmative, however, there is no change of form, and the *i*-adjective is followed by *desu*. Unlike the copula *desu* "to be," the *desu* used with *i*-adjectives does not conjugate.§

Ii desu.	It is good.	*Ookii desu.*	It is big.
Warui desu.	It is bad.	*Chiisai desu.*	It is small.
Takai desu.	It is expensive.	*Akarui desu.*	It is bright.
Yasui desu.	It is inexpensive.	*Kurai desu.*	It is dark.

---

  * *Na*-adjectives are introduced in Lesson 4.
  † *Ii* is much more common than *yoi*.
  ‡ The present negative form of *i*-adjectives is discussed in Lesson 5, and the past tense in Lesson 6.
  § For further explanation of *desu* with *i*-adjectives, see Lessons 13 and 15.

Shimadaya no kutsu wa yasui desu.
   Shimadaya's shoes are inexpensive.

   Sometimes *n* is used between the *i*-adjectives and *desu* to make the sentence more emphatic, or to mean "the fact is that . . ." or "indeed."

Yasui n desu.
   [The fact is that] it is inexpensive.

Hanabishi no kutsu wa takai n desu.
   [Indeed] Hanabishi's shoes are expensive.

5. QUESTION WORDS

   As in yes-no questions (see Lesson 1, C7), the sentence particle *ka* stands at the end of questions containing question words such as *nani* "what," *doko* "where," and *dono* "which."

   a. *Nani* "what"

   In the following examples, *nani* "what" is the direct object, so the particle *o* follows it.

Nani o shimashoo ka.
   What should we do?

Nani o tabemasu ka.
   What will you eat?

Udon o tabemasu.
   I will eat noodles.

Nani o kaimashoo ka.
   What should we buy?

Pan to jamu o kaimashoo.
   Let's buy bread and jam.

   b. *Doko* "where"

   In the following examples, note that *doko* "where" is followed by *e, de,* or *no* after *doko.*

Doko e ikimashoo ka.
   Where [to what place] should we go?

Hanabishi e ikimashoo.
   Let's go to Hanabishi.

Ashita doko de asagohan to hirugohan o tabemasu ka.
   Where will you have breakfast and lunch tomorrow?

Uchi de tabemasu.
    I will eat at home.

Doko no mise desu ka.
    Which store is it? [What place's store is it?]

Shinjuku no mise desu.
    It is a store in Shinjuku.

c. *Dono* "which" (out of three or more choices)

Dono "which" should always be used before the noun.

Dono sakana o tabemashoo ka.
    Which fish should we eat?

Maguro o tabemashoo.
    Let's eat tuna.

Dono hana o kaimashoo ka.
    Which flowers should we buy?

Bara o kaimashoo.
    Let's buy roses.

*Dono depaato de.**
    At which department store?

When the noun following *dono* indicates location, you may also say *doko no*.

Doko no depaato de.
    At which department store? [At what place's department store?]

6. PARTICLES

a. The sentence particle *yo*

Yo is a sentence particle like *ka*. Placed at the end of a sentence, *yo* implies that the speaker is trying to give new information, attract the listener's attention, or emphasize the statement. The English equivalents would be "you know" or "certainly."

Shimadaya no kutsu wa yasui desu yo.
    Shimadaya's shoes are certainly inexpensive.

Suzuki san wa depaato e ikimashita yo.
    Ms. Suzuki went to the department store, you know.

---

* This is a sentence fragment. The whole sentence could be *Dono depaato de kaimashita ka.* "At which department store did you buy them?"

Tatta sen'en deshita yo.
It was only one thousand yen, you know.

b. The clause particle *kedo* "but"

Wa, e, etc. are phrase particles, and *ka* and *yo* are sentence particles. Clause particles, such as *kedo* "but," come after a clause.

Watashi no kutsu wa tatta nisen'en deshita kedo, kookyuuhin desu.
My shoes were only two thousand yen, but they are high-quality merchandise.

Hanabishi no kutsu wa takai desu kedo, yoofuku wa yasui desu.
Shoes at Hanabishi are expensive, but their apparel is inexpensive.

Suzuki san wa dekakemasu kedo, watashi wa dekakemasen.
Ms. Suzuki is going out, but I am not.

7. *DEMO* "BUT"

Demo can also mean "but." However, *demo* and *kedo* are used differently. *Demo* is not a particle, but a conjunction used at the beginning of a sentence. Compare:

Maguro wa yasui desu kedo, unagi wa takai desu.
The tuna is inexpensive, but the eel is expensive.

Maguro wa yasui desu. Demo, unagi wa takai desu.
The tuna is inexpensive. However, the eel is expensive.

8. DELETION OF THE DIRECT OBJECT

Just like subjects, direct objects can be deleted if the context allows it.

Doko de kutsu o kaimasu ka.
Where are you going to buy shoes?

Shimadaya de kaimasu.
I am going to buy [them] at Shimadaya.

Kinoo booshi o kaimashita.
I bought a hat yesterday.

Watashi mo kaimashita yo.
I bought [one], too.

D. MOJI (Characters)

Here are the final basic *hiragana* characters, representing the syllables in the sixth through the eleventh lines of Table I (page 5).

LINE 6	ha は	hi ひ	fu ふ	he へ	ho ほ
LINE 7	ma ま	mi み	mu む	me め	mo も
LINE 8	ya や	(i) い	yu ゆ	(e) え	yo よ
LINE 9	ra ら	ri り	ru る	re れ	ro ろ
LINE 10	wa わ	(i) い	(u) う	(e) え	o を
LINE 11	n' ん				

The syllables in parentheses, *i* い and *e* え on line 8 and *i* い, *u* う and *e* え on line 10, are redundant, that is, they are the same syllables as the ones on line 1 (see Lesson 1). Since each line has five syllables (except for line 11), to maintain the same pattern, the blank spots are filled in with these redundant syllables.

There are two *hiragana* characters for *o* — お on line 1 and を on line 10. を is used only to write the particle *o*. The other *o* (お) is used to represent everything else.

STROKE ORDER

ha	し に は	*ma*	ー = ま
hi	ひ	*mi*	み み
fu	丶 ふ ふ ふ	*mu*	ー む む
he	へ	*me*	し め
ho	し 1 に ほ	*mo*	ー = も

35

ya	つ ゔ	や
yu	い	ゆ
yo	゛	よ

ra	`	ら
ri	'	り
ru		る
re	l	れ
ro		ろ

wa	l	わ
o	˜ ち	を
n'		ん

Read the following:

くつ   *kutsu*
                        shoes

わたし   *watashi*
                        I

はい、ほんを　かいました。   *Hai, hon o kaimashita.*
                        Yes, I bought books.

いきましたか。   *Ikimashita ka.*
                        Did you go?

The Japanese comma and period are 、 and 。, respectively. No space is needed between words, but normally there is a space after a comma or a period. To help you read more easily, spaces between phrases are provided in this book. Other punctuation marks such as question marks or exclamation marks are unnecessary, although some writers use them.

E. TANGO TO HYOOGEN (Vocabulary and Expressions)

mise	store
depaato	department store
kutsu	shoes
booshi	hat, cap
kasa	umbrella
pan	bread

jamu	jam
sakana	fish
maguro	tuna
unagi	eel
hana	flower
bara	rose
asagohan	breakfast
hirugohan	lunch
yoofuku	clothes
kookyuuhin	quality goods
shimasu	to do
dekakemasu	to go out
ii/yoi	good, nice, fine, okay
warui	bad
takai	expensive
yasui	inexpensive
ookii	big
chiisai	small
akarui	bright
kurai	dark
tatta	only
totemo	very
tokidoki	sometimes
demo	but
tokoro de	by the way
itsu ka	sometime, someday
nani	what
doko	where
dono	which

RENSHUU (EXERCISES)

A. Fill in the blanks with particles, basing your answers on the English equivalents.

1. *Kutsu _____ yasui desu _____.*
   The shoes are inexpensive, you know.
2. *Doko _____ depaato _____ kaimashoo ka.*
   At which department store should we buy it?
3. *Nani _____ nomimasu ka.*
   What will you drink?
4. *Yamada san _____ gakusei desu _____, Suzuki san _____ gakusei ja arimasen.*
   Mr. Yamada is a student, but Ms. Suzuki is not.

You have bought the following things at a department store. Fill in the blanks.

hat	¥2000
eel	¥1000
pencil	¥100
shoes	¥2000

1. *Enpitsu wa* _____ *en deshita.*
2. _____ *wa sen'en deshita.*
3. *Booshi wa* _____ *en deshita.*
4. _____ *mo nisen'en deshita.*

C. Fill in the blanks with the appropriate form of the verbs or the copula.

1. a: *Moo gohan o tabemashita ka.*
   b: *Iie, kore kara* _____.
2. Salesclerk: *Kore wa nisen'en desu.*
   Customer: *Kinoo sen'en* _____ *yo.*
3. a: *Kore kara nani o shimashoo ka.*
   b: *Depaato e* _____ *mashoo.*

D. Write the antonym of each word.

1. *akarui*
2. *chiisai*
3. *ii*
4. *yasui*

E. Compliment your friend's new house using *i*-adjectives.

1. big house
2. wide living room
3. bright kitchen

F. Fill in the blanks choosing from the box below, and complete the sentences.

1. _____ *e ikimashoo ka.*
2. _____ *o tabemashoo ka.*
3. _____ *depaato ga ii desu ka.*

dono nani doko

G. Choose the sentence in each pair from which the direct object can be eliminated.

1. A: *Doko de <u>sono kutsu o</u> kaimashita ka.*
   B: *Hanabishi de <u>kutsu o</u> kaimashita yo.*
2. A: *Eiga o mimashoo ka?*
   B: *Soo desu ne. Eiga o mimashoo.*
3. A: *Shimadaya de yoofuku o kaimashita.*
   B: *Watashi mo Shimadaya de yoofuku o kaimashita.*

KARUCHAA NOOTO
(Cultural Note)

Department stores in Japan are much bigger than their American counterparts. Many of them have five, six, seven, or even more floors, and you can buy almost anything there. Usually they have groceries such as meat, fish, and vegetables, and snack bars in the basement. A large restaurant and a few smaller specialty restaurants can be found on the upper floors, and coffee shops may be found in the same building. Some stores even have playgrounds for children on the roof. In the summer the roof is converted to a "beer garden" serving popular Japanese food such as *yaki-tori* (skewered grilled chicken), beer, and other drinks. These are popular after work and evening spots in larger cities.

Generally, the service in department stores is good. Some of them even have uniformed young women operating the elevators. Each store has its own distinctive wrapping paper and will wrap your purchase without any additional cost. Since the wrapping paper reveals where you shop, some people are quite concerned about the prestige of a store, especially when they are buying gifts.

An *ichiba* is a non-enclosed market arcade. *Ichiba* contain a variety of small shops, stalls, and restaurants. The owners of small neighborhood businesses often live behind or above their shops, so they tend to know their local customers well. As in other countries, supermarkets and department stores may drive out many of the smaller retailers, yet they can still be found in many places.

KOTAE (ANSWERS)

A. 1. *wa, yo* 2. *no, de* 3. *o* 4. *wa, kedo, wa*
B. 1. *hyaku* 2. *Unagi* 3. *nisen'* 4. *Kutsu*
C. 1. *tabemasu* 2. *deshita* 3. *iki*
D. 1. *kurai* 2. *ookii* 3. *warui* 4. *takai*
E. 1. *ookii uchi desu ne.* 2. *hiroi ima desu ne.* 3. *akarui kitchin (daidokoro) desu ne.*
F. 1. *doko* 2. *nani* 3. *dono*
G. 1. (B) 2. (B) 3. (B)

DAI YONKA
Lesson 4
SUMOO.   Sumo Wrestling.

A. DAIAROOGU (Dialogue)

SUMOO FAN TO NO KAIWA.

Mr. White is visiting Mr. Mori, a colleague, at his home.

MORI: **Kinoo térebi de sumoo o mimáshita ka.**

HOWAITO: **Iie, mimasén deshita kedo. Mori san wa sumoo ga sukí desu ka.**

MORI: **Ée, dáisuki desu.**

HOWAITO: **Íma, dáre ga tsuyói desu ka.**

MORI: **Sóo desu ne. Kono goro Wakayagi ga tsuyói desu ne. Sumoo no hón desu. Mimásu ka.**

HOWAITO: **Ée. Rippa na hón desu née. Dóre ga Wakayagi désu ka.**

MORI: **Kore ga Wakayagi désu.**

HOWAITO: **Ookíi karada désu ne. Kore wa dáre desu ka.**

MORI: **Fujinoyama désu. Fujinoyama mo tsuyói desu kedo, kinoo makemáshita yo.**

HOWAITO: **Sumoo wa akkenái desu kedo, omoshirói n desu ka.**

MORI: **Ée, totemo omoshirói desu yo.**

HOWAITO: **Hee.**

CONVERSING WITH A SUMO FAN.

MORI: Did you watch the sumo wrestling on TV yesterday?

WHITE: No, I didn't. Do you like sumo wrestling, Mr. Mori?

MORI: Yes, I like it very much.

WHITE: Who's doing well [strong] at the moment?

MORI: Well, recently Wakayagi has been doing well. Here's a book on sumo wrestling. Would you like to look at it?

40

WHITE: Yes. What a magnificent book! Which one is Wakayagi?

MORI: This [one] is Wakayagi.

WHITE: He has a large body, doesn't he? And who is this?

MORI: Fujinoyama. He's also strong, but yesterday he lost.

WHITE: Sumo seems [is] short and simple. Is it really interesting?

MORI: Yes, it's very interesting.

WHITE: Really?

B. HATSUON (Pronunciation)

CONSONANTS AS PARTS OF SYLLABLES

k	like the English k	**kasa** umbrella; **kutsu** shoes; **kyuu** nine
s	like the English s	**saka** slope; **susu** soot; **sekai** world
sh	like the English sh	**shashin** photograph; **shichi** seven; **shooko** proof
t	like the English t	**tamago** egg; **te** hand; **to** door
ch	like the ch in cheese	**ocha** tea; **uchi** house; **chuui** caution
ts	like the ts in cats	**natsu** summer; **tsunami** tidal wave
n	like the English n	**nana** seven; **niku** meat; **nyuuin** hospitalization

C. BUNPOO TO YOOHOO (Grammar and Usage)

1. VERBS

a. *-masen deshita*

The past tense of a verb in the negative is formed by adding *deshita* to the present negative form. Compare:

Mimasen.
I do not see.

Mimasen deshita.
I did not see.

Kinoo depaato e ikimasen deshita.
I did not go to a department store yesterday.

Kyoo dekakemasen deshita.
I did not go out today.

Kinoo sumoo o mimashita ka.
   Did you watch sumo yesterday?

Iie, mimasen deshita.
   No, I did not watch it.

   b. *-masu ka*

-masu ka can be used as a suggestion or invitation as well as a simple question.

Mimasu ka.
   Would you like to look at it? (I invite you to/suggest you look at it.)

   -masu ka conveys a slightly weaker suggestion or invitation than *-masen ka* (see Lesson 1, C7).

Terebi o mimasu ka.
   Would you like to watch TV?

Shashin o torimasu ka.
   Would you like to take a picture?

2. *NA*-ADJECTIVES

Unlike *i*-adjectives, *na*-adjectives do not have to end in *-i*.

kirei	pretty, clean
rippa	magnificent
shizuka	quiet
suki	to like
daisuki	to like very much
kirai	to dislike
daikirai	to dislike very much
joozu	skillful, good (at)
heta	not skillful, poor (at)

Note that *suki* "to like," *daisuki* "to like very much," *kirai* "to dislike," and *daikirai* "to dislike very much" are adjectives, not verbs, in Japanese.
   Although *kirei* "pretty, clean" ends in *-i*, it cannot be an *i*-adjective because, as explained in Lesson 3, *i*-adjectives never end in *-ei*. As *kirai* "to dislike" and *daikirai* "to dislike very much" end in *-ai,* you cannot tell whether they are *i*-adjectives or *na*-adjectives. However, there are very few *na*-adjectives that look like *i*-adjectives, and you can simply memorize them as exceptions.
   Na-adjectives, unlike *i*-adjectives, do not change their forms depending on the tense or whether the sentence is affirmative or negative. As

with nouns, *desu* follows the *na*-adjective to express the present affirmative, and *desu* changes its form to express the past tense, the negative, and the affirmative.*

Kirei desu.
   It is pretty/clean.

Rippa desu.
   It is magnificent.

Rikishi no karada wa rippa desu.
   The sumo wrestlers' bodies are magnificent.

Shokudoo wa kirei desu ka.
   Is the cafeteria clean?

3. ADJECTIVES MODIFYING NOUNS

So far adjectives have been introduced as predicates.

Sumoo wa omoshiroi desu.   (*i*-adjective)
   Sumo is interesting.

Shokudoo wa shizuka desu.   (*na*-adjective)
   The cafeteria is quiet.

When used as modifiers of nouns, the two types of adjectives behave as follows.

a. *I*-adjectives

When an *i*-adjective modifies a noun, it precedes the noun just like in English.

Ookii karada desu.
   He has a big body. [It's a big body.]

Yasui terebi o kaimashoo.
   Let's buy an inexpensive TV.

Omoshiroi shiai deshita.
   It was an interesting tournament.

b. *Na*-adjectives

When a *na*-adjective modifies a noun, it also precedes the noun, but *na* stands between the adjective and the noun.

* The present negative form of *na*-adjectives will be discussed in Lesson 5, and the past tense in Lesson 6.

Rippa na hon desu.
    It is a magnificent book.

Kirei na shashin desu.
    It is a pretty photograph.

Shizuka na tokoro e ikimashoo.
    Let's go to a quiet place.

To summarize, when the first type of adjective modifies a noun, *-i* (part of the adjective) stands before the noun. When the second type of adjective modifies a noun, *na* stands before the noun. Thus, the former are called "*i*-adjectives" and the latter "*na*-adjectives."

4. PARTICLES

a. *Ga* (with subject)

Ga both marks the subject and emphasizes it. If the subject is followed by *wa*, on the other hand, it is not emphasized.

Wakayagi ga tsuyoi desu.
    Wakayagi is strong. (emphasis on *Wakayagi*)

Wakayagi wa tsuyoi desu.
    Wakayagi is strong. (*Wakayagi* is not emphasized.)

In the following question, *nani* "what" is followed by *ga* because *nani* is the subject, and furthermore, the emphasis is clearly on the question word. When a question word is the subject of a sentence, it is always followed by *ga*, never by *wa*.

Nani ga omoshiroi desu ka.
    What is interesting?

To answer the question above, the new information, which is supposed to be emphasized, has to be followed by *ga*.

Sumoo ga omoshiroi desu.
    Sumo is interesting.

Here are a few more examples.

Doko ga shizuka desu ka.
    What place is quiet?

Toshokan ga shizuka desu.
    The library is quiet.

Nani ga yasui desu ka.
    What is inexpensive?

Kutsu ga yasui desu.
    Shoes are inexpensive.

   b. *Ga* (in an adjectival sentence structure)

   Ga is used in another way, too. Consider the following.

Sumisu san wa joozu desu.
    Mr. Smith is skillful.

The noun denoting what Mr. Smith is skillful in is used with *ga*. The sentence pattern is:

someone (or something)	*wa*	something (or someone)	*ga*	adjective

Sumisu san wa tenisu ga joozu desu.
    Mr. Smith is good at tennis. [Mr. Smith tennis skillful/good.]

Mori san wa sumoo ga suki desu. *
    Mr. Mori likes Sumo.

Watashi wa koohii ga kirai desu.
    I don't like [dislike] coffee.

   c. *De* "by means of"

   In addition to corresponding to "at" or "in" (see Lesson 2, C3), *de* is also used to signify the means of an action. The English equivalents can be "by," "by means of," "with," or "by using."

Terebi de sumoo o mimashita ka.
    Did you see sumo wrestling on [by means of] TV?

Enpitsu de hiragana to katakana o kakimashita.
    I wrote *hiragana* and *katakana* with a pencil.

* Note that *suki* and *kirai* are adjectives, not verbs.

Watashi no kamera de shashin o torimashita.
I took the picture with my camera [not with yours].

d. *Ne* (sentence particle)

Ne, which is a sentence particle like *ka* or *yo*, is used in several different ways. First, *ne* can form a tag question.

Ookii karada desu ne.
He has a big body, doesn't he?

Kore wa sumoo no hon desu ne.
This is a book on sumo, isn't it?

Kinoo terebi o mimasen deshita ne.
You didn't watch TV yesterday, did you?

Second, *ne* is used when the speaker expresses his or her personal feelings, opinions, or judgments. Usually, this expression is used when answering a question.

Dare ga tsuyoi desu ka.
Who is strong?

Kono goro Wakayagi ga tsuyoi desu ne.
Recently, Wakayagi has been strong [in my opinion].

Nani ga kirai desu ka.
What do you not like?

Gyuunyuu ga kirai desu ne.
[I feel] I don't like milk.

Terebi o yoku mimasu ka.
Do you often watch TV?

Iie, mimasen ne.
No, I don't watch it [I don't think I watch it].

Nee can be used instead of *ne*, whether it is in a tag question or to express feelings, or judgments. *Nee* implies surprise on the part of the speaker.

Rippa na hon desu nee.
It's a magnificent book, isn't it? [I am surprised.]

e. *Kedo* "but"

As mentioned before, *kedo* "but" is a clause particle that follows a clause, <u>and</u> is followed by another clause (see Lesson 3, C6).

Kutsu wa takai desu kedo, yoofuku wa yasui desu.
Shoes are expensive, but apparel is inexpensive.

If the context allows it, you may omit the second clause.

Kutsu wa takai desu kedo ...
Shoes are expensive, but ... [apparel is inexpensive.]

In many cases when *kedo* is at the end of a sentence, the original meaning "but" fades away, and it simply functions as a softener to avoid an abrupt remark.

Kinoo terebi de sumoo o mimashita ka.
Did you watch sumo wrestling on TV yesterday?

Iie, mimasen deshita kedo.
No, I didn't watch it.

Sumoo ga suki desu ka.
Do you like sumo wrestling?

Ee, suki desu kedo.
Yes, I like it.

When making a phone call and identifying yourself, *kedo* is often used as a softener.

Yamada desu kedo.
This is Yamada.

5. QUESTION WORDS

a. *Dare* "who" and *donata* "who"

Both *dare* and *donata* mean "who," but *donata* is more polite than *dare*. Whether *dare* or *donata* is used often depends on the speaker or the circumstances. For example, women tend to use the honorific *donata* more often than men do.

Dare ga tsuyoi desu ka.
Who is strong?

Dare desu ka.
Who is it? [(It) is who?]

Kore wa dare desu ka.
Who is this? [As for this, (it) is who?]

Dare ga ashita ikimasu ka.
     Who is going tomorrow?

Donata ga sensei desu ka.
     Who is the teacher?

Donata no terebi desu ka.
     Whose TV is it?

Donata ga sumoo ga suki desu ka.
     Who likes sumo wrestling?

b. *Dore* "which one"

While *dono* "which" must be followed by a noun (see Lesson 3, C5), *dore*, "which" out of three or more, cannot be followed by a noun. Compare:

Dono kamera ga yasui desu ka.
     Which camera is inexpensive?

Dore ga yasui desu ka.
     Which one is inexpensive?

Dore ga Wakayagi desu ka.
     Which one is Wakayagi?

Dore o kaimashoo ka.
     Which one should we buy?

6. OMITTING THE HONORIFIC *SAN*

When you refer to somebody who is a historical figure, an athlete, or a celebrity with whom you are not personally acquainted, you usually do not use *san*. Compare:

Yamada san ga tsuyoi desu.
     Mr. Yamada is strong. (The speaker knows Mr. Yamada.)

Wakayagi ga tsuyoi desu.
     Wakayagi is strong. (Wakayagi is a sumo wrestler.)

Fujinoyama mo tsuyoi desu kedo, kinoo makemashita.
     Fujinoyama is also strong, but yesterday he lost.

Watashi wa Kawabata Yasunari no shoosetsu ga suki desu.
     I like Kawabata Yasunari's novels.

D. MOJI (Characters)

For the syllables in Table II (page 6), variations of the basic *hiragana* characters are used. The following represents the syllables in line 1 through line 5.

HIRAGANA WITH TWO DOTS   cf.

LINE 1	*ga* が	*gi* ぎ	*gu* ぐ	*ge* げ	*go* ご	*ka* か	*ki* き	*ku* く	*ke* け	*ko* こ
LINE 2	*za* ざ	*ji* じ	*zu* ず	*ze* ぜ	*zo* ぞ	*sa* さ	*shi* し	*su* す	*se* せ	*so* そ
LINE 3	*da* だ	*(ji)* ぢ	*(zu)* づ	*de* で	*do* ど	*ta* た	*chi* ち	*tsu* つ	*te* て	*to* と
LINE 4	*ba* ば	*bi* び	*bu* ぶ	*be* べ	*bo* ぼ	*ha* は	*hi* ひ	*fu* ふ	*he* へ	*ho* ほ

HIRAGANA WITH A CIRCLE   cf.

LINE 5	*pa* ぱ	*pi* ぴ	*pu* ぷ	*pe* ぺ	*po* ぽ	*ha* は	*hi* ひ	*fu* ふ	*he* へ	*ho* ほ

On line 3 in Table II, *d* occurs only with *a*, *e*, and *o*, because Japanese does not have the syllables *di* and *du*. For *hiragana*, these two empty positions are filled with *ji* and *zu*. Note that line 2 also has *ji* and *zu*. The pronunciations of *ji* and *zu* on line 2 and on line 3 are identical. However, the *hiragana ji* じ and *zu* ず on line 2 are used most of the time, while ぢ and づ are used only in limited cases. (See Lesson 22.) Unless otherwise mentioned, always use じ and ず for *ji* and *zu*.

Read the following:

ちず
chizu
map

えんぴつ
enpitsu
pencil

たかいです。
Takai desu.
It is expensive.

ひるごはんを　たべましたか。
Hirugohan o tabemashita ka.
Did you have lunch?

E. TANGO TO HYOOGEN
(Vocabulary and Expressions)

sumoo	sumo wrestling
rikishi	sumo wrestler
karada	body
tenisu	tennis
shiai	tournament, match, game
terebi	television
kamera	camera
shashin	photograph
toshokan	library
shoosetsu	novel
koohii	coffee
gyuunyuu	cow's milk
tokoro	place
makemasu	to be defeated, lose
mimasu	to see, watch, look at
kakimasu	to write
torimasu	to take, get, obtain
tsuyoi	strong
akkenai	short and simple
omoshiroi	interesting
rippa	magnificent
shizuka	quiet
kirei	pretty, clean
joozu	skillful, good (at)
heta	unskillful, poor (at)
suki	to like (adj.)
daisuki	to like very much (adj.)
kirai	to dislike (adj.)
daikirai	to dislike very much (adj.)
dare	who
donata	who (honorific)
dore	which one
ima	now, at this moment
kono goro	recently
hee	dear me, really?
Soo desu ne.	Well./Let's see.

RENSHUU (EXERCISES)

A. Change the present-tense sentences to the past tense and vice versa.

1. *Mori san wa ikimasen.*
2. *Sakana o tabemasu ka.*
3. *Kore wa kissaten desu.*
4. *Watashi wa mimasen deshita.*

B. Insert the appropriate question words.

1. ———— *kutsu ga yasui desu ka.*
2. ———— *ga makemashita ka.*
   (*Miki san ga makemashita.*)
3. ———— *e ikimashoo ka.*
4. ———— *de terebi o mimasu ka.*

C. Translate the following into English.

1. *Watashi wa tenisu ga heta desu.*
2. *Kore wa donata no kamera desu ka.*
3. *Sumoo no hon wa omoshiroi desu.*
4. *Dore ga watashi no koohii desu ka.*

D. State whether the following are *i*-adjectives (I) or *na*-adjectives (N).

1. *ookii*
2. *shizuka*
3. *omoshiroi*
4. *takai*
5. *kirei*
6. *yuumei* "well-known"
7. *shinsetsu* "kind"
8. *tsuyoi*

E. Compliment your friend's new house using *na*-adjectives.

1. very (use different word) gate *(mon)*
2. very clean kitchen
3. very quiet neighborhood *(chiiki)*

F. Complete the sentences below in Japanese.

Example: I, negative, past, watch TV, yesterday.
   → *watashi wa kinoo, terebi o <u>mimasen deshita</u>.*

1. Question, you, present, like, sumo.
2. I, negative, past, eat, sushi.
3. I, negative, drink, coffee

G. Fill in the blanks with either *dore* or *dono*.

1. _____ *kamera ga yasui desu ka.*
2. _____ *ga ii kamera desu ka.*
3. _____ *kuruma o kau n desu ka.*
4. _____ *ga ii kuruma desu ka.*

KARUCHAA NOOTO
(Cultural Note)

Sumo wrestling is a very popular traditional national spectator sport, dating back to the sixth or seventh century. Today, sumo tournaments are held six times a year for fifteen days each. Two hefty competitors wrestle each other inside a circular ring measuring 14.9 feet in diameter. The wrestler who is pushed out of the ring or has any part of his body except for the soles of his feet touch the ground loses. Wrestlers are ranked according to their number of victories. The highest rank is *yokozuna* "grand champion."

The tournaments are televised and broadcast, and many Japanese people, both men and women, get excited about them. High-ranked sumo wrestlers are as popular as movie stars. A few non-Japanese sumo wrestlers have become popular, such as Akebono and Konishiki, both of whom are from Hawaii. No women are allowed to join mainstream sumo, although there may be female sumo wrestlers in some off-beat arenas.

KOTAE (ANSWERS)

A. 1. *ikimasen deshita.* 2. *tabemashita ka.* 3. *kissaten deshita.*
4. *mimasen.*
B. 1. *Dono* 2. *Dare or Donata* 3. *Doko* 4. *Doko*
C. 1. I play tennis poorly. 2. Whose camera is this? 3. The book on sumo wrestling is interesting. 4. Which one is my coffee?
D. 1. I 2. N 3. I 4. I 5. N 6. N 7. N 8. I
E. 1. *totemo rippa na mon desu ne.* 2. *totemo kirei na kitchin (daidokoro) desu ne.* 3. *totemo shizuka na chiiki desu ne.*
F. 1. *sumoo ga suki desu ka.* 2. *watashi wa (o)sushi o tabemasen deshita.*
3. *watashi wa koohii o nomimasen.*
G. 1. *dono* 2. *dore* 3. *dono* 4. *dore*

DAI GOKA
Lesson 5

EIGA.   Movies.

A. DAIAROOGU (Dialogue)

EIGA NO KOOKOKU.

Mr. Jones and Mr. Hara, who are colleagues, are chatting in the park during their lunch break.

JOONZU: **Sono kamí wa nán desu ka.**

HARA: **Eiga no kookoku désu. Ano eigákan no desu. Jóonzu san wa eiga o yóku mimásu ka.**

JOONZU: **Kono goro zenzen mimasén kedo, dáisuki desu.**

HARA: **Kono eiga o mimáshita ka. Nihon no eiga désu.**

JOONZU: **Tsubakíhime . . . Iie. Sore wa furúi desu ka.**

HARA: **Iie, fúruku arimasén. Amari yuumei ja arimasén kedo, omoshirói desu yo. Jáa, kore wa?**

JOONZU: **Áa, Kurosawa Ákira no Rashóomon desu ne. Háwai de mimáshita.**

HARA: **Watashi mo máe mimáshita kedo, mata mimasén ka.**

JOONZU: **Íi desu ne. Ikimashóo.**

A MOVIE ADVERTISEMENT.

JONES: What's that flyer [the paper] you have?

HARA: It's an advertisement for movies at that movie theater over there. Do you go to the movies?

JONES: Even though I haven't seen any at all recently, I really like movies.

HARA: Have you seen this one? It's a Japanese movie.

JONES: *Tsubakihime* . . . No, is it an old one?

HARA: No, it's not. It's not very well known, but it's interesting. Well then, how about this one?

JONES: Oh, it's Kurosawa Akira's *Rashomon*, isn't it? I saw it in Hawaii.

HARA: I've seen it [before], too, but would you like to see it again?

JONES: Why don't we? Let's go.

B. HATSUON (Pronunciation)

CONSONANTS AS PARTS OF SYLLABLES

h	like the English <u>h</u>	**hana** flower; **hon** book; **hyooshi** rhythm
f	different from the English <u>f</u>; force air out between the lips as if blowing out a candle	**fune** ship; **futa** lid
m	like the English <u>m</u>, but without tightening the lips as much	**machi** town; **michi** road; **myaku** pulse
r	pronounce by first placing the tip of the tongue at the back of the upper teeth and then flapping it	**riku** land; **renga** brick; **ryokan** inn

C. BUNPOO TO YOOHOO (Grammar and Usage)

1. ADJECTIVES IN THE PRESENT NEGATIVE

a. *I*-adjectives

To negate the present form, drop the final *-i* and add *-ku*. The result of this is called "KU form." Then, add *arimasen* to the KU form. Compare:

Furui desu.
It is old.

Furuku arimasen.
It is not old.

Kono eiga wa omoshiroku arimasen.
This movie is not interesting.

Nyuuyooku wa tooku arimasen.
New York is not far away.

Kono kutsu wa yoku arimasen.
These shoes are not good.

Note that both *yoi* and *ii* mean "good," but that the conjugated forms such as the present negative are derived only from *yoi*.

b. *Na*-adjectives

To negate the present form, change the copula *desu* to *ja arimasen* or *de wa arimasen*, as you do with nouns.

NOUNS:

Gakusei desu.
    I am a student.

Gakusei ja arimasen or *Gakusei de wa arimasen.*
    I am not a student.

NA-ADJECTIVES:

Yuumei desu.
    It is well-known.

Yuumei ja arimasen or *Yuumei de wa arimasen.*
    It is not well-known.

Kono puuru wa kirei ja arimasen.
    This swimming pool is not clean.

Watashi wa nihongo ga joozu ja arimasen.
    I am not good at Japanese.

2. *KO-SO-A-DO* WORDS

Some Japanese words indicating location come in sets of four that are usually pronounced alike, except for the first syllable. These sets of words are called "*ko-so-a-do* words" because the first syllable is always either: *ko-, so-, a-,* or *do-.*
    Ko- words refer to things at the same place as both the speaker and the listener, or at the same place as the speaker but away from the listener.
    So- words refer to things near the listener, or at the same place as the listener but away from the speaker.
    A- words refer to things outside of the immediate reach of both the speaker and the listener.
    Do- words are question words.

kono kami	this paper (by both of us)
sono kami	that paper (by you)
ano kami	that paper over there
dono kami	which paper (see Lesson 3, C5)

Kono, sono, ano, dono are so-called prenominal modifiers. They cannot stand alone but have to be followed by the noun that they modify. The following four words, on the other hand, cannot be followed by a noun.

kore	this one
sore	that one
are	that one over there
dore	which one (see Lesson 4, C5)

Kono eiga o mimashita ka.
  Did you see this movie?

Sore wa kookoku desu ka.
  Is that an advertisement?

Are wa eigakan desu.
  That one over there is a movie theater.

Dore ga yasashii desu ka.
  Which one is easy?

Dono tatemono ga chikai desu ka.
  Which building is near?

3. *NAN* "WHAT" PRECEDING *DESU, NO,* OR *DE* "BY MEANS OF"

The question word *nani* "what" changes to *nan* before *desu* and *no*. Before *de* "by means of," *nani* can, but doesn't have to, change to *nan*.

Sono kami wa nan desu ka.
  What is that paper? [That paper is what?]

Sore wa nan no kookoku desu ka.
  What advertisement is that? [That's an advertisement of what?]

Ashita nan de Nyuuyooku e ikimasu ka.
  How [by what means] will you go to New York tomorrow?

4. ADVERBS IN NEGATIVE SENTENCES

Adverbs modify verbs, adjectives, or adverbs. For example, *moo* "already," *yoku* "often," and *totemo* "very" are adverbs. Some adverbs are used only in negative sentences.

a. *Amari* "(not) very," "(not) often," "(not) much"

Compare:

Totemo yuumei desu.
    It is very well known.

Amari yuumei ja arimasen.
    It is not very well known.

Watashi wa amari atarashii eiga o mimasen.
    I don't see new movies often.

Kinoo amari tabemasen deshita.
    I didn't eat much yesterday.

b. *Zenzen* "(not) at all"

Kono goro zenzen mimasen.
    I don't see them at all these days.

Kono zasshi wa zenzen muzukashiku arimasen.
    This magazine is not difficult at all.

Kore wa zenzen yoku arimasen.
    This is not good at all.

5. THE PARTICLE *NO*

The particle *no* is used between two nouns to indicate possession, relation, and location (see Lesson 1, C7). The second noun can be omitted if the context allows it.

watashi no hon	→	*watashi no*
my book		mine

Ano eigakan no desu.
    It's that movie theater's (advertisement).

Kore wa donata no kaban desu ka.
    Whose bag is this?

Hara san no desu.
    It's Mr. Hara's.

D. MOJI (Characters)

In this lesson, you will learn *hiragana* characters for the rest of the syllables in Table II (page 6). *Ya* や, *yu* ゆ or *yo* よ should be smaller than the preceding *hiragana*, e.g., *kya* きゃ. If や, ゆ or よ have the same size as the preceding *hiragana*, the combination represents two syllables. Compare:

ONE SYLLABLE		TWO SYLLABLES	
きゃ	*kya*	きや	*kiya*
きゅ	*kyu*	きゆ	*kiyu*
きょ	*kyo*	きよ	*kiyo*

LINE 6	*kya* きゃ	*kyu* きゅ	*kyo* きょ	cf. *ki* き
LINE 7	*sha* しゃ	*shu* しゅ	*sho* しょ	cf. *shi* し
LINE 8	*cha* ちゃ	*chu* ちゅ	*cho* ちょ	cf. *chi* ち
LINE 9	*nya* にゃ	*nyu* にゅ	*nyo* にょ	cf. *ni* に
LINE 10	*hya* ひゃ	*hyu* ひゅ	*hyo* ひょ	cf. *hi* ひ
LINE 11	*mya* みゃ	*myu* みゅ	*myo* みょ	cf. *mi* み
LINE 12	*rya* りゃ	*ryu* りゅ	*ryo* りょ	cf. *ri* り
LINE 13	*gya* ぎゃ	*gyu* ぎゅ	*gyo* ぎょ	cf. *gi* ぎ
LINE 14	*ja* じゃ （ぢゃ）	*ju* じゅ （ぢゅ）	*jo* じょ （ぢょ）	cf. *ji* じ （ぢ）

Like *ji* ぢ (see Lesson 4), *ja* ぢゃ, *ju* ぢゅ and *jo* ぢょ are also used only in limited cases.

LINE 15	bya びゃ	byu びゅ	byo びょ	cf. bi び
LINE 16	pya ぴゃ	pyu ぴゅ	pyo ぴょ	cf. pi ぴ
LINE 17	p	t	k	s

P, t, k, and *s* on line 17 are single-consonant syllables. For these syllables, you write *tsu* つ. But this つ should be smaller than the other *hiragana*, e.g., *kissaten* きっさてん .

Read the following:

どなたが　がくちょうの　ひしょですか。
Donata ga gakuchoo no hisho desu ka.
 Who is the university president's secretary?

たった　にひゃくえんでした。
Tatta nihyakuen deshita.
 It was only 200 yen.

E. TANGO TO HYOOGEN

eiga	movie
eigakan	movie theater
tatemono	building
puuru	swimming pool
kami	paper
kookoku	advertisement
zasshi	magazine
kaban	totebag, briefcase
nihongo	Japanese language
furui	old
atarashii	new
muzukashii	difficult
yasashii	easy
tooi	far
chikai	near
yuumei	famous, well known
amari	(not) very, (not) often, (not) much
zenzen	(not) at all
nan (<nani)	what

mae	previously, before, in front
mata	again
jaa	well then
kono	this
sono	that
ano	that over there
sore	that one
are	that one over there

RENSHUU (EXERCISES)

A. Mark the statements T (true) or F (false) on the basis of the dialogue.

1. *Joonzu san wa eiga ga daisuki desu.*
2. *Hara san wa mae Rashoomon o mimashita.*
3. *Joonzu san wa Rashoomon o Ginza de mimashita.*

B. Transform the affirmative into the negative, and vice versa.

1. *Shokudoo wa shizuka de wa arimasen.*
2. *Depaato wa tooi desu.*
3. *Kinoo Nyuuyooku e ikimashita.*
4. *Watashi no kamera wa atarashiku arimasen.*
5. *Uchi wa ookiku arimasen.*

C. Choose the correct word.

1. *(Ano/Are) tatemono wa furui desu.*
2. *(Dono/Dore) ga muzukashii desu ka.*
3. *(Dono/Dore) eiga ga yuumei desu ka.*
4. *(Sono/Sore) hon wa omoshiroi desu yo.*
5. *(Kono/Kore) wa Yamada san no terebi desu.*

D. Fill in the blanks.

Example: *Kissaten wa ookii desu ka.*
     Iie, <u>ookiku</u> arimasen. <u>Chiisai</u> desu.

1. *Kono hon wa yasashii desu ka.*
   Iie, _____ arimasen. _____ desu.
2. *Eigakan wa chikai desu ka.*
   Iie, _____ arimasen. _____ desu.
3. *Moroo san wa nihongo ga joozu desu ka.*
   Iie, _____ arimasen. _____ desu.
4. *Uchi wa furui desu ka.*
   Iie, _____ arimasen. _____ desu.

E. Complete the sentences using either *i*-adjectives or *na*-adjectives.

1. *depaato* in Tokyo, negative, small
2. the actor *(haiyuu)*, negative, famous
3. Mr. Jones' house, affirmative, expensive
4. the book, negative, interesting

F. Choose the appropriate adverb(s) for the following sentences.

1. *kono kuruma wa (totemo/amari/zenzen) takai desu.*
2. *watashi no uchi wa eki kara (totemo/amari/zenzen) tooi desu.*
3. *sono eiga wa (totemo/amari/zenzen) omoshiroku arimasen.*
4. *kono kamera wa atarashii desu kedo (totemo/amari/zenzen) yoku arimasen.*

KARUCHAA NOOTO
(Cultural Note)

Both Japanese and Western movies are popular in Japan. American movies and their stars are especially well known, for example, Gary Cooper and Audrey Hepburn in the past, and Tom Cruise, Jodie Foster, Julia Roberts, and other stars that are popular in the USA, today. Some Japanese movies have won international acclaim. Movie directors such as Kurosawa Akira, Kinugasa Teinosuke, Mizoguchi Kenji, and Ozu Yasujiro are highly regarded. *Rashomon*, directed by Kurosawa Akira, won the Grand Prix at the Venice Film Festival in 1951. Since then, many Japanese movies have received awards at international film festivals. For example, *Gates of Hell* by Kinugasa and *Kagemusha* by Kurosawa won the Grand Prix at the Cannes Film Festival in 1964 and 1980, respectively.

KOTAE (ANSWERS)

A. 1. T   2. T   3. F
B. 1. *shizuka desu.*   2. *tooku arimasen.*   3. *ikimasen deshita.*   4. *atarashii desu.*   5. *ookii desu.*
C. 1. *Ano*   2. *Dore*   3. *Dono*   4. *Sono*   5. *Kore*
D. 1. *yasashiku, Muzukashii*   2. *chikaku, Tooi*   3. *joozu ja* or *joozu de wa, Heta*   4. *furuku, Atarashii*
E. 1. *Tookyoo no depaato wa chiisaku arimasen.* 2. *sono haiyuu wa yuumei dewa arimasen.* 3. *Joonzu san no uchi wa takai desu.* 4. *sono hon wa omoshiroku arimasen.*
F. 1. *totemo*   2. *totemo*   3. *amari* or *zenzen*   4. *amari* or *zenzen*

FUKUSHUU 1 (FIRST REVIEW)

A. Fill in the blanks with *wa* or *ga*.

1. *Mori san* _____ *nihonjin desu.* (emphasis on *Mori san*)
2. *Kore* _____ *watashi no hon desu.* (*Kore* is not emphasized.)
3. *Ashita dare* _____ *kimasu ka.*
4. *Doko* _____ *shizuka desu ka.*

B. Fill in the blanks with the appropriate form of the word given in parentheses.

1. *Kutsu wa amari* _____ *arimasen.* (*takai*)
2. *Kinoo gakkoo e* _____ *deshita.* (*ikimasu*)
3. *Ano kissaten wa* _____ *arimasen.* (*shizuka*)

C. Each pair consists of a question and its answer. Fill in the blanks.

1. _____ *o nomimasu ka.*
   Juusu _____ *nomimasu.*
2. *Dono tatemono desu* _____.
   Ano tatemono _____.
3. *Nani* _____ *shimashita ka.*
   Terebi o mi _____.

D. Choose from the particles in parentheses to match the English translation.

1. *Tanaka san wa gakusei desu (ne, yo, ka).*
   Ms. Tanaka is a student, isn't she?
2. *Kamera (de, o, ga) kaimashita.*
   I bought a camera.
3. *Depaato (o, de, wa) mimashita.*
   I saw it in the department store.
4. *Watashi (wa, mo, to) nihon no eiga (mo, ga, de) suki desu.*
   I like Japanese movies.

E. Match the Japanese and the English.

1. _____ *Irasshai.*   a. Good night.
2. _____ *Hee.*   b. Not too bad.
3. _____ *Oyasumi nasai.*   c. Welcome.
4. _____ *Hajimemashite.*   d. How do you do?
5. _____ *Maa maa.*   e. Dear me.

F. Match a word or phrase in Group I with Group II to form a sentence.

I
1. *Hara san o* _____
2. *Furui desu kedo, ii* _____
3. *Kono* _____
4. *Depaato e* _____
5. *Nani o* _____
6. *Doko ga* _____

II
a. *desu yo.*
b. *ikimashoo ka.*
c. *kirei desu ka.*
d. *kaimashoo ka.*
e. *kissaten ga ookii desu.*
f. *mimashita.*

G. Choose the correct word.

1. _____ *o nomimashita.*
   a. *Ocha* b. *Bara* c. *Shashin*
2. _____ *de oyogimashita.*
   a. *Kissaten* b. *Sakana* c. *Puuru*
3. _____ *tomodachi ga kimasu.*
   a. *Ototoi* b. *Kinoo* c. *Ashita*
4. *Ano* _____ *wa akarui desu.*
   a. *toshokan* b. *ocha* c. *enpitsu*

H. Write the English equivalents.

Example: あした tomorrow

1. ともだち

2. なまえ

3. みせ

4. ざっし

5. ひゃくえん

KOTAE (ANSWERS)

A. 1. *ga* 1. *wa* 3. *ga* 4. *ga*
B. 1. *takaku* 2. *ikimasen* 3. *shizuka ja* or *shizuka de wa*
C. 1. *Nani, o* 2. *ka, desu* 3. *o, mashita*
D. 1. *ne* 2. *o* 3. *de* 4. *wa, ga*
E. 1. c 2. e 3. a 4. d 5. b
F. 1. f 2. a 3. e 4. b 5. d 6. c
G. 1. a 2. c 3. c 4. a
H. 1. friend 2. name 3. store 4. magazine 5. one hundred yen

DAI ROKKA
Lesson 6
TENKOO, KISETSU.   Weather, Seasons.

A. DAIAROOGU

ARU SAMUI HI NI.

Ms. Brown and Mr. Nakai are members of a youth group in their neighborhood. They run into each other in town.

BURAUN: **Okaerinasái. Kyóoto wa dóo deshita ka.**

NAKAI: **Kankoo ryókoo ja arimasén deshita kedo, kékkoo tanóshikatta desu yo. Yudóofu o takusan tabemáshita.**

BURAUN: **Áa, watashi mo yudóofu ga sukí desu. Oténki wa yókatta desu ka.**

NAKAI: **Sóo desu ne. Yukí ga furimáshita kedo, amari sámuku arimasén deshita. Ryokan no niwa ga yukí de totemo kírei deshita yo.**

BURAUN: **Otera ya jínja mo mimáshita ka.**

NAKAI: **Iie, mitákatta n desu kedo, jikan ga arimasén deshita. Ítsuka yukkúri mitái desu. Buráun san mo Kyóoto ga sukí desu ka.**

BURAUN: **Ée, watashi wa kotoshi no háru Kyóoto e ikimáshita. Kyóoto no machí wa amari kírei ja arimasén deshita kedo, yamá ya shokubutsúen ga totemo yókatta desu. Choodo shóobu no kisétsu deshita. Tookyoo mo háru subarashíi desu kedo.**

NAKAI: **Ée, sore ni shitémo, Tookyoo wa kono fuyu hontoo ni samúi desu née.**

BURAUN: **Ée, watashi no apáato wa totemo samúi n desu. Sutóobu ya móofu ya kotatsu o kaimáshita kedo, sore démo samúi n desu.**

NAKAI: **Kissáten de koohíi o nomimasén ka. Atatamaritái n desu.**

BURAUN: **Íi desu ne.**

ON A COLD DAY.

BROWN: Welcome back. How was Kyoto?

NAKAI: It was not a sight-seeing trip, but it was a lot of fun anyway. I ate a lot of *yudoofu*.*

BROWN: Oh, I like *yudoofu*, too. Was the weather nice?

NAKAI: Well, it snowed, but it wasn't too cold. The garden at the inn was very pretty with the snow.

BROWN: Did you also see any temples and shrines [and the like]?

NAKAI: No, I wanted to, but I didn't have time. Someday I want to take my time seeing them. Do you like Kyoto, too?

BROWN: Yes, I went there this spring [in the spring this year]. The city [of Kyoto] was not very clean, but the mountains and botanical gardens [and the like] were very nice. I went there right in the middle of iris season. Tokyo is wonderful, in the spring, too, though.

NAKAI: Well, be that as it may, this winter Tokyo is really cold.

BROWN: Yes, my apartment is very cold. I bought a space heater, blankets, a *kotatsu*† [and so on], but I'm still cold.

NAKAI: Why don't we get [drink] some coffee in a coffee shop? Maybe that will warm us up [I want to warm myself].

BROWN: That sounds nice.

B. HATSUON

CONSONANTS AS PARTS OF SYLLABLES

g	at the beginning of a word, pronounced like the g in go	**gaikoku** foreign country; **gin** silver ‡
z	like the English z	**zubon** pants; **zehi** by all means
j	like the English j	**jikan** time; **jagaimo** potato
d	like the English d, but less explosive	**dare** who; **denwa** telephone

* *Yudoofu* is a tofu dish.
† A *kotatsu* is a heated table.
‡ In the middle of a word, *g* usually has a nasal quality and sounds similar to the *ng* in sin*g*er: *hagaki* postcard; *kagi* key. The nasalization of *g* is optional. You will be understood if you use a hard *g*.

b	generally pronounced like the English *b,* but less explosive	**ban** evening; **bijutsu** art
p	like the English *p,* but less explosive	**pan** bread; **sanpun** three minutes

C. BUNPOO TO YOOHOO

1. THE PAST NEGATIVE OF THE COPULA WITH NOUNS

To form the past negative of the copula (*desu*), add *deshita* to its present negative form *ja arimasen* or *de wa arimasen* (see Lesson 1, C3). Compare:

Kankoo ryokoo ja/de wa arimasen.
    It's not a sight-seeing trip.

Kankoo ryokoo ja/de wa arimasen deshita.
    It was not a sight-seeing trip.

Otera ja arimasen deshita. Jinja deshita.
    It was not a temple. It was a shrine.

Hara san no apaato ja arimasen deshita.
    It was not Ms. Hara's apartment.

2. THE PAST TENSE OF *I*-ADJECTIVES

a. Affirmative

To form the past affirmative of an *i*-adjective, replace the final -*i* with *katta* and add *desu.* Compare:

Tanoshii desu.   *Tanoshikatta desu.*
    It is fun.   It was fun.

Ryokan wa takakatta desu.
    The inn was expensive.

Otenki wa totemo yokatta desu.
    The weather was very good.

As in the case of the present affirmative, *n* can be inserted before *desu* for emphasis or to mean "the fact was that . . ." or "indeed" (see Lesson 3, C4).

Totemo suzushikatta n desu.
[Indeed,] it was very cool.

Otenki ga warukatta n desu.
[Indeed,] the weather was bad.

Ryokan wa takakatta n desu.
[Indeed,] the inn was expensive.

b. Negative

In the past negative of an *i*-adjective, *deshita* is added to the present negative *-ku arimasen* (see Lesson 5, C1). Compare:

Samuku arimasen.	*Samuku arimasen deshita.*
It is not cold.	It was not cold.

Tomodachi no apaato wa ookiku arimasen deshita.
My friend's apartment was not big.

Ano kissaten wa atatakaku arimasen deshita.
That coffee shop over there was not warm.

3. THE PAST TENSE OF *NA*-ADJECTIVES

The past affirmative and negative forms of the copula used with *na*-adjectives are the same as those used with nouns: *deshita* (affirmative) and *ja/de wa arimasen deshita* (negative). The form of the *na*-adjective does not change.

a. Affirmative

Kirei deshita.
It was pretty.

Ryokan no niwa wa rippa deshita.
The garden of the inn was magnificent.

Shokubutsuen wa shizuka deshita.
The botanical garden was quiet.

b. Negative

Kyooto no machi wa amari kirei ja arimasen deshita.
The city of Kyoto was not very clean.

Kissaten wa shizuka ja arimasen deshita.
The coffee shop was not quiet.

Amari suki ja arimasen deshita.
I did not like it very much.

4. CONJUGATION SUMMARY

The following is a summary of the forms of verbs, adjectives, and nouns in the affirmative and negative of the present and past tenses.

	PRESENT AFFIRMATIVE	PRESENT NEGATIVE	PAST AFFIRMATIVE	PAST NEGATIVE
VERB	*Tabemasu.* (I) eat. (I) will eat.	*Tabemasen.* (I) don't eat. (I) will not eat.	*Tabemashita.* (I) ate.	*Tabemasen deshita.* (I) didn't eat.
I-ADJECTIVE	*Ookii desu* (It) is big.	*Ookiku arimasen.* (It) is not big.	*Ookikatta desu.* (It) was big.	*Ookiku arimasen deshita.* (It) was not big.
NA ADJECTIVE +COPULA	*Shizuka desu.* (It) is quiet.	*Shizuka ja/de wa arimasen.* (It) is not quiet.	*Shizuka deshita.* (It) was quiet.	*Shizuka ja/de wa arimasen deshita.* (It) was not quiet.
NOUN +COPULA	*Gakusei desu.* (I) am a student.	*Gakusei ja/de wa arimasen.* (I) am not a student.	*Gakusei deshita.* (I) was a student.	*Gakusei ja/de wa arimasen deshita.* (I) was not a student.

5. TIME EXPRESSIONS

The following words are the most common expressions of time.

haru	spring
natsu	summer
aki	fall
fuyu	winter
asa	morning
hiru	noon
ban	evening
yoru	night

mainichi	*kyoo*	*kinoo*	*ashita*
every day	today	yesterday	tomorrow
maishuu	*konshuu*	*senshuu*	*raishuu*
every week	this week	last week	next week
maitsuki or	*kongetsu*	*sengetsu*	*raigetsu*
maigetsu			
every month	this month	last month	next month
maitoshi or	*kotoshi*	*kyonen*	*rainen*
mainen			
every year	this year	last year	next year

Usually the time expressions above are not followed by any particle.*

Tookyoo mo haru subarashii desu.
Tokyo is also wonderful in the spring.

Tookyoo wa kono fuyu hontoo ni samui desu nee.
Tokyo is really cold this winter, isn't it?

Dewa mata raishuu.
See you next week [Well then, next week again].

6. PARTICLES

a. *Ya*

Ya connects two or more nouns similar to *to*. *To* simply means "and," but *ya* implies at least one additional item that is not specifically mentioned. Compare:

Otera to jinja o mimashita.
I saw temples and shrines.

Otera ya jinja o mimashita.
I saw temples, shrines, and other things like that.

Sutoobu ya moofu ya kotatsu o kaimashita.
I bought a space heater, blankets, a *kotatsu*, and so on.

Yama ya shokubutsuen e ikimashita.
I went to the mountains, the botanical garden, and other places.

b. *De*

Another meaning of *de* is "because of" or "for."

---

* The cases where particles do follow these time nouns are explained in C6 of this lesson and in later lessons.

Ryokan no niwa ga yuki de totemo kirei deshita.
  The garden of the inn was very pretty with [because of] the snow.

Kono shokubutsuen wa shoobu de yuumei desu.
  This botanical garden is famous for irises.

Kono resutoran wa oishii koohii de yuumei desu.
  This restaurant is famous for delicious coffee.

c. *Ga*

One meaning of the verb *arimasu* is "to have." In those cases, the item which is possessed (comparable to the direct object in English) is followed by *ga*, not by *o* (see Lesson 2, C3).

Watashi wa jikan ga arimasu.
  I have the time.

Zenzen jikan ga arimasen deshita.
  I did not have the time at all.

Watashi wa okane ga arimasen.
  I don't have any money.

With *wakarimasu* "to understand" and *dekimasu* "to be able to do," the item serving as a direct object (in English) is followed by *ga* as well, not by *o*.

Watashi wa Nihongo ga wakarimasu.
  I understand Japanese.

Tomodachi wa hon'yaku ga dekimasu.
  My friend can translate [can do translation].

d. *Mo*

So far, *mo*, which means "also," "too," or "either," has been used with the subject.

Shikago mo samukatta desu.
  Chicago was cold, too.

Mo can be used with other parts of the sentence as well.

Yamada san wa okane ga arimasu. Sore ni hima mo arimasu.
  Mr. Yamada has money. Besides, he has free time, too.

Otera ya jinja mo mimashita ka.
  Did you also see temples and shrines?

The English sentence "Ms. Brown bought a blanket, too." is ambiguous. It could mean "Someone bought a blanket, and so did Ms.

Brown." or "Ms. Brown bought a blanket, and something else, too." In Japanese, no ambiguity occurs, because the placement of the particle clarifies the meaning.

Buraun san mo moofu o kaimashita.
Ms. Brown bought a blanket [someone else did, too].

Buraun san wa moofu mo kaimashita.
Ms. Brown bought a blanket [as well as something else].

e. *No*

No is used between two nouns describing time.

kotoshi no haru
this spring [(in) the spring of this year]

Buraun san wa kyonen no aki Nihon e kimashita.
Ms. Brown came to Japan last fall [in the fall of last year].

Kinoo no asa ame ga furimashita.
It rained yesterday morning.

Kinoo no ame wa hidokatta desu.
Yesterday's rain was awful.

7. THE QUESTION WORD *DOO*

Doo, translated as "how" or "how about," is often used before the copula.

Kyooto wa doo deshita ka.
How was Kyoto?

Otenki wa doo deshita ka.
How was the weather?

Dono kissaten e ikimashoo ka.
Which coffee shop shall we go to?

Ano kissaten wa doo desu ka.
How about that coffee shop over there?

The verbs *omoimasu* "to think" and *shimasu* "to do" are often used with *doo*.

Doo omoimasu ka.
What [how] do you think?

Doo shimashita ka.
What happened?

8. *-TAI** "TO WANT TO—"

-tai "to want to . . ." is an *i*-adjective and conjugated like other *i*-adjectives. It follows the pre-*masu* form (e.g., *tabe* from *tabemasu*) of a verb.

tabetai
    want to eat

Tabetai desu.
    I want to eat.

Watashi wa pan o tabetai desu.
    I want to eat the bread.

Atatamaritai n desu.
    I want to warm myself.

Otera ya jinja o mitakatta n desu.
    I wanted to see temples and shrines [etc.].

Amari tabetaku arimasen deshita.
    I didn't want to eat very much.

-tai is normally used to indicate the speaker's desire. It should be avoided when asking about an addressee's desire if he or she is a superior. *-Tai* is not used to talk about a third person's desire. These rules hold true for all expressions with "want."†

9. THE POLITE MARKER *O-*

The prefix *o-* can be used with certain nouns to make them more polite. *O-* has two functions. One is to elevate another person's belongings to show your respect for that person. The other is simply to show overall politeness, whether the thing referred to is the speaker's or someone else's. Whether *o-* shows respect or simple politeness depends on the word. For example, *o-* attached to *namae* "name" shows respect, and thus, you cannot say *watashi no onamae* "my name," because it is considered inappropriate for the speaker to elevate him or herself.

---

* For "to want" plus noun (e.g., "I want the bread"), see Lesson 7. For "to want someone to . . ." (e.g., I want you to eat the bread), see Lesson 32.

† Not all verbs can be used with *-tai*. See Lesson 7 for *arimasu* ("to want to have") and Lesson 30 for *dekimasu* ("to want to be able to") and *wakarimasu* ("to want to understand").

The following cases of *o-* show simple politeness.

otenki	weather
otera	temple
osushi	sushi
omizu	water
ocha	tea
okane	money

The use of *o-* is optional depending on the item referred to, regardless of whether its function is respect or simple politeness. Among the examples above, "tea" (*cha*) and "money" (*kane*) without *o-* sound harsh, while *mizu* "water" does not.

Native speakers may differ in their notions of politeness. In general, women tend to use *o-* more frequently than men.

There are also words that are never used with *o-*.

gakkoo	school
tatemono	building
terebi	TV

O- can also be used with adjectives, verbs, and adverbs.*

Mainichi osamui desu ne. (simple politeness)
　It is cold every day, isn't it?

Buraun san wa yudoofu ga osuki desu. (respect)
　Ms. Brown likes *yudoofu.*

10. SENTENCES WITH QUANTITY EXPRESSIONS

The typical word order in quantity expressions such as *takusan* "many, much" or *sukoshi* "a few, a little" is noun + particle + quantity . . . verb.

Yudoofu o takusan tabemashita.
　I ate a lot of *yudoofu.*

Mainen gaikokujin ga takusan Kyooto e ikimasu.
　Many foreigners go to Kyoto every year.

Yuki ga sukoshi furimashita.
　It snowed a little.

* For verbs with *o-*, see Lesson 26.

D. MOJI

DOUBLE VOWELS IN *HIRAGANA*

The second vowels *a, i, u, e* are written as あ、い、う、え、respectively.

aa	*okaasan* (mother)	*o*	*ka*	*a*	*sa*	*n*
		お	か	あ	さ	ん

ii	*oishii* (tasty)	*o*	*i*	*shi*	*i*
		お	い	し	い

uu	*kuuki* (air)	*ku*	*u*	*ki*
		く	う	き

ee	*oneesan* (older sister)	*o*	*ne*	*e*	*sa*	*n*
		お	ね	え	さ	ん

However, to write *oo*, you almost always use the *hiragana* for the vowel-syllable *u* (う) in place of the second *o*.

Tookyoo (Tokyo)	*To*	*o*	*kyo*	*o*
	と	う	きょ	う

gakkoo (school)	*ga*	*k*	*ko*	*o*
	が	っ	こ	う

For some words, お (*o*) is used instead of う, but these exceptions are not numerous. Memorize them. Here are the ones among the words you have already learned.

ookii	big	おおきい
tooi	far	とおい

Other exceptions include:

too	ten	とお
ookami	wolf	おおかみ
toorimasu	to pass	とおります
koori	ice	こおり
ooi	many	おおい
toori	street	とおり

Read the following:

いきましょうか。
Should we go?

ゆうめいです。
It is well-known.

ああ、そうですか。
I see.

E. TANGO TO HYOOGEN

(o)tenki	weather
ame	rain
yuki	snow
kisetsu	season
haru	spring
natsu	summer
aki	fall
fuyu	winter
asa	morning
hiru	noon
ban	evening
yoru	night
maishuu	every week
konshuu	this week
senshuu	last week
raishuu	next week
maitsuki/maigetsu	every month

kongetsu	this month
sengetsu	last month
raigetsu	next month
maitoshi/mainen	every year
kotoshi	this year
kyonen	last year
rainen	next year
machi	town, downtown, city
(o)tera	Buddhist temple
jinja	Shinto shrine
apaato	apartment
ryokan	inn, Japanese hotel
niwa	garden
shokubutsuen	botanical garden
yama	mountain
shoobu	iris
sutoobu	space heater
kotatsu	heater attached to a table for warming the legs and feet
moofu	blanket
okane	money
(o)mizu	water
yudoofu	tofu dish cooked with broth and eaten with condiments
(o)sushi	sushi
gaikokujin	foreigner
hon'yaku	translation
jikan	time
hima	free time
furimasu	to fall (precipitation)
atatamarimasu	to warm oneself
omoimasu	to think
arimasu	to have
wakarimasu	to understand
dekimasu	to be able to do
atsui	hot
samui	cold
atatakai	warm
suzushii	cool
subarashii	wonderful
tanoshii	fun
hidoi	awful
-tai	to want to . . .
doo	how, how about

takusan	many, much
sukoshi	a few, a little
yukkuri	leisurely, by taking time
kekkoo	quite, very well, well enough
choodo	right, exactly, just
dewa	well then (more formal than *jaa*)
sore ni	besides, in addition
sore ni shite mo	nevertheless, however, be that as it may
sore de mo	still
hontoo ni	really
Okaeri(nasai).	Welcome back.
o-	honorific marker

RENSHUU

A. Mr. Smith's friend asked him how his trip to Japan was. His responses follow. Translate the statements into Japanese.

   1. It rained a lot.
   2. Tokyo was warm.
   3. The mountains in Kyoto were pretty.
   4. The inn in Kyoto was not very expensive.

B. It is very cold today. Four people would like to do the following. Translate their statements.

   1. *Yudoofu o takusan tabetai desu.*
   2. *Kissaten de atsui koohii o nomitai desu.*
   3. *Depaato de kotatsu o kaitai desu.*
   4. *Hawai e ikitai desu.*

C. Fill in the blanks with particles according to the English equivalents.

   1. *Shoobu* _____ *bara* _____ *kaimashita.*
     I bought irises, roses, etc.
   2. *Kono ryokan wa yudoofu* _____ *yuumei desu.*
     This inn is famous for *yudoofu.*
   3. *Ashita* _____ *ban jikan* _____ *arimasu ka.*
     Do you have time tomorrow evening?
   4. *Abe san wa tenisu* _____ *dekimasu.*
     Ms. Abe can play tennis.

D. Fill in the blanks according to the English equivalents.

1. _____ *Kyooto e* _____ *n desu.*
   I wanted to go to Kyoto last month.
2. *Uchi e* _____ *arimasen.*
   I don't want to go home.
3. *Juusu o* _____ *nomimashita.*
   I drank a little juice.
4. *Ryokoo wa* _____ *deshita ka.*
   How was the trip?

KARUCHAA NOOTO

Japan consists of four main islands and more than four thousand small ones. Tokyo and Kyoto (which was the capital from the eighth century to the nineteenth century, when the modern era started and Tokyo became the capital) are on the largest island, *Honshuu.* Since Japan is a long narrow country stretching from northeast to southwest, the climate varies quite a bit from place to place. The southern regions are warmer than the northern ones. Furthermore, since mountain ranges run down the center from north to south, the climates on the Pacific side and on the Japan Sea side are different. The Japan Sea side has much more snow in winter. Generally speaking, however, Japan has four distinct seasons. It is cold in winter. Tokyo can have below-freezing temperatures, but the average temperature in the winter is between 4° and 6° Celsius. It is hot and humid in the summer, with an average summer temperature of around 25°C. Since not many homes have central heating or air-conditioning, the best time to visit Japan may be in May, when new green leaves abound and beautiful flowers blossom everywhere, or in October, when the leaves turn. Sports fans, however, may enjoy summer and winter sports.

KOTAE

A. 1. *Ame ga takusan furimashita.* 2. *Tookyoo wa atatakakatta (n) desu.*
3. *Kyooto no yama wa kirei deshita.* 4. *Kyooto no ryokan wa amari takaku arimasen deshita.*
B. 1. I want to eat a lot of *yudoofu.* 2. I want to drink hot coffee in a coffee shop. 3. I want to buy a *kotatsu* in a department store. 4. I want to go to Hawaii.
C. 1. *ya, o* 2. *de* 3. *no, ga* 4. *ga*
D. 1. *Sengetsu, ikitakatta* 2. *kaeritaku* 3. *sukoshi* 4. *doo*

DAI NANAKA
Lesson 7
IFUKU, IRO.   Clothing, Colors.

A. DAIAROOGU

FUJINFUKUTEN DE.

A young woman enters a boutique in Kobe looking for a suit.

TEN'IN: **Irasshaimáse.**

KYAKU: **Súutsu ga hoshíi n desu kedo.**

TEN'IN: **Takusan arimásu. Dóozo. Dónna iró ga osuki désu ka.**

KYAKU: **Sóo desu ne. Pínku ya áka ga sukí desu kedo.**

TEN'IN: **Kore wa dóo desu ka. Kono kurói botan wa atarashíi sutáiru desu.**

KYAKU: **Kawaíi súutsu desu ne. Sukáato ga chótto mijikái desu ne.**

TEN'IN: **Jáa, kore wa dóo desu ka. Sukáato wa nagái desu.**

KYAKU: **Kono sáizu wa nána desu ne. Sóo desu ne. Chótto shichaku shitái n desu kedo.**

TEN'IN: **Hái, ano shichakúshitsu e dóozo.**

Shibaraku shite.

TEN'IN: **Dóo deshita ka.**

KYAKU: **Totemo íi n desu kedo, chótto kitsúi n desu. Kyúu ka juuichí mo arimásu ka.**

TEN'IN: **Kyúu ka juuichí desu ka. Ainiku íma wa arimasén ne. Ráigetsu hairimásu kedo.**

KYAKU: **Jáa, mata kimásu.**

TEN'IN: **Hái, arígatoo gozaimasu.**

AT A BOUTIQUE.

CLERK: May I help you?

CUSTOMER: Yes, I'm looking for a suit [I want a suit].

CLERK: We have lots of them. Please take a look. What [kind of] color would you like?

CUSTOMER: Well, I like [colors like] pink or red.

CLERK: How about this one? These black buttons are the new style.

CUSTOMER: It's a cute suit. But the skirt is a little short, isn't it?

CLERK: Well then, how about this one? The skirt is longer [long].

CUSTOMER: This one is a size seven, isn't it? Yes, why not? I'd like to try it on.

CLERK: Okay. You can use that dressing room over there.

A little later.

CLERK: How was it?

CUSTOMER: It's very nice, but it's a little tight. Do you have size nine* or perhaps eleven, too?

CLERK: Nine or eleven? Unfortunately, we don't have those sizes now. They'll be coming in next month.

CUSTOMER: All right, I'll come back then.

CLERK: Very well. Thank you very much.

B. HATSUON

SEMI-VOWELS

y	pronounced like the English *y* in *yacht* before the vowel *a, u* or *o*	**yama** mountain; **yuki** snow; **yoru** night; **hiyoo** cost
	between a consonant and a vowel, consonant palatalized (said with the	**hyaku** one hundred; **kyuu** nine; **ryoo** dorm; **hihyoo** criticism

---

* Sizes seven, nine, and eleven are women's clothing sizes, which are assigned in odd numbers. Sizes three through seven are considered "small," sizes nine through thirteen are considered "medium," and sizes above fifteen are considered "large."

| | tongue approaching or touching the palate) | |
| w | pronounced somewhat like the English $\underline{w}$ in $\underline{want}$, but without rounding or protruding the lips | **watashi** I; **kawa** river |

C. BUNPOO TO YOOHOO

1. *HOSHII* "TO WANT" PLUS NOUNS

In the previous lesson, you learned how to say "to want to . . ." plus verb (see Lesson 6, C8).

Kimono o kitai n desu.
　I want to wear a kimono.

The English verb "to want" followed by a noun is translated as *hoshii*, which is an *i*-adjective. The word for the item desired is followed by *ga*. Sentences with *hoshii* "to want" are formed exactly like the ones with *suki* "to like" (see Lesson 4, C4).

> Someone *wa* something *ga hoshii (n) desu*

Suutsu ga hoshii desu.
　I want a suit.

Atarashii fuku ga hoshikatta n desu.
　I wanted new clothes.

Seetaa to sukaafu ga hoshii n desu.
　I want a sweater and a scarf.

Hoshii is only used when dealing with the speaker's desire.
　As you may remember from the previous lesson, *arimasu* "to have" cannot be used with *-tai* "to want to. . . ." To say "I want to have money," simply use *hoshii*.

Okane ga hoshii desu.
　I want (to have) money.

Nagai beruto ga hoshikatta n desu.
　I wanted (to have) a long belt.

2. *SHIMASU* VERBS

Some nouns are activity nouns, which denote actions, rather than physical objects. In English, they are expressed either with the -ing form (gerund), as for example, "studying," or with regular nouns, such as "laundry."

Studying Japanese is fun.
I have to do laundry today.

In Japanese, the combination of an activity noun and the verb *shimasu* "to do" becomes one verb, called a "*shimasu* verb."

NOUN		VERB
shichaku trying something on + *shimasu*	→	*shichaku shimasu* to try something on
sentaku laundry + *shimasu*	→	*sentaku shimasu* to do laundry
benkyoo studying + *shimasu*	→	*benkyoo shimasu* to study

Shichaku shitai n desu.
   I want to try it on.

Kinoo seetaa o sentaku shimashita.
   I washed the sweater yesterday.

Toshokan de nihongo o benkyoo shimashita.
   I studied Japanese at the library.

O can be inserted between the activity noun and *shimasu*. Then the activity noun becomes the direct object and only *shimasu* is the verb.

NOUN (direct object)		VERB
Benkyoo	*o*	*shimasu.*

When *o* is inserted, you cannot have another direct object before the activity noun. Use *no* instead. Compare the same sentence with and without *o* between the activity noun and *shimasu*.

Nihongo no benkyoo o shimashita.
Nihongo o benkyoo shimashita.
   I studied Japanese.

3. COLORS

In English, colors are treated as adjectives or nouns. In Japanese, all colors are treated as nouns.

aka	red	*shiro*	white
kuro	black	*ao* or *buruu*	blue
kiiro	yellow	*chairo*	brown
murasaki	purple	*midori* or *guriin*	green
nezumiiro or *haiiro* or *guree*	gray	*pinku*	pink

When a color modifies a noun, *no* follows it. Compare:

Midori ga suki desu.
I like green.

Midori no suutsu o kimashita.
I wore a green suit.

Chairo no kutsu ga hoshii n desu.
I want brown shoes.

The following colors have alternate *i*-adjective forms.

aka	→	*akai*	red
shiro	→	*shiroi*	white
kuro	→	*kuroi*	black
ao	→	*aoi*	blue
kiiro	→	*kiiroi*	yellow
chairo	→	*chairoi*	brown

Watashi no kooto wa akai/aka desu.
My coat is red.

Kono kuroi botan/kuro no botan wa atarashii sutairu desu.
These black buttons are the new style.

Shiroi burausu/shiro no burausu o kaimashita.
I bought a white blouse.

In cases like those above, the *i*-adjective and noun forms of colors are equally common. However, in some cases, one form will be more natural or even obligatory. For example, when talking about colors in connection with natural phenomena, *i*-adjectives should be used.

akai sora
red sky

aoi umi
blue sea

4. PARTICLES

a. *Ka* "or"

Ka occurring between nouns may be translated as "or."

Kyuu ka juuichi mo arimasu ka.
  Do you have size nine or size eleven, as well?

Suutsu ka wanpiisu o kaimasu.
  I will buy a suit or a one-piece dress.

Mainichi uchi ka toshokan de benkyoo shimasu.
  I study at home or at the library every day.

b. Particles with time expressions

The time expressions that have been introduced so far usually do not take particles.

Kinoo sukaato o kaimashita.
  I bought a skirt yesterday.

Ima isogashii desu.
  I am busy now.

However, depending on the situation, particles can be used. As mentioned before, *no* can be used between two time expressions or after a time expression (see Lesson 6, C6). The particles *wa, mo, ka* and *to* can also be used with them.
  When *wa*, a topic marker, follows a time expression, the phrase becomes a topic.

Ima wa arimasen.
  [As for] now, we don't have them.

Haru wa isogashii desu.
  [As for] in spring, I am busy.

When *mo* follows a time expression, the phrase means "also/too."

Kyoo mo ame ga furimashita.
  It rained today, as well.

Ashita no ban mo dekakemasu.
  I am going out tomorrow evening, too.

Ka is used between two time expressions to mean "or."

Kotoshi ka rainen Nihon e ikimasu.
  I am going to Japan this year or next year.

84

Tanaka san wa kyoo ka ashita kimasu.
  Ms. Tanaka will come today or tomorrow.

To is used between two time expressions to mean "and."

Kinoo to kyoo kimono o kimashita.
  I wore a kimono yesterday and today.

Konshuu to raishuu mise o shimemasu.
  We will close the store this week and next week.

5. THE QUESTION WORD *DONNA*

Donna "what kind of" precedes the noun it modifies.

Donna iro ga osuki desu ka.
  What [kind of] color do you like?

Aka ka pinku ga suki desu.
  I like red or pink.

Donna kaban desu ka.
  What kind of bag is it?

Ookii kaban desu.
  It's a big bag.

Donna mise desu ka.
  What kind of store is it?

Modan na mise desu.
  It's a modern store.

6. *CHOTTO* AND *SUKOSHI*

Both *chotto* and *sukoshi* mean "a few" or "a little." *Chotto* is more informal than *sukoshi*. They are both used in the same word order:
noun+particle+*chotto/sukoshi* . . . verb (see Lesson 6, C10).

Yuki ga chotto furimashita.
  It snowed a little yesterday.

Chotto and *sukoshi* may also modify an adjective.

Sukaato ga chotto mijikai desu ne.
  The skirt is a little too short, isn't it?

Totemo ii n desu kedo, chotto kitsui n desu.
  It's very nice, but it's a little tight.

Kono mise wa sukoshi takai desu yo.
This store is a little expensive.

Chotto and *sukoshi* may mean "for a moment" or "for a little while."

Umi de chotto oyogimashita.
I swam in the ocean for a little while.

Koko de sukoshi yasumimashoo.
Let's rest here for a moment.

However, unlike *sukoshi, chotto* may be used as a mere softener.

Chotto shichaku shitai n desu kedo.
I would like to try it on.

Chotto depaato e ikimashita.
I went to a department store.

7. ... *DESU KA*

To confirm your understanding of a person's remark, repeat what has been said and add ... *desu ka*. It has the same function as the English "I see" or "right?"

A: *Kyuu ka juuichi mo arimasu ka.*
Do you have size nine or size eleven, also?

B: *Kyuu ka juuichi desu ka.*
Nine or eleven [I see].

A: *Kono sukaafu wa sen'en desu.*
This scarf is one thousand yen.

B: *Sen'en desu ka.*
One thousand yen [right?].

D. MOJI

は (*ha*) and へ (*he*) have dual functions. Besides representing *ha,* は is also used to write *wa* in the following cases.

particle *wa*	これは いいんです。	This is good.
Konnichi wa.	こんにちは。	Hello.
Konban wa.	こんばんは。	Good evening.

| *dewa* | では | well, then |
| *de wa arimasen* | しずかではありません。 | It is not quiet. |

へ (*he*) is also used to write the particle *e*.

Nihon e ikimashita.
にほんへ いきました。
I went to Japan.

Read the following:

わたしは にほんじんではありません。
I am not Japanese.

やまださんは うちへ かえりました。
Mr. Yamada went home.

E. TANGO TO HYOOGEN

kimono	kimono
fuku	clothes
kooto	coat
suutsu	suit
wanpiisu	(one-piece) dress
seetaa	sweater
burausu	blouse
sukaato	skirt
sukaafu	scarf
beruto	belt
botan	button
saizu	size
sutairu	style
iro	color
aka(i)	red
shiro(i)	white
kuro(i)	black
ao(i)	blue
buruu	blue

kiiro(i)	yellow
chairo(i)	brown
murasaki	purple
midori	green
guriin	green
nezumiiro	gray
haiiro	gray
guree	gray
pinku	pink
ten'in	store clerk
kyaku	customer, guest
sora	sky
umi	sea
shichakushitsu	dressing room
shichaku	trying something on
shichaku shimasu	to try something on
benkyoo	studying
benkyoo shimasu	to study
sentaku	laundry
sentaku shimasu	to do laundry
kimasu	to wear
hairimasu	to come in, go in, enter
yasumimasu	to rest
shimemasu	to close
hoshii	to want
kawaii	lovely, cute
nagai	long
mijikai	short
kitsui	tight
isogashii	busy
modan	modern-style
chotto	a few, a little, for a moment, for a little while, (softener)
sukoshi	a few, a little, for a moment, for a little while
donna	what kind of
ainiku	unfortunately

A. Some customers are talking to the salesclerk in a boutique. Match the words or combinations of words in Group I and Group II to form a sentence.

I

1. *Shiroi burausu ga*
2. *Guree*
3. *Watashi no saizu wa*
4. *Akai*

II

a. *nana ka kyuu desu.*
b. *no beruto mo arimasu ka.*
c. *hoshii n desu.*
d. *sukaafu mo hoshii n desu.*

B. Translate the following sentences about Ms. Brown's activities today.

1. *Asa sentaku shimashita.*
2. *Depaato de pinku no burausu o kaimashita.*
3. *Yoru wa nihongo o benkyoo shimashita.*

C. Fill in the blanks with the appropriate question word.
Dore, Dare, Donna

1. _____ *no kutsu desu ka.*
2. _____ *seetaa ga arimasu ka.*
3. _____ *o tabemashoo ka.*
4. _____ *hana desu ka.*

D. Fill in the blanks with particles according to the English equivalents.

1. *Koohii* _____ *ocha o nomimasu.*
   I will drink coffee or tea.
2. *Kimono* _____ *hoshii n desu.*
   I want a kimono.
3. *Mainichi asa* _____ *ban nihongo* _____ *benkyoo* _____ *shimasu.*
   Every day I study Japanese in the morning and evening.
4. *Kyoo* _____ *atsukatta desu.*
   It was hot today, too.

E. Describe the bag that you want.

Question: *"Donna kaban ga hoshii desu ka."*
Example: *chiisai kaban ga hoshii desu.*

1. big
2. black
3. not very expensive

F. Choose the appropriate particle for the following sentences.

1. *watashi* _____ *kinoo depaato* _____ *kutsu* _____ *kaimashita.*
   (I bought a pair of shoes at a department store yesterday, too.)
2. *ashita, uchi* _____ *benkyoo* _____ *suru tsumori desu.*
   (I will study at home tomorrow.)
3. *Tanaka san* _____ *watashi* _____ *kinoo eiga* _____ *mimashita.*
   (Mr. Tanaka and I saw a movie yesterday.)

KARUCHAA NOOTO

The traditional dress in Japan is the kimono, a robe secured around the waist with a sash called an *obi*. There are different kinds of kimonos, ranging from those for daily wear to extremely formal ones. Kimonos, especially formal ones, may be very complicated to put on, so women may need somebody else to help them. There are even kimono classes providing instruction on how to wear them properly. Kimonos are extremely expensive and may cost thousands of dollars. Very few women wear kimonos today, except on special occasions such as New Year's or weddings.

Men's kimonos are simpler and some men even wear them at home after work. However, nowadays, men's kimonos are becoming less popular as well.

Western clothes, which are the usual attire now, began to be worn at the beginning of the modern era in the nineteenth century. Young Japanese follow fashion trends very closely. People wear formal clothes or casual clothes according to place, time, and occasion, but compared to Americans, the Japanese tend to dress more conservatively in public.

KOTAE

A. 1c, 2b, 3a, 4d
B. 1. She did laundry in the morning. 2. She bought a pink blouse in the department store. 3. As for at night, she studied Japanese.
C. 1. *Dare* 2. *Donna* 3. *Dore* 4. *Donna*
D. 1. *ka* 2. *ga* 3. *to, no, o* 4. *mo*
E. 1. <u>*ookii*</u> *kaban ga hoshii desu.* 2. <u>*kuroi*</u> *kaban ga hoshii desu.* 3. <u>*amari takakunai*</u> *kaban ga hoshii desu.*
F. 1. *mo, de, o* 2. *de, o* 3. *to, wa, o*

DAI HACHIKA
Lesson 8
KUUKOO DE.   At the Airport.

A. DAIAROOGU

KUUKOO DE NO DEMUKAE.

Ms. Moore is moving to Japan from the U.S. for business. Ms. Kimura, a representative of the company, meets her at the airport.

KIMURA: **Múua san desu ka.**

MUUA: **Hái, sóo desu.**

KIMURA: **Kimura désu. Hajimemáshite.**

MUUA: **A, hajimemáshite. Oisogashii tokoro arígatoo gozaimasu.**

KIMURA: **Iie, dóo itashimáshite. Jáa, ikimashóo ka.**

MUUA: **Anoo, ryoogae shitái n desu kedo, kono hen de dekimásu ka.**

KIMURA: **Ée, dekimásu yo. Asoko ni ginkoo ga arimásu.**

MUUA: **Áa, asoko désu ka. Sore kara, denwa wa dóko ni arimásu ka.**

KIMURA: **Denwa désu ka. Áa, asoko ni otoko no hitó ga imásu ne. Anó hito no ushiro ni arimásu.**

MUUA: **Jáa, sumimasén. Súgu modorimásu.**

KIMURA: **Dóozo goyukkúri.**

Shibaraku shite.

MUUA: **Omatase shimáshita.**

KIMURA: **Iie. Oshokuji wa móo sumimáshita ka.**

MUUA: **Ee, hikóoki no náka de.**

KIMURA: **Jáa, kono kissáten de chótto yasumimashóo ka. Koko no koohíi wa oishíi n desu.**

91

Meeting at the airport.

KIMURA: Are you Ms. Moore?

MOORE: Yes, I am.

KIMURA: I am Ms. Kimura. How do you do?

MOORE: [Oh,] how do you do? Thank you very much for coming. [Thank you very much although you are busy.]

KIMURA: Don't mention it. Well, are you ready to go? [Well, shall we go?]

MOORE: Uh, I would like to exchange some money first. Can I do that somewhere around here?

KIMURA: Yes, of course. The bank is over there.

MOORE: Oh, over there. And where is a telephone?

KIMURA: A telephone. Let me see. Oh, do you see that man over there? [A man is over there, isn't he?] It's right behind him [that person].

MOORE: Well, excuse me. I'll be right back.

KIMURA: Take your time.

A little later.

MOORE: Thanks for waiting.

KIMURA: No problem. Have you eaten already? [Did a meal finish already?]

MOORE: Yes, on the plane [inside the plane].

KIMURA: Then, do you want to [shall we] rest at this coffee shop for a while? The coffee here is delicious.

B. HATSUON

THE SYLLABIC CONSONANTS *P, T, K, S*

P, t, k, and *s* can be syllables by themselves. The identical consonant always follows.

kippu	ticket
ittoo	first class
nikki	diary
kassai	applaud

itchi	agreement
ittsuu	one letter
zasshi	magazine

In *itchi* "agreement" and *ittsuu* "one letter," the *t* is not followed by the identical consonant, that is, *t* in *itchi* is followed by *ch* and in *ittsuu* it is followed by *ts*. However, these examples do not violate the restriction stated above because *t, ch,* and *ts* are in the same consonant group (see *ta chi tsu te to* in the syllabary chart). The same is true for *zasshi* "magazine": the *s* is followed by *sh*, which is in the same consonant group as *s* (see *sa shi su se so* in the syllabary chart).

To pronounce syllabic consonants such as these, hold the tongue position for one extra beat before pronouncing the next syllable.

Syllabic *p, t, k,* and *s* never occur at the beginning of a word.

C. BUNPOO TO YOOHOO

1. THE VERBS FOR "TO EXIST" AND THE PARTICLE *NI*

A

Mr. Tsuda is a student.
I am a student.
Ms. Tanaka and Ms. Brown are students.

B

Mr. Tsuda is at the airport.
I am at the airport.
Ms. Tanaka and Ms. Brown are at the airport.

The sentences in group A and group B use forms of "to be": "is," "am," and "are." In group A, these words serve as the copula, a linking word, but in group B, they are verbs of existence. In Japanese, the equivalents are different words. The former, as you have learned, is the copula *desu*.

Tsuda san wa gakusei desu.
Mr. Tsuda is a student.

The equivalent of "is," "am," or "are" in group B is the verb *imasu* "to exist," and the word referring to the place of existence is followed by the particle *ni* "at" or "in."

Tsuda san wa
Watashi wa   *kuukoo ni imasu.*
Tanaka san to Buraun san wa
     Mr. Tsuda
     I   is/am/are at the airport.
     Ms. Tanaka and Ms. Brown.

93

Neko wa niwa ni imasen deshita.
    The cat was not in the garden.

When the subject is inanimate, use the verb *arimasu* instead of *imasu*.

Asoko ni ginkoo ga arimasu.
    The bank is over there.

Denwa wa doko ni arimasu ka.
    Where is the telephone?

Terebi wa watashi no heya ni arimasen.
    The television is not in my room.

The particle *ni*, "at" or "in," is used for place names along with a stative verb such as *arimasu* or *imasu*. On the other hand, the particle *de* for "at" or "in," introduced in Lesson 2, is used for the location where an action takes place.

Kuukoo de chizu o kaimashita.
    I bought a map at the airport.

Ano ginkoo de ryoogae shimashita.
    I exchanged money at that bank over there.

2. *IMASU* "TO HAVE"

As explained already, *arimasu* can mean "to have" (see Lesson 6, C6) when used with inanimate objects. *Imasu* can also mean "to have" when the noun in the position of the direct object is animate.

Kono gakkoo wa ii sensei ga imasu.
    This school has good teachers.

Kawaii inu ga imashita.
    I had a cute dog.

3. LOCATION NOUNS

In addition to particles, nouns can also indicate locations.

ue	top	*shita*	bottom
ushiro	back	*mae*	front
naka	inside	*soto*	outside
tonari	next	*mukai*	opposite side
soba	vicinity		

Naka wa akarui desu.
   The inside is bright.

In many cases, these location nouns are preceded by a noun plus *no*.

Hikooki no naka de tabemashita.
   I ate on the plane [inside the plane].

Ano onna no hito no ushiro ni arimasu.
   It is behind that woman over there.

Kuukoo no soba ni ki ga takusan arimasu.
   There are many trees in the vicinity of the airport.

4. *KO-SO-A-DO* WORDS

Another set of *ko-so-a-do* words (see in Lesson 5, C2) is:

koko	this place, here
soko	that place, there
asoko	that place over there
doko	what place, where

Koko no koohii wa oishii n desu.
   This place's coffee is delicious.

Ginkoo wa doko ni arimasu ka.
   Where is the bank?

Asoko ni arimasu.
   It's over there.

Soko de kookuuken o kaimashita.
   I bought a plane ticket there.

5. *SOO DESU*

For an affirmative reply to a question with a noun plus the copula, you can use the short answer *soo desu*.

Muua san desu ka.	*Hai, soo desu.*
Are you Ms. Moore?	Yes, I am.
Are wa ginkoo desu ka.	*Hai, soo desu.*
Is that a bank?	Yes, it is.

D. MOJI

The *katakana* characters are used primarily for (a) writing words borrowed from other languages (mainly from Western languages), (b) giving special emphasis to certain words in much the same way that italics are used in English, (c) writing certain onomatopoetic words, and (d) telegrams. First, study the basic *katakana*, whose *hiragana* equivalents you have already learned. The first line is (see Table I, page 5):

LINE 1	*a*	*i*	*u*	*e*	*o*
KATAKANA	ア	イ	ウ	エ	オ
HIRAGANA	あ	い	う	え	お

STROKE ORDER

a	⁻ ア	
i	ノ イ	
u	' ﾞ ウ	
e	‐ エ エ	
o	‐ ナ オ	

E. TANGO TO HYOOGEN

kuukoo	airport
hikooki	airplane
kookuuken	plane ticket
ginkoo	bank
denwa	telephone
hito	person
otoko no hito	man
onna no hito	woman
inu	dog
neko	cat
heya	room
chizu	map
ki	tree

(o)shokuji	meal
hen	area (dependent noun, i.e., *hen* should be used with another word preceding it, *kono hen* "this area")
soko	there
asoko	over there
ue	top
ushiro	behind
naka	inside
tonari	next
soba	vicinity
shita	bottom
mae	front
soto	outside
mukai	opposite side
ryoogae shimasu	to exchange money
arimasu	to exist, be situated
imasu	to exist, have
sumimasu	to finish
modorimasu	to return
oishii	delicious
soo	so, right
sugu	soon, right away, immediately
sore kara	and (then)
anoo	um, uh
Oisogashii tokoro arigatoo gozaimasu.	Thank you very much for your time [although you are busy].
Doozo goyukkuri.	Take your time.
Omatase shimashita.	Sorry to have kept you waiting.

RENSHUU

A. Fill in the blanks with *arimasu* or *imasu*.

1. *Suzuki san wa ima ginkoo ni* _____ .
2. *Neko wa doko ni* _____ *ka.*
3. *Ginkoo wa depaato no tonari ni* _____ .
4. *Dare ga* _____ *ka.*

B. Fill in the blanks according to the English equivalents.

1. *Kissaten wa gakkoo no* _____ *ni arimasu.*
   The coffee shop is on the opposite side of the school.
2. *Mise no* _____ *wa kirei desu ka.*
   Is the inside of the store clean?
3. *Ginkoo wa depaato no* _____ *ni arimashita.*
   The bank was next to the department store.
4. *Ki no* _____ *de yasumimashita.*
   I rested under the tree.

C. Fill in the blanks with *kono* or *koko.*

1. _____ *no sakana wa yasui desu.*
2. *Chizu wa* _____ *ni arimasu.*
3. _____ *mise de kaimashoo ka.*
4. _____ *hikooki wa Oosaka e ikimasu.*

D. Fill in the blanks with *ni* or *de.*

1. *Kuukoo no ginkoo* _____ *ryoogae shimashita.*
2. *Kimura san wa doko* _____ *imasu ka.*
3. *Gakkoo no toshokan* _____ *benkyoo shimashita.*
4. *Enpitsu wa terebi no soba* _____ *arimashita.*

KARUCHAA NOOTO

Upon landing in Japan, you will first have to go through Immigration and Customs. In Immigration, your passport and visa are verified, and in Customs, your baggage is inspected. Depending on what you bring with you, you may have to pay duty. The New Tokyo International Airport (Narita Airport) is about a two-hour drive from Tokyo. It is very expensive to travel from the airport to Tokyo by taxi. Both the airport limousine bus, which takes you to many major hotels in Tokyo, and the new train system, the Narita Express, which takes you from the airport to Tokyo Station in under an hour, are much faster and cheaper.

To meet the needs of the increasing number of plane travelers, another big airport, Kansai International Airport, was opened in 1994. It is near Osaka, Kobe, and Kyoto.

KOTAE

A. 1. *imasu* 2. *imasu* 3. *arimasu* 4. *imasu*
B. 1. *mukai* 2. *naka* 3. *tonari* 4. *shita*
C. 1. *koko* 2. *koko* 3. *kono* 4. *kono*
D. 1. *de* 2. *ni* 3. *de* 4. *ni*

DAI KYUUKA
Lesson 9
APAATO O KARIRU.   Renting an Apartment.

A. DAIAROOGU

FUDOOSAN'YA DE.

Mr. Minami is looking for an apartment not too far from his office.

FUDOOSAN'YA: **Hankyuu énsen ga íi n desu ne.**

MINAMI: **Ée, dekíreba, éki no sóba ni sumitái n desu.**

FUDOOSAN'YA: **Íma Ashiyá Eki no sóba ni hitótsu arimásu kedo.**

MINAMI: **Dónna apáato desu ka.**

FUDOOSAN'YA: **Wari to atarashíi apáato desu. Iriguchi ni sakura no kí ga níhon arimásu kara, háru totemo kírei desu yo.**

MINAMI: **Heyá wa íkutsu arimásu ka.**

FUDOOSAN'YA: **Futatsu arimásu. Sore kara, ookíi dainingu kítchin ga arimásu.**

MINAMI: **Yáchin wa íkura desu ka.**

FUDOOSAN'YA: **Hachiman'en désu. Sore kara shikikin to kenrikin ga juu rokuman'en zútsu desu.**

MINAMI: **Áa, sóo desu ka. Ítsu akimásu ka.**

FUDOOSAN'YA: **Juugatsú ni akimásu. Goran ni narimásu ka.**

MINAMI: **Ée, onegai shimásu. Kyóo wa chótto tsugoo ga warúi n desu kedo.**

FUDOOSAN'YA: **Jáa, doyóobi wa dóo desu ka.**

MINAMI: **Eetto, doyóobi wa juu ichinichí desu ne. Ée, daijóobu desu. Nánji ni kimashóo ka.**

FUDOOSAN'YA: **Jáa, sánji ni koko de aimashóo ka.**

MINAMI: **Ée, íi desu.**

FUDOOSAN'YA: **Jáa, doyóobi ni.**

AT THE REAL ESTATE AGENT'S OFFICE.

AGENT: So you're looking for an apartment along the Hankyu Line?

MINAMI: Yes, if possible, I want to live near a station.

AGENT: There is one available near Ashiya Station now.

MINAMI: What kind of apartment is it?

AGENT: It is a relatively new apartment. There are two cherry trees by the entrance, so it is very pretty in the spring.

MINAMI: How many rooms does it have?

AGENT: Two plus a big dine-in kitchen.

MINAMI: How much is the rent?

AGENT: It is 80,000 yen. Plus 160,000 yen each for the deposit and the key money.

MINAMI: I see. And when will it be available [become vacant]?

AGENT: It will be available in October. Would you like to see it?

MINAMI: Yes, please. But it would be a little inconvenient today [the convenience is a little bad].

AGENT: Well then, how about Saturday?

MINAMI: Let's see, Saturday is the eleventh, isn't it? Yes, that will be all right. What time should I come?

AGENT: How about meeting here at three o'clock?

MINAMI: Yes, that'll be fine.

AGENT: See you Saturday, then.

B. HATSUON

THE NASAL SYLLABIC CONSONANT *N'**

The syllabic *n'* is different from the *n* as part of a syllable. The syllabic *n'* is always held as long as one full syllable, and its pronunciation changes depending on the sound that follows.

Before *t, ch, ts, n, r, z, d,* or *j,* it is pronounced like the English n in pen:

hanzai   crime   **ondo**   temperature

---

* *N'* is written as *n*, except when there is ambiguity. For more, see page 6.

Before *m, b*, or *p*, it is pronounced like the English m̲:

shinbun   newspaper   **kanpai**   toast (when drinking)

Before every other sound, and at the end of a word, it is pronounced like the English ng in singer:

sensei   teacher   **ten'in**   salesclerk

Normally, *n'* never occurs at the beginning of a word, and unlike *p, t, k*, or *s*, it is never followed by another syllabic n̲'.

C. BUNPOO TO YOOHOO

1. NUMBERS

The numbers with a sound change are underscored.

juuichi (10 *juu* + 1 *ichi*)	11	*hyaku*	100
juuni	12	*hyakuichi* (100 *hyaku* + 1 *ichi*)	101
juusan	13	*hyakujuu*	110
juushi, juuyon	14	*nihyaku* (2 *ni* × 100 *hyaku*)	200
juugo	15	*sanbyaku*	300
juuroku	16	*yonhyaku*	400
juushichi, juunana	17	*gohyaku*	500
juuhachi	18	*roppyaku*	600
juuku, juukyuu	19	*nanahyaku, (shichihyaku *)*	700
nijuu (2 *ni* × 10 *juu*)	20	*happyaku*	800
nijuuichi (20 *nijuu* + 1 *ichi*)	21	*kyuuhyaku*	900
nijuuni	22	*sen, issen* (1 *ichi* × 1000 *sen*)	1,000
nijuusan	23	*nisen* (2 *ni* × 1000 *sen*)	2,000
	•	*nisen'ichi*	2,001
	•	*nisenjuu*	2,010
sanjuu (3 *san* × 10 *juu*)	30	*nisenhyaku*	2,100
yonjuu, (shijuu *)	40	*nisenhyakujuu*	2,110
gojuu	50	*sanzen*	3,000
rokujuu	60	*yonsen*	4,000
shichijuu, nanajuu	70	*gosen*	5,000
hachijuu	80	*rokusen*	6,000
kyuujuu	90	*nanasen, (shichisen *)*	7,000

* *Yonjuu* (40), *nanahyaku* (700), and *nanasen* (7,000) are much more common than *shijuu*, *shichihyaku*, and *shichisen*.

hassen	8,000	_hachiman_	80,000
kyuusen	9,000	_kyuuman_	90,000
ichiman	10,000	_juuman_	100,000
niman	20,000	_nijuuman_	200,000
sanman	30,000		•
yonman	40,000		•
goman	50,000	_hyakuman_	1,000,000
rokuman	60,000	_senman, issenman_	10,000,000
nanaman, shichiman	70,000	_ichioku_	100,000,000

2. COUNTERS

Compare:

A	B
There are two trees.	There are two sheets of paper.
I bought two tickets.	I drank two cups of tea.

In group A, the number comes immediately before the noun modified, while in group B, words such as "sheets of" or "cups of" stand between the number and the noun. These words are similar to Japanese counters used in quantity expressions. In Japanese, you need to use a counter even for sentences like those in group A. There are numerous counters, and which one you use depends on the features of the items counted.

-hon	for long, narrow items such as trees, pencils, bottles, sticks, etc.
-mai	for thin, flat items such as paper, tickets, handkerchiefs, sliced things, etc.
_-en_	for Japanese currency (See Lesson 3, C1.)
_-ji_	for "o'clock" (e.g., _sanji_ "three o'clock")
-nichi	for the date or for counting days (e.g., _sanjuunichi_ "the thirtieth of the month" or "thirty days"); for counting days, _-kan_ is attached to _-nichi_ optionally.
-gatsu	for names of months (e.g., _ichigatsu_ "January")
-kagetsu(kan)	for counting months (e.g., _nikagetsu_ "two months")
-nen	for the year or for counting years (e.g., _nisennen_ "the year 2000" or "2000 years"); for counting years, _-kan_ is optionally attached to the year.

There are two kinds of counters. One indicates quantity (_-hon, -mai, -en, -nichi_ [for counting days], _-kagetsu_ and _-nen_ [for counting years]), and the other, a specific point (*-ji, -nichi* [for the date], *-gatsu*, and *-nen* [for the year]).

A typical sentence pattern with counters indicating quantity is noun + particle + quantity . . . verb (see Lesson 6, C10).

Ki ga nihon arimasu.
There are two trees.

Chiketto o nimai kaimashita.
I bought two tickets.

Kyooto ni juu ichinichi imashita.
I was in Kyoto for eleven days.

Nihongo o gokagetsu benkyoo shimashita.
I studied Japanese for five months.

Kono mise de ninen hatarakimashita.
I worked in this store for two years.

In a typical sentence pattern with *-en* "yen," the amount of money is followed by the copula or a verb.

Yachin wa hachiman'en desu.
The rent is 80,000 yen.

Shikikin wa juurokuman'en deshita.
The deposit was 160,000 yen.

Nisen'en haraimashita.
I paid 2,000 yen.

Counters indicating specific points are followed by the copula.

Ima sanji desu.
It is three o'clock now.

Ashita wa nijuu ninichi desu.
Tomorrow is the twenty-second.

Watashi no tanjoobi wa juugatsu juu gonichi desu.
My birthday is October fifteenth.

The particle *ni* is used to denote a specific point in time and translates as "at," "on," or "in."

Sanji ni dekakemashoo ka.
Should we go out at three?

Apaato wa juugatsu ni akimasu.
The apartment will be available in October.

Hachigatsu sanjuu ichinichi ni kimashita.
She came on August thirty-first.

Sen kyuuhyaku hachijuunen ni uchi o kaimashita.
I bought the house in 1980.

3. JAPANESE NATIVE NUMBERS

The numbers you have learned so far are mostly Sino-Japanese (of Chinese origin) numbers.* In addition to them, there is a set of native Japanese numbers. The native numbers are limited to one through ten.

hitotsu	1	*futatsu*	2
mittsu	3	*yottsu*	4
itsutsu	5	*muttsu*	6
nanatsu	7	*yattsu*	8
kokonotsu	9	*too*	10

Certain items are counted with native numbers. Since the native numbers are no longer used above ten, use Sino-Japanese numbers without counters for numbers above ten.

a. Intangible things (in many cases)

Hoohoo wa futatsu arimasu. (native number)
There are two methods.

Hoohoo wa juuichi arimasu. (Sino-Japanese number without a counter)
There are eleven methods.

b. Rooms

Counters for rooms (*-heya* or *-shitsu*) are usually not used.

Heya wa <u>mittsu</u> arimasu. (native number)
There are three rooms.

Heya wa juuni arimasu. (Sino-Japanese number without a counter)
There are twelve rooms.

c. Apartments

The counter for apartments *-ken* is usually not used, either.

---

* Although the numbers in the first set are not all Sino-Japanese (*yon* "four" and *nana* "seven" have native origins), we will call them Sino-Japanese numbers as opposed to the native numbers introduced here, to make explanations less complicated.

Apaato wa ima hitotsu arimasu. (native number)
There is one apartment now.

Apaato wa ima nijuu arimasu. (Sino-Japanese number without a counter)
There are twenty apartments now.

d. Age

The counter for age, *-sai*, is optional.

Watashi no kodomo wa itsutsu desu. (native number) or *gosai desu.* (Sino-Japanese number plus the counter *-sai*)
My child is five years old.

Yamada san wa nijuusan desu. (Sino-Japanese number without the counter *-sai*) or *nijuu sansai desu.* (Sino-Japanese number plus the counter *-sai*)
Mr. Yamada is twenty-three years old.

e. Small and round things

The counter for things like apples, candy, and marbles, *-ko*, is optional.

Ringo o futatsu tabemashita. (native number) or *niko tabemashita.* (Sino-Japanese number plus the counter *-ko*)
I ate two apples.

Ringo o juugo kaimashita. (Sino-Japanese number without the counter *-ko*) or *juu goko kaimashita.* (Sino-Japanese number plus the counter *-ko*)
I bought fifteen apples.

4. QUESTION WORDS

a. *Nan*

The question word *nan* plus a counter translates into "how many," "what," etc.

Nanji ni kimashoo ka.
What time should I come?

Kono apaato wa nannichi ni akimasu ka.
When [On what date] will this apartment become available?

Nannichi arimasu ka.
How many days are there?

Chiketto o nanmai kaimashoo ka.
How many tickets should we buy?

When the counter *-hon* is used with *nan*, *-hon* becomes *-bon*.

Ki wa nanbon arimasu ka.
How many trees are there?

Nan is used with *-yoobi* to ask "what day."

Kyoo wa nanyoobi desu ka.
What day is today?

b. *Ikutsu*

Ikutsu "how many" is used with items that can be counted with native numbers.

Hoohoo wa ikutsu arimasu ka.
How many methods are there?

Heya wa ikutsu arimasu ka.
How many rooms are there?

Apaato wa ikutsu arimasu ka.
How many apartments are there?

Yamada san wa ikutsu (or *nansai*) *desu ka.*
How old is Mr. Yamada?

Ringo o ikutsu (or *nanko*) *kaimashoo ka.*
How many apples should we buy?

c. *Ikura*

Ikura "how much" is used mainly with money.

Yachin wa ikura desu ka.
How much is the rent?

Shikikin wa ikura desu ka.
How much is the deposit?

Okane wa ikura arimasu ka.
How much money is there?

d. *Itsu*

Itsu is used to ask "when."

Itsu akimasu ka.
When will it become available (vacant)?

Itsu tsugoo ga warui n desu ka.
When will you be unavailable?

Tanaka san no tanjoobi wa itsu desu ka.
When is Ms. Tanaka's birthday?

5. PARTICLES

a. *Ni* (with location)

Ni "at" or "in" is used with the stative verbs *imasu* "to exist" or *arimasu* "to exist," after a noun referring to a place (see Lesson 8, C1).

Minami san no apaato wa ano hen ni arimasu.
Mr. Minami's apartment is in that area over there.

Ni is also used with a noun indicating location, if used with the stative verb *sumimasu* "to live."

Eki no soba ni sumitai n desu.
I want to live near a station.

b. *Ni* (with time)

As mentioned before, *ni* is used to indicate a specific point in time and translates into "at," "on," "in," or "during." The following time nouns also take *ni.*

yasumi ni
during the vacation

tanjoobi ni
on the birthday

Natsuyasumi ni apaato o karimashita.
I rented an apartment during the summer vacation.

Watashi no tanjoobi ni yuki ga furimashita.
It snowed on my birthday.

Ni is optional with seasonal terms but necessary with days of the week.

aki (ni)
in the fall

kin'yoobi ni
on Friday

Kono apaato wa kotoshi no haru (ni) akimasu.
This apartment becomes available in the spring of this year.

c. *Kara* "because"

The clause particle *kara* "because," "since," "so," or "therefore" follows the clause that gives the reason.

Sakura no ki ga nihon arimasu kara, haru totemo kirei desu.
There are two cherry trees; therefore, it is very pretty in spring.

Kono apaato wa shizuka desu kara, karitai n desu.
  Since this apartment is quiet, I want to rent it.

Kyoo wa tsugoo ga warui desu kara, ashita kimasu.
  It is inconvenient today, so I will come tomorrow.

D. MOJI

The following *katakana* are for syllables on the second line through the fifth line of Table I (page 5).

	ka	ki	ku	ke	ko
LINE 2	*ka*	*ki*	*ku*	*ke*	*ko*
KATAKANA	カ	キ	ク	ケ	コ
HIRAGANA	か	き	く	け	こ
LINE 3	*sa*	*shi*	*su*	*se*	*so*
KATAKANA	サ	シ	ス	セ	ソ
HIRAGANA	さ	し	す	せ	そ
LINE 4	*ta*	*chi*	*tsu*	*te*	*to*
KATAKANA	タ	チ	ツ	テ	ト
HIRAGANA	た	ち	つ	て	と
LINE 5	*na*	*ni*	*nu*	*ne*	*no*
KATAKANA	ナ	ニ	ヌ	ネ	ノ
HIRAGANA	な	に	ぬ	ね	の

STROKE ORDER

ka	フ カ	*sa*	一 十 サ
ki	一 二 キ	*shi*	` ` ` ` シ
ku	ノ ク	*su*	フ ス
ke	ノ レ ケ	*se*	一 セ
ko	フ コ	*so*	` ソ

ta	ノ ク タ	
chi	／ 二 チ	
tsu	` ´´ ツ	
te	一 二 テ	
to	l ト	

na	一 ナ	
ni	- 二	
nu	フ ヌ	
ne	` ヲ ネ ネ	
no	ノ	

E. TANGO TO HYOOGEN

fudoosan'ya	real estate agent
dainingu kitchin	dine-in kitchen
iriguchi	entrance
yachin	rent for a residence
shikikin	deposit for renting a residence
kenrikin	key money
eki	station (for public transportation)
ensen	area along a train line
sakura	cherry (tree or blossoms, not fruit)
sakura no ki	cherry tree
ringo	apple
kodomo	child
chiketto	ticket
hoohoo	method
tsugoo	convenience
yasumi	vacation
natsuyasumi	summer vacation
tanjoobi	birthday
nichiyoobi	Sunday
getsuyoobi	Monday
kayoobi	Tuesday
suiyoobi	Wednesday
mokuyoobi	Thursday
kin'yoobi	Friday
doyoobi	Saturday
ichigatsu	January
nigatsu	February
sangatsu	March
shigatsu	April (never *yongatsu*)
gogatsu	May
rokugatsu	June
shichigatsu	July (never *nanagatsu*)

hachigatsu	August
kugatsu	September (never *kyuugatsu*)
juugatsu	October
juuichigatsu	November
juunigatsu	December
karimasu	to rent, borrow
akimasu	to become vacant
sumimasu	to live
aimasu	to meet
hatarakimasu	to work
haraimasu	to pay
wari to	relatively
dekireba	if possible
eetto	let me see, well
zutsu	each (dependent noun)
nan-	how many, what
ikutsu	how many
ikura	how much
itsu	when
Goran ni narimasu ka.	Would you like to see it? (respect)
Daijoobu desu.	That'll be fine.
Onegai shimasu.	Please help me./I'd like to ask you a favor.

RENSHUU

A. Choose the correct counter.

1. *Seetaa o ni (mai/hon/nichi) kaimashita.*
2. *Roku (ji/mai/sai) ni bangohan o tabemashita.*
3. *Shigatsu nijuu go (nichi/ko/ji) ni kaerimashita.*
4. *Enpitsu wa nan (hon/ko/mai/bon) arimasu ka.*

B. Write out these numbers in Japanese.

1. 250
2. 3,168
3. 84,351
4. 126,600

C. Write out these numbers using the Japanese native numbers.

1. 3
2. 10
3. 8
4. 2
5. 7
6. 1

D. Translate the following.

1. *Kinoo wa nannichi deshita ka.*
2. *Kono ki wa ikura desu ka.*
3. *Ashita wa mokuyoobi desu ne.*
4. *Kyoo wa doyoobi desu kara, gakkoo e ikimasen deshita.*

KARUCHAA NOOTO

Most big cities in Japan are overcrowded. Finding an apartment, therefore, is very difficult. Rent is sometimes extremely high, and apartments are relatively small. It may be difficult or impossible to find an inexpensive and spacious apartment near a train station in cities like Tokyo or Osaka. Compared to the United States, apartments in Japan are smaller for the same amount of money. The typical small apartment has a kitchen or a dine-in kitchen and one small room, which functions as a bedroom and living room.

To find an apartment, consult a real estate agent, the classified ads of newspapers, and magazines specializing in housing. When you have finally found a suitable apartment, you will most likely have to pay a refundable deposit and sometimes even "key money." The deposit may be as high as six months' rent. The key money, about one to two months' rent, is a nonrefundable "gift" to the owner. In addition, you may have to pay a fee of about one month's rent to the real estate agent.

Often you will be asked to name a guarantor who will vouch for you as a tenant. Ask an established resident who knows you well, such as a relative or colleague. When signing the lease, you may need a personal seal, called an *inkan*, since signatures are usually not accepted in legal transactions. If your family name is written in *kanji* and is not uncommon, ready-made seals can be purchased in stationery (and other) stores. If your family name is not written in *kanji* or is uncommon, you can have a seal made. Take the seal to the local government office to have it registered. Foreigners are often allowed to use signatures.

KOTAE

A. 1. *mai* 2. *ji* 3. *nichi* 4. *bon*
B. 1. *nihyaku gojuu* 2. *sanzen hyaku rokujuu hachi* 3. *hachiman yonsen sanbyaku gojuu ichi* 4. *juuniman rokusen roppyaku*
C. 1. *mittsu* 2. *too* 3. *yattsu* 4. *futatsu* 5. *nanatsu* 6. *hitotsu*
D. 1. What was the date yesterday? 2. How much is this tree? 3. Tomorrow is Thursday, isn't it? 4. Today is Saturday, so I didn't go to school.

DAI JUKKA
Lesson 10
KAZOKU. Family.

A. DAIAROOGU

FURUI KAZOKU SHASHIN.

Ms. Hata, who lives in the neighborhood, is visiting Ms. Oda's house in Tokyo.

HATA: **Gokázoku no shashin désu ka.**

ODA: **Ée, mukashi no shashin désu. Kore wa Nágoya no uchí desu.**

HATA: **Itsu goro désu ka.**

ODA: **Eetto, Shoowa yonjuunen góro desu ne. Watashi wa máda íssai deshita kara.**

HATA: **Áa, kono ákachan desu ka. Kore wa okáasan desu ne.**

ODA: **Iie, sore wa sóbo desu. Háha wa koko ni imásu.**

HATA: **Kírei na okáasan desu ne.**

ODA: **Sóo desu ka.**

HATA: **Takusan irasshaimásu née.**

ODA: **Ée, áni ga hitóri to ane ga sannin imásu.**

HATA: **Otóosan mo okáasan mo yóku Tookyoo e irasshaimásu ka.**

ODA: **Iie, amari. Futari tomo shigoto de isogashíi n desu. Démo, áni ya anétachi wa yóku kimásu kara, ítsumo kékkoo nigíyaka desu yo.**

HATA: **Íi desu née. Watashi wa hitoríkko desu kara, urayamashíi desu.**

AN OLD FAMILY PICTURE.

HATA: Is this a picture of your family?

ODA: Yes, it's an old picture. This is our house in Nagoya.

HATA: When was it taken [around when]?

112

ODA: Let's see. I was still one year old, so it was [is] around the fortieth year of Showa.

HATA: Oh, you are this baby? This is your mother, isn't it?

ODA: No, that's my grandmother. My mother is here.

HATA: She is beautiful.

ODA: Do you think so? [Is that so?]

HATA: You have a big family.

ODA: Yes. I have one older brother and three older sisters.

HATA: Do both your father and your mother come to Tokyo often?

ODA: No, not very often. Both of them are busy with their jobs. But my older brother and sisters come often. It is always quite lively.

HATA: How nice! I am so envious of you. [Because] I am an only child.

B. HATSUON

DEVOICED VOWELS

The vowels *i* and *u* are often just whispered or even disappear altogether in rapid conversation unless they are accented.

Devoicing usually occurs when these vowels are between the voiceless consonants *k, s, sh, t, ch, ts, h, f,* and *p*; or at the end of a word immediately following one of these voiceless consonants. In the following examples, the underlined vowels are devoiced.

k<u>i</u>tté	postage stamp
k<u>u</u>tsú	shoes
zéh<u>i</u>	by all means
s<u>u</u>kkári	entirely

Not all native speakers use devoiced vowels. Whether or not a vowel is devoiced does not affect the meaning of the word.

C. BUNPOO TO YOOHOO

1. KINSHIP TERMS

Different terms are used for family members depending on whether the person referred to is part of the speaker's own family or not. The terms for someone else's family members are more polite. Note, also, the terms for directly addressing members of the speaker's family and those used to talk about someone within the family.

	THE SPEAKER'S FAMILY	SOMEONE ELSE'S FAMILY	1. ADDRESS 2. REFERENCE WITHIN THE FAMILY
FATHER	chichi	otoosan	otoosan
MOTHER	haha	okaasan	okaasan
OLDER BROTHER	ani	oniisan	oniisan
OLDER SISTER	ane	oneesan	oneesan
YOUNGER BROTHER	otooto	otootosan	
YOUNGER SISTER	imooto	imootosan	
GRANDFATHER	sofu	ojiisan	ojiisan
GRANDMOTHER	sobo	obaasan	obaasan
HUSBAND	otto (shujin)	goshujin	
WIFE	tsuma (kanai)	okusan	

As you can see, there are no forms of address for younger siblings and spouses. When addressing or referring to them within the family, you normally use their names.

There are no general words for "brother" or "sister," but there is a word for "sibling."

kyoodai
  sibling

otoko (no) kyoodai
  male sibling

onna (no) kyoodai
  female sibling

Otoko no kyoodai wa imasen.
  I have no brothers [male siblings].

The usage of *kyoodai, otoko (no) kyoodai*, and *onna (no) kyoodai*, however, is limited. You cannot use them in the sense that English "brothers" and "sisters" are used. When you refer to a specific brother, you should use *ani* "older brother" or *otooto* "younger brother."

Shujin "husband" literally means "master," and *kanai* "wife" literally means "inside the house." Some people tend to avoid these terms, because they are obviously undesirable from a feminist perspective. Therefore, they prefer to use *otto* "husband" and *tsuma* "wife." The terms for someone else's husband and wife, *goshujin* "husband" (polite for "master") and *okusan* "wife" (literally, someone in the back of the

114

house), while politically incorrect as well, are used anyway because there are no alternatives.

2. COUNTERS

a. *-nin*

-nin is used for counting people.

Ane ga sannin imasu.
I have three older sisters.

Tomodachi ga gonin koko e kimashita.
Five friends came here.

Nihonjin wa nannin imasu ka.
How many Japanese people are there?

b. Counters with numbers from one to ten

The following are the counters you have learned so far.* Note that some of the combinations of numbers and counters are irregular (**boldface**). Note also that for numbers which may be represented by more than one term, often only one of the terms can be used with a certain counter. For example, *ku* "nine," not *kyuu* "nine," should be used with *-ji* "o'clock."

COUNTERS NUMBERS	*-HON*	*-MAI*	*-EN*	*-SAI*	*-KO*	*-NIN*
1 *ichi*	**ippon**	*ichimai*	*ichien*	**issai**	**ikko**	**hitori**
2 *ni*	*nihon*	*nimai*	*nien*	*nisai*	*niko*	**futari**
3 *san*	**sanbon**	*sanmai*	*san'en*	*sansai*	*sanko*	*sannin*
4 *yon*	*yonhon*	*yonmai*	*yon'en*	*yonsai*	*yonko*	
yo-†		*yomai*	*yoen*			*yonin*
5 *go*	*gohon*	*gomai*	*goen*	*gosai*	*goko*	*gonin*
6 *roku*	**roppon**	*rokumai*	*rokuen*	*rokusai*	**rokko**	*rokunin*
7 *shichi*	*shichihon*	*shichimai*	*shichien*	*shichisai*	*shichiko*	*shichinin*
nana	*nanahon*	*nanamai*	*nanaen*	*nanasai*	*nanako*	*nananin*
8 *hachi*	*hachihon*	*hachimai*	*hachien*	*hachisai*	*hachiko*	*hachinin*
	happon			**hassai**	**hakko**	
9 *ku*	*kyuuhon*	*kyuumai*	*kyuuen*	*kyuusai*	*kyuuko*	*kyuunin*
kyuu						*kunin*
10 *juu*	**juppon**	*juumai*	*juuen*	**jussai**	**jukko**	*juunin*
	jippon			**jissai**	**jikko**	

* For the names of the months, see *Tango to hyoogen* in Lesson 9.

† *Yo-* also means "four" besides *yon* and *shi*, but it is always followed by a counter. Not many counters can be used with *shi* "four."

115

COUNTERS NUMBERS	-JI	-KAGETSU	-NEN
1 *ichi*	*ichiji*	**ikkagetsu**	*ichinen*
2 *ni*	*niji*	*nikagetsu*	*ninen*
3 *san*	*sanji*	*sankagetsu*	*sannen*
4 *yon*		*yonkagetsu*	
yo-	*yoji*		*yonen*
5 *go*	*goji*	*gokagetsu*	*gonen*
6 *roku*	*rokuji*	**rokkagetsu**	*rokunen*
7 *shichi*	*shichiji*	*shichikagetsu*	*shichinen*
nana	*nanaji*	*nanakagetsu*	*nananen*
8 *hachi*	*hachiji*	*hachikagetsu*	*hachinen*
		hakkagetsu	
9 *ku*	*kuji*		
kyuu		*kyuukagetsu*	*kyuunen*
10 *juu*	*juuji*	**jukkagetsu**	*juunen*
		jikkagetsu	

Enpitsu ga sanbon arimasu.
There are three pencils.

Hankachi o nimai kaimashita.
I bought two handkerchiefs.

Juuen arimasu ka.
Do you have ten yen?

Otooto wa ima kyuusai desu.
My younger brother is nine now.

Ringo wa jukko arimasu.
There are ten apples.

Onna no hito wa yonin imasu.
There are four women.

Kinoo uchi e kuji ni kaerimashita.
I went home at nine yesterday.

Igirisu ni ikkagetsu imashita.
I was in the United Kingdom for a month.

Moo yonen tachimashita.
Four years have passed already.

c. Counters with dates

While the regular counter is *-nichi*, the first ten days of the month, as well as the fourteenth, the twentieth, and the twenty-fourth, are irregular.

1	2	3	4	5	6	7
tsuitachi	**futsuka**	**mikka**	**yokka**	**itsuka**	**muika**	**nanoka**
8	9	10	11	12	13	14
yooka	**kokonoka**	**tooka**	*juu ichinichi*	*juu ninichi*	*juu sannichi*	**juu yokka**
15	16	17	18	19	20	21
juu gonichi	*juu roku-nichi*	*juu shichi-nichi*	*juu hachi-nichi*	*juu kunichi*	**hatsuka**	*nijuu ichi-nichi*
22	23	24	25	26	27	28
nijuu ni-nichi	*nijuu san-nichi*	**nijuu yokka**	*nijuu go-nichi*	*nijuu rokunichi*	*nijuu shichi-nichi*	*nijuu hachi-nichi*
29	30	31				
nijuu kunichi	*sanjuu nichi*	*sanjuu ichinichi*				

Tomodachi wa hatsuka ni kimashita.
My friend came on the twentieth.

Shigatsu yooka wa haha no tanjoobi desu.
April eighth is my mother's birthday.

When talking about duration in days, the above terms for dates can be used. For "one day," however, use *ichinichi*.

Kyoo wa ichinichi uchi ni imashita.
I was at home all day long [for one day].

Kan can be optionally attached to the terms expressing numbers of days, except for *ichinichi* "one day."

futsuka(kan)
two days

juu ichinichi(kan)
eleven days

Itsukakan machimashita kedo, tegami wa kimasen deshita.
I waited for five days, but the letter didn't come.

3. "APPROXIMATELY"

Goro, a dependent noun, is used following a specific point in time to mean "approximately."

Itsu goro desu ka.
When approximately is it?

Sangatsu tooka goro desu.
It's around March tenth.

In a sentence with *ni* "at, on, in," *goro* can replace the particle *ni*, or both *goro* and *ni* can be used. When *goro* is used, *ni* is optional. *Ni* always follows *goro*.

Yoji goro (ni) ikimashoo.
Let's go around four o'clock.

While *goro* is used with a specific point in time, *gurai* (or *kurai*) is used in other contexts.

Gonen gurai Kanada ni imashita.
I was in Canada for about five years.

Niwa ni ki ga juu gohon gurai arimasu.
There are about fifteen trees in the garden.

Although you may hear people replacing *goro* with *gurai* (or *kurai*) for a specific point in time, the standard term is *goro*.

4. JAPANESE YEARS

Although the Western system of counting years (e.g., 1997) is common, the Japanese system is even more common, which divides years into eras. Each era is the reign of an emperor. To count individual years, the name of the era is followed by the year.

Heisei hachinen
the eighth year of Heisei (1996)

Shoowa yonjuunen goro desu.
It's around Showa forty (1965).

This system originates in the modern period in the nineteenth century. The eras are the following:

Meiji	1868–1912	*Shoowa*	1926–1989
Taishoo	1912–1926	*Heisei*	1989–present

118

5. THE HONORIFIC VERB *IRASSHAIMASU*

Japanese is rich in honorific expressions. Honorific verbs can be classified into three categories: those expressing respect, those expressing
humbleness, and those expressing simple politeness. An honorific
verb of respect elevates the subject of the sentence. A humble honorific verb, on the other hand, humbles it.

Honorific verbs are either regular or irregular. Irregular ones
should be memorized individually. In this lesson, you will deal with one
irregular respectful honorific verb, *irasshaimasu*. The neutral (non-
honorific) equivalents of *irasshaimasu* are *imasu* "to exist," *kimasu* "to
come," and *ikimasu* "to go." Therefore, sometimes, a sentence may be
ambiguous, but usually the context clarifies its meaning.

NEUTRAL EQUIVALENTS:

Takusan irasshaimasu.
There are many people.   *(imasu)*
Many people come.   *(kimasu)*
Many people go.   *(ikimasu)*

Yamada san wa yoku koko e irasshaimasu ka.
Does Mr. Yamada come here often?   *(kimasu)*

Sensei wa kinoo Nagoya e irasshaimasen deshita.
The teacher did not go to Nagoya yesterday.   *(ikimasen deshita)*

Since *irasshaimasu* is a respectful honorific word, the subject of a sentence with this verb should not be the speaker or someone closely connected to the speaker (a family member, for example).

6. THE POLITE MARKER *GO-*

Like the polite marker *o-* (see Lesson 6, C9), *go-* is also used as a prefix
to express respect or simple politeness. It is attached to a noun, an adjective, or an adverb. Usually, words that take *go-* do not take *o-*, and
vice versa.

Gokazoku wa Kamakura ni irasshaimasu.
Her family is in Kamakura.

Gokyoodai wa nannin irasshaimasu ka.
How many brothers and sisters do you have?

Kochira wa Oda san no goshujin desu.
This is Ms. Oda's husband.

Doozo goyukkuri.
Take your time. [Please be slowly.]

7. PARTICLES

a. ... *mo* ... *mo*- "both ... and ..."

When *mo* "also" occurs twice with two nouns, it means "both ... and ..." in an affirmative sentence, and "neither ... nor ..." in a negative sentence.

Otoosan mo okaasan mo yoku Tookyoo e irasshaimasu ka.
Do both your father and mother come to Tokyo often?

Ane mo imooto mo furansugo o hanashimasu.
Both my older sister and my younger sister speak French.

Chichi mo haha mo kinoo dekakemasen deshita.
Neither my father nor my mother went out yesterday.

b. *Kara* "because"

Kara "because" can come at the end of a sentence. This construction is used mainly in spoken Japanese.

Watashi wa mada issai deshita kara.
Because I was still one year old.

Compare:

Ame ga furimashita kara, chichi wa kimasen deshita.
Because it rained, my father didn't come.
My father didn't come because it rained.

Chichi wa kimasen deshita. Ame ga furimashita kara.
My father didn't come. Because it rained.

Uchi wa itsumo nigiyaka deshita. Kyoodai ga takusan imashita kara.
My house was always lively. Because there were many brothers and sisters.

8. -*TACHI*

In Lesson 1, you learned that -*tachi* is attached to a pronoun to indicate plurality. For example:

watashi (I) → *watashitachi* (we)

-*tachi* can also be used with regular nouns referring to animate beings, usually people. Attachment of -*tachi* is obligatory or optional, depending on the word.

Gakusei(tachi) ga takusan kimashita.
Many students came.

With a person's name or a specific noun such as *kono hito* "this person," *-tachi* is obligatory to show that the person mentioned and at least one more person are involved. In the following sentence, adding *-tachi* to *Oda san* changes the meaning to Ms. Oda and at least one more unspecified person, usually someone closely associated with her.

Oda santachi wa resutoran de shokuji shimashita.
 Ms. Oda and another person (or other people) dined in the restaurant.

In the following cases, the meaning of *-tachi* is ambiguous.

Anitachi wa yoku kimasu.
 My older brothers come often.
  or
 My older brother(s) and another person (or other people) come often.

Ani ya anetachi wa yoku kimasu.
 My older brother(s) and older sister(s) come often.
  or
 My older brother(s), older sister(s), and another person (or other people) come often.

Imootosantachi wa ogenki desu ka.
 Are your younger sisters fine?
  or
 Are your younger sister(s) and another person (or other people) fine?

D. MOJI

The following are the remaining basic *katakana* characters as shown in Table I, lines six through eleven (page 5):

LINE 6	*ha*	*hi*	*fu*	*he*	*ho*
KATAKANA	ハ	ヒ	フ	ヘ	ホ
HIRAGANA	は	ひ	ふ	へ	ほ
LINE 7	*ma*	*mi*	*mu*	*me*	*mo*
KATAKANA	マ	ミ	ム	メ	モ
HIRAGANA	ま	み	む	め	も
LINE 8	*ya*	*(i)*	*yu*	*(e)*	*yo*
KATAKANA	ヤ	(イ)	ユ	(エ)	ヨ
HIRAGANA	や	(い)	ゆ	(え)	よ

	ra	ri	ru	re	ro
LINE 9	ra	ri	ru	re	ro
KATAKANA	ラ	リ	ル	レ	ロ
HIRAGANA	ら	り	る	れ	ろ
LINE 10	wa	(i)	(u)	(e)	o
KATAKANA	ワ	(イ)	(ウ)	(エ)	ヲ
HIRAGANA	わ	(い)	(う)	(え)	を
LINE 11	n'				
KATAKANA	ン				
HIRAGANA	ん				

The *katakana* in parentheses—*i* イ and *e* エ on line 8; and *i* イ, *u* ウ and *e* エ on line 10— are redundant. Like the *hiragana* in parentheses (see Lesson 3), they are the same syllables as the ones on line 1.

As in *hiragana*, there are two *katakana* for *o* — オ and ヲ. The *hiragana* お and を are both for the syllable *o*, and を is used only to write the particle *o*. Since particles are always written in *hiragana*, you do not often need to use the *katakana* ヲ, (*o*) except when *katakana* are used for emphasis or telegrams.

STROKE ORDER

ha	ノ ハ	ma	フ マ
hi	ー ヒ	mi	ヽ ミ ミ
fu	フ	mu	ム ム
he	ヘ	me	ノ メ
ho	一 ナ オ ホ	mo	一 二 モ

ya	ヤ ヤ	ra	ー ラ
yu	フ ユ	ri	ヽ リ
yo	ヨ ヨ ヨ	ru	ノ ル
		re	レ
		ro	ヽ 冂 ロ

wa	' ワ
o	一 ニ ヲ
n'	ヽ ン

122

Some *katakana* are similar to each other. Compare the following:

ソ	*so*	ン	*n'*
ツ	*tsu*	シ	*shi*
ア	*a*	マ	*ma*
ナ	*na*	メ	*me*
コ	*ko*	ユ	*yu*
ク	*ku*	ワ	*wa*

Read the following:

カメラ	*kamera*	camera
アメリカ	*Amerika*	America
フランス	*Furansu*	France

E. TANGO TO HYOOGEN

(go)kazoku	family
chichi/otoosan	father
haha/okaasan	mother
ani/oniisan	older brother
ane/oneesan	older sister
otooto/otootosan	younger brother
imooto/imootosan	younger sister
sofu/ojiisan	grandfather
sobo/obaasan	grandmother
otto/shujin/goshujin	husband
tsuma/kanai/okusan	wife
(go)kyoodai	sibling
otoko (no) kyoodai	male sibling
onna (no) kyoodai	female sibling
hitorikko/hitorigo	only child in the family

akachan	baby
shigoto	job, work
tegami	letter
hankachi	handkerchief
mukashi	old days
futari tomo	both people
shokuji shimasu	to have a meal
hanashimasu	to speak, talk
machimasu	to wait
tachimasu	to elapse
irasshaimasu	to exist, come, go (honorific)
urayamashii	envious
nigiyaka	lively
(o)genki	healthy, well, fine
itsumo	always, usually
mada	still
go-	honorific marker
goro	approximately (dependent noun)
gurai	approximately (dependent noun)

RENSHUU

A. Mark each statement T (true) or F (false) on the basis of the dialogue.

1. *Oda san no otoosan mo okaasan mo shigoto de isogashii desu.*
2. *Oda san wa hitorikko desu.*
3. *Oda san wa Shoowa yonjuunen goro mada akachan deshita.*

B. Fill in the blanks with the appropriate kinship terms.

1. _____ *wa ogenki desu ka.*
   Is your mother well?
2. _____ *wa ima eki ni imasu.*
   My younger brother is at the station now.
3. _____, *watashi wa koko ni imasu.*
   Grandfather, I am here.
4. *Kore wa* _____ *no onamae desu ka.*
   Is this your older brother's name?

C. Fill in the blanks with the date in parentheses.

1. *Watashi no tanjoobi wa* _____ *desu.*
   (May 1)
2. *Sobo wa* _____ *ni kimasu.*
   (April 6)
3. _____ *wa doyoobi desu yo.*
   (December 24)
4. *Kono apaato wa* _____ *ni akimasu.*
   (September 30)

D. Choose the correct words.

1. *Watashi wa Nagoya ni (irasshaimashita/imashita/arimashita).*
2. *Gakusei ga (ninin/futari) kimashita.*
3. *Watashi no (gokyoodai/kyoodai) wa eiga ga suki desu.*
4. *Ima (kuji/kyuuji) desu.*

KARUCHAA NOOTO

The traditional Japanese family was a stem family, with one couple of each generation in the household: Grandparents and possibly great grandparents may all live with the married couple and their children. However, the number of nuclear families has drastically increased in Japan since World War II.

The traditional Japanese family structure mirrors Japan's hierarchical society. Older people had a higher status than younger ones, and males were regarded as higher than females. For example, at one time, only the oldest son had the right to inherit the family property. Japanese kinship terms still reflect the traditional family structure. After World War II, family laws were changed a great deal: the traditional hierarchical nature is now fading away, and the role of women in the family as well as in society at large is changing. The concept that older people should be respected, however, is still prevalent not only within the family but in Japanese society as a whole. It is reflected in the use of honorifics to address older people.

KOTAE

A. 1. T   2. F   3. T
B. 1. *Okaasan*   2. *Otooto*   3. *Ojiisan*   4. *oniisan*
C. 1. *gogatsu tsuitachi*   2. *shigatsu muika*   3. *Juunigatsu nijuu yokka*
4. *kugatsu sanjuunichi*
D. 1. *imashita*   2. *futari*   3. *kyoodai*   4. *kuji*

FUKUSHUU 2

A. Fill in the blanks according to the English in parentheses.

1. *Imooto ga* ——— *imasu.* (two)
2. *Nagoya ni* ——— *imashita.* (three days)
3. *Ima* ——— *desu.* (four o'clock)
4. *Kami o* ——— *kaimashita.* (twenty)

B. Fill in the blanks with particles according to the English equivalents.

1. *Natsuyasumi* ——— *yama e ikitai desu.*
   I want to go to the mountains during the summer vacation.
2. *Sofu* ——— *sobo* ——— *genki desu.*
   Both my grandfather and grandmother are well.
3. *Shashin wa watashi* ——— *heya* ——— *arimasu.*
   The photograph is in my room.
4. *Buruu* ——— *burausu* ——— *hoshii n desu.*
   I want a blue blouse.

C. Insert the appropriate question word.

1. *Kyoo wa* ——— *yoobi desu ka.*
   Doyoobi desu.
2. *Ringo o* ——— *kaimashoo ka.*
   Mittsu kaimashoo.
3. *Kono suutsu wa* ——— *desu ka.*
   Niman'en desu.
4. ——— *de shashin o torimashoo ka.*
   Uchi no mae de torimashoo.

D. Answer the questions using the clues in parentheses.

1. *Kyoo wa nannichi desu ka.* (August 9)
2. *Ginkoo wa doko ni arimasu ka.* (behind the library)
3. *Donna machi ga suki desu ka.* (old town)
4. *Moofu wa nanmai arimasu ka.* (three)

E. Choose the correct word.

1. ——— *wa ima uchi ni imasen.*
   a. *Apaato* b. *Otto* c. *Seetaa*
2. *Tookyoo e* ——— *de ikimashita.*
   a. *hikooki* b. *kinoo* c. *chichi*
3. *Kuukoo no kissaten de* ———
   a. *ikimashita* b. *imashita* c. *yasumimashita*
4. *Kore kara uchi e* ——— *n desu.*
   a. *hoshii* b. *kaeritai* c. *isogashii*

F. Fill in the blanks.

mimasu	1	*mimashita*	2
3	*oishiku arimasen*	4	5
6	7	8	*joozu ja arimasen deshita*

G. Match the Japanese and the English.

1. *Doozo goyukkuri.*
2. *Omatase shimashita.*
3. *Irasshaimase.*
4. *Shibaraku desu nee.*

a. Can I help you?
b. Take your time.
c. I haven't seen you for a long time.
d. Sorry to have kept you waiting.

H. Write the English equivalents.

Example: パン bread

1. しゃしん

2. かぞく

3. しょうせつ

4. アメリカじん

5. フランスご

KOTAE

A. 1. *futari*   2. *mikka(kan)*   3. *yoji*   4. *nijuumai*
B. 1. *ni*   2. *mo, mo*   3. *no, ni*   4. *no, ga*
C. 1. *nan*   2. *ikutsu*   3. *ikura*   4. *Doko*
D. 1. (*Kyoo wa*) *hachigatsu kokonoka desu.* 2. (*Ginkoo wa*) *toshokan no ushiro ni arimasu.* 3. *Furui machi ga suki desu.* 4. (*Moofu wa*) *sanmai arimasu.*
E. 1. b   2. a   3. c   4. b
F. 1. *mimasen*   2. *mimasen deshita*   3. *oishii desu*   4. *oishikatta desu*
5. *oishiku arimasen deshita*   6. *joozu desu*   7. *joozu ja arimasen*   8. *joozu deshita*
G. 1. b   2. d   3. a   4. c
H. 1. photograph   2. family   3. novel   4. American person   5. French language

YOMU RENSHUU (READING PRACTICE)

ある¹どようび

　　わたしの　うちは　かまくらの　うみの　そばに　あります。とても
しずかな　ところです。きょうは　あまり　さむく　ありませんでした。
それで、あねと　いっしょに²かいがん³へ　いきました。　そらと
うみが　とても　きれいでした。　しゃしんを　たくさん　とりました。
きょうは　どようびでしたけど、ひとは　あまり　いませんでした。
おおきい　きの　したで　おべんとう⁴を　たべました。
　　それから、にじはんごろ、とうきょうへ　いきました。ぎんざで
かいもの　しました。⁵わたしは　ハンカチを　にまい　かいました。
あねは　かびん⁶と　かさを　かいました。それから、レストランで
しょくじを　しました。わたしは　てんぷらを　たべました。あねは
おすしを　たべました。そして、かまくらの　うちへ　よる　かえりまし
た。すこし　つかれました⁷けど、たのしい　いちにちでした。

TANGO TO HYOOGEN

1.	ある	one, a certain
2.	と　いっしょに	together with
3.	かいがん	seashore
4.	(お)べんとう	box lunch
5.	かいものします	to go shopping
6.	かびん	vase
7.	つかれます	to get tired

DAI JUU IKKA
Lesson 11
PUREZENTO.   Presents.

A. DAIAROOGU

KEKKON IWAI.

A mutual friend of Ms. Yabe and Ms. Tani, Ms. Maeda, is getting married.

YABE: **Maeda san kara kekkónshiki no shootaijoo o moraimáshita ka.**

TANI: **Ée, moraimáshita. Moo súgu desu ne. Oiwai o kaitái n desu kedo . . .**

YABE: **Ée, watashi mo. Démo, tekitoo na monó ga mitsukarimasén née.**

TANI: **Issho ni agemasén ka.**

YABE: **Sóo desu ne. Náni o agemashóo ka.**

TANI: **Shokki wa dóo desu ka.**

YABE: **Ée, íi desu ne. Takaraya ni takusan arimásu ne.**

TANI: **Takaraya. Éki no sóba no misé desu ka.**

YABE: **Ée, sóo desu. Ane ga tokidoki Takaraya no osara ya owan o kuremásu kedo, iró ya dezáin ga totemo íi n desu.**

TANI: **Jáa, kore kara mí ni ikimashóo ka.**

Takaraya de.

YABE: **Kírei na owan désu née. Dóo omoimásu ka.**

TANI: **Ée, subarashíi desu née. Sumimasén. Kono owan no sétto wa íkura desu ka.**

TEN'IN: **Nimán gosen'en désu.**

TANI: **Dóo desu ka.**

YABE: **Ée, íi desu ne.**

TANI: **Jáa, kore o itadakimásu.**

THE WEDDING PRESENT.

YABE: Did you get a wedding invitation from Ms. Maeda?

TANI: Yes, I got one. The wedding is going to be pretty soon, isn't it? I want to get [buy] a [congratulatory] present for her, but . . .

YABE: Yes, me too. But I can't find an appropriate one.

TANI: Why don't we give her a present together?

YABE: Yes, I would like to. But what? [What shall we give to her?]

TANI: How about dishes?

YABE: Yes, that's a good idea. Takaraya usually has a good selection, right?

TANI: Takaraya? Is that the store near the station?

YABE: Yes, that's right. My older sister sometimes gives me plates and bowls from there. Their colors and designs are very nice.

TANI: Well then, should we go take a look at them now?

At Takaraya.

YABE: What pretty bowls! What [how] do you think?

TANI: Yes, they are wonderful. Excuse me. How much is this set of bowls?

CLERK: They are 25,000 yen.

TANI: Okay?

YABE: Yes, that's fine.

TANI: Well then, we will get these.

B. BUNPOO TO YOOHOO

1. *AGEMASU* AND *KUREMASU* "TO GIVE"

"To give" can be translated in different ways.

a. *Agemasu*

While the typical English sentence pattern with "to give" is "giver gives recipient something," the typical Japanese pattern with *agemasu* is:

> giver *wa* (or *ga*)   recipient *ni*   something *o agemasu*

Yamada san wa Maeda san ni purezento o agemashita.
　Mr. Yamada gave Ms. Maeda a present.

Watashi wa minna ni omiyage o agemashita.
　I gave everybody a souvenir.

Issho ni Maeda san ni purezento o agemasen ka.
　Why don't we give Ms. Maeda a present together?

Nani o agemashoo ka.
　What should we give her?

b. *Kuremasu*

Kuremasu is used when the recipient is the speaker or is in the speaker's in-group (e.g., a family member). The sentence pattern remains the same.

Ane ga tokidoki watashi ni osara ya owan o kuremasu.
　My older sister sometimes gives me plates, bowls, etc.

Otooto ga shatsu o kuremashita.
　My younger brother gave me a shirt.

Kono mise wa itsumo kuupon o kuremasu.
　This store always gives us coupons.

Yamada san wa watashi no kodomo ni ningyoo o kuremashita.
　Mr. Yamada gave my child a doll.

However, even when the recipient is in the speaker's in-group, if the giver is the speaker, use *agemasu*, not *kuremasu*. Compare:

Yamada san wa haha ni kaban o kuremashita.
　Mr. Yamada gave my mother a bag.

Watashi wa haha ni kaban o agemashita.
　I gave my mother a bag.

If both the giver and the recipient are in the speaker's in-group, it is often not clear whether to use *agemasu* or *kuremasu*. Consider the following two sentences:

Chichi wa sofu ni saifu o agemashita.
　My father gave my grandfather a wallet.

Chichi wa watashi no kodomo ni konpyuutaa o kuremashita.
　My father gave my child a computer.

In the above sentences, *agemasu* is more appropriate than *kuremasu* in the first, but *kuremasu* is more appropriate in the second. One explanation is that in the second sentence, the child is in the speaker's custody, so the speaker has feelings of gratitude toward the father.

In general, the decision between *agemasu* and *kuremasu* depends on the relationship among in-group people, as exemplified in the above two sentences. Sometimes, even native speakers get confused.

2. *YARIMASU* "TO GIVE"

Yarimasu "to give" is used in the same instances as *agemasu* except that the recipient is humbled by the speaker.

Watashi wa kodomo ni okashi o yarimashita.
  I gave the child sweets.

Suzuki san wa neko ni sakana o yarimashita.
  Ms. Suzuki gave the cat a fish.

Hana ni mizu o yarimashoo.
  Let's give the flowers water.

Be careful with your use of *yarimasu*, because it may be impolite to use it when the recipient is a person.

Kuremasu has no replacement that humbles the recipient the way that *yarimasu* does.

3. *MORAIMASU* "TO RECEIVE"

The typical sentence pattern with *moraimasu* "to receive/get" is:

recipient *wa* (or *ga*)   giver *kara* (or *ni*)   something *o moraimasu*

Unlike in sentences with *agemasu* or *kuremasu*, the recipient is the subject.

Watashi wa Maeda san kara shootaijoo o moraimashita.
  I received an invitation from Ms. Maeda.

Watashi wa ane kara ochawan o moraimashita.
  I got rice bowls from my older sister.

Otooto wa tomodachi ni kawaii neko o moraimashita.
  My younger brother got a cute cat from his friend.

4. "TO GIVE" AND "TO RECEIVE": HONORIFIC VERBS

Three honorific verbs for "to give" and "to receive" are introduced here (see Lesson 10, C5).

a. *Sashiagemasu* "to give"

This verb is a humble honorific verb: The giver (the subject) is humbled and the recipient is elevated. The neutral equivalent is *agemasu*.

Ima otsuri o sashiagemasu.
I will give you the change now.

Haha wa sensei ni shootaijoo o sashiagemashita.
My mother gave an invitation to the teacher.

Maeda san ni purezento o sashiagetai n desu.
I want to give Ms. Maeda a present.

b. *Kudasaimasu* "to give"

This verb is a respectful honorific verb: The giver (the subject) is elevated and the recipient, who is the speaker or a member of the speaker's in-group, is humbled. The neutral equivalent is *kuremasu*.

Tani san wa watashi ni osara o kudasaimashita.
Ms. Tani gave me plates.

Maeda san wa imooto ni kirei na e o kudasaimashita.
Ms. Maeda gave my younger sister a pretty picture.

Sensei ga tegami o kudasaimashita.
The teacher gave me a letter.

c. *Itadakimasu* "to receive"

This verb is a humble honorific verb: The recipient (the subject) is humbled and the giver elevated. The neutral equivalent is *moraimasu*.

Kore o itadakimasu.
I will take this. (in a store, for example)

Watashitachi wa sensei kara omiyage o itadakimashita.
We got a souvenir from the teacher.

Sain o itadakitai n desu.
I would like to get your signature.

Itadakimasu.
I will receive it.

Itadakimasu is a fixed expression if it is used just before eating (or drinking). After eating (or drinking), use *Gochisoosama* (*deshita*) "I appreciate the food."

5. SUMMARY OF "TO GIVE" AND "TO RECEIVE"

	HUMBLING THE RECIPIENT	NEUTRAL	HONORIFIC
TO GIVE	*yarimasu*	*agemasu*	*sashiagemasu* (humble)
TO GIVE	————	*kuremasu*	*kudasaimasu* (respectful)
TO RECEIVE	————	*moraimasu*	*itadakimasu* (humble)

6. PURPOSE

The English "to/in order to" has several Japanese equivalents. One of them is the following:

> pre-*masu* form + *ni* ... motion verb

Here, the pre-*masu* form functions as a noun derived from a verb. The motion verb denotes moving from one place to another. The most common motion verbs are *ikimasu* "to go," *kimasu* "to come," and *kaerimasu* "to return."

Depaato e shokki o kai ni ikimashita.
I went to the department store to buy dishes.

Tomodachi ga orei o ii ni kimashita.
My friend came to express [say] his gratitude.

Mi ni ikimashoo.
Let's go to see it.

Ginkoo e ryoogae shi ni ikimashita.
I went to the bank to exchange money.

With a *shimasu* verb (see Lesson 7, C2), like *ryoogae shimasu* "to exchange money," the pre-*masu* form *shi* can be deleted.

Ginkoo e ryoogae (shi) ni ikimashita.
I went to the bank to exchange money.

Uchi e shokuji (shi) ni kaerimashita.
I went home to have a meal.

C. MOJI

The *katakana* equivalents of the *hiragana* characters with two dots or a circle (see Lesson 4) are also written with two dots or a circle. The following represents the syllables in Table II (page 6), lines one through five.

KATAKANA WITH TWO DOTS

LINE 1	ga	gi	gu	ge	go
KATAKANA	ガ	ギ	グ	ゲ	ゴ
HIRAGANA	が	ぎ	ぐ	げ	ご
LINE 2	za	ji	zu	ze	zo
KATAKANA	ザ	ジ	ズ	ゼ	ゾ
HIRAGANA	ざ	じ	ず	ぜ	ぞ
LINE 3	da	(ji)	(zu)	de	do
KATAKANA	ダ	ヂ	ヅ	デ	ド
HIRAGANA	だ	ぢ	づ	で	ど
LINE 4	ba	bi	bu	be	bo
KATAKANA	バ	ビ	ブ	ベ	ボ
HIRAGANA	ば	び	ぶ	べ	ぼ

Like the *hiragana ji* ぢ and *zu* づ, the *katakana ji* ヂ, and *zu* ヅ are used only in limited cases.

KATAKANA WITH A CIRCLE

LINE 5	pa	pi	pu	pe	po
KATAKANA	パ	ピ	プ	ペ	ポ
HIRAGANA	ぱ	ぴ	ぷ	ぺ	ぽ

Read the following:

テレビ	*terebi*	television
イギリス	*Igirisu*	the United Kingdom
カナダ	*Kanada*	Canada
ドイツ	*Doitsu*	Germany
ピンク	*pinku*	pink
プレゼント	*purezento*	present
ブラウス	*burausu*	blouse
パン	*pan*	bread
デザイン	*dezain*	design

135

D. TANGO TO HYOOGEN

purezento	present
oiwai	congratulatory present
kekkonshiki	wedding ceremony
shootaijoo	(letter of) invitation
shokki	dish
(o)sara	plate
(o)wan	bowl
(o)chawan	rice bowl
(o)kashi	sweets
(o)miyage	souvenir
shatsu	shirt
kuupon	coupon
ningyoo	doll
e	picture, painting (not a photograph)
saifu	wallet
konpyuutaa	computer
min(n)a	everybody
mono	thing
(o)rei	gratitude
setto	set
(o)tsuri	change (money)
sain	signature
dezain	design
agemasu	to give
kuremasu	to give
yarimasu	to give
moraimasu	to receive
sashiagemasu	to give (honorific: equivalent of *agemasu*)
kudasaimasu	to give (honorific: equivalent of *kuremasu*)
itadakimasu	to receive (honorific: equivalent of *moraimasu*)
iimasu	to say
mitsukarimasu	to be found
tekitoo	appropriate
moo sugu	before long, pretty soon
Itadakimasu.	Thank you for the food. (before eating)
Gochisoosama (deshita).	Thank you for the food. (after eating)

RENSHUU

A. Answer the following questions based on the dialogue.

   1. *Tani san to Yabe san wa dare kara shootaijoo o moraimashita ka.*
   2. *Yabe san no oneesan wa tokidoki nani o Yabe san ni agemasu ka.*
   3. *Takaraya wa doko ni arimasu ka.*
   4. *Owan no setto wa ikura deshita ka.*

B. Using the verbs provided, fill in the blanks according to the English equivalents.
   a. *agemashita* b. *kuremashita* c. *moraimashita*

   1. *Haha ga watashi ni kutsu o* ———.
      My mother gave me shoes.
   2. *Yamada san wa Abe san ni kirei na e o* ———.
      Mr. Yamada received a pretty picture from Ms. Abe.
   3. *Yabe san wa imooto ni okashi o* ———.
      Mr. Yabe gave my younger sister sweets.
   4. *Ani wa Yamada san ni saifu o* ———.
      My older brother gave Mr. Yamada a wallet.

C. Choose the appropriate verb from the following, and fill in the blanks.

   a. *sashiagemashita* b. *kudasaimashita* c. *itadakimashita*

   1. *Sensei wa otooto ni hon o* ———.
   2. *Tani san no otoosan kara shootaijoo o* ———.
   3. *Chichi wa sensei ni shashin o* ———.
   4. *Sumisu san kara kirei na shokki o* ———.

D. Fill in the blanks with the appropriate particles.

   1. *Sobo wa watashi* ——— *shatsu* ——— *kuremashita.*
   2. *Haha wa Miki san* ——— *ningyoo* ——— *moraimashita.*
   3. *Depaato* ——— *purezento o kai* ——— *ikitai n desu.*

E. Combine two sentences as shown in the following example.

Example: *tabemasu + ikimasu* → *tabe ni ikimasu*

   1. *eiga o mimasu + ikimasu.* (go to see a movie)
   2. *booshi o torimasu + uchi ni kaerimasu.* (go home to get a hat)
   3. *konpyuutaa o shimasu + gakkoo ni ikimasu.* (go to school to use the computer)

KARUCHAA NOOTO

Giving gifts is an important part of Japanese culture. Besides the usual birthday and Christmas presents, which are popular among young people, there are other occasions that are noted by giving gifts. You receive presents when you start school or graduate, when you get a new job, and when you leave on a long trip. When coming back from vacation or a short trip, some people bring an *omiyage* (souvenir) to friends and co-workers. Brides and grooms receive wedding presents, parents receive gifts for a newborn baby, and children receive money, called *otoshi-dama*, as a New Year present. On Valentine's Day, women give chocolates to men (husbands, boyfriends, or colleagues). When a woman gives chocolates to a man because she feels obligated to do so, it is known as *giri-choko* (obligation chocolate). Men usually do not give presents on Valentine's Day. On "White Day" (March 14), however, men return the favor and give presents to women.

Traditions unique to Japan are the *ochuugen* and the *oseibo*, gifts given to show gratitude in summer and December, respectively. These gifts are given to your relatives, teachers, business acquaintances, customers, supervisors at work, and the go-between who did the match-making for your wedding. The recent trend is to give practical items such as food, soap, or towels. Some people argue that giving presents to a teacher or supervisor at work is ethically questionable, since they may be mistaken for bribes. Summer and December are also bonus seasons, when employees receive special monetary bonuses in addition to their regular salaries. Many employees use their bonuses to buy the *ochuugen* and the *oseibo*.

KOTAE

A. 1. *Maeda san kara moraimashita.* 2. *Osara ya owan o agemasu.* 3. *Eki no soba ni arimasu.* 4. *Niman gosen'en deshita.*
B. 1. b 2. c 3. b 4. a
C. 1. b 2. c 3. a or c 4. c
D. 1. *ni, o* 2. *kara* or *ni, o* 3. *e, ni*
E. 1. *eiga o <u>mi ni</u> ikimasu.* 2. *booshi o <u>tori ni</u> uchi ni kaerimasu.* 3. *konpyuu-taa o <u>shi ni</u> gakkoo ni ikimasu.*

138

DAI JUU NIKA
Lesson 12
KANKOO RYOKOO.   A Sight-seeing Trip.

A. DAIAROOGU

Nihonkai engan.

Mr. Imai and Mr. Taylor, an American, teach in the same high school.

IMAI: **Natsuyásumi ni náni o suru tsumori désu ka.**

TEERAA: **Isshuukan gúrai ryokoo suru tsumori désu.**

IMAI: **Dóko e.**

TEERAA: **Nihónkai o mitái n desu. Dóko ga íi desu ka.**

IMAI: **Kinósaki wa dóo desu ka.**

TEERAA: **Kinósaki desu ka.**

IMAI: **Ée, watashi wa kyónen Kinósaki made shigoto de ikimáshita kedo, onsen ga arimásu kara, yókatta desu yo.**

TEERAA: **Kinósaki wa Áma-no-hashidate kara tooí desu ka.**

IMAI: **Iie, chikái desu. Áa, soo soo. Hajime wa hoka no tokoró e ikanai tsumori déshita kedo, jikan ga arimáshita kara, Áma-no-hashidate mo mí ni ikimáshita.**

TEERAA: **Áma-no-hashidate wa kírei na késhiki de yuumei désu ne.**

IMAI: **Ée, úmi to mátsu no ki no choowa ga subaráshikatta desu yo.**

TEERAA: **Áa, sóo desu ka. Watashi mo kenbutsu shitái desu ne.**

IMAI: **Uchi ni Kinósaki ya Áma-no-hashidate no shashin ga arimásu kara, kore kara mí ni kimasén ka.**

The coast of the Japan Sea.

IMAI: What are you planning to do during your summer vacation?

TAYLOR: I am planning to go on a trip for about a week or so.

IMAI: Where are you going?

TAYLOR: I want to see the Japan Sea. Where should I go? [Which place is nice?]

IMAI: How about Kinosaki?

TAYLOR: Kinosaki?

IMAI: Yes. I went to [as far as] Kinosaki last year on business. There are hot springs there, so I really enjoyed my stay.

TAYLOR: Is Kinosaki far from Ama-no-hashidate?

IMAI: No, it's close. Oh, that's right. At first, I did not plan to go to any other places, but since I had the time, I went to see Ama-no-hashidate, also.

TAYLOR: Ama-no-hashidate is famous for its pretty scenery, isn't it?

IMAI: Yes, the combination [harmony] of the sea and the pine trees was splendid.

TAYLOR: Is that right? I'd like to visit there, too.

IMAI: I have pictures from my trip to Kinosaki and Ama-no-hashidate at home, so why don't you come with me now to see them?

B. BUNPOO TO YOOHOO

1. NORMAL AND PLAIN FORMS OF VERBS

So far, you have learned normal forms of verbs, that is, forms that end in -*masu* and conjugated forms of -*masu*.*

There is another set of forms, plain forms, which are also conjugated according to tense and whether they are affirmative or negative. For now let's focus on the plain forms in the present tense. For example, the normal present form in the affirmative for "to go" is *ikimasu*. The plain present form in the affirmative, on the other hand, is *iku*. While both *ikimasu* and *iku* mean "to go," certain sentence structures require plain forms instead of normal forms.

The plain present affirmative form such as *iku* "to go" is called the dictionary form, because these are the forms that are listed as entries in the dictionary. From now on, when you learn verbs, memorize these forms, and you will be able to make other forms from them by using the appropriate rules. The following is a list of the dictionary forms of the verbs appearing in Lessons 1 through 11.

The symbols C, V, and I mean "consonant verb," "vowel verb," and "irregular verb," respectively. They are explained in section 2 below.

---

* -*mashoo* "let's" is also a normal form. Its plain equivalent is introduced in Lesson 35.

	DICTIONARY FORM (PLAIN PRESENT AFFIRMATIVE)		NORMAL PRESENT AFFIRMATIVE FORM
V	*ageru*	to give	*agemasu*
C	*aku*	to be vacated	*akimasu*
C	*aru*	to have, exist	*arimasu*
C	*atatamaru*	to warm oneself	*atatamarimasu*
C	*au*	to meet	*aimasu*
V	*dekakeru*	to go out	*dekakemasu*
V	*dekiru*	to be able to do	*dekimasu*
C	*furu*	to fall	*furimasu*
C	*hairu*	to enter	*hairimasu*
C	*hanasu*	to talk	*hanashimasu*
C	*harau*	to pay	*haraimasu*
C	*hataraku*	to work	*hatarakimasu*
C	*iku*	to go	*ikimasu*
C	*irassharu*	to go, come, be	*irasshaimasu*
V	*iru*	to exist, have	*imasu*
C	*itadaku*	to receive	*itadakimasu*
C	*iu**	to say	*iimasu*
C	*kaeru*	to return	*kaerimasu*
C	*kaku*	to write	*kakimasu*
V	*kariru*	to borrow	*karimasu*
C	*kau*	to buy	*kaimasu*
V	*kiru*	to wear	*kimasu*
C	*kudasaru*	to give	*kudasaimasu*
V	*kureru*	to give	*kuremasu*
I	*kuru*	to come	*kimasu*
V	*makeru*	to be defeated	*makemasu*
C	*matsu*	to wait	*machimasu*
V	*miru*	to see	*mimasu*
C	*mitsukaru*	to be found	*mitsukarimasu*
C	*morau*	to receive	*moraimasu*
C	*nomu*	to drink	*nomimasu*
C	*omou*	to think	*omoimasu*
C	*oyogu*	to swim	*oyogimasu*
V	*sashiageru*	to give	*sashiagemasu*
V	*shimeru*	to close	*shimemasu*
C	*sumu*	to finish, live	*sumimasu*
I	*suru*	to do	*shimasu*
V	*taberu*	to eat	*tabemasu*
C	*tatsu*	to lapse	*tachimasu*

* The actual pronunciation is *yuu*.

c	*toru*	to take	*torimasu*
c	*wakaru*	to understand	*wakarimasu*
c	*yaru*	to give	*yarimasu*
c	*yasumu*	to rest	*yasumimasu*

2. VERB CLASSIFICATION: CONSONANT VERBS, VOWEL VERBS, AND IRREGULAR VERBS

Verbs can be classified into three groups: consonant verbs, vowel verbs, and irregular verbs. There are only two irregular verbs, *suru* "to do" and *kuru* "to come." All others are either consonant or vowel verbs.

To understand the terms "consonant verb" and "vowel verb," you need to know what "base form" means. The base form is what is left-over after the final *-u* has been dropped from the dictionary form of a consonant verb and the final *-ru* has been dropped from the dictionary form of a vowel verb.

| CONSONANT VERB | *ik* | ← | *iku* |
| VOWEL VERB | *dekake* | ← | *dekakeru* |

The base form of a consonant verb ends in a consonant, and the base form of a vowel verb ends in a vowel, hence the terms. Verb classifications may decide a verb's conjugation rules.

You can often tell whether the verb is a consonant or vowel verb from the dictionary form. All verbs (except for the two irregular verbs *suru* "to do" and *kuru* "to come") whose dictionary forms do not end in *-eru* or *-iru* are consonant verbs. Those with dictionary forms ending in *-eru* or *-iru* are usually vowel verbs, but there are some consonant verbs whose dictionary forms end in *-eru* or *-iru*. Memorize such verbs, which include *hairu* "to enter" and *kaeru* "to return" among the verbs listed above.*

3. CONJUGATION RULES

You can derive the other conjugated verb forms from the dictionary form of a verb by following certain rules. The two irregular verbs (*suru* "to do" and *kuru* "to come") often have no rules for conjugation, and each conjugated form has to be memorized.

a. The normal present affirmative form (=*masu* form)

The base form (the remaining after the final *-u* has been dropped from the dictionary form) of consonant verbs is followed by *-imasu*.

* From now on such verbs will be thus indicated in *Tango to hyoogen*. See also the Glossary (Japanese-English).

iku	→	*ikimasu*	to go
aru	→	*arimasu*	to exist
hairu	→	*hairimasu*	to enter

If the dictionary form of the verb ends in *-su*, when the final *-u* is dropped and *-imasu* is added, the syllable before *-masu* is *si*. Since Japanese does not have the syllable *si*, it becomes *shi*:

hanasu	→	*hanasimasu*	→	*hanashimasu*	to talk

If the dictionary form of the verb ends in *-tsu*, when the final *-u* is dropped and *-imasu* is added, the syllable before *-masu* is *tsi*. Since Japanese does not have the syllable *tsi*, it becomes *-chi*, e.g.:

matsu	→	*matsimasu*	→	*machimasu*	to wait

There are two exceptions among the verbs listed in section 1.

irassharu	→	*irasshaimasu* (not *irassharimasu*)	to be, come, go
kudasaru	→	*kudasaimasu* (not *kudasarimasu*)	to give

The base form of vowel verbs (the part leftover after the final *-ru* has been dropped from the dictionary form) is followed by *-masu*.

dekakeru	→	*dekakemasu*	to go out
dekiru	→	*dekimasu*	to be able
kiru	→	*kimasu*	to wear

The normal present affirmative of the two irregular verbs is:

suru	→	*shimasu*	to do
kuru	→	*kimasu*	to come

b. The plain present negative form

The base form of consonant verbs is followed by *-anai*.

iku	→	*ikanai*	not to go
hairu	→	*hairanai*	not to enter
irassharu	→	*irassharanai*	not to be, come, go

If the dictionary form ends in the single vowel syllable *-u*, the *-u* is dropped, and *-wanai* is added.

kau	→	*kawanai*	not to buy
morau	→	*morawanai*	not to receive

There is one exception.

aru → *nai* (not *aranai*) not to exist/not have

The base form of vowel verbs is followed by *-nai*.

dekakeru	→	*dekakenai*	not to go out
taberu	→	*tabenai*	not to eat
kiru	→	*kinai*	not to wear

The plain present negative of the two irregular verbs is:

suru	→	*shinai*
kuru	→	*konai*

4. INTENTION

Tsumori, used to express an intention or plan, is a dependent noun. It cannot be used by itself, but is always modified. Here are its various structures.

dictionary form (plain present aff.)	+	*tsumori desu*	intend to . . .
dictionary form	+	*tsumori deshita*	intended to . . .
plain present negative	+	*tsumori desu*	intend not to . . .
plain present negative	+	*tsumori deshita*	intended not to . . .

Ryokoo suru tsumori desu.
I plan to travel.

Densha de iku tsumori deshita.
I planned to go by train.

Natsuyasumi ni kuni e kaeranai tsumori desu.
I don't intend to [intend not to] go back to my home country during summer vacation.

Hoka no tokoro e ikanai tsumori deshita.
I didn't plan to [planned not to] go to any other places.

Natsuyasumi ni nani o suru tsumori desu ka.
What do you plan to do during summer vacation?

Hon o takusan yomu tsumori desu.
I plan to read lots of books.

5. THE COUNTER -*SHUUKAN*

-*shuukan* is the counter for "week." The irregular forms are in boldface.

one week	**isshuukan**	six weeks	*rokushuukan*
two weeks	*nishuukan*	seven weeks	*nanashuukan, shichishuukan*
three weeks	*sanshuukan*	eight weeks	**hasshuukan**
four weeks	*yonshuukan*	nine weeks	*kyuushuukan*
five weeks	*goshuukan*	ten weeks	**jusshuukan, jisshuukan**

Isshuukan gurai ryokoo suru tsumori desu.
I plan to travel for about a week.

Kinosaki ni nishuukan imashita.
I was in Kinosaki for two weeks.

Nihongo o rokushuukan benkyoo shimashita.
I studied Japanese for six weeks.

Nihon ni nanshuukan gurai iru tsumori desu ka.
[For about] how many weeks do you intend to be in Japan?

Sanshuukan gurai iru tsumori desu.
I plan to stay for about three weeks.

6. PARTICLES

a. *Kara* ("from" with location and time noun)

In Lesson 11, we discussed *kara* "from" used with the giver in sentences with *morau* "to receive" or *itadaku* "to receive." *Kara* "from" is also used with location and time nouns.

Kinosaki wa Ama-no-hashidate kara tooi desu ka.
Is Kinosaki far from Amanohashidate?

Ashita kara isshuukan ryokoo shimasu.
Starting [from] tomorrow, I am going to travel for one week.

b. *Made* (with location and time noun)

When *made* is used with a location, it is translated as "to," like the particle *e*, but it implies "as far as."

Kinosaki made shigoto de ikimashita.
I went to Kinosaki on business.

When *made* is used with a time noun, it means "until."

Doyoobi made koko ni imasu.
I am going to be here until Saturday.

c. *Kara* and *made*

Kara and *made* can be used together to indicate the beginning and end points of a sequence of motion or a period of time.

Taiheiyoo kara Nihonkai made kuruma de ikimashita.
I went from the Pacific Ocean to the Japan Sea by car.

Goji kara rokuji made benkyoo shimashita.
I studied from five to six o'clock.

C. MOJI

For the syllables consisting of a consonant, *y,* and a vowel, *katakana* characters (Table II, page 6, lines six through seventeen) follow the same pattern as *hiragana* characters (see Lesson 5).

LINE 6	*kya*	*kyu*	*kyo*
KATAKANA	キャ	キュ	キョ
HIRAGANA	きゃ	きゅ	きょ
LINE 7	*sha*	*shu*	*sho*
KATAKANA	シャ	シュ	ショ
HIRAGANA	しゃ	しゅ	しょ
LINE 8	*cha*	*chu*	*cho*
KATAKANA	チャ	チュ	チョ
HIRAGANA	ちゃ	ちゅ	ちょ
LINE 9	*nya*	*nyu*	*nyo*
KATAKANA	ニャ	ニュ	ニョ
HIRAGANA	にゃ	にゅ	にょ
LINE 10	*hya*	*hyu*	*hyo*
KATAKANA	ヒャ	ヒュ	ヒョ
HIRAGANA	ひゃ	ひゅ	ひょ

LINE 11	mya	myu	myo
KATAKANA	ミャ	ミュ	ミョ
HIRAGANA	みゃ	みゅ	みょ
LINE 12	rya	ryu	ryo
KATAKANA	リャ	リュ	リョ
HIRAGANA	りゃ	りゅ	りょ
LINE 13	gya	gyu	gyo
KATAKANA	ギャ	ギュ	ギョ
HIRAGANA	ぎゃ	ぎゅ	ぎょ
LINE 14	ja	ju	jo
KATAKANA	ジャ	ジュ	ジョ
	(ヂャ)	(ヂュ)	(ヂョ)
HIRAGANA	じゃ	じゅ	じょ
	(ぢゃ)	(ぢゅ)	(ぢょ)
LINE 15	bya	byu	byo
KATAKANA	ビャ	ビュ	ビョ
HIRAGANA	びゃ	びゅ	びょ
LINE 16	pya	pyu	pyo
KATAKANA	ピャ	ピュ	ピョ
HIRAGANA	ぴゃ	ぴゅ	ぴょ
LINE 17	p, t, k, s		

For the single-consonant syllables *p*, *t*, *k*, and *s*, the small *tsu* ッ is used as in *hiragana*.

Read the following:

ジャム	*jamu*	jam
シャツ	*shatsu*	shirt
セット	*setto*	set

D. TANGO TO HYOOGEN

densha   train
kuruma   car
takushii   taxi
ryokoosha   travel agency

147

Nihonkai	the Japan Sea
Taiheiyoo	the Pacific Ocean
keshiki	scenery
matsu	pine
matsu no ki	pine tree
onsen	hot spring
kuni	hometown
choowa	harmony
tsumori	intention
ryokoo suru	to travel
kenbutsu suru	to go sight-seeing
yomu	to read
hoka no	(an)other
hajime wa	at first
(Aa,) soo soo.	(Oh,) that's right. (when you remember something suddenly)

RENSHUU

A. Answer the following questions based on the dialogue.

1. *Teeraa san wa natsuyasumi ni nanshuukan gurai ryokoo suru tsumori desu ka.*
2. *Doko ni onsen ga arimasu ka.*
3. *Imai san wa doko e shigoto de ikimashita ka.*

B. Fill in the blanks.

iku	*ikimasu*
kaeru	1
kudasaru	2
kasu "to lend"	3
katsu "to win"	4
ryokoo suru	5
kuru	6
okiru "to get up"	7
akeru "to open"	8

148

C. Fill in the blanks.

iku	ikanai
nomu	1
matsu	2
aru	3
kuru	4
miru	5
kureru	6
sentaku suru	7

D. Fill in the blanks according to the English equivalents.

1. *Kyoo puuru de ——— tsumori ———.*
   I plan to swim in the swimming pool.
2. *——— ryokoo shimashita.*
   I traveled for five weeks.
3. *Kinoo kimono o ——— tsumori ———.*
   I intended not to wear a kimono yesterday.
4. *——— wa kuukoo ——— tooi desu ka.*
   Is the station far from the airport?

KARUCHAA NOOTO

Japan has many beautiful coastal locations. Ama-no-hashidate, located north of Kyoto, is one of the so-called *Nihon sankei* "the three beauty spots in Japan." The other two are Matsushima in northern Japan and Miyajima near Hiroshima. All three locations have beautiful coastal scenery and are visited by many tourists. There are also many mountains, rivers, lakes, and gorges to visit. Since Japan has many volcanoes, there are many hot springs to enjoy. Many beautiful places are designated as national or quasi-national parks. For example, Fuji-Hakone-Izu National Park is around Mt. Fuji and some islands near Tokyo.

KOTAE

A. 1. *Isshuukan gurai ryokoo suru tsumori desu.* 2. *Kinosaki ni onsen ga arimasu.* 3. *Kinosaki e ikimashita.*
B. 1. *kaerimasu* 2. *kudasaimasu* 3. *kashimasu* 4. *kachimasu* 5. *ryokoo shimasu* 6. *kimasu* 7. *okimasu* 8. *akemasu*
C. 1. *nomanai* 2. *matanai* (← *matsanai*) 3. *nai* 4. *konai* 5. *minai* 6. *kurenai* 7. *sentaku shinai*
D. 1. *oyogu, desu* 2. *Goshuukan* 3. *kinai, deshita* 4. *Eki, kara*

DAI JUU SANKA
Lesson 13
SUPOOTSU. Sports.

A. DAIAROOGU

YAKYUU TO TENISU.

Mr. Ueda and Ms. Takagi are colleagues at work.

UEDA: **Ashita Hokkáidoo kara tomodachi ga kúru n desu. Issho ni Kamakura e ikú n desu kedo, Takagi san mo ikimasén ka.**

TAKAGI: **Áa, sumimasén. Démo, ashitá wa tsugoo ga warúi n desu. Kookoo no doosóokai no hitótachi to issho ni yakyuu o mí ni ikú n desu.**

UEDA: **Áa, sóo desu ka. Zannén desu ne. Chíketto wa móo áru n desu ka.**

TAKAGI: **Ée, íi séki no chíketto o kau kotó ga dékita n desu. Ueda san wa yakyuu wa mínai n desu ka.**

UEDA: **Iie, térebi de ítsumo mimásu yo. Mukashi wa amari supootsu bángumi wa mínakatta n desu kedo, kono goro wa yóku míru n desu.**

TAKAGI: **Supóotsu o surú no mo sukí desu ka.**

UEDA: **Ée, bóku wa ténisu ga sukí desu kara, kaisha no tenisu kóoto de tokidoki renshuu surú n desu.**

TAKAGI: **Watashi mo ténisu o surú n desu. Amari joozú ja arimasén kedo.**

UEDA: **Bóku mo hetá desu yo. Kóndo issho ni shimasén ka.**

TAKAGI: **Ée, onegai shimásu.**

UEDA: **Raishuu no doyóobi wa dóo desu ka.**

TAKAGI: **Ée, daijóobu desu.**

UEDA: **Juu ichiji góro ni tenisu kóoto de aimashóo ka.**

TAKAGI: **Sóo desu ne. Jáa, mata.**

BASEBALL AND TENNIS.

UEDA: A friend of mine is coming from Hokkaido tomorrow. We are going to Kamakura together. Would you like to come with us [go, too]?

TAKAGI: Oh, thanks. But I can't tomorrow. [It is inconvenient tomorrow.] I am going to see a baseball game with people in my high school alumni association.

UEDA: Is that right? That's too bad. Do you have tickets already?

TAKAGI: Yes, we were able to buy tickets for good seats. You don't watch baseball games, do you?

UEDA: Yes, I do. [No] I watch them all the time on TV. In the past, I did not watch sports [programs] often, but I do these days.

TAKAGI: Do you like to play sports, too?

UEDA: Yes, [since] I like tennis. I sometimes practice at the company tennis court.

TAKAGI: I play tennis, too. I'm not very good at it, though.

UEDA: Neither am I. Why don't we play together sometime?

TAKAGI: Yes. I would like to. [I would like to ask you.]

UEDA: How about next [week] Saturday?

TAKAGI: Sounds good.

UEDA: Should we meet at the tennis court at, say, eleven o'clock?

TAKAGI: Yes, fine. See you there.

B. BUNPOO TO YOOHOO

1. PLAIN FORMS OF VERBS IN THE PAST AFFIRMATIVE

a. Consonant verbs

The plain past affirmative form of a consonant verb depends on the final syllable of the dictionary form. If the dictionary form ends in *-ku*, *-ku* is replaced by *-ita*.

kaku	→	*kaita*	wrote
saku	→	*saita*	bloomed

There is one exception.

iku	→	*itta*

went

If the dictionary form ends in *-gu*, *-gu* is replaced by *-ida*.

oyogu	→	*oyoida*	swam
isogu	→	*isoida*	hurried

If the dictionary form ends in *-su*, *-su* is replaced by *-shita*.

hanasu	→	*hanashita*	talked
kasu	→	*kashita*	lent

If the dictionary form ends in *-u* (a single vowel syllable), *-tsu*, or *-ru*, the final syllable is replaced by *-tta*.

kau	→	*katta*	bought
morau	→	*moratta*	received
matsu	→	*matta*	waited
katsu	→	*katta*	won
furu	→	*futta*	fell
hairu	→	*haitta*	entered

If the dictionary form ends in *-bu*, *-mu*, or *-nu*, the last syllable is replaced by *-nda*.

tobu	→	*tonda*	flew
asobu	→	*asonda*	played
nomu	→	*nonda*	drank
amu	→	*anda*	knitted
shinu*	→	*shinda*	died

b. Vowel verbs

The final syllable *-ru* is replaced by *-ta*.

* *Shinu* is the only verb whose dictionary form ends in *nu*.

taberu	→	*tabeta*	ate
miru	→	*mita*	saw

c. Irregular verbs

suru	→	*shita*	did
kuru	→	*kita*	came

2. PLAIN FORMS OF VERBS IN THE PAST NEGATIVE

The plain past negative form of a verb is derived from the plain present negative form. Drop the final *-i* of the latter, and add *-katta*.

ikanai	→	*ikanakatta*	did not go
yomanai	→	*yomanakatta*	did not read
agenai	→	*agenakatta*	did not give
dekakenai	→	*dekakenakatta*	did not go out
shinai	→	*shinakatta*	did not do
konai	→	*konakatta*	did not come

3. SUMMARY OF NORMAL AND PLAIN FORMS

	NORMAL				PLAIN			
	pres. aff.	pres. neg.	past aff.	past neg.	pres. aff. (dic. form)	pres. neg.	past aff.	past neg.
C	*ikimasu* go	*ikimasen* don't go	*ikimashita* went	*ikimasen deshita* didn't go	*iku* go	*ikanai* don't go	*itta* went	*ikanakatta* didn't go
V	*mimasu* see	*mimasen* don't see	*mimashita* saw	*mimasen deshita* didn't see	*miru* see	*minai* don't see	*mita* saw	*minakatta* didn't see
I	*shimasu* do	*shimasen* don't do	*shimashita* did	*shimasen deshita* didn't do	*suru* do	*shinai* don't do	*shita* did	*shinakatta* didn't do
I	*kimasu* come	*kimasen* don't come	*kimashita* came	*kimasen deshita* didn't come	*kuru* come	*konai* don't come	*kita* came	*konakatta* didn't come

4. EXPLANATORY PREDICATES

You have learned that *n* can occur between an *i*-adjective and *desu* (see Lesson 3, C4).

Takai n desu.
    [The fact is that] it's expensive.

Takakatta n desu.
    [The fact is that] it was expensive.

The *n desu* above is an explanatory predicate. *N* itself does not have a meaning, but with *desu*, the phrase shows emphasis and means "the fact is . . ." or "indeed."
    N desu can be used with verbs for the same purpose. The verb before *n* must be in the plain form.

Tomodachi ga kuru n desu.
    [The fact is that] my friend is coming.

Moo katta n desu.
    [The fact is that] we already bought them.

Minakatta n desu.
    [The fact is that] I didn't see them.

A yes-no question with *n desu* implies that the speaker assumes or has reason to assume that he or she may know the answer. Compare:

Ashita Yamada san wa kimasu ka. (simple question)
    Is Mr. Yamada coming tomorrow?

Ashita Yamada san wa kuru n desu ka.
    Is Mr. Yamada coming tomorrow? [I think he is, therefore, I'm asking you to confirm.]

Tenisu no booru o kawanakatta n desu ka.
    You didn't buy a tennis ball, did you? [I don't think you did.]

Samui n desu ka.
    Are you cold? [You look like you are cold.]

Sumoo wa akkenai desu kedo, omoshiroi n desu ka.
    Sumo tournaments are short and simple, but are they so interesting? [I know sumo is interesting to you.]

And from the dialogue, you know the following sentence:

Ueda san wa minai n desu ka.
    You don't watch them (baseball games), do you?
    [You are not going to see the game tomorrow, but you are going somewhere else, so I assume you don't watch baseball games.]

In a wh-question, too, the use of *n* implies that the speaker has some previous knowledge about the matter in question. Compare:

Dore ga oishii n desu ka.
　　Which one is tasty? [I heard that something is tasty.]

Dore ga oishii desu ka.
　　Which one is tasty? [It is not the case that I heard that something is tasty.]

N is a contracted form of *no*. Instead of *n*, *no* can be used. With *no*, the sentence sounds more formal; thus, it is mainly used in written Japanese or formal speech.

Watashitachi no chiimu ga katta no desu.
　　[The fact is that] our team won.

5. *KOTO GA DEKIRU* "TO BE ABLE TO"

You learned how to say "to be able to do . . ." using the verb *dekiru* (see Lesson 6, C6).

Watashi wa karate ga dekimasu.
　　I can do karate.

Another potential expression uses the verb *dekiru* as well, but in a different structure.

> dictionary form   + *koto ga dekiru*

Ii seki no chiketto o kau koto ga dekita n desu.
　　We were able to buy tickets for good seats.

Watashi wa tenisu o suru koto ga dekimasu.
　　I can play [do] tennis.

Kono chiketto o tsukau koto ga dekimasen deshita.
　　I could not use this ticket.

6. THE DEPENDENT NOUN *NO*

The dependent noun *no* "act" is preceded by a dictionary form. The English equivalent of the phrase is "to do," "-ing," or "the act of -ing."

Oyogu no wa muzukashii desu.
　　Swimming is difficult.

Yakyuu o miru no wa tanoshii desu.
Watching baseball is fun.

Rajio o kiku no o wasuremashita.
I forgot to listen to the radio.

Takai desu kara, iku no o yameta n desu.
I quit going because it is expensive.

7. PARTICLES

a. *To* "with (somebody)"

You have learned that the particle *to* means "and" (see Lesson 2, C3). Another meaning of *to* is "with (somebody)."

Kookoo no doosookai no hitotachi to issho ni yakyuu o mi ni iku n desu.
I am going to see a baseball game together with people in my high school alumni association.

Tomodachi to Kamakura e iku tsumori desu.
I plan to go to Kamakura with a friend of mine.

Donata to tenisu o suru n desu ka.
With whom are you going to play tennis?

b. *Wa* (with non-subjects)

You have learned that the particle *wa* is a topic marker used instead of *ga* with the subject.

Ano kyuujoo wa ookii desu.
That stadium is big.

Wa, as a topic marker, can also replace *ga* even when *ga* is not with the subject. Compare:

Chiketto ga moo aru n desu ka.
Chiketto wa moo aru n desu ka. (as for tickets . . .)
Do you have tickets already?

Otooto san mo tenisu ga suki desu ka.
Otooto san mo tenisu wa suki desu ka. (as for tennis . . .)
Does your younger brother like tennis, too?

Raketto ga hoshii desu.
Raketto wa hoshii desu. (as for a racket . . .)
I want the racket.

Koko de oyogu koto ga dekimasen.
Koko de oyogu koto wa dekimasen. (Speaking of swimming here . . .)
　　We cannot swim here.

　　Wa, as a topic marker, also replaces *o*.

Yakyuu wa minai n desu ka. (as for baseball . . .)
　　You don't watch baseball, do you?

Supootsu bangumi wa amari minakatta n desu. (as for sports . . .)
　　I used to not watch sports [programs] often.

Chiketto wa kaimashita ka. (as for a ticket . . .)
　　Did you buy a ticket?

　　So far, you have learned to use *wa*, as a topic marker, in the following
cases: (1) to replace *ga*, (2) to replace *o*, and (3) with a time noun that
usually takes no particle (see Lesson 7, C4).
　　Beyond its function as a topic marker, *wa* is used to show contrast,
usually between two things.

*Mukashi wa amari supootsu bangumi wa minakatta n desu kedo, kono goro
wa yoku miru n desu.*
　　I didn't watch sports [programs] often in the past, but these days, I
　　often watch them.

　　In this sentence, *mukashi* "in the past" and *kono goro* "these days" are
in contrast.

Tenisu wa shimasu kedo, gorufu wa shimasen.
　　I play tennis, but not golf.

Nihongo wa naraimashita kedo, furansugo wa naraimasen deshita.
　　I learned Japanese, but I didn't learn French.

　　It is possible to use *wa* for contrast even when only one item is mentioned in the sentence; the second item is implied.

Kyoo wa benkyoo shimasen deshita.
　　I did not study today (although I did on another day).

　　Whether *wa* is a simple topic marker on one hand, or announces contrast added to the topic meaning, on the other, depends on the context
and/or the intonation.

8. ANSWERS TO YES/NO QUESTIONS

When a yes-no question is in the negative, Japanese speakers and English speakers answer in opposite ways.

Yakyuu wa minai n desu ka.
You don't watch baseball, do you?

Iie, yoku mimasu yo.
No [your assumption is wrong], I watch it often.
→ Yes, I watch it often.

Kinoo kimasen deshita ka.
Didn't you come yesterday?

Hai, kimasen deshita.
Yes [your assumption is right], I didn't come.
→ No, I didn't come.

In the following cases, however, the Japanese yes-no distinction is the same as that in English.
   When the sentence with -*masen ka* is a suggestion, not a simple negative question:

Sakkaa o mi ni ikimasen ka.
Why don't we go watch soccer?

Ee, ikimashoo.
Yes, let's go.

When the negative question means "you mean . . . ," or "I am sure . . .":

Eki no soba ni ii kissaten ga aru n desu.
There is a nice coffee shop near the station.

Aa, Sakura ja arimasen ka.
Oh, isn't it Sakura?

Ee, soo desu.
Yes, that's right.

C. MOJI

For the second vowel of a double vowel in *katakana*, use a bar ー. In a text written vertically, write ｜.*

apaato	アパート	ア パ ー ト	apartment
guriin	グリーン	グ リ ー ン	green
puuru	プール	プ ー ル	pool
guree	グレー	グ レ ー	gray
booru	ボール	ボ ー ル	ball

Read the following:

コート	*kooto*	coat
ブルー	*buruu*	blue
スカート	*sukaato*	skirt
スーツ	*suutsu*	suit

* When *katakana* are used for giving special emphasis to certain words or in a telegram, a bar is not used. Instead, *katakana* are used in the manner of *hiragana* (see Lesson 8), e.g., *Tookyoo* トウキョウ.

D. TANGO TO HYOOGEN

supootsu	sports
bangumi	program
supootsu bangumi	sports (program on TV or radio)
yakyuu	baseball
tenisu	tennis
tenisu kooto	tennis court
gorufu	golf
sakkaa	soccer
karate	karate
kyuujoo	stadium
chiimu	team
booru	ball
raketto	racket
seki	seat
rajio	radio
boku	I (used only by males)
doosookai	alumni association, alumni meeting
kookoo	high school
kaisha	company
renshuu suru	to practice
suru	to do, play (sports)
kasu	to lend
katsu	to win
narau	to learn
tsukau	to use
kiku	to listen, hear
saku	to bloom
isogu	to hurry
tobu	to fly, jump
asobu	to play (not sports), enjoy oneself
amu	to knit
shinu	to die
yameru	to quit
wasureru	to forget
zannen	too bad
kondo	sometime

A. Fill in the blanks.

kaku	kaita
taberu	1
kaeru	2
kau	3
benkyoo suru	4
kuru	5

B. Fill in the blanks.

kaku	kakanai	kakanakatta
renshuu suru	1	2
aru	3	4
yomu	5	6
kuru	7	8
katsu	9	10
kiru	11	12

C. Rewrite line b of each dialogue in the *n desu* form.

1. a: *Otoosan wa ima uchi ni irasshaimasu ka.*
   b: *Iie, ima imasen. Hokkaidoo e ikimashita.*
   _____

2. a: *Yamada san to hanashimashita ka.*
   b: *Iie, Yamada san wa kinoo koko e kimasen deshita.*
   _____

3. a: *Chiketto wa soko ni arimasu ka.*
   b: *Iie, arimasen.*
   _____

D. Fill in the blanks with the appropriate form of the verb given in parentheses.

1. *Pan o _____ no o wasuremashita.*   (to buy)
2. *Hiragana o _____ koto ga dekimasu ka.*   (to write)
3. *Koohii o _____ ni ikimashita.*   (to drink)
4. *Kyoo _____ nai tsumori desu.*   (to go out)

E. Rewrite the sentences to say "I can _____."

1. *konpyuutaa de risaachi o shimasu.*
2. *nihongo o hanashimasu.*
3. *kanji o kakimasu.*

KARUCHAA NOOTO

Both spectator and participatory sports are very popular in Japan, especially among younger people. The most popular spectator sports have been sumo wrestling and baseball, although soccer has become tremendously popular recently with the development of a professional soccer league known as J-League and the acquisition of European soccer stars. While sumo wrestling is a traditional Japanese exercise, baseball was not introduced to Japan until 1873. Professional baseball started in 1934, but student baseball had become popular long before then. The most famous Japanese tournaments are the professional baseball tournaments, the league competition of Tokyo's "Big Six" universities, and high school tournaments. High school baseball is especially popular. Some say the only time people stop working is to watch the high school tournaments on TV, which are held twice a year, in spring and summer.

KOTAE

A. 1. *tabeta* 2. *kaetta* 3. *katta* 4. *benkyoo shita* 5. *kita*
B. 1. *renshuu shinai* 2. *renshuu shinakatta* 3. *nai* 4. *nakatta*
5. *yomanai* 6. *yomanakatta* 7. *konai* 8. *konakatta* 9. *katanai*
10. *katanakatta* 11. *kinai* 12. *kinakatta*
C. 1. *Iie, ima inai n desu. Hokkaidoo e itta n desu.* 2. *Iie, Yamada san wa kinoo koko e konakatta n desu.* 3. *Iie, nai n desu.*
D. 1. *kau* 2. *kaku* 3. *nomi* 4. *dekake*
E. 1. *konpyuutaa de resaachi o suru koto ga dekimasu.* 2. *nihongo o hanasu koto ga dekimasu.* 3. *kanji o kaku koto ga dekimasu.*

DAI JUU YONKA
Lesson 14
BIYOOIN DE.   At the Beauty Parlor.

A. DAIAROOGU

HEAKATTO.

In a beauty parlor in Shinjuku in Tokyo. A female student comes in.

BIYOOSHI 1: **Irasshaimáse.**

KYAKU: **Kátto o onegai shimásu.**

BIYOOSHI 1: **Hái, dóozo. Achira de omachi kudasái.**

KYAKU: **Jikan wa dono gurai kakarimásu ka. Íma sánji júppun desu ne. Yoji hán made ni dekimásu ka.**

BIYOOSHI: **Ée, daijóobu desu. Kóoto wa sochira ni kákete kudasai.**

Shibaraku shite.

BIYOOSHI 2: **Omatase shimáshita. Kochira e dóozo. Kono isu ni kákete kudasai. Dónna kamigata ni shimashóo ka.**

KYAKU: **Nagái kamí o araú no wa mendóo desu kara, mijikái kamí ni shitái n desu. Mimi no shita gúrai ga íi desu.**

BIYOOSHI 2: **Jáa, jussenchi gúrai kirimásu. Íi desu ka.**

KYAKU: **Sóo desu ne.**

BIYOOSHI 2: **Maegami mo kirimashóo ka.**

KYAKU: **Sóo desu ne. Maegami wa íma choodo íi desu. Démo chótto soróete kudasai.**

BIYOOSHI 2: **Hái, wakarimáshita.**

A HAIRCUT.

HAIRDRESSER 1: Hello!

CLIENT: I'd like a haircut.

HAIRDRESSER 1: Sure. Please wait over there.

164

CLIENT: How long will it take? It's 3:10 now, isn't it? Can you do it by 4:30?

HAIRDRESSER 1: Yes, that will be no problem. You can hang your overcoat there.

A little later.

HAIRDRESSER 2: Sorry to have kept you waiting. This way, please. Take a seat right here [in this chair]. What kind of hairstyle would you like [shall I make]?

CLIENT: Washing long hair is too much trouble, so I want to try a short cut now. Could you cut it to just below my ears?

HAIRDRESSER 2: Then I will cut about ten centimeters, okay?

CLIENT: Yes, that will be fine.

HAIRDRESSER 2: Do you also want me to cut the bangs?

CLIENT: Let me see. The bangs are just fine now. But you could trim them a little?

HAIRDRESSER 2: All right. [Yes, I understood.]

B. BUNPOO TO YOOHOO

1. TE FORMS OF VERBS

The TE form of verbs is one of several other verb forms besides the normal and plain forms you have already learned. Unlike normal and plain forms, the TE form by itself does not indicate tense. Its form is the same as that of the plain past affirmative except for the final syllable. If the plain past affirmative ends in *ta*, the TE form ends in *te*, and if the plain past affirmative ends in *da*, the TE form ends in *de*. Compare:

PLAIN PAST AFFIRMATIVE FORM	TE FORM
kaita	*kaite*
nonda	*nonde*
tonda	*tonde*
tabeta	*tabete*
mita	*mite*
shita	*shite*
kita	*kite*

The TE form itself cannot be translated into English. It derives its meaning only from the structures it forms part of, such as requests.

165

2. REQUESTS AND INVITATIONS (TE *KUDASAI*)

TE *kudasai*, one example of a TE form structure, is used to express a request or an invitation.

Kitte kudasai.
Please cut it.

Kami o aratte kudasai.
Please wash my hair.

Chotto matte kudasai.
Please wait a while.

There is one exception: the TE form of *kureru* "to give" cannot be used with *kudasai*. Instead, use:

Kudasai.
Please give it to me.

Shanpuu o kudasai.
Please give me the shampoo.

3. REQUESTS AND INVITATIONS
(*O-PRE-MASU* FORM *KUDASAI*)

The *o*-pre-*masu* form followed by *kudasai* also expresses a request or an invitation.

Omachi kudasai.
Please wait.

Ohairi kudasai.
Please come in.

Kono kondishonaa o otsukai kudasai.
Please use this conditioner.

Again, *kureru* "to give" cannot be used in this structure.

There are some differences between TE *kudasai* and the *o*-pre-*masu* form *kudasai*. First, the *o*- pre-*masu* form *kudasai* is more polite. Second, the *o*-pre-*masu* form *kudasai* carries a stronger connotation of extending an invitation than TE *kudasai*. There is, however, no clear distinction between the two meanings since the notions of request and invitation are often mixed within a sentence. Third, the *o*-pre-*masu* form *kudasai* is more limited in usage. It cannot be used with verbs that have one-syllable pre-*masu* forms. For example, for *suru* "to do, make," or *miru* "to see," whose pre-*masu* forms are one-syllable (*shi* and *mi*, respectively), this structure is unacceptable. Also, honorific verbs such as *irassharu* "to be, go, come" cannot be used with it. TE *kudasai*, on the other hand, can be used in all these cases.

4. MAKING A CHOICE *(NI SURU)*

When you choose something from among alternatives, the chosen noun is followed by the particle *ni* plus the verb *suru*. Here, *suru* means "to make."

Donna kamigata ni shimashoo ka.
　　What kind of hairstyle would you like [shall we make]?

Sandoitchi ni shimasu.
　　I will have a sandwich. (in a restaurant, for example)

Donna purezento o katta n desu ka.
　　What kind of present did you buy?

Sukaafu ni shita n desu.
　　I decided on a scarf.

　　Nani "what" can be changed to *nan*.

Nan(i) ni shimasu ka?
　　What are you going to choose?

5. COUNTERS

a. *-fun*

-fun is a counter for "minute." It can be used to express a specific time or a duration. For duration, *-kan* may be attached optionally. The irregular forms are in boldface.

ippun	1	**roppun**	6
nifun	2	nanafun, shichifun	7
sanpun	3	**happun,** hachifun	8
yonpun	4	kyuufun	9
gofun	5	**juppun, jippun**	10

nanpun
　　how long [how many minutes]?

Ima sanji juppun desu ne.
　　It is 3:10 now, isn't it?

Goji juu gofun ni biyooin e ikimashita.
　　I went to the beauty parlor at 5:15.

167

Nijuppunkan oobun de yakimasu.
   Bake it for twenty minutes in the oven. (in a recipe)

Nanpun kakarimasu ka.
   How long [How many minutes] will it take?

   The dependent noun *han* means "half."

yoji han or *yoji sanjuppun/sanjippun*
   4:30

Mainichi shichiji han ni okimasu.
   I get up at 7:30 every day.

   b. *-senchi*

   -senchi is a counter for "centimeter."

1 centimeter (cm)	=	0.3937 inch
1 meter (m)	=	3.28084 feet
1 kilometer (km)	=	0.62137 mile

   Irregular forms are in boldface.

	SENCHI CENTIMETER	*MEETORU* METER	*KIRO* (*MEETORU*) KILOMETER
1	**issenchi**	*ichimeetoru*	*ichikiro* (*meetoru*)
2	*nisenchi*	*nimeetoru*	*nikiro* (*meetoru*)
3	*sansenchi*	*sanmeetoru*	*sankiro* (*meetoru*)
4	*yonsenchi*	*yonmeetoru*	*yonkiro* (*meetoru*)
5	*gosenchi*	*gomeetoru*	*gokiro* (*meetoru*)
6	*rokusenchi*	*rokumeetoru*	**rokkiro (meetoru)**
7	*nanasenchi*	*nanameetoru*	*nanakiro* (*meetoru*)
	shichisenchi	*shichimeetoru*	*shichikiro* (*meetoru*)
8	**hassenchi**	*hachimeetoru*	*hachikiro* (*meetoru*)
9	*kyuusenchi*	*kyuumeetoru*	*kyuukiro* (*meetoru*)
10	*jussenchi*	*juumeetoru*	*jukkiro* (*meetoru*)

Jussenchi gurai kirimasu.
   I will take [cut] about ten centimeters off.

Ichimeetoru wa hyakusenchi desu.
   One meter is one hundred centimeters.

Kinoo sankiro gurai arukimashita.
   Yesterday I walked about three kilometers.

6. *KO-SO-A-DO* WORDS

Another set of *ko-so-a-do* words is *kochira, sochira, achira,* and *dochira.* They have different meanings depending on the context. One is to indicate a direction to a location.

kochira	this way
sochira	that way
achira	that way over there
dochira	which way

Kochira e doozo.
    This way, please.

Another use of this set is as the polite equivalent of the *kore* group.

POLITE	REGULAR	
kochira	*kore*	this one
sochira	*sore*	that one
achira	*are*	that one over there
dochira	*dore*	which one

Kochira wa watashi no tomodachi desu.
    This is a friend of mine. (See Lesson 1.)

This set is also the polite equivalent of the *koko* group.

POLITE	REGULAR	
kochira	*koko*	this place
sochira	*soko*	that place
achira	*asoko*	that place over there
dochira	*doko*	where

Achira de omachi kudasai.
    Please wait over there.

Finally, if you add *no* to each word, this set becomes the polite equivalent of the *kono* group.

POLITE	REGULAR	
kochira no	*kono*	this
sochira no	*sono*	that
achira no	*ano*	that over there
dochira no	*dono*	which

Yamada san wa dochira no heya ni irasshaimasu ka.

Which room is Mr. Yamada in?

7. THE QUESTION WORD *DONO GURAI*

Dono gurai (or *dono kurai*) means "how long," "how much," or "how many," depending on the context.

Eki kara biyooin made dono gurai arimasu ka.
How far is it from the station to the beauty parlor?

Nihon ni dono gurai ita n desu ka.
How long did you stay in Japan?

Maegami wa dono gurai kirimashoo ka.
How much should I cut off your bangs?

Ringo wa dono gurai kaimashoo ka.
How many apples should we buy?

8. PARTICLES

a. *Made ni* "by"

Made ni "by" is used with time nouns.

Yoji han made ni dekimasu ka.
Can you do it by 4:30?

Doyoobi made ni repooto o kaite kudasai.
Please write a report by Saturday.

Ashita made ni kuruma o arau tsumori desu.
I intend to wash the car by tomorrow.

b. *Ni* "on"

Ni "on" is used when a motion or action is directed at or onto an object or place.

Kooto wa sochira ni kakete kudasai.
Please hang your overcoat there.

Kono isu ni kakete kudasai.
Please sit in this chair.

Kokuban ni kanji o kakimashita.
I wrote *kanji* on the blackboard.

Hasami to kushi wa ano doraiaa no soba ni okimashita.
I put the scissors and the comb near that dryer.

C. MOJI

Some syllables that are not used in native Japanese words can be used for borrowed words, which are written in *katakana*.

fa	ファ	ファースト	*faasuto*	first
fi	フィ	フィクション	*fikushon*	fiction
fe	フェ	フェミニスト	*feminisuto*	feminist
fo	フォ	フォーク	*fooku*	fork
va	ヴァ	ヴァイオリン	*vaiorin*	violin
		or バイオリン	or *baiorin*	
vi	ヴィ	ヴィオラ	*viora*	viola
		or ビオラ	or *biora*	
vu	ヴ	カーヴ	*kaavu*	curve
		or カーブ	or *kaabu*	
ve	ヴェ	ヴェランダ	*veranda*	veranda
		or ベランダ	or *beranda*	
vo	ヴォ	ヴォランティア	*vorantia*	volunteer
		or ボランティア	or *borantia*	
ti	ティ	パーティー	*paatii*	party
tu	テュ	テューバ	*tuuba*	tuba
tsa	ツァ	ツァー	*tsaa*	czar
tse	ツェ	ツェツェばえ	*tsetsebae*	tsetse fly
di	ディ	コンディショナー	*kondishonaa*	conditioner
du	デュ	デュエット	*duetto*	duet
she	シェ	シェークスピア	*Sheekusupia*	Shakespeare
che	チェ	チェス	*chesu*	chess

171

je	ジェ	ジェット	*jetto*	jet
d	ッ	ベッド	*beddo*	bed
g	ッ	バッグ	*baggu*	bag
f	ッ	スタッフ	*sutaffu*	staff

D. TANGO TO HYOOGEN

biyooin	beauty parlor
biyooshi	hairdresser
kami	hair
kamigata	hairstyle
maegami	bangs
(hea)katto	haircut
hasami	scissors
kushi	comb
shanpuu	shampoo
kondishonaa/rinsu	conditioner
kagami	mirror
doraiaa	dryer
mimi	ear
sandoitchi	sandwich
oobun	oven
isu	chair
kokuban	blackboard
repooto	report
han	half (dependent noun)
kochira	this (way, one, place, person)
sochira	that (way, one, place, person)
achira	that (way, one, place, person) over there
dochira	which (way, one, place, person)
dono gurai (or **kurai**)	how (long, far, much, many)
arau	to wash
kiru	to cut (consonant verb)
soroeru	to trim
suru	to make
kakaru	to take (time)
kakeru	to hang, sit (in a chair)
yaku	to bake
oku	to put on, place

okiru	to get up
aruku	to walk
mendoo	troublesome

RENSHUU

A. Fill in the blanks.

miru	mita	mite
suru	1	2
kiru "to cut"	3	4
kiru "to wear"	5	6
kuru	7	8
yobu "to call"	9	10
yomu	11	12

B. Fill in the blanks with the appropriate form of the verb given in parentheses.

1. *Kono hon o o—— kudasai.* (to read)
2. *Koko de o—— kudasai.* (to rest)
3. *Sugu —— kudasai.* (to go)
4. *Tegami o —— kudasai.* (to write)
5. *Chotto o—— kudasai.* (to wait)

C. Fill in the blanks with particles according to the English equivalents.

1. *Achira no isu —— okake kudasai.*
   Please sit in the chair over there.
2. *Kinoo juuji —— benkyoo shita n desu.*
   I studied until twelve o'clock yesterday.
3. *Watashi wa maguro —— shimasu.*
   I will have a tuna. (in a sushi restaurant, for example)
4. *Suiyoobi —— shite kudasai.*
   Please do it by Wednesday.

D. Write the following in Japanese.

1. 8:05
2. 9:03
3. sixteen meters
4. ninety centimeters
5. eleven kilometers

E. Write the following in *katakana*, and try to figure out what they mean.

1. *jesuchaa*

2. *sherii*

3. *ferii*

4. *fookasu*

5. *chero*

KARUCHAA NOOTO

Up until the beginning of the modern era in the middle of the nineteenth century, male and female Japanese hairstyles were quite elaborate. Men used to wear long hair tied back in a topknot, and women used to wear their hair up in elaborate chignons. Although men were ordered by the government to cut off their topknots in the 1870s, traditional female hairstyles continued to be worn. However, with the introduction of Western hairstyles, the traditional chignon styles became less and less popular. Today only brides during their wedding ceremonies and geishas, who entertain people at sake parties with music and dancing, may choose to wear them.

Nowadays, many women have permanent waves, *paama*. Beauty parlors are as popular in Japan as in the United States. Japanese beauty parlors and their American counterparts are similar, but in Japan, customers do not tip. Tipping in general is not a custom in Japan.

KOTAE

A. 1. *shita* 2. *shite* 3. *kitta* 4. *kitte* 5. *kita* 6. *kite* 7. *kita* 8. *kite*
9. *yonda* 10. *yonde* 11. *yonda* 12. *yonde*
B. 1. *yomi* 2. *yasumi* 3. *itte* 4. *kaite* 5. *machi*
C. 1. *ni* 2. *made* 3. *ni* 4. *made ni*
D. 1. *hachiji gofun* 2. *kuji sanpun* 3. *juu rokumeetoru* 4. *kyuujussenchi*
5. *juu ichikiromeetoru*
E. 1. ジェスチャー gesture 2. シェリー sherry 3. フェリー ferry
4. フォーカス focus 5. チェロ cello

DAI JUU GOKA
Lesson 15
SHIGOTO SAGASHI.   Job Hunting.

A. DAIAROOGU

PAATII DE.

Mr. Kojima and Ms. Murai are alumni of the same university. They meet each other at a party.

KOJIMA: **Shibáraku desu née.**

MURAI: **Ée, hontoo ni. Máinichi oisogashíi desu ka.**

KOJIMA: **Konpyúutaa no gakkoo de oshiete irú n desu kedo, íma natsuyásumi desu kara, amari isogáshiku nái n desu. Murai san wa.**

MURAI: **Watashi wa íma shigoto o sagashite irú n desu.**

KOJIMA: **Dónna shigoto ga íi n desu ka.**

MURAI: **Jaanarízumu no shigoto o mitsuketái n desu.**

KOJIMA: **Áa, sóo desu ka. Bóku no ane ga zasshísha ni tsutómete irú n desu. Sono kaisha ga moo súgu atarashíi hitó o boshuu suru sóo desu yo. Ane ni kiite mimashóo ka.**

MURAI: **Sono kaisha wa dónna zasshi o dáshite irú n desu ka.**

KOJIMA: **Ómo ni bíjutsu no zasshi da sóo desu. Kaisha no namae wa Mikawásha desu.**

MURAI: **Mikawásha desu ka. Watashi mo yóku shitte imásu. Ano kaisha wa iroiro na omoshirói bíjutsu no zasshi o dáshite imásu ne.**

KOJIMA: **Ée, mukashi wa chiisái kaisha dátta sóo desu kedo. Jitsú wa ane mo kono páatii ni kíte irú n desu. A, asoko ni imásu. Aimásu ka.**

MURAI: **Ée, onegai shimásu.**

AT A PARTY.

KOJIMA: I haven't seen you for a long time.

MURAI: Yes, that's true. I guess you are busy these days. (Are you busy every day?)

KOJIMA: I teach at a computer school, but since it's summer vacation now, I'm not too busy. How about you?

MURAI: I'm looking for a job.

KOJIMA: What kind of job are you looking for?

MURAI: I want to find a job in journalism.

KOJIMA: Oh, really? My older sister works for a magazine publisher. I heard they are going to recruit new people before long. Should I ask her about it (to find out)?

MURAI: What kind of magazines do they (does that company) publish?

KOJIMA: I understand they're mainly magazines on fine arts. The name of the company is Mikawasha.

MURAI: It's Mikawasha (I see). I know it well, too. That company publishes a variety of interesting fine arts magazines, doesn't it?

KOJIMA: Yes. I understand it started out (was) as a small company a long time ago. In fact, my older sister is here at this party, also. Oh, she is over there! Would you like to meet her?

MURAI: Yes, please. That would be great.

B. BUNPOO TO YOOHOO

1. TE *IRU*

While *iru* "to exist" is a main verb, *iru* in TE *iru*, which cannot be translated by itself, is not. When *iru* follows the TE form of a verb, the combination is progressive, habitual, or stative. It is a vowel verb and is conjugated just like regular vowel verbs.

a. Progressive

TE *iru* is used to indicate that an action is ongoing (i.e., in progress). The English equivalent is "to be . . . -ing."

Ima shigoto o sagashite iru n desu.
I am looking for a job now.

Koko de matte ite kudasai.
Please wait [be waiting] here.

b. Habitual

TE *iru* is also used to indicate repeated or habitual actions.

Donna zasshi o dashite iru n desu ka.
What kind of magazines do they publish?

Mukashi wa iroiro na shinbun o yonde imashita.
I used to read several newspapers.

c. Stative

The results of an action are also expressed with TE *iru*.

Ane wa kekkon shite imasu.
My older sister is married. [The event of my older sister getting married took place and she has been married ever since.]

Ane mo kono paatii ni kite iru n desu.
My older sister is at [has come to] this party, also.

Kono mushi wa shinde imasu.
This insect is dead.

In many cases, the context decides whether the TE *iru* means progressive, habitual, or stative. The following sentence, for example, can be interpreted in three different ways.

Haha wa kimono o kite imasu.
My mother is putting on a kimono. (progressive)
My mother wears a kimono regularly. (habitual)
My mother has a kimono on. (stative)

Some verbs, for example, *kekkon suru* "to get married" and *shinu* "to die," cannot be used to indicate actions expressed with "–ing" in English. *Kekkon shite imasu* and *Shinde imasu* never mean "She is getting married" and "She is dying." Naturally, these verbs cannot be used to express one person's habitual activities, either.

2. *SHIRU* "TO KNOW"

Shiru is a unique verb. TE *iru* is used in the affirmative, but not in the negative.

	PRESENT	PAST
AFFIRMATIVE	*Shitte imasu.* I know.	*Shitte imashita.* I knew.
NEGATIVE	*Shirimasen.* I don't know.	*Shirimasen deshita.* I didn't know.

Watashi mo yoku shitte imasu.
    I know it well, too.

Kojima san no oneesan o shitte imashita ka.
    Did you know Mr. Kojima's older sister?

Iie, zenzen shirimasen deshita.
    No, I did not know her at all.

3. TE *MIRU*

When the dependent verb *miru* is used with the TE form, it means "someone does something to find out . . . ."

Kiite mimashoo ka.
    Shall I ask her [to find out the answer]?

Kono biiru o nonde mite kudasai.
    Please drink this beer [to find out how it is].

Tenpura o tabete mimashita.
    I ate tempura [to find out how it was].

4. THE PLAIN FORMS OF *I*-ADJECTIVES

Like verbs, *i*-adjectives also have plain forms in addition to normal forms.

	PRESENT AFFIRMATIVE	PRESENT NEGATIVE	PAST AFFIRMATIVE	PAST NEGATIVE
	is expensive	is not expensive	was expensive	was not expensive
NORMAL	*takai desu*	*takaku arimasen*	*takakatta desu*	*takaku arimasen deshita*
PLAIN	(dictionary form) *takai*	*takaku nai*	*takakatta*	*takaku nakatta*

5. EXPLANATORY PREDICATES WITH *I*-ADJECTIVES

As mentioned before (see Lesson 13, B4), the explanatory predicate *n desu* or *no desu* follows the plain form of a verb.

Ashita iku n desu.
    [The fact is that] I am going tomorrow.

You have also learned that explanatory predicates can follow the plain present affirmative and the plain past affirmative of an *i*-adjective.

Takai n desu.
[The fact is that] it is expensive.

Takakatta n desu.
[The fact is that] it was expensive.

In addition to the affirmative forms, explanatory predicates can also follow the plain negative forms of an *i*-adjective.

Takaku nai n desu.
[The fact is that] it is not expensive.

Takaku nakatta n desu.
[The fact is that] it was not expensive.

Amari isogashiku nai n desu.
I am not very busy.

Okyuuryoo wa waruku nakatta n desu.
My salary was not bad.

6. THE PLAIN COPULA

The copula *desu*, which follows a *na*-adjective or a noun, is a normal form. It has plain forms as well.

	PRESENT AFFIRMATIVE	PRESENT NEGATIVE	PAST AFFIRMATIVE	PAST NEGATIVE
	is quiet is a student	is not quiet is not a student	was quiet was a student	was not quiet was not a student
NORMAL	*shizuka desu* *gakusei desu*	*shizuka ja/de wa arimasen* *gakusei ja/de wa arimasen*	*shizuka deshita* *gakusei deshita*	*shizuka ja/de wa arimasen deshita* *gakusei ja/de wa arimasen deshita*
PLAIN	*shizuka da* *gakusei da*	*shizuka ja/de (wa) nai* *gakusei ja/de (wa) nai*	*shizuka datta* *gakusei datta*	*shizuka ja/de (wa) nakatta* *gakusei ja/de (wa) nakatta*

7. *SOO DESU* (HEARSAY)

To express "I understand . . . ," "I heard . . . ," or "The rumor is . . . ,"
use *soo desu* following the plain form.

Atarashii hito o boshuu suru soo desu.
I heard that they will recruit new people.

Omo ni bijutsu no zasshi da soo desu.
I understand they are mainly magazines on fine arts.

Mukashi wa chiisai kaisha datta soo desu.
I understand it was a small company a long time ago.

Yamada san no kaisha wa amari furuku nai soo desu.
I understand Mr. Yamada's company is not very old.

Soo desu is an expression that informs the addressee about hearsay
containing previously unknown information. If, however, you talk about
something the addressee knows about, use *ne* at the end.

Ginkoo o yameta soo desu ne.
I heard you quit your job at the bank [am I right?].

Takeda san wa jaanarisuto da soo desu ne.
I heard Mr. Takeda is a journalist [am I right?].

8. PARTICLES

a. *Ni* "to" (with destination)

Ni, like *e*, can be used for "to" when indicating a destination.

Sugu uchi ni kaerimashita.
I went home right away.

Daigakuin ni itte iru n desu.
I go to graduate school.

In most cases, *ni* and *e* can be interchanged. If the destination is an
event, however, such as a party or a movie, *ni* is preferred.

Ane mo kono paatii ni kite iru n desu.
My older sister is at [has come to] this party, also.

Kinoo eiga ni ikimashita.
I went to a movie yesterday.

b. *Ni* "to" (with recipient)

As explained in Lesson 11, *ni* is translated as "to" when it is used with the recipient of the action of giving.

Watashi wa Suzuki san ni pen o agemashita.
I gave a pen to Ms. Suzuki.

Likewise, *ni* "to" can be used with recipient(s) of the action of other verbs.

Ane ni kiite mimashoo ka.
Should I ask my older sister?

Yamada san ni soo itta n desu.
I said so to Mr. Yamada.

Jooshi ni moo hanashita n desu.
I talked to my boss already.

Oji to oba ni tegami o kaku tsumori desu.
I intend to write a letter to my uncle and aunt.

Kono e o Yamada san ni misetai n desu.
I want to show this picture to Mr. Yamada.

c. *Ni* (with place of work)

When the verb *tsutomeru* "to work" is used, *ni* follows the word denoting the place of employment.

Boku no ane ga zasshisha ni tsutomete iru n desu.
My older sister works for a magazine publishing company.

Depaato no sendenbu ni tsutomete ita n desu.
I worked for the publicity department of a department store.

9. *TSUTOMERU* AND *HATARAKU* "TO WORK"

Both *tsutomeru* and *hataraku* can mean "to work," but they are used differently. *Ni* is used following the place of employment with *tsutomeru*, but *de* is used with *hataraku*.

Depaato ni tsutomete imasu.
Depaato de hataraite imasu.
I work at a department store.

While *tsutomeru* refers to the work you do at your place of employment only, *hataraku* can refer to any kind of work, regardless of whether it is work done at or for your place of employment.

Yuubinkyoku de hataraite imasu. (employment)
I work for the post office.

Kinoo asa kara ban made uchi de hatarakimashita. (non-employment)
I worked at home from morning till evening yesterday.

In Japanese, unlike in English, "to work" does not mean "to study."

10. *KO-SO-A-DO* WORDS

So far you have seen various sets of *ko-so-a-do* words. They are based on the physical distance from the speaker and the addressee's perspective. There are also cases where psychological distance is involved. When something that is in the vicinity of neither the speaker nor the addressee is referred to, there is the following difference between *so-* and *a*-words.

SO-: *So*-words refer to things that either the speaker or the addressee is not familiar with.
A-: *A*-words refer to things that both the speaker and the addressee are familiar with.

Consider the sentences used in the dialogue.

Boku no ane ga zasshisha ni tsutomete iru n desu. Sono kaisha ga moo sugu atarashii hito o boshuu suru soo desu yo.
My older sister works for a magazine publishing company. I heard that company is going to recruit new people before long.

Here the speaker is talking about a company that he assumes the addressee is not familiar with. Thus, he says *sono kaisha* "that company."

Sono kaisha wa donna zasshi o dashite iru n desu ka.
What kind of magazines does that company publish?

In this sentence, the speaker is asking about the company that the addressee mentioned. At this point, the speaker does not know about the company. Thus, she says *sono kaisha* "that company."

Mikawasha desu ka. Watashi mo yoku shitte imasu. Ano kaisha wa iroiro na omoshiroi bijutsu no zasshi o dashite imasu ne.
It's Mikawasha [I see]. I know it well, too. That company publishes a variety of interesting fine arts magazines, doesn't it?

Now the speaker knows which company the addressee means. Since both the speaker and the addressee know about the company, she says *ano kaisha* "that company." Here are some more examples.

The addressee is not familiar with the *tomodachi* "friend."

Tomodachi ga ashita kuru n desu kedo, <u>sono</u> tomodachi to iku tsumori desu.
A friend of mine is coming tomorrow. I plan to go with that friend.

The speaker B is not familiar with the *kooen* "park."

A: *Uchi no soba ni kooen ga aru n desu.*
There is a park near my house.

B: <u>*Sono*</u> *kooen wa ookii desu ka.*
Is that park big?

Both the speaker and the addressee are familiar with Ms. Suzuki.

A: *Ototoi Suzuki san to denwa de hanashita n desu.*
The day before yesterday I talked with Ms. Suzuki on the phone.

B: <u>*Ano*</u> *hito wa ima byooin ni tsutomete iru soo desu ne.*
I heard she [that person] works for a hospital now.

C. MOJI

Both *hiragana* and *katakana* are classified as *kana*. *Kanji* are often referred to as "Chinese characters," because the vast majority of these characters are of Chinese origin, unlike *kana,* which were created in Japan based on abbreviated forms of the *kanji*.

There are a huge number of *kanji*; no one knows exactly how many. Nearly 2,000 *kanji* are designated as *Jooyoo Kanji* "*Kanji* for common use." In this book, you will learn 147 of them.

As stated in Lesson 1, each *kanji* is an ideographic symbol representing a concept or a thing. If you do not know or have forgotten a *kanji*, you can write the word in *kana*. Therefore, one might say that *kanji* are unnecessary. However, one effective aspect of *kanji* is that by looking at a *kanji*, you can get its meaning directly as you can from a picture, so you can read Japanese much faster.

KANJI	READING (IN HIRAGANA)	MEANING
[1] 木	き	tree
[2] 人	ひと	person
[3] 山	やま	mountain

[1]	一 十 才 木
[2]	ノ 人
[3]	｜ 山 山

Since each *kanji* is associated with a certain meaning(s), use the *kanji* only with the proper association. For example, 木, whose pronunciation is *ki*, is used for the meaning of "tree." Do not use 木 for *ki* in *kimasu* "to come" or *ki* in *kiiro* "yellow," for example.

Read the following:

さくらの 木
cherry tree

木は なんぼん ありますか。
How many trees are there?

あの人の なまえは なんですか。
What is that person's name?

人が たくさん いました。
There were many people.

きれいな 山です。
It's a pretty mountain.

きのう 山を みに いったんです。
I went to see the mountain yesterday.

D. TANGO TO HYOOGEN

(o)kyuuryoo	salary
jooshi	boss
sendenbu	publicity department
jaanarizumu	journalism
jaanarisuto	journalist
shinbun	newspaper
zasshisha	magazine publisher

yuubinkyoku	post office
byooin	hospital
daigakuin	graduate school
pen	pen
bijutsu	fine arts
kooen	park
paatii	party
mushi	insect, worm
tenpura	tempura (deep-fried seafood or vegetables)
biiru	beer
oji	uncle
ojisan	uncle (somebody else's)
oba	aunt
obasan	aunt (somebody else's)
boshuu suru	to recruit
kekkon suru	to get married
tsutomeru	to be employed
sagasu	to look for
mitsukeru	to find
dasu	to publish
kiku	to ask, inquire
oshieru	to teach
miseru	to show
shiru	to know (consonant verb)
iroiro	various
yoku	well
soo	so, that way
omo ni	mainly
jitsu wa	in fact

RENSHUU

A. Rewrite the following sentences using the TE *iru* form.

Examples: *Hon o yomimasu.* → *Hon o yonde imasu.*
Hon o yomimashita. → *Hon o yonde imashita.*

1. *Tegami o kakimasu.*
2. *Denwa de hanashimashita.*
3. *Toshokan de benkyoo shimashita.*
4. *Terebi o mimasu.*

B. Fill in the blanks.

PLAIN PRESENT AFF.	PLAIN PRESENT NEG.	PLAIN PAST AFF.	PLAIN PAST NEG.
samui	1	2	3
4	*waruku nai*	5	6
7	8	*furukatta*	9
10	11	12	*ookiku nakatta*

C. Fill in the blanks.

PLAIN PRESENT AFF.	PLAIN PRESENT NEG.	PLAIN PAST AFF.	PLAIN PAST NEG.
kirei da	1	2	3

D. Transform the sentences using *soo desu*.

Example. *Ame ga furimasu.* → *Ame ga furu soo desu.*

1. *Chichi wa Nagoya e ikimasu.*
2. *Okashi wa oishikatta desu.*
3. *Muua san wa Amerikajin desu.*
4. *Heya wa atatakaku arimasen deshita.*
5. *Suzuki san wa kekkon shimashita.*
6. *Asoko wa kooen deshita.*
7. *Depaato de hataraite imasu.*

KARUCHAA NOOTO

The Japanese Constitution, which went into effect in 1947, states that men and women are equal. Since then, of course, the status of Japanese women has improved. Nevertheless, women are often still seen as subordinate to men in the workplace. To try to improve the situation, in 1986, the Equal Employment Opportunity Law, which requires employers to give women the same opportunities and treatment as men, went into effect. Now, women are expected to work as hard and as long as men do. However, it is also true that the majority of women are expected to be primarily concerned with their families and cannot be committed to their jobs. To solve this dilemma, many companies offer women the choice of two tracks: ordinary jobs (the traditional type) and comprehensive jobs (the career type) to women, although men are supposed to take the comprehensive track. Women who choose the comprehensive option are supposed to be treated the same as men but often they are not. There is still job discrimination and inequality in the workplace.

KOTAE

A. 1. ——*kaite imasu.* 2. ——*hanashite imashita.* 3. ——*benkyoo shite imashita.* 4. ——*mite imasu.*

B. 1. *samuku nai*   2. *samukatta*   3. *samuku nakatta*   4. *warui*
5. *warukatta*   6. *waruku nakatta*   7. *furui*   8. *furuku nai*   9. *furuku nakatta*   10. *ookii*   11. *ookiku nai*   12. *ookikatta*

C. 1. *kirei ja nai* or *kirei de (wa) nai*   2. *kirei datta*   3. *kirei ja nakatta* or *kirei de (wa) nakatta*

D. 1. ——*iku soo desu.* 2. ——*oishikatta soo desu.* 3. ——*Amerikajin da soo desu.* 4. ——*atatakaku nakatta soo desu.* 5. ——*kekkon shita soo desu.*
6. ——*kooen datta soo desu.* 7. ——*hataraite iru soo desu.*

FUKUSHUU 3

A. Fill in the blanks with particles according to the English equivalents.

1. *Yamada san wa otooto _____ chiketto _____ kuremashita.*
   Mr. Yamada gave my younger brother a ticket.
2. *Ashita _____ shite kudasai.*
   Please do it by tomorrow.
3. *Haha _____ Hokkaidoo e ryokoo shitai desu.*
   I want to travel to Hokkaido with my mother.
4. *Kinoo hachiji _____ goji _____ hatarakimashita.*
   I worked from eight o'clock to five o'clock yesterday.
5. *Sensei _____ tegami _____ kakimashita.*
   I wrote a letter to the teacher.

B. Rewrite the following sentences using *n desu.*

1. *Depaato de shokki o kaimashita.*
2. *Ashita tomodachi to tenisu o shimasu.*
3. *Umi wa koko kara amari tooku arimasen.*
4. *Kyoo zenzen benkyoo shimasen deshita.*

C. Fill in the blanks with the appropriate form of the verb given in parentheses.

1. *Watashi no uchi ni* _____ *kudasai.* (*kuru*)
2. *Purezento o* _____ *ni ikimashoo ka.* (*kau*)
3. *Ashita* _____ *nai tsumori desu.* (*dekakeru*)
4. *Otooto wa puuru de* _____ *imasu.* (*oyogu*)

D. Choose the appropriate answer from the following expressions.

a. *Gochisoosama.*
b. *Soo desu ne.*
c. *Itadakimasu.*
d. *Ojama shimasu.*
e. *Onegai shimasu.*

1. What do you say after you have a meal?
2. What do you say when you agree with someone?
3. What do you say when you ask someone a favor?
4. What do you say before you have a meal?

E. Match a combination of words in Group I with one in Group II to form a sentence.

I

1. *Kono isu ni*
2. *Ane wa moo*
3. *Nihonkai ni*
4. *Apaato o karinai*
5. *Kochira de oyasumi*

II

a. *kekkon shite imasu.*
b. *ikitai desu.*
c. *tsumori deshita.*
d. *kakete kudasai.*
e. *kudasai.*

F. Fill in the blanks.

DICTIONARY FORM	TE FORM	PLAIN PRESENT NEGATIVE FORM
naku "to cry"	1	2
sakebu "to shout"	3	4
tsukau "to use"	5	6
shimeru "to shut"	7	8

G. Fill in the blanks to complete the dialogue according to the English equivalent.

    a. Why don't we go swimming?
    b. Yes, which swimming pool should we go to?
    a. There is one near the station, isn't there?
    b. Yes, I heard that swimming pool is clean. Oh, it's raining. That's too bad.
    a. Should we go tomorrow? [Shall we choose tomorrow?]
    b. Yes, I would like to.

    a. _____¹ *ni ikimasen ka.*
    b. *Ee, dono puuru ni ikimashoo ka.*
    a. _____² *no* _____³ *ni arimasu ne.*
    b. *Ee, ano puuru wa* _____⁴ *ne. A, ame ga* _____⁵ *imasu yo.* _____⁶ *desu ne.*
    a. *Ashita* _____⁷ *shimashoo ka.*
    b. *Soo desu ne.*

H. Translate the following:

1. 山へ　木を　きりに　いきました。

2. どんな　スポーツが　すきですか。

3. パーティーに　ほっかいどうの　人が　たくさん　きていました。

KOTAE

A. 1. *ni, o* 2. *made ni* 3. *to* 4. *kara, made* 5. *ni, o*

B. 1. ——*katta n desu.* 2. ——*suru n desu.* 3. ——*tooku nai n desu.*
4. ——*shinakatta n desu.*

C. 1. *kite* 2. *kai* 3. *dekake* 4. *oyoide*

D. 1. a 2. b 3. e 4. c

E. 1. d 2. a 3. b 4. c 5. e

F. 1. *naite* 2. *nakanai* 3. *sakende* 4. *sakebanai* 5. *tsukatte*
6. *tsukawanai* 7. *shimete* 8. *shimenai*

G. 1. *Oyogi* 2. *Eki* 3. *soba* 4. *kirei da soo desu* 5. *futte* 6. *Zannen*
7. *ni*

H. 1. I went to the mountains to cut trees. 2. What kind of sports do you like? 3. There were many people from Hokkaido at the party.

DAI JUU ROKKA
Lesson 16
KOOTSUU.   Transportation.

A. DAIAROOGU

TSUUKIN DENSHA NO NAKA DE.

Mr. Sano and Mr. Toda are both *sarariiman* (company employees) who live in the same neighborhood.

SANO: **Ohayoo gozaimásu.**

TODA: **A, Ohayoo gozaimásu. Ítsumo kono densha de ikú n desu ka.**

SANO: **Iie, taitei kyuukoo de ikú n desu. Démo, kyuukoo wa komimásu kara, tama ni futsuu dénsha de nonbíri to ikitái n desu.**

TODA: **Sóo desu née. Bóku wa kono densha o órite kara, chikatetsu ni norú n desu kedo, sono chikatetsu ni norú no ga taihen ná n desu. Sore ni oríru no mo namayasashíi kotó ja nái desu yo.**

SANO: **Hontoo ni kono tsuukin jígoku wa karada ni yóku nái desu ne. Saiwai bóku wa ashitá kara isshúukan kyuuka o tóru n desu.**

TODA: **Sóo desu ka. Ryokoo démo surú n desu ka.**

SANO: **Ée, bóku no shusshínchi wa Hímeji na n desu kédo, soko de, imootó ga kekkon surú n desu.**

TODA: **Áa, sore wa omedetoo gozaimásu. Hímeji made nanjikan gúrai desu ka.**

SANO: **Sóo desu ne. Shinkánsen de gojikan gúrai desu ne.**

TODA: **Bóku wa Hímeji wa shiranái n desu kedo, Kakogawa máde ichido itta kotó ga áru n desu.**

SANO: **Áa, Kakogawa désu ka. A, bóku wa koko de orimásu.**

TODA: **Jáa, mata.**

ON THE COMMUTER TRAIN.

SANO: Good morning.

TODA: Oh, good morning. Do you always take this train?

SANO: No, usually I take the express. But since the express gets so crowded, I occasionally like to go comfortably on the local train.

TODA: Yes, I know. I take the subway after I get off this train. Getting on that subway is terribly hard, and getting off is not a simple thing, either.

SANO: Really, this commuting hell is not good for us [our bodies]. Fortunately, I'm taking a week off starting tomorrow.

TODA: Is that right? Are you going somewhere [to take a trip or something]?

SANO: Yes, my younger sister is getting married in our hometown of Himeji. [My hometown is Himeji, and my younger sister is getting married there.]

TODA: That calls for congratulations. How long [how many hours] does it take to get to Himeji?

SANO: Well, if you take the Shinkansen Lines, it's about five hours.

TODA: I don't know Himeji, but I've been to Kakogawa.

SANO: Kakogawa [I see]. Oh, I am getting off here.

TODA: See you.

B. BUNPOO TO YOOHOO

1. NEGATIVE FORMS

The following is a summary of the negative forms you have learned so far.

	PLAIN AFF.	NORMAL NEG.		PLAIN NEG.	
	PRESENT	PRESENT	PAST	PRESENT	PAST
VERB	*iku*	*ikimasen*	*ikimasen deshita*	*ikanai*	*ikanakatta*
	goes	doesn't go	didn't go	doesn't go	didn't go
I- ADJECTIVE	*oishii*	*oishiku arimasen*	*oishiku arimasen deshita*	*oishiku nai*	*oishiku nakatta*
	is tasty	isn't tasty	wasn't tasty	isn't tasty	wasn't tasty
NA- ADJECTIVE PLUS COPULA	*shizuka da*	*shizuka ja/de wa arimasen*	*shizuka ja/de wa arimasen deshita*	*shizuka ja/de (wa) nai*	*shizuka ja/de (wa) nakatta*
	is quiet	isn't quiet	wasn't quiet	isn't quiet	wasn't quiet
NOUN PLUS COPULA	*gakusei da*	*gakusei ja/de wa arimasen*	*gakusei ja/de wa arimasen deshita*	*gakusei ja/de (wa) nai*	*gakusei ja/de (wa) nakatta*
	is a student	isn't a student	wasn't a student	isn't a student	wasn't a student

There is another set of normal-negative forms: Add *desu* to each plain-negative form of the *i*-adjective and the copula.

	NORMAL NEGATIVE	
	PRESENT	PAST

I-ADJECTIVE	*oishiku arimasen*
	   or
	oishiku nai desu
	is not tasty
		oishiku arimasen deshita
		   or
		oishiku nakatta desu
		was not tasty

NA-ADJECTIVE
PLUS
COPULA
	shizuka ja/de wa arimasen
	
	   or
	shizuka ja/de (wa) nai desu
	
	is not quiet
		shizuka ja/de wa
		   arimasen deshita
		   or
		shizuka ja/de (wa)
		   nakatta desu
		was not quiet

NOUN
PLUS
COPULA
	gakusei ja/de wa arimasen
	
	   or
	gakusei ja/de (wa) nai desu
	
	is not a student
		gakusei ja/de wa arimasen
		   deshita
		   or
		gakusei ja/de (wa)
		   nakatta desu
		was not a student

Yoku nai desu.
   It is not good.

Oriru no mo namayasashii koto ja nai desu.
   To get off is not a simple thing, either.

Purattohoomu wa kirei ja nakatta desu.
   The platform was not clean.

Kippu wa amari takaku nakatta desu.
   The ticket was not very expensive.

2. EXPLANATORY PREDICATES WITH *NA*-ADJECTIVES AND NOUNS

N desu or *no desu* can be used with *na*-adjectives and nouns just as with *i*-adjectives and verbs to form an explanatory predicate. The plain copula follows the *na*-adjective or noun and is in turn followed by *n desu* or *no desu* (see Lesson 15, B6). When the copula is in the present affirmative (*da*), it changes to *na* before *n desu* or *no desu*.

193

Taihen <u>na</u> n desu. (*na*-adjective)
It is terribly hard.

Boku no shusshinchi wa Himeji <u>na</u> n desu. (noun)
My hometown is Himeji.

For present-negative, past-affirmative, and past-negative forms, *n desu* and *no desu* simply follow the plain copula.

Are wa kyuukoo <u>ja nai</u> n desu.
That one is not an express.

Watashi no ani wa mae densha no shashoo <u>datta</u> n desu.
My older brother used to be a train conductor.

Kankoo ryokoo <u>datta</u> n desu ka.
Was it a sight-seeing trip?

Iie, soo <u>de wa nakatta</u> n desu.
No, it was not [so].

3. EXPERIENCE

To express your experiences, you often use the present-perfect tense in English, e.g., "I have climbed that mountain." In Japanese, the following sentence pattern is used.

> plain-past form + *koto ga* (or *wa*) *aru*

Kakogawa made itta koto ga aru n desu.
I have been to Kakogawa. [I have had the experience of going to Kakogawa.]

Himeji no oshiro o mita koto ga arimasu ka.
Have you ever seen the Himeji Castle?

Ee, arimasu.
Yes, I have.

Abe san wa kuruma o unten shita koto ga nai soo desu.
I heard Ms. Abe has never driven a car.

Watashi wa kyuuka o totta koto wa arimasen.
I have never taken a vacation.

Though it is much less common, the plain-past-negative form of a verb can also be used before *koto*.

Shukudai o shinakatta koto wa arimasu ka.
Have you ever forgotten to do your homework? [Do you have an experience of not doing your homework?]

Iie, arimasen. Itsumo shimashita yo.
No, never. I always did it.

4. TE *KARA* "AFTER"

When the particle *kara* follows the TE form of a verb, it translates best as "after. . . ." As mentioned earlier, the TE form itself does not indicate tense. The tense is determined by and corresponds to the tense of the final (main) clause.

Uchi ni kaette kara, denwa shimasu.
After I go home, I will call you.

Shuuten de orite kara, juppun gurai arukimashita.
I walked for about ten minutes after I got off at the terminal.

The subject in the subordinate clause should be followed by *ga*, not by *wa*. In the following sentences, *kyuukoo* "express" and *watashi* "I" are the subjects in the subordinate clauses.

Kyuukoo ga dete kara, futsuu densha ga tsuku n desu.
The local train arrives after the express leaves.

Haha wa, watashi ga nete kara, dekakemashita.
My mother went out after I went to bed.

5. COUNTERS

a. *-jikan*

When *jikan* "time" is used as a counter, it means "hour."

Gojikan gurai desu.
It takes (is) about five hours.

Nanjikan unten shita n desu ka.
How many hours did you drive?

Kuruma de yojikan han kakarimasu.
It takes four and a half hours by car.

When you specify minutes and hours, the optional *-kan* following *-fun* "minute" cannot be used (see Lesson 14, B5).

yojikan juu gofun
　　four hours and fifteen minutes.

Ano basutei de ichijikan juppun machimashita.
　　I waited for an hour and ten minutes at that bus stop.

　　b. *-do*

The counter *-do* is used to express frequency.

Kakogawa made ichido itta koto ga aru n desu.
　　I have been to Kakogawa once.

Kono kuruma wa katte kara, moo yondo koshoo shimashita.
　　This car has broken down four times already since I bought it.

6. PARTICLES

　　a. *Ni* "for" (with adjectives)

Adjectives such as *ii* "good" or *warui* "bad" are used with *ni* following a noun. In these cases, *ni* can be translated as "for."

Kono tsuukin jigoku wa karada ni yoku nai desu ne.
　　This commuting hell is not good for our health.

Norimono no naka de hon o yomu no wa me ni warui desu yo.
　　Reading books while in a vehicle is bad for your eyes.

Kono undoo wa akachan no ashi no hattatsu ni ii soo desu.
　　I understand this exercise is good for the development of babies' legs.

　　b. *Ni* (with *noru*)

When the verb *noru* "to ride/get on" is used, the noun describing the means of transportation is followed by *ni*.

Mainichi densha ni norimasu.
　　I ride a train every day.

Chikatetsu ni noru no wa taihen na n desu.
　　It is hard to get on the subway.

Nihon no fune ni notta koto ga arimasu ka.
　　Have you ever taken a Japanese ship?

　　c. *O* (with *oriru*)

When the verb *oriru* "to get off" is used, the particle *o* follows the noun referring to the means of transportation.

Ginza de basu o orimashita.
   I got off the bus at Ginza.

Boku wa kono densha o orite kara, chikatetsu ni noru n desu.
   I take a subway after I get off this train.

O can also be used with other nouns besides those referring to methods of transportation.

Kono shigoto o orimashita.
   I quit this job.

   d. *Demo*

To indicate that something is an example or a possibility, use *demo*. It can be translated as "something," "for example," or "perhaps." Compare:

Ryokoo o suru n desu ka.
   Are you going to take a trip?

Ryokoo demo suru n desu ka.
   Are you going to take a trip perhaps?

Tsumetai mono demo nomimashoo ka.
   Should we drink something cold?

C. MOJI

In order to understand *kanji* characters fully, you need to be familiar with two terms: *on yomi* (Sino-Japanese pronunciation) and *kun yomi* (native Japanese pronunciation). When *kanji* characters were introduced from China, approximations of their pronunciations were adopted along with the characters themselves. The Chinese characters were also matched with the pronunciations of existing Japanese words with the same meanings as the Chinese characters. Take 山, for example. This *kanji* means "mountain." One pronunciation is *san*, whose pronunciation is from Chinese. The Japanese pronunciation is *yama*. Thus, *san* is the *on yomi,* and *yama* is the *kun yomi.* Which reading is used depends on the environment in which the *kanji* character is used. When 山 is used by itself, it is *yama*, and when it is used in a compound such as ふじ山 "Mt. Fuji," it is *san*.

   In listing *kanji* in this book, the *on yomi* of a *kanji* will be written in capital letters and the *kun yomi* in lower case. Among the 147 *kanji* in this book, some are introduced only with their *kun yomi* or *on yomi*, and others are introduced with both (possibly in different lessons).

The following *kanji* were introduced in Lesson 15.

[1]　木　*ki*　　　　　　　　　　　tree

[2]　人　*hito*　　　　　　　　　　person

[3]　山　*yama*　　　　　　　　　mountain

New *kanji* in this lesson are:

[4]　水　*mizu*　　　　　　　　　water

[5]　本　*HON*　　　　　　　　　book

[6]　中　*naka*　　　　　　　　　inside

STROKE ORDER

[4]　亅　ず　ず　水

[5]　一　十　才　木　本

[6]　丶　宀　口　中

Read the following dialogue that uses the *kanji* you have learned.

1. 山の 中で　　　*yama no naka de*　　in the mountains

　a. きれいな 水ですね。
　　Kirei na mizu desu ne.
　　It's clean water.

　b. あ、中に ちいさい むしが たくさん いますよ。
　　A, naka ni chiisai mushi ga takusan imasu yo.
　　Oh, there are many small insects in it.

2. a. これは だれの 本ですか。
　　Kore wa dare no hon desu ka.
　　Whose book is this?

　b. あの 人の 本です。
　　Ano hito no hon desu.
　　It's her [that person's] book.

198

D. TANGO TO HYOOGEN

norimono	vehicle, means of transportation
futsuu densha	local train
kyuukoo	express (train, bus)
Shinkansen	Shinkansen Line, bullet train
chikatetsu	subway
fune	ship
basu	bus
basutei	bus stop
shuuten	terminus, last stop
(puratto)hoomu	platform
tsuukin	commuting
jigoku	hell
tsuukin jigoku	commuting hell
shashoo	conductor of a train or bus
kippu	ticket (for transportation)
cf. **chiketto**	ticket (for entertainment)
undoo	physical exercise
shusshinchi	hometown
me	eye
ashi	leg, foot
hattatsu	development, growth
kyuuka	vacation
(o)shiro	castle
shukudai	homework
koto	thing (abstract, intangible)
cf. **mono**	thing (concrete, tangible)
unten suru	to drive
koshoo suru	to break (a mechanical object)
denwa suru	to make a phone call
komu	to get crowded
noru	to ride, get on
oriru	to get off
tsuku	to arrive
deru	to go out, leave
cf. **dekakeru**	to go out (from home or the place where one belongs)
toru	to take (a vacation, class)
neru	to go to bed, sleep
namayasashii	simple

tsumetai	cold (for a tangible object or a human personality)
cf. **samui**	cold (weather)
taihen	hard, terrible
taitei	generally, usually
tama ni	occasionally
nonbiri (to)	comfortably, leisurely
saiwai	fortunately
Omedetoo gozaimasu.	Congratulations./Happy-.
Sore wa omedetoo gozaimasu.	That calls for congratulations.

RENSHUU

A. Answer the following questions based on the dialogue.

1. *Sano san wa taitei kyuukoo ni norimasu ka.*
2. *Toda san wa itsu chikatetsu ni norimasu ka.*
3. *Dare ga ashita kara kyuuka o torimasu ka.*
4. *Himeji wa dare no shusshinchi desu ka*
5. *Toda san wa Kakogawa ni nando itta koto ga arimasu ka.*

B. Transform the following negative sentences using negative forms with *desu*.

1. *Basutei wa amari tooku arimasen.*
2. *Namayasashii koto ja arimasen deshita.*
3. *Watashi wa Amerikajin ja arimasen.*
4. *Kinoo wa samuku arimasen deshita.*

C. Transform the following sentences using *n desu*.

1. *Watashi no kuruma ja arimasen.*
2. *Himeji wa oshiro de yuumei desu.*
3. *Kyuukoo wa sugu kimashita.*
4. *Ashita wa imooto no kekkonshiki desu.*

D. Fill in the blanks according to the English equivalents.

1. *Uchi ni _____ kara, shukudai o shimashita.*
   I did homework after I went home.
2. *Shinkansen ni _____ koto ga arimasu ka.*
   Have you ever taken the Shinkansen Line?
3. *Takusan _____ no wa karada ni yoku nai desu.*
   It is not good for your health to eat a lot.
4. *Tanaka san wa ichijikan gurai _____ soo desu.*
   I understand Ms. Tanaka walked for about an hour.

E. Read and translate the following:

1. 中は さむいです。

2. 木に 水を やりました。

3. 本を よみました。

4. ゆうめいな 人

KARUCHAA NOOTO

Although the number of people in Japan who own cars has been increasing, it is still easy to get around without a car. Public transportation is well developed, taking you almost anywhere.

You can commute by train or bus. In major cities, subways are available, too. Because of the convenient transportation system and the lack of parking, not many people commute by car. Therefore public commuting facilities are notoriously crowded in big cities during rush hours, and passengers are packed in so tightly that it is hard to move. The crowding is so distasteful to many people that it has come to be called *tsuukin jigoku* "commuting hell." In most big cities white-gloved conductors stand on the subway platforms and literally pack passengers into subway cars.

The lines of so-called "bullet trains," the Shinkansen, make up the most convenient and extensive system available for long-distance travel. For example, a five- or six-hour car trip from Tokyo to Nagoya takes just two hours by Shinkansen. The Shinkansen Lines are owned by JR (Japan Railways).

KOTAE

A. 1. *Hai, norimasu.* 2. *Densha o orite kara, norimasu.* 3. *Sano san ga torimasu.* 4. *Sano san no shusshinchi desu.* 5. *Ichido itta koto ga arimasu.*
B. 1. ——*tooku nai desu.* 2. ——*namayasashii koto ja nakatta desu.*
3. ——*Amerikajin ja nai desu.* 4. ——*samuku nakatta desu.*
C. 1. ——*kuruma ja nai n desu.* 2. ——*yuumei na n desu.* 3. ——*sugu kita n desu.* 4. ——*kekkonshiki na n desu.*
D. 1. *kaette/modotte* 2. *notta* 3. *taberu* 4. *aruita*
E. 1. *Naka wa samui desu.* It's cold inside. 2. *Ki ni mizu o yarimashita.*
I gave the tree water. 3. *Hon o yomimashita.* I read books. 4. *yuumei na hito* a famous person

DAI JUU NANAKA
Lesson 17
MICHI O TAZUNERU.   Asking for Directions.

A. DAIAROOGU

Shiyakusho Made Ikitai n desu.

A woman asks a man for directions on the street.

A: **Chótto sumimasén. Shiyákusho made ikitái n desu kedo, dóo it-tára íi desu ka.**

B: **Arúite ikú n desu ka.**

A: **Ée, dono gurai kakarimásu ka.**

B: **Sóo desu ne. Níjuu gofun gúrai desu ne. Toókattara, básu mo arimásu yo. Kono toorí o tóotte irú n desu.**

A: **Níjuu gofun gúrai dattara, arukimásu.**

B: **Jáa, kono toorí o massúgu ikú n desu. Gofun gúrai ittára, hón'ya ga arimásu. Sono kádo o higashi, tsúmari, migi ni magatte, ni-sanpun ittára, shingoo ga áru n desu. Soko o watatte, shi-gofun arúite ikú n desu. Suruto, hidari ni gasorin sutándo ga arimásu. Soko kara chótto fukuzatsu ná n desu. Gasorin sutándo de moo ichido kiite míte kudasai.**

A: **Áa, sóo desu ka. Wakarimáshita.**

B: **A, chótto mátte kudasai. Shiyákusho wa moo súgu shimarimásu yo.**

A: **Sore wa íi n desu. Shiyákusho no tonari ni funsui ga áru sóo desu kedo, sono funsui máde ikitái n desu.**

Looking for City Hall.

A: Excuse me. I'd like to go to city hall. What's the best way to get there?

B: Are you going to walk?

A: Yes, how long will it take?

B: Well, it's about twenty-five minutes away. If that's too far for you, you can take the bus [there is a bus, also]. It runs on this street.

202

A: If it only takes about twenty-five minutes, I'll walk.

B: Well then, okay, go straight on this street. In about five minutes, you'll see a bookstore. Turn east, that is, right at that corner, and go two or three minutes until you get to a traffic light. Cross the street there and continue walking for four or five minutes until you reach a gas station on the left. From there, it's a little complicated. Ask for directions again at the gas station.

A: All right.

B: Oh, wait a minute. The city hall will be closed before long.

A: That's fine. I understand there's a fountain next to it, and that's where I want to go.

B. BUNPOO TO YOOHOO

1. -TARA "IF . . ./WHEN . . ."

The TARA form can be used to express "if . . ." or "when. . . ." To get to the TARA form, attach *ra* to the plain past form.

PLAIN PAST			TARA
itta	went	→	*ittara*
ikanakatta	did not go	→	*ikanakattara*
oishikatta	was tasty	→	*oishikattara*
oishiku nakatta	was not tasty	→	*oishiku nakattara*
shizuka datta	was quiet	→	*shizuka dattara*
shizuka ja/de (wa) nakatta	was not quiet	→	*shizuka ja/de (wa) nakattara*
gakusei datta	was a student	→	*gakusei dattara*
gakusei ja/de (wa) nakatta	was not a student	→	*gakusei ja/de (wa) nakattara*

Gofun gurai ittara, hon'ya ga arimasu.
　　If you continue [go] for about five minutes, there is a bookstore.

Doo ittara ii desu ka.
　　How do I get there? [If I go how, will it be good?]

Tookattara, basu mo arimasu.
　　If it is [too] far, there is also a bus.

Nijuu gofun gurai dattara, arukimasu.
　　If it only takes about twenty-five minutes, I'll walk.

Wakaranakattara, kiite kudasai.
　　Please ask me if you don't understand.

The word *moshi* "in case" can be used before a TARA form for emphasis.

Moshi tooku nakattara ikitai desu.
    If it is not far, I want to go.

Ashita moshi ame ga futtara, shiai wa yamemashoo.
    If it rains tomorrow, let's call off the game.

Just like the TE form, the TARA form itself does not have a tense. The tense is determined by the tense of the main clause. In the following sentence, the TARA clause must be in the past, because *aka deshita* "it was red" is in the past tense.

Shingoo o mitara, aka deshita.
    When I saw the traffic light, it was red.

In the subordinate TARA clause, the subject should be followed by *ga* if it is not identical to the subject of the main clause (see Lesson 16, B4). If the subject covers both the main and the subordinate clauses, it can be followed by *wa*.

Shigoto ga owattara, kite kudasai.
    Please come when your work is finished.

Imooto wa Ginza e ittara, itsumo ano pan'ya e iku n desu.
    My younger sister always goes to that bakery when she goes to Ginza.

2. THE TE FORM OF A VERB FOR TWO SEQUENTIAL ACTIONS

When two actions take place in sequence, the first action is expressed in the TE form. Here, TE can be translated as ". . . and then."

Sono toori o watatte, gofun gurai aruku n desu.
    Cross the street there, and then walk for about five minutes.

Migi ni magatte, sanpun gurai ittara, shingoo ga aru n desu.
    If you turn to the right and then continue [go] for about three minutes, you'll get to a traffic light.

Gasorin sutando e itte, kikimashita.
    I went to the gas station and asked them.

Hoteru e kaette, shokuji shimashita.
    I went back to my hotel and then had a meal.

TE *kara* (see Lesson 16, B4) can be used to express sequence as well. However, TE *kara* carries the meaning "after" rather than merely "and."

Depaato ni itte kara, shiyakusho ni ikimashita.
After I went to the department store, I went to city hall.

Depaato ni itte, chizu o kaimashita.
I went to the department store and bought a map.

Note that *to* "and" cannot be used to link verbs, *i*-adjectives, or the copula; it is used only for connecting nouns and noun phrases (see Lesson 18).

3. THE TE FORM USED WITH MOTION VERBS

The TE form is also used with motion verbs when you are referring to the manner in which the motion is accomplished.

Aruite iku n desu ka.
Are you going on foot?

Jitensha ni notte ikimashita.
I bicycled there.

Uchi e hashitte kaerimashita.
I ran home.

Shiyakusho made isoide ikimashita.
I hurried to city hall.

4. THE PARTICLE *O* EXPRESSING LOCATION

A noun referring to a location can be followed by *o* to express that a motion covers the entire location. Often the English equivalents are "along," "on," "at," "around," or "through."

Basu wa kono toori o tootte iru n desu.
Buses run along this street.

Kono toori o massugu iku n desu.
You go straight on this street.

Sono kado o nishi ni magarimasu.
You turn west at that corner.

Funsui no mawari o arukimashita.
I walked around the fountain.

Compare the use of *o* with the use of *de*:

Kawa o oyogimashita.
I swam along/across the river.

Kawa de oyogimashita.
I swam in the river.

5. NUMERALS IN SUCCESSION EXPRESSING RANGE

To express a somewhat indefinite number such as "one or two," or "two or three," use both numerals. The second numeral takes a counter in the same way it would without the first numeral. The first one does not.

ichi-nifun (cf. *nifun* two minutes)	one or two minutes
ni-sanpun (cf. *sanpun* three minutes)	two or three minutes
juusan-yonpun (cf. *yonpun* four minutes)	thirteen or fourteen minutes
ni-sanjuppun (cf. *sanjuppun* thirty minutes)	twenty or thirty minutes

When the numeral "four" occurs as the first numeral, *shi* is used instead of *yon*.

shi-gofun	four or five minutes

However, for the following combinations, use *ka* "or" between the two numerals.

happun ka kyuufun	eight or nine minutes
kyuufun ka juppun	nine or ten minutes
juppun ka juu ippun	ten or eleven minutes
juu kyuufun ka nijuppun	nineteen or twenty minutes
nijuppun ka nijuu ippun	twenty or twenty-one minutes

With other counters, the same rules apply.

ni-sanmai	two or three (tickets)
shi-gonin	four or five people
juuichi-nihon	eleven or twelve (trees)
ni-sanjuppon	twenty or thirty (pencils)

For days, the regular counter *nichi* is used except for numerals with "four" as the first digit (see Lesson 10, B2, for counting days).

ni-sannichi	two or three days
san-yokka	three or four days
shi-gonichi	four or five days
juusan-yokka	thirteen or fourteen days
nijuusan-yokka	twenty-three or twenty-four days

For dates, use *ka* "or."

futsuka ka mikka	the second or third day of the month

C. MOJI

Some words are never written in *kanji*. Particles and the copula, for example, are always written in *hiragana*. *Kanji* can be used for most nouns. The non-conjugated parts of verbs and *i*-adjectives can usually be written in *kanji* as well. Their conjugated parts, however, are written in *hiragana*. The vast majority of *na*-adjectives can be written in *kanji* (some only partially).

行く	*iku* (verb)	to go (-*ku* is written in *hiragana*.)
古い	*furui* (*i*-adjective)	old (-*i* is written in *hiragana*.)
好き	*suki* (*na*-adjective)	to like (-*ki* is written in *hiragana*.)

The *hiragana* part, such as *ku*, *i*, or *ki* above, is called *okurigana*. When *kanji* are listed, the *okurigana* are shown in parentheses.

[7]	行	*i(ku)*	to go
[8]	古	*furu(i)*	old
[9]	好	*su(ki)*	to like

STROKE ORDER

[7]	´ ﾉ 彳 彳 彳 行
[8]	一 十 十 古 古
[9]	く 乡 女 女 好

D. TANGO TO HYOOGEN

toori	street
kado	corner
shingoo	traffic light
shiyakusho	city hall
funsui	fountain
hon'ya	bookstore
pan'ya	bakery
gasorin	gasoline
gasorin sutando	gas station
hoteru	hotel
kawa	river
jitensha	bicycle
hidari	left

207

migi	right
kita	north
minami	south
higashi	east
nishi	west
mawari	around
tooru	to pass
wataru	to cross
hashiru	to run
owaru	to end
shimaru	to close
fukuzatsu	complicated
massugu	straight
suruto	just then
tsumari	that is, namely
moo "—"	more
moshi	in case

RENSHUU

A. Fill in the blanks based on the dialogue.

1. _____ wa kado ni arimasu.
2. Shingoo wa _____ no nishi ni arimasu.
3. _____ wa shiyakusho no tonari ni arimasu.

B. Fill in the blanks according to the English equivalents.

1. Ame ga _____, ikimasen.
   If it rains, I will not go.
2. _____, nido mitai desu.
   If it is interesting, I want to see it twice.
3. Yasui _____, kaimasu.
   If it is an inexpensive bicycle, I will buy it.
4. Gasorin sutando ni _____, Tanaka san ga imashita.
   When I went to the gas station, Ms. Tanaka was there.

C. Combine the two sentences with the TE form, and translate the sentences into English.

Example: Uchi ni kaerimasu.
        Shokuji shimasu.
        → Uchi ni kaette, shokuji shimasu.
          I will go home and have a meal.

1. *Shiyakusho ni ikimasu.*
   Kiite mimasu.
2. *Ano kado o magarimasu.*
   Gofun gurai aruku n desu.
3. *Shuuten de orimashita.*
   Takushii o sagashimashita.

D. Fill in the blanks according to the following map.

post office

traffic lights

beauty parlor

a. *Yuubinkyoku made ikitai n desu kedo, doo* _____[1] *ii desu ka.*
b. *Kono toori* _____[2] *massugu iku n desu. Suruto kado ni* _____[3]
   ga arimasu.
   Sono kado o _____[4] *ni magatte, shi-gofun ittara,* _____[5] *ga*
   arimasu.
   Soko o wattatte, chotto aruku n desu. Yuubinkyoku wa _____[6]
   ni arimasu.

E. Read and translate the following:

1. 古い 本

2. 山へ 行きました。

3. さくらの 木が 好きです。

F. Write the following using *kanji*:

1. *ikanai.*

2. *Furuku arimasen.*

3. *Suki desu.*

G. Choose the most appropriate numbers from the box below.

1. *Sumimasen ga, ———— matte kudasai.* (at the restaurant)
   (Please wait for another twenty to thirty minutes.)
2. ———— *de dekimasu yo.* (at the laundry)
   (The laundry will be done in a few days.)
3. *Hon wa ———— de todokimasu yo.* (at the bookstore)
   (The book will arrive in <u>about two weeks</u>.)

> A: *ni-san nichi*   B: *juusan-yokka*   C: *ni-san juppun*

KARUCHAA NOOTO

Generally speaking, it is harder to find a building or a street address in Japan than in the United States. In many places, streets are not laid out in a grid pattern, and often the address signifies the name of the area rather than that of the street. For example, in the following address, *Ashiya-shi, Kasugachoo, 1–25* (1–25 Kasugacho, Ashiya), *Kasugachoo* is an area in the city of *Ashiya.* Thus, while public places may be found relatively easily, private residences are difficult to locate, even though each house has a nameplate on the front. The best person to ask for directions is most likely the mail carrier.

If you are not lucky enough to run into one, go to the local police post, which has a detailed map of area. Police posts are located all over Japan to serve and protect the people in trouble. For example, they lend money to people who are stranded or umbrellas to those caught in the rain. Most people return the money or umbrellas at a later date. In rural areas, the policeman and his family live in the police post. The relationship between police officers and the community tends to be personal, and both sides cooperate to create a better living environment, although in larger cities, this kind of relationship is unusual.

KOTAE

A. 1. *Hon'ya*   2. *gasorin sutando*   3. *Funsui*
B. 1. *futtara*   2. *Omoshirokattara*   3. *jitensha dattara*   4. *ittara*
C. 1. *Shiyakusho ni itte, kiite mimasu.* I will go to city hall and ask them to find out. 2. *Ano kado o magatte, gofun gurai aruku n desu.* You turn at that corner and walk on for about five minutes. 3. *Shuuten de orite, takushii o sagashimashita.* I got off at the terminal and looked for a taxi.
D. 1. *ittara*   2. *o*   3. *biyooin*   4. *migi*   5. *shingoo*   6. *hidari*
E. 1. *furui hon* old book 2. *Yama e ikimashita.* I went to the mountains.
3. *Sakura no ki ga suki desu.* I like cherry trees.
F. 1. 行かない don't go 2. 古く ありません It's not old.
3. 好きでした I liked it.
G. 1. C   2. A   3. B

DAI JUU HACHIKA
Lesson 18

HOOMON.   Paying a Visit to a Home.

A. DAIAROOGU

SAKAIKE O TAZUNERU.

Ms. Turner, an American, is studying at a Japanese university. Today she is visiting the Sakais, her host family, for the first time.

SAKAI: **Irasshai. Dóozo oagari kudasái.**

TAANAA: **Ojama shimásu.**

SAKAI: **Dóozo kochira e. Súgu wakarimáshita ka.**

TAANAA: **Ée. Kono hen wa shízuka de kírei na juutákuchi desu ne. Sore ni mídori ga óokute, arúku no ga tanóshikatta desu.**

SAKAI: **Mukashi wa tanbo ya hatake ga átte, nódoka na inaka dátta n desu yo. Dóozo kochira ni okake kudasái. Otto wa hón'ya made itte, musumé wa eiga o mí ni ittá n desu. Sore ni musuko mo tomodachi no uchí ni itte íma inái n desu kedo, minna moo súgu modóru hazu désu kara, kyóo wa yukkúri nasátte kudasai.**

TAANAA: **Arígatoo gozaimasu.**

SAKAI: **Kono heyá wa chótto samúi desu ne. Tatami no heyá e ikimashóo ka. Hi ga attatte, atatakái desu kara.**

TAANAA: **Áa, sóo desu ka. Démo, anoo, tatami ni suwarú no wa chótto nigate ná n desu kedo.**

SAKAI: **Zabúton ga arimásu kara, daijóobu desu yo. Móshi damé dattara, engawa ni isu mo arimásu kara.**

TAANAA: **Sóo desu ka. Jáa, ganbátte mimasu.**

VISITING THE SAKAIS.

SAKAI: Welcome. Please come in [step up].

TURNER: Thank you.

SAKAI: This way, please. Did you find the house easily?

TURNER: Yes. This is a quiet and pretty neighborhood [residential area], isn't it? And there's lots of green around. It was a nice walk.

SAKAI: Years ago, there were rice and vegetable fields all around, and it was a peaceful rural area. Please take a seat here. My husband went to the bookstore, and my daughter went to see a movie. And my son went to his friend's house, so he's not home either, but all of them are supposed to be back before long. Please stay and relax [today].

TURNER: Thank you very much.

SAKAI: This room is a little bit cold, isn't it? Should we go to the *tatami* room? The sun shines into it, so it's warm.

TURNER: All right. But, uh, I'm not good at sitting on *tatami*.

SAKAI: We have cushions, so you won't have a problem. If it's no good, there are chairs on the porch, too.

TURNER: Really? Well, I'll try.

B. BUNPOO TO YOOHOO

1. THE TE FORM OF A VERB FOR PARALLEL AND CAUSAL RELATIONSHIPS

Note that the TE verb form is used for a sequence of actions.

Uchi e kaette, terebi o mimashita.
    I went home and watched TV.

The TE verb form can also indicate parallel and causal relationships.

a. Parallel relationships (events happening at the same time)

Here the TE form can be translated as ". . . and" or "while . . ."

Otto wa hon'ya made itte, musume wa eiga o mi ni itta n desu.
    My husband went to the bookstore, and my daughter went to see a movie.

Rajio o kiite, benkyoo shimashita.
    I studied while listening to the radio.

Musume wa hatake de hataraite, watashi wa sentaku shimashita.
    My daughter worked in the field, and I did the laundry.

b. Causal relationships

The TE form can be translated as ". . . and (therefore)" or ". . . so."

Mukashi wa tanbo ya hatake ga atte, nodoka na inaka datta n desu.
  Years ago, there were rice and vegetable fields, and so it was a peaceful rural area.

Musuko wa tomodachi no uchi ni itte, ima inai n desu.
  My son went to his friend's house, so he's not here now.

Hi ga attatte, atatakai desu.
  The sun shines, and therefore it is warm.

  Kara "because" can also be used to express causal relationships (see Lesson 9, C5). The causal relationship expressed by a TE form is not as strong as one with *kara*. Furthermore, *kara* can be used for a sentence expressing a request or a suggestion, whereas the TE form cannot. This restriction is also true for the TE forms of *i*-adjectives and the copula, which are introduced below.

Sugu modorimasu kara, matte ite kudasai.
  Please wait [be waiting], because I will be right back.

Ame ga futte imasu kara, uchi ni imashoo.
  Since it's raining, let's stay home.

2. THE TE FORM OF AN *I*-ADJECTIVE FOR PARALLEL AND CAUSAL RELATIONSHIPS

  Add *-te* to the KU form. (The KU form is derived by replacing the final *-i* of an *i*-adjective with *-ku*.)

i-ADJECTIVES		TE FORMS	
ookii	→	*ookikute*	big
tooi	→	*tookute*	far
ii	→	*yokute* (not *ikute*)	good

  a. Parallel relationships

Ano heya wa ookikute, akarui desu.
  That room is big and bright.

Niwa wa hirokute, kirei desu.
  The garden is spacious and pretty.

Shinshitsu wa semakute, kurakatta desu.
  The bedroom was small and dark.

b. Causal relationships

Midori ga ookute, aruku no ga tanoshikatta desu.
There was so much green, and it was fun to walk.

Uchi wa totemo takakute, kau koto ga dekimasen deshita.
The house was so expensive that I could not buy it.

Mado ga ookikute, hi ga yoku atarimasu.
The window is big, so we get a lot of sun.

3. THE TE FORM OF THE COPULA FOR PARALLEL AND CAUSAL RELATIONSHIPS

The TE form of the copula, used with a *na*-adjective or a noun, is *de*.

a. Parallel relationships

Shizuka de, kirei na juutakuchi desu.
It is a quiet and pretty residential area.

Ima wa yooma de, shinshitsu wa nihonma desu.
The living room is a Western-style room, and the bedroom is a Japanese-style room.

Suzuki san no uchi wa nihonfuu de, Murai san no uchi wa yoofuu desu.
Ms. Suzuki's house is Japanese style, and Ms. Murai's house is Western style.

b. Causal relationships

Kono kaban wa benri de, itsumo tsukatte iru n desu.
This bag is handy, so I always use it.

Kono hen wa totemo shizuka de, yoru chotto kowai desu.
This area is very quiet, so it is a little scary at night.

Musume wa jaanarisuto de, yoku ryokoo suru n desu.
My daughter is a journalist, so she travels often.

4. EXPECTATION *(HAZU)*

Hazu "expectation" is a dependent noun like *tsumori* "intention" (see Lesson 12, B4). In the sentence patterns below, *hazu* means "to be expected to" or "to be supposed to."

verb (dictionary form)	+	*hazu desu*	is expected to ...
	+	*hazu deshita*	was expected to ...
verb (plain present negative form)	+	*hazu desu*	is expected not to ...
	+	*hazu deshita*	was expected not to ...

Hazu is used when the speaker has a reason to assume that his or her expectation will come true. It should be avoided when the action is under the speaker's control.

Futari tomo moo sugu modoru hazu desu.
I expect both of them to come back before long [and I have reason to do so].

Ashita ame wa furanai hazu desu. Rajio de soo itte imashita yo.
It is not expected to rain tomorrow. The radio said so.

Shigoto wa sanji made ni owaranai hazu deshita.
The work was not supposed to be finished by three o'clock.

5. HONORIFIC VERBS

You have already learned some honorific verbs: *irassharu, sashiageru, kudasaru,* and *itadaku.* Here are a few additional ones.

| *suru* | → | *nasaru* | (respect) | to do |
| *iu* | → | *ossharu* | (respect) | to say |

Nasaru and *ossharu* are consonant verbs. Their *masu* forms are *nasaimasu* and *osshaimasu* (without the *r* between *a* and *i*), like *irasshaimasu* and *kudasaimasu* (see Lesson 12, B3).

HOST: *Kyoo wa yukkuri nasatte kudasai.*
Please stay and relax [today]. (*yukkuri nasaru*: to stay and relax)

GUEST: *Arigatoo gozaimasu.*
Thank you very much.

WAITER: *Nani ni nasaimasu ka.*
What would you like to order?

CUSTOMER: *Osushi ni shimasu.*
I would like to have sushi.

A: *Oniisan ga soo osshatta n desu.*
　　Your older brother said so.

B: *Ani ga soo itta n desu ka.*
　　My older brother said so?

A: *Hayashi san ga orei o osshatte imashita yo.*
　　Ms. Hayashi was expressing her gratitude to you.

B: *Watashi mo orei o iitakatta n desu.*
　　I wanted to express my gratitude to her, also.

6. *MINNA* "EVERYONE"

Minna "everyone" or "all" is an informal variation of *mina. Minasan* is a respectful word used only for people. Like other quantity expressions, *mina, minna, minasan* can be used without a particle (see Lesson 9, C2).

Minna moo sugu modoru hazu desu.
　　All of them are supposed to return before long.

Gokazoku wa minasan ogenki desu ka.
　　Is everybody in your family fine?

Kono hen no uchi wa mina yoofuu desu.
　　The houses in this area are all Western-style.

C. MOJI

Here are ten more *kanji* characters.

[10]	一	*ICHI*	*hito(tsu)*	one
[11]	二	*NI*	*futa(tsu)*	two
[12]	三	*SAN*	*mit(tsu)*	three
[13]	四	*SHI*	*yon, yo-, yot(tsu)*	four
[14]	五	*GO*	*itsu(tsu)*	five
[15]	六	*ROKU*	*mut(tsu)*	six
[16]	七	*SHICHI*	*nana, nana(tsu)*	seven
[17]	八	*HACHI*	*yat(tsu)*	eight
[18]	九	*KU, KYUU*	*kokono(tsu)*	nine
[19]	十	*JUU*	*too*	ten

[10]	一
[11]	⼀ 二
[12]	一 二 三
[13]	丨 冂 冚 四 四
[14]	一 丁 五 五
[15]	丶 亠 广 六
[16]	一 七
[17]	丿 八
[18]	丿 九
[19]	一 十

Note that the pronunciations of some *kanji* undergo a sound change in certain combinations.

一ぽん	*ippon*	一さい	*issai*
六ぽん	*roppon*		
八ぽん	*happon*	八さい	*hassai*
十ぽん	*juppon, jippon*	十さい	*jussai, jissai*

Hito 人 "person" (introduced in Lesson 15) has other readings.

[1]	人	*hito*	person
	NIN		person, counter for people
	JIN		person

三人	*sannin*	three people
なん人	*nannin*	how many people
アメリカ人	*amerikajin*	American (person)
にほん人	*nihonjin*	Japanese (person)

The following are irregular readings.

| 一人 | *hitori* | one person |
| 二人 | *futari* | two people |

D. TANGO TO HYOOGEN

juutaku	residence
juutakuchi	residential area
inaka	rural area, countryside
tanbo	rice field
hatake	vegetable field
tatami	tatami mat
engawa	Japanese-style porch
ima	living room
shinshitsu	bedroom
mado	window
nihonma	Japanese-style room
yooma	Western-style room
nihonfuu	Japanese style
yoofuu	Western style
zabuton	floor cushion
hi	sun, sunshine
musume	daughter (the speaker's)
ojoosan	daughter (somebody else's)
musuko	son (the speaker's)
musukosan	son (somebody else's grown-up sons)
botchan	son (somebody else's male child)
minasan	everybody (respect)
agaru	to step up, go up, rise
suwaru	to sit (in a chair or on the floor)
cf. **kakeru**	to sit (in a chair)
ganbaru	to make efforts, persevere
ataru	to hit
nasaru	to do (honorific)
ossharu	to say (honorific)
ooi	many, much
hiroi	spacious, wide
semai	not spacious, narrow
kowai	scary
nodoka	peaceful

218

nigate	weak in, poor at
benri	convenient, handy
dame	no good
sugu	easily
Ojama shimasu.	I will visit you. [I am going to bother you.]

RENSHUU

A. Answer the following questions based on the dialogue.

1. *Taanaa san wa Sakai san no uchi made kuruma ni notte kimashita ka.*
2. *Taanaa san wa nani ga nigate desu ka.*
3. *Tatami no heya ni nani ga arimasu ka.*

B. Fill in the blanks with TE forms according to the English equivalents.

1. *Musume wa tenisu o _____, musuko wa yakyuu o shimasu.*
My daughter plays tennis, and my son plays baseball.
2. *Mise ga _____, benri desu.*
Stores are close, therefore it is convenient.
3. *Ame ga _____, shiai o suru koto ga dekimasen deshita.*
It rained, so we could not play the game.
4. *Watashi no uchi wa _____, tanoshii desu.*
My house is lively, and it is fun.

C. Transform part b using *hazu desu.*

1. a: *Kore kara Yamada san no uchi ni iku n desu.*
   b: *Yamada san wa kyoo uchi ni imasen yo.*
2. a: *Kono densha wa itsu deru n desu ka.*
   b: *Kuji ni demasu.*
3. a: *Suzuki san wa Sakai san o shitte imasu ne.*
   b: *Iie, shirimasen yo.*

D. Transform the following dialogues using honorific verbs whenever appropriate.

1. a: *Otootosan wa tenisu o shimasu ka.*
   Does your younger brother play tennis?
   b: *Iie, tenisu wa shimasen.*
   No, he does not play tennis.
2. a: *Kirei na hana desu nee.*
   What pretty flowers!
   b: *Bara wa haha ga kurete, shoobu wa Sakai san ga kureta n desu.*
   My mother gave me the roses, and Ms. Sakai gave me irises.

3. a: *Ashita nanji ni kimasu ka.*
   When are you coming tomorrow?
   b: *Juuji goro iku tsumori desu.*
   I plan to come around ten o'clock.

E. Read the following:

1. へやが 九つ あります。

2. アメリカ人が 五人 います

F. Write the following using *kanji*:

1. おとうとは やっつです。

2. ちゅうごくじんは なんにん いますか。 よにん います。

G. Comment on the following items using the TE form of the
i-adjectives.

Example: the bag; cheap, good → *kono kaban wa yasukute ii desu ne.*

1. this room; small, expensive.
2. the kitchen; bright, clean
3. the car; big, good

H. Write the following telephone numbers using *kanji*.

1. 03-3943-6758
2. 03-9914-0524
3. 06-6231-0243

KARUCHAA NOOTO

Japan began adopting customs from Western cultures in the late nineteenth century, and houses combining Japanese and Western features
became popular. In such houses, the majority of rooms were decorated
according to the Japanese tradition and furnished with *tatami* mats.
Typically, however, the parlor was a room decorated according to Western traditions, and it had a wooden floor. More recently, houses tend to
have more than one Western room: the parlor, the dining room, the living room, and the foyer are usually Western style. However, the Japanese still like to have their *tatami* rooms, too. The standard size of a
tatami is six feet long by three feet wide and two inches thick. It is
made of rice straw with a finished cover of woven rush greens. The bor-
ders are covered with strips of cloth. Small rooms take three to six
tatami mats, and large ones take eight or more.
    When you enter a house, you have to take off your shoes. You may

wear slippers, but when you enter a *tatami* room, you take even them off. It may be hard to sit on the *tatami* for a long time, but a *zabuton* cushion may help. Traditionally, the main *tatami* room has a porch called an *engawa* attached, which faces the garden.

As for the exterior, Japanese houses tend to have more elaborate fences and gates than American ones. Unlike in America, where you can usually see the yards easily from outside, Japanese houses tend to be more secluded.

KOTAE

A. 1. *Iie, aruite kimashita.* 2. *Tatami ni suwaru no ga nigate desu.*
3. *Zabuton ga arimasu.*
B. 1. *shite*   2. *chikakute*   3. *futte*   4. *nigiyaka de*
C. 1. ——*inai hazu desu yo.* 2. ——*deru hazu desu.* 3. ——*shiranai hazu desu yo.*
D. 1. a: ——*nasaimasu ka.* 2. b: ——*Sakai san ga kudasatta n desu.*
3. a: ——*irasshaimasu ká.*
E. 1. *Heya ga kokonotsu arimasu.* There are nine rooms. 2. *Amerikajin ga gonin imasu.* There are five Americans.
F. 1. おとうとは 八つです。 My younger brother is eight. 2. ちゅうごく人は なん人 いますか。 How many Chinese are there? 四人 います。 There are four.
G. 1. *kono heya wa <u>chiisakute</u> takai desu ne.* 2. *kono kitchin (daidokoro) wa <u>akarukute</u> kirei desu ne.* 3. *kono kuruma wa <u>ookikute</u> ii desu ne.*
H. 1. ○三-三九四三-六七五八 2. ○三-九九一四-○五二四
3. ○六-六二三一-○二四三

DAI JUU KYUUKA
Lesson 19
IRYOO SEIDO.   Medical Care.

A. DAIAROOGU

SHINSATSUSHITSU DE.

Mr. Okada has hurt his leg and has come to the doctor's office in his neighborhood.

OKADA: **Senséi, gobusata shite orimásu.**

ISHA: **A, Okada san, shibáraku desu née.**

OKADA: **Ashí o kegá shita n desu.**

ISHA: **Itasóo desu ne. Dóo shita n desu ka.**

OKADA: **Kinoo jiténsha ni notte itára, michi ga sémakute, sóba no ogawa ni óchita n desu. De, soko ni átta iwá ni ashí o butsuketa n desu.**

ISHA: **Abunái desu née.**

OKADA: **Fúdan tóoru michi de, nárete itá n desu kedo. . . . Honé wa órete imásu ka.**

ISHA: **Iie, daijóobu da to omoimásu yo. Démo, nen no tamé ni rentógen o tótte mimashóo.**

Shibaraku shite.

ISHA: **Honé wa órete imasén deshita ne. Kizu wa isshuukan gúrai de naóru to omoimásu.**

OKADA: **Áa, sóo desu ka.**

ISHA: **Itamidome o agemásu kara, shokugo, ichinichí ni nido nónde kudasai. Ashita moo ichido kíte kudasai.**

OKADA: **Hai, wakarimáshita. Arígatoo gozaimáshita.**

AT THE DOCTOR'S OFFICE.

OKADA: Doctor, I haven't been to see you for a long time.

DOCTOR: Oh, Mr. Okada. Yes it has been a long time.

OKADA: I've hurt my leg.

DOCTOR: It looks painful. How did this happen?

OKADA: I was riding my bicycle yesterday, but the road was too narrow, and I fell into the stream beside the road. [And then,] I hit my leg on a rock [that was there].

DOCTOR: Terrible.

OKADA: I've taken this road so often [It is a road which I take so often] that I'm [was] used to it, but . . . Is the bone broken?

DOCTOR: No, I think it's all right. But, to make sure, let's take an X ray.

A little later.

DOCTOR: The bone is [was] not broken. I think the wound will heal in about a week.

OKADA: Really?

DOCTOR: I'll give you a painkiller. Take it twice a day after eating. And please come back tomorrow.

OKADA: All right. Thank you very much (for what you have done).

B. BUNPOO TO YOOHOO

1. RELATIVE CLAUSES

Relative clauses modify a noun. While the English relative clause follows the noun it modifies, the Japanese relative clause precedes the noun. Where English uses relative pronouns such as "who," "which," "where," and "that," no such pronouns are used in Japanese. The clauses in brackets in the following sentences are the relative clauses.

[Asoko ni iru] hito wa Suzuki san no otoosan desu.
The person [who is over there] is Ms. Suzuki's father.

Are wa [Yamamoto san ga tateta] byooin desu.
That's the hospital [that Mr. Yamamoto built].

[I o arasanai] kusuri o kudasai.
Please give me some medicine [that will not hurt my stomach].

[Tsukawanakatta] hootai wa doko ni arimasu ka.
Where is the bandage [which we didn't use]?

Relative clauses are always in plain form, except in highly polite speech. As in other subordinate clauses, *wa* cannot be used in relative clauses.

[Tomodachi ga kureta] itamidome wa yoku kikimashita.
The painkiller [that my friend gave me] worked well.

The particle *ga* in the relative clause can be changed to *no*.

[Tomodachi no kureta] itamidome wa yoku kikimashita.
The painkiller [that my friend gave me] worked well.

When the main clause is in the past tense, the relative clause does not have to be in the past tense when the clause has a negative, stative, or habitual meaning.

Tomodachi ga kawanakatta (past tense)/*kawanai* (present tense) *hon o kaimashita.*
I bought the book which my friend did not buy.

Here are more examples of sentences with relative clauses.

Soko wa fudan tooru michi de, narete ita n desu.
I take that road so often [That place is a road that I take so often] that I am [was] used to it.

Soko ni atta iwa de kega o shita n desu.
Because of the rock that was there, I got injured.

Kore wa Yamada san ga nyuuin shite iru byooin desu.
This is the hospital where Mr. Yamada is hospitalized.

2. -*SOO* "IT LOOKS . . ." OR "IT SEEMS . . ."

When -*soo* is attached to an adjective or a verb, it means "it looks . . ." or "it seems. . . ." A phrase with -*soo* behaves like a *na*-adjective.

a. -*soo* with an *i*-adjective in the affirmative

The final -*i* is replaced by -*soo*.

Itasoo desu.
It looks painful.

Abunasoo na michi desu ne.
It's a dangerous-looking road, isn't it?

b. *-soo* with a *na*-adjective in the affirmative

-soo directly follows the *na*-adjective.

Byooin e iku no ga iyasoo deshita.
He seemed to be reluctant to go to the hospital.

Genkisoo na inu desu.
It is a healthy-looking dog.

c. *-soo* with a verb in the affirmative

-soo is attached to the pre-*masu* form of a verb and means "Something seems to be happening or about to happen."

Netsu ga arisoo desu.
He seems to have a fever.

Kizu wa sugu naorisoo desu.
The wound looks as if it will heal soon.

d. *-soo* with a verb in the negative

The usage of *-soo* with a verb in the negative is avoided except for certain weather predictions. The final *-i* is replaced by *-soo*, just as in *i*-adjectives.

Ame wa furanasoo desu.
It appears that it will not rain.

e. Insertion of *sa*

With *ii (yoi)* "good," *nai* "to be not, to have not," and the present negative forms of both *i*-adjectives and the copula, *sa* is inserted before *-soo*.

Ano byooin wa yosasoo (not *isasoo*) *desu.*
That hospital seems good.

Jikan ga nasasoo desu.
There seems to be no time.

Kizu wa itaku nasasoo deshita.
The wound seemed not to be painful.

Ano isha wa joozu ja nasasoo desu.
That doctor doesn't seem to be good.

Although *-soo* cannot be used with a noun plus copula in the affirmative, it can be used with a noun plus copula in the negative.

Ano hito wa kangofu ja nasasoo desu.
She [that person] doesn't seem to be a nurse.

Note that -*soo* in this lesson is different from the *soo* introduced in Lesson 15. The latter follows a plain form and expresses hearsay. Compare:

Kizu wa itasoo desu.
The wound looks painful.

Kizu wa itai soo desu.
I heard the wound is painful.

3. PARTICLES

a. *To* (for quotations)

The clause particle *to* preceding the verbs "to think" or "to say" signifies the end of a quote. *To* is normally preceded by a plain form.

Rainen iryoohi wa agaru to omoimasu.
I think medical costs will go up next year.

Kono byooki wa sugu naoranai to itte imashita.
She said that this disease will not heal right away.

Yamada san ga kono kusuri wa yoku nai to itte imasu yo.
Mr. Yamada is saying that this medicine is not good.

Daijoobu da to omoimasu.
I think it's all right.

Nan "what," not *nani* is used before *to*.

Isha wa nan to itte imashita ka.
What did the doctor say?

A word or a phrase that is not part of the quoted clause can come between *to* and the main verb.

Isha ga shujutsu wa seikoo shita to itte iru n desu.
    or
Shujutsu wa seikoo shita to isha ga itte iru n desu.
The doctor is saying that the surgery was successful.

<u>*Okaasan ni*</u> *byooin no iriguchi de matte iru to osshatte kudasai.*
    or
Byooin no iriguchi de matte iru to <u>*okaasan ni*</u> *osshatte kudasai.*
Please tell your mother that I am waiting at the entrance of the hospital.

Unlike in English, the tense of the quoted clause is not affected by the tense of the main verb. Compare:

Hone ga orete iru (present tense) *to omotta n desu.*
I thought the bone was [is] broken.

Hone ga orete ita (past tense) *to omotta n desu.*
I thought the bone had been broken.

Yamada san wa otooto san ga byooki da (present tense) *to itta n desu.*
Mr. Yamada said that his younger brother was [is] sick.

Yamada san wa otooto san ga byooki datta (past tense) *to ittan desu.*
Mr. Yamada said that his younger brother had been sick.

b. *De* "within"

De used after an expression of duration means "within" or "in."

Isshuukan gurai de naoru to omoimasu.
I think it will heal in about a week.

Shujutsu wa nijuppun de owaru hazu desu.
The surgery is supposed to be over in twenty minutes.

Mikka de taiin suru koto ga dekimashita.
I was able to leave the hospital in three days.

c. *Ni* "per"

Ni "per" is used with a frequency expression.

Kusuri o ichinichi ni nido nonde kudasai.
Please take the medicine twice a day.

Isshuukan ni futsuka yakkyoku de hataraite imasu.
I work two days a week at a pharmacy.

Ichijikan ni ikutsu tsukuru koto ga dekimasu ka.
How many can you make per hour?

d. *Ni* (with *butsukeru*)

With the verb *butsukeru* "to bump, hit," the thing hit is followed by *ni*.

Iwa ni ashi o butsuketa n desu.
I bumped my leg on a rock.

Kuruma o hei ni butsuketa n desu.
I ran my car into the fence.

4. SENSEI

Although the word *sensei* means "teacher," it is also used when addressing or referring to physicians or clergy, and sometimes even for politicians or lawyers. Use *sensei* after the name instead of *san*. Use the family name, although the given or full name is possible as well. *Sensei* can also be used to address someone without using any name, whereas *san* cannot.

Sensei, gobusata shite orimasu.
Doctor, I haven't seen you for a long time.

Kochira wa Takagi sensei desu.
This is Professor Takagi.

Kyoo sensei wa oheya ni irasshaimasu ka.
Is she going to be in her room today? (talking about a teacher)

C. MOJI

Here are the *kanji* representing the larger numbers.

[20]　百　*HYAKU [-BYAKU] [-PYAKU]* hundred

[21]　千　*SEN [-ZEN]*　　　　　　thousand

[22]　万　*MAN*　　　　　　　ten thousand

STROKE ORDER

[20]　一　丁　丆　万　丆　百

[21]　ノ　二　千

[22]　一　丆　万

二百	*nihyaku*	200
三百	*sanbyaku*	300
六百	*roppyaku*	600
八百	*happyaku*	800
百九十二	*hyaku kyuujuuni*	192
二千六百四十	*nisen roppyaku yonjuu*	2,640
三千	*sanzen*	3,000
一千五百	*issen gohyaku*	1,500
or	or	

千五百	sengohyaku	
一万三千八百五十六	ichiman sanzen	13,856
	happyaku gojuuroku	

Hon 本 "book" is also used as the counter *-hon*.

[5]　本　*HON* (Lesson 16)　　　book

COUNTER *-HON*

一本	*ippon*	one (tree)
二本	*nihon*	two (trees)
三本	*sanbon*	three (trees)
百一本	*hyaku ippon*	101 (trees)

D. TANGO TO HYOOGEN

hone	bone
i	stomach
kizu	wound
kega	injury
byooki	ailment
netsu	fever
isha	physician
kangofu	nurse
yakkyoku	pharmacy
kusuri	medicine
itamidome	painkiller
hootai	bandage
rentogen	X ray
shujutsu	surgery
iryoohi	medical costs
michi	road
ogawa	brook, stream
iwa	rock
hei	fence
shokugo	after a meal
kega o suru	to get injured

nyuuin suru	to be hospitalized
taiin suru	to leave a hospital (be released)
seikoo suru	to succeed
oreru	to break
arasu	to damage
naoru	to heal
nomu	to take (medicine)
kiku	to work well, be effective
ochiru	to fall down
tateru	to build
tsukuru	to make
butsukeru	to bump, crash
nareru	to get used to
itai	painful
abunai	dangerous
iya	reluctant
fudan	usually, normally
de	and then
nen no tame ni	to make sure, for caution's sake
Gobusata shite orimasu.	I haven't kept in touch with you.

RENSHUU

A. Mark the statements T (true), F (false), or X (cannot tell) based on the dialogue.

1. *Okada san wa michi no soba no ogawa ni ochimashita.*
2. *Isha wa Okada san no ashi no rentogen o torimashita.*
3. *Okada san ga tootte ita michi wa kurakatta desu.*
4. *Okada san wa ichinichi ni ichido kusuri o nomimasu.*

B. Fill in the blanks according to the English equivalents.

1. *Otooto ga ———— o nomimashita.*
   I took the medicine my younger brother bought.
2. *Watashi no amari ———— desu.*
   It is a road I don't take often.
3. *Kore wa Suzuki san ga hataraite ———— desu.*
   This is the hospital where Ms. Suzuki is working.
4. *Watashi ga yoku ———— wa kyoo imasen deshita.*
   The nurse I know well was not there today.

C. Choose the correct form in parentheses.

Example: *Kono kusuri wa (takai/taka) soo desu.*
  I understand that this medicine is expensive.
  takai

1. *Ano heya wa (samui/samu) soo desu ne.*
   That room looks cold.
2. *Soko wa (nigiyaka da/nigiyaka) soo desu.*
   I understand that place is lively.
3. *Yuki ga (furu/furi) soo desu ne.*
   It looks like it will snow.
4. *Kono hon wa (muzukashiku nai/muzukashiku nasa) soo desu.*
   This book does not seem to be difficult.

D. The following are the first impressions of tourists visiting a town. Fill in the blanks according to the English equivalents.

1. *Michi ga ———— to omoimasu.*
   I think the roads are narrow.
2. *Byooin ga ———— to omoimasu.*
   I think the hospital is magnificent.
3. *Michi ga kurakute, ———— to omoimasu.*
   I think the roads are dark, and thus dangerous.
4. *———— ga ———— to omoimasu.*
   I think the water in the brook is clean.
5. *———— ga takusan ———— to omoimasu.*
   I think there are many pretty trees.

E. Read and translate the following:

1. 木が 十二本 あります。

2. このまちに アメリカ人が 二万三千五百人 います。

3. a. フランス人は なん人 きましたか。

   b. 二人 きました。

F. Rewrite the following numbers with Kanji. (¥=円)

1. ¥13,580
2. ¥39,800
3. ¥1,980

KARUCHAA NOOTO

For medical treatment, you can go to a large general hospital, a smaller clinic, or a private doctor's office. Many private practitioners have their offices in their homes. Since they and their families live in the community, the relationship between the doctor and the patients can become quite close and personal.

Whether you are a Japanese citizen or not, you can buy health insurance. You can join the insurance plan your employer offers, or if you are not employed, you can join the National Health Insurance. Applications can be obtained at the local government office. Of course, there are also private insurance policies available, regardless of whether or not you are employed. Medical costs are much lower than in the United States. Some critics say this is because the care in hospitals is not as good and fewer comforts are available.

In case of an emergency, call 119 for an ambulance or the fire department. The ambulance will take you to the hospital free of charge.

KOTAE

A. 1. T 2. T 3. X 4. F
B. *kureta kusuri* 2. *tooranai michi* 3. *iru byooin* 4. *shitte iru kangofu*
C. 1. *samu* 2. *nigiyaka da* 3. *furi* 4. *muzukashiku nasa*
D. 1. *semai* 2. *rippa da* 3. *abunai* 4. *Ogawa no mizu, kirei da*
5. *Kirei na ki, aru*
E. 1. *Ki ga juu nihon arimasu.* There are twelve trees. 2. *Kono machi ni amerikajin ga niman sanzen gohyakunin imasu.* There are 23,500 Americans in this town. 3. a. *Furansujin wa nannin kimashita ka.* How many French came? b. *Futari kimashita.* Two people came.
F. 1. 一万三千五百八十円 2. 三万九千八百円 3. 千九百八十円

232

DAI NIJUKKA
Lesson 20
DENWA NO KAIWA.   Telephone Conversations.

A. DAIAROOGU

KAISHA NI DENWA O KAKERU.

Mr. Toyoda is trying to reach Mr. Fujii, who is from his hometown, at his office at a company in Tokyo.

UKETSUKE: **Hái, Uematsu Shóoji desu.**

TOYODA: **Móshi moshi, jinjika ni denwa shite irú n desu ga, zutto hanashichuu ná n desu. Denwa bángoo o kakunin shitái n desu ga.**

UKETSUKE: **Hái, jinjika no bangóo wa san, yón, hachi, sán no nana, róku, roku, kyúu desu.**

TOYODA: **Dóomo. Jáa, sumimasén, tsunaide kudasái.**

SHAIN: **Hái, jinjika desu.**

TOYODA: **Móshi moshi, Fujii san to hanashitái n desu ga.**

SHAIN: **Fujii wa futari orimásu ga.**

TOYODA: **A, kachoo no Fujii san désu.**

SHAIN: **Shóoshoo omachi kudasái.**

FUJII: **Móshi moshi, Fujii désu ga.**

TOYODA: **A, Fujii san, Tóyoda desu.**

FUJII: **Konnichi wá. Móo Tookyóo Eki ni tsúita n desu ka.**

TOYODA: **Ée, tatta íma. Sochira ni goji góro ukagaitái n desu ga, íi desu ka.**

FUJII: **Ée kootsuu no bénri na tokoró desu kara, nijuppun gúrai de koraremásu yo.**

TOYODA: **Dónna tatémono desu ka.**

FUJII: **Iriguchi no dóa ga kurói tatémono na n desu. Básu o óritara, súgu miemásu yo.**

TOYODA: **Sóo desu ka. Jáa, nochihodo.**

CALLING AN OFFICE.

RECEPTIONIST: Hello, Uematsu Trading Company.

TOYODA: I'm trying to reach personnel, but the line has been busy. I would like to make sure I have the right phone number.

RECEPTIONIST: All right. The personnel department's [section's] number is 3483-7669.

TOYODA: Thanks. Could you transfer me, please?

COMPANY EMPLOYEE: Personnel.

TOYODA: I'd like to speak to Mr. Fujii.

COMPANY EMPLOYEE: There are two Fujiis here.

TOYODA: Oh, I'd like to speak to the Mr. Fujii who's the section manager.

COMPANY EMPLOYEE: Just a moment.

FUJII: Hello, Fujii speaking.

TOYODA: Hello, Mr. Fujii, this is Toyoda.

FUJII: Hi, how are you? Are you at the Tokyo Station already [Have you arrived at the Tokyo Station already]?

TOYODA: Yes, I arrived just now. I would like to come over to your office around five o'clock. Is that okay?

FUJII: Sure. We are conveniently located, so you can get here in twenty minutes.

TOYODA: What does the building look like?

FUJII: The building has a black entrance door. [It's a building whose entrance door is black.] When you get off the bus, you'll see it right away.

TOYODA: Really? Well then, I'll see you later on.

B. BUNPOO TO YOOHOO

1. RELATIVE CLAUSES WITH *I*-ADJECTIVES

Relative clauses ending in *i*-adjectives follow the rules already discussed (see Lesson 19, B1).

[Iriguchi no doa ga kuroi] tatemono na n desu.
It's a building with a black entrance door. [It's a building (whose entrance door is black.)]

234

[Otenki no yoku nai] hi ga tsuzukimashita.
> The bad weather continued. [The days (when the weather is bad) continued.]

2. RELATIVE CLAUSES WITH THE COPULA

The rules of relative clauses with verbs and *i*-adjectives also apply to relative clauses with the copula.

a. A *na*-adjective plus the copula

In the present affirmative, the copula *da* (plain form) in the relative clause changes to *na*.

[Kootsuu no benri na] tokoro desu.
> It is a place [where transportation is convenient].

[Me no kirei na] hito desu ne.
> She has beautiful eyes. [She is a person (whose eyes are beautiful.)]

[Gyuunyuu ga suki ja nai] hito wa takusan imasu.
> There are many people [who do not like milk].

b. A noun plus the copula

In the present affirmative, the copula *da* in the relative clause changes to *no*.

[Kachoo no Fujii san] desu.
> It is Mr. Fujii, [(who is) the section manager].

A: *Dono Tanaka san desu ka.*
> Which Tanaka are you referring to?

B: *[Isha no] Tanaka san desu.*
> I am referring to Ms. Tanaka [who is a doctor].

Koko wa [mae oshiro datta] tokoro desu.
> This place used to be a castle. [This is a place (that was a castle before.)]

3. POTENTIAL VERBS: *-(RAR)ERU* "TO BE ABLE TO"

The structure "dictionary form + *koto ga dekiru*" expresses ability and possibility (see Lesson 13, B5).

Iku koto ga dekimasu.
> I can go.

Another way to express ability and possibility is to use the potential form of the verb, which is more common than *koto ga dekiru*. Potential verbs are all vowel verbs, so they conjugate just like other vowel verbs.

a. Consonant verbs

The final *-u* of the dictionary form is replaced by *-eru*.

iku	→	*ikeru*	can go
kau	→	*kaeru*	can buy
hanasu	→	*hanaseru*	can speak
matsu	→	*materu (tse → te)*	can wait

Doko de terehon kaado o kaemasu ka.
Where can we buy telephone cards?

Suzuki san wa doitsugo o hanaseru n desu.
Ms. Suzuki can speak German.

b. Vowel verbs

The final *-ru* of the dictionary form is replaced by *-rareru*.

taberu	→	*taberareru*	can eat
deru	→	*derareru*	can leave
neru	→	*nerareru*	can sleep

Goji ni deraremasu.
I can leave at five o'clock.

Kyoo amari taberarenai n desu.
I can't eat much today.

Often *-ra* is dropped and you may hear, for example, *tabereru* instead of *taberareru*. Although both forms are widely used, the standard form is *taberareru*.

c. Irregular verbs

suru	→	*dekiru*	can do
kuru	→	*korareru* or *koreru*	can come

236

Nijuppun gurai de koraremasu.
  You can come in about twenty minutes.

Kyoo zenzen benkyoo dekinakatta n desu.
  I couldn't study at all today.

For *miru* "to see," and *kiku* "to hear," there are two potential forms.

miru	→	*mirareru*	can see, can watch, can look
		mieru	can see (is visible)
kiku	→	*kikeru*	can hear, can listen
		kikoeru	can hear (is audible)

Mieru and *kikoeru* do not involve voluntary actions. As with *dekiru* "can do" (see Lesson 6, C6), the particle *o* cannot be used. Use *ga* instead.

Ano kado o magattara, ookii tatemono ga miemasu.
  When you turn that corner, you can see a big building.

Denwa no beru ga kikoemasen deshita.
  I could not hear the telephone ringing. (The ring of the telephone was not audible.)

Koko de shokuji ga dekimasu ka.
  Can we eat here?

With other potential verbs, *ga* may be used instead of *o*.

Dono kooshuu denwa de kokusai denwa o/ga kakeraremasu ka.
  With which public phone can I make an international call?

Denwa bangoo o/ga zenzen oboeraremasen.
  I can't memorize the phone numbers at all.

Kono rabo de nihongo no teepu o/ga kikemasu.
  You can listen to Japanese language tapes in this lab.

Ano bijutsukan de yuumei na e o/ga takusan miraremasu.
  You can see many famous pictures in that museum.

There are no potential verbs for *aru* "to exist, have," *kureru* "to give," and *wakaru* "to understand."

4. PARTICLES

a. *Ni* (with *tsuku*)

With the verb *tsuku* "to arrive," the location arrived at is followed by *ni*.

Ima Tookyoo Eki ni tsuita n desu.
I arrived at the Tokyo Station a while ago.

Kesa shichiji ni kaisha ni tsukimashita.
I arrived at the company at seven this morning.

b. *Ni* (with recipient of phone call)

With the verb meaning "to phone" (*denwa (o) suru, denwa o kakeru*), the recipient of the call is followed by *ni*.

Tomodachi ni denwa o kakemashita.
I called my friend.

Ashita boku no uchi ni denwa shite kudasai.
Please call my house tomorrow.

c. *Ga* ("but," "and," and softener)

When *ga* is used as a clause particle, it is similar to *kedo* ("but," "and"). They both can also serve as a softener at the end of a sentence. *Ga* is more formal than *kedo*.

Denwa bangoo o kakunin shitai n desu ga.
I want to confirm the phone number.

Moshi moshi, Fujii desu ga.
Hello, this is Fujii.

Ofisu ni denwa shite iru n desu ga, tsunagaranai n desu.
I am trying to call the office, but the call isn't going through.

Kinoo isha ni denwa shita n desu ga, kodomo no kega wa sugu naoru soo desu.
Yesterday I called the doctor, and I learned that my child's injury will heal soon.

d. *No* (in a phone number)

When you provide a phone number, the symbol "-" between numbers is pronounced as *no*.

San, yon, hachi, san no nana, nana, roku, kyuu
3483-7769

Watashi no denwa bangoo wa zero, san no san, nana, ichi, nana no zero, kyuu, hachi, yon desu.
My phone number is 03-3717-0984.

5. HONORIFIC VERBS

a. *Ukagau*

The non-honorific equivalent of the humble honorific verb *ukagau* is *iku* "to go," *kuru* "to come," or *kiku* "to hear, to listen, to ask."

Goji goro ni ukagaimasu.
I will come around five o'clock.

Kinoo sensei no otaku ni ukagaimashita.
I went to the teacher's house yesterday.

Hai, moo ukagaimashita.
Yes, I heard that already.

Buchoo ni denwa o kakete, ukagatta n desu.
I called the department head and asked him.

b. *Oru*

The non-honorific equivalent of the humble hororific verb *oru* is *iru* "to be."

Fujii wa futari orimasu.
There are two Fujiis.

Mainichi rokuji goro made ofisu ni orimasu.
I am in my office until around six o'clock every day.

Only the normal forms of *oru* are used. Other forms such as the plain forms, the TE and TARA forms, are avoided in standard Japanese.

Otooto wa uchi ni iru (not *oru*) *hazu desu.*
I expect my younger brother to be home.

6. OMITTING THE HONORIFIC *SAN*

When referring to someone in your in-group, such as a colleague at work, omit *san* when you talk to an outsider. In the dialogue, for example, when talking to Mr. Toyoda, an outsider, on the phone, the company employee uses the name Fujii without *san* because she is referring to people in her own workplace.

Fujii wa futari orimasu.
There are two Fujiis.

Tanaka wa ima orimasen ga.
Tanaka is not in now.

When, however, both the addressee and the person referred to are in your workplace, *san* should be used.

Kachoo, Suzuki san wa kyoo yasumu soo desu.
Kachoo, I heard Ms. Suzuki will be absent today.

When you refer to a younger member of your family, *san* or its equivalent* may also be omitted.

Hideko wa tomodachi no uchi e itta n desu.
Hideko went to her friend's house.

This sentence might be uttered by a mother referring to her daughter when speaking to her husband. Unlike at work, even when both the speaker and the addressee are in the same family, *san* or its equivalent can be omitted.

When referring to an older member of your family, use the kinship term (see Lesson 10, C1).

C. MOJI

Here are seven additional *kanji* characters.

[23]	日	*NICHI, ka, hi [-bi]*	day, sun(light)
		NI	(for NIHON "Japan" 日本)
[24]	今	*KON,* ima	now
[25]	出	*de(ru), de(kakeru)*	to go out, to leave (a place)
[26]	思	*omo(u)*	to think
[27]	月	*GATSU*	month
[28]	時	*JI*	time, o'clock
[29]	分	*FUN[-PUN]*	minute

* One of the equivalents of *san* is *chan. Chan* is used for a small child, or a grown-up whom the speaker has known since he or she was small.

STROKE ORDER

[23]	丨 冂 月 日
[24]	丿 八 今 今
[25]	丨 屮 中 出 出
[26]	丶 冂 皿 冊 田 甲 思 思
[27]	丿 刀 月 月
[28]	日 日― 旪 昧 昨 時 時
[29]	丿 八 分 分

二十三日	*nijuusannichi*	23d day of the month, 23 days
二日	*futsuka*	2d, 2 days
三日	*mikka*	3d, 3 days
四日	*yokka*	4th, 4 days
五日	*itsuka*	5th, 5 days
六日	*muika*	6th, 6 days
七日	*nanoka*	7th, 7 days
八日	*yooka*	8th, 8 days
九日	*kokonoka*	9th, 9 days
十日	*tooka*	10th, 10 days
三月十一日	*sangatsu juu ichinichi*	March 11

あめが ふる 日
ame ga furu hi
  rainy day

たんじょう日
tanjoobi
  birthday

日が よく あたります。
Hi ga yoku atarimasu.
  The sun shines brightly.

241

今 行きます。
Ima ikimasu.
   I am going now.

今日は。
Konnichi wa.
   Hello.

きのう 出かけました。
Kinoo dekakemashita.
   I went out yesterday.

でんしゃは もう 出ました。
Densha wa moo demashita.
   The train left already.

だいじょうぶだと 思います。
Daijoobu da to omoimasu.
   I think it will be all right.

三時	*sanji*	3 o'clock
五分	*gofun*	5 minutes
一分	*ippun*	1 minute
三分	*sanpun*	3 minutes
四時十五分	*yoji juu gofun*	4:15
九時三十分	*kuji sanjuppun*	9:30

The following are irregular readings.

一日	*tsuitachi*	1st day of the month
cf. 一日	*ichinichi*	1 day
二十日	*hatsuka*	20th day of the month, 20 days
今日	*kyoo*	today

D. TANGO TO HYOOGEN

bangoo	number
denwa bangoo	phone number
terehon kaado	telephone card (prepaid)
beru	ring, bell
kooshuu denwa	public phone
kokusai denwa	international call
hanashichuu	The line's busy.
kootsuu	traffic
kachoo	section manager
buchoo	department head
shain	company employee
uketsuke	reception desk, receptionist
jinjika	personnel department
ofisu	office
doa	door
hi	day
bijutsukan	museum
rabo	language lab
teepu	tape
doitsugo	German (language)
otaku	house (somebody else's)
kakunin suru	to confirm
tsunagaru	to be connected, go through
tsunagu	to connect
tsuzuku	to continue
kakeru	to call (on the phone)
mieru	to be visible
kikoeru	to be audible
yasumu	to be absent
oboeru	to memorize, learn
ukagau	to go, come, hear, listen, ask (honorific)
orimasu	to be (honorific)
nochihodo	later on
zutto	continuously
shooshoo	a little, for a while
moshi moshi	hello (on the phone)
chan	affectionate form of *san*

A. Answer the following questions based on the dialogue.

1. *Fujii san no tsutomete iru kaisha no namae wa nan desu ka.*
2. *Sono kaisha no tatemono wa donna tatemono desu ka.*
3. *Toyoda san wa nanji goro Fujii san no kaisha ni ikimasu ka.*
4. *Tookyoo Eki kara Fujii san no kaisha made dono gurai kakarimasu ka.*

B. Fill in the blanks according to the English in parentheses.

1. *Donna kissaten desu ka.*
   Koohii no _____ kissaten desu. (delicious)
2. *Donna kaisha desu ka.*
   _____ kaisha desu. (old and famous)
3. *Dono Maeda san desu ka.*
   _____ Maeda san desu. (department head)
4. *Donna heya desu ka.*
   Mado ga _____ heya desu. (big)

C. Rewrite the sentences using potential verbs.

1. *Koko de kippu o kau koto ga dekimasu.*
2. *Nihongo no shinbun o yomu koto ga dekimasu ka.*
3. *Zenzen oyogu koto ga dekimasen.*
4. *Kinoo kuru koto ga dekinakatta n desu.*

D. Fill in the blanks with particles, and translate the sentences.

1. *Itsu ofisu _____ denwa shita n desu ka.*
2. *Doa _____ kuruma o butsuketa n desu.*
3. *Niji _____ Oosaka _____ tsukimashita.*
4. *Denwa _____ kakete mimashita _____, tsunagarimasen deshita.*

E. Write the entire dialogue from this lesson in Japanese characters, using *kanji* that you have already learned.

KARUCHAA NOOTO

When using a public phone, you need at least a ten-yen coin, which pays for a local call of one minute. You will hear a warning chime when your time is running out. If you do not put in more coins, the line is cut off. Unused coins are returned after you hang up. You can also use a telephone card, which can be purchased from a vending machine or at a convenience store for a fixed value. Telephone cards can be customized, for example, by putting a picture on them. Some companies even use them as marketing tools.

It allows you to make calls until the value of your card is exhausted.

Telephone cards may be used for domestic and international calls, but they are particularly handy for international calls, which are quite expensive. Green public phones with a golden panel can be used for international calls. To call Japan from the United States, dial 011-81 plus the number, deleting the first zero (0) of the area code. To call the United States from Japan, one possible way is to dial 0041-1 plus the number.

KOTAE

A. 1. *Uematsu Shooji desu.* 2. *Iriguchi no doa ga kuroi tatemono desu.*
3. *Goji goro ikimasu.* 4. *Nijuppun gurai kakarimasu.*
B. 1. *oishii* 2. *furukute, yuumei na* 3. *buchoo no* 4. *ookii*
C. 1. *Koko de kippu ga/o kaemasu.* 2. *Nihongo no shinbun ga/o yome masu ka.* 3. *Zenzen oyogemasen.* 4. *Kinoo korarenakatta/korenakatta n desu.*
D. 1. *ni* When did you call the office? 2. *ni* I hit the door with the car.
3. *ni, ni* I arrived in Osaka at 2:00. 4. *o, ga/kedo* I tried to call, but I couldn't get through.
E. はい、うえまつ しょうじです。

　もしもし、じんじかに でんわ しているんですが、ずっと
　　はなしちゅうなんです。

　でんわばんごうを かくにん したいんですが。

　はい、じんじかの ばんごうは、三、四、八、三、の 七、六、六、
　　九です。*

　どうも、じゃあ、すみません、つないで ください。

　はい、じんじかです。

　もしもし、ふじいさんと はなしたいんですが。

　ふじいは 二人 おりますが。

　あ、かちょうの ふじいさんです。

　しょうしょう おまちください。

　もしもし ふじいですが。

　あ、ふじいさん、とよだです。

　今日は。(*Konnichi wa.*) もう とうきょうえきに ついたんですか。

　ええ、たった 今。そちらに 五時ごろ うかがいたいんですが、
　　いいですか。

　ええ、こうつうの べんりな ところですから、二十分ぐらいで
　　こられますよ。

　どんな たてものですか。

　いりぐちの ドアが くろい たてものなんです。バスを おりたら、
　　すぐ みえますよ。

　そうですか。じゃあ、のちほど。

*Note that when written horizontally, phone numbers are usually written in Arabic numerals rather than in *kanji*: 3483-7669.

FUKUSHUU 4

A. Choose from the following words to fill in the blanks.

soo   irasshaimasen   gobusata   haha   otaku   orimasen
okaasan   Tanaka san   shibaraku

    1: *Moshi moshi, Tanaka Hideko san no _____ desu ka.*
    2: *Hai _____ desu. Demo Hideko wa ima _____ ga.*
    3: *Hideko san no _____ desu ka. Suzuki desu.*
    4: *A Suzuki san, _____ shite orimasu.*

B. Fill in the blanks with the appropriate form of the word given in parentheses.

    1. *Eki ni _____ ra, denwa shimasu.   (tsuku)*
    2. *Shokuji o _____ kara, _____ tsumori desu.   (suru, dekakeru)*
    3. *Ano heya wa _____ te, akarui desu.   (hiroi)*
    4. *Ashita yuki ga _____ to omoimasu.   (furu)*

C. Fill in the blanks according to the English equivalents.

    1. *Isshuukan _____ ichido haha _____ denwa o kakeru n desu.*
        I call my mother once a week.
    2. *Shiyakusho made juppun _____ ikemasu.*
        You can reach city hall in ten minutes.
    3. *Denwa bangoo wa san, nana, roku _____ yon, yon, ichi zero desu.*
        My phone number is 376-4410.
    4. *Ano resutoran de sandoitchi _____ tabemashoo ka.*
        Should we have sandwiches or something at that restaurant?

D. Which word does not fit in the group?

Example: *Yamada*
         Suzuki
         Tanaka
         <u>*uchi*</u>
         Hayashi

1	2	3	4
kaisha	*chikatetsu*	*mimi*	*shingoo*
byooin	*densha*	*me*	*hidari*
kusuri	*Shinkansen*	*inaka*	*higashi*
shiyakusho	*hikooki*	*karada*	*nishi*
biyooin	*juutakuchi*	*ashi*	*migi*

E. Answer the following questions, according to the English cues.

Example: *Donna michi desu ka.*
    narrow and dangerous
    Semakute, abunai michi desu.

1. *Donna kaisha desu ka.*
    a large and famous company
2. *Donna uchi desu ka.*
    the house with a large garden [the house whose garden is large]
3. *Soko kara nani ga miemasu ka.*
    the museum that my mother likes
4. *Dono isha desu ka.*
    the Japanese doctor [the doctor who is Japanese]

F. Combine the two sentences following the cues in parentheses, and then translate.

1. *Shigoto ga owarimashita. Eiga o mi ni ikimashita.* (Use TE *kara*)
2. *Uchi ni modorimashita. Tomodachi ga matte imashita.* (Use TARA)
3. *Kuruma ga koshoo shimashita. Sanji made ni ikemasen deshita.* (Use TE)
4. *Ane wa kangofu desu. Imooto wa jaanarisuto desu.* (Use TE)

G. When speaking with some of her friends about another friend's new home, Ms. Sakai gives the following information.

Eki kara aruite shi-gofun de ikeru n desu.
Yoofuu no uchi na n desu kedo, tatami no heya mo futatsu aru n desu.
Ima ga totemo hirokute, akarui n desu.
Benrisoo na dainingu kitchin na n desu.
Ookikute kowasoo na inu ga iru n desu.

Mark the statements T (true), F (false), or X (cannot tell) based on the above description.

1. There are two bedrooms.
2. The house is conveniently located within a fifteen-minute walk from the station.
3. The house is Western-style, but it has Japanese features, too.
4. They have a big dog that barks a lot.
5. The living room faces south.
6. The dine-in kitchen appears to be inconvenient to use.

H. Write the *kanji* that are indicated by the *hiragana* below the parentheses, and then translate the sentences.

1. (   ) まで まっていました。

    しちじじゅうごふん

2. この(   ) は (   ) えんです。

    ほん   ろくせんさんびゃく

3. (   ) とも (   ) (   ) かけているんです。

   ふたり   いま   で

4. (   ) に (   ) くつもりです。

   よっか   い

KOTAE

A. 1. *otaku* 2. *soo* 3. *orimasen* 4. *okaasan* 5. *gobusata*
B. 1. *tsuita* 2. *shite, dekakeru* 3. *hiroku* 4. *furu*
C. 1. *ni, ni* 2. *de* 3. *no* 4. *demo*
D. 1. *kusuri* 2. *juutakuchi* 3. *inaka* 4. *shingoo*
E. 1. *Ookikute, yuumei na kaisha desu.* 2. *Niwa ga/no ookii uchi desu.*
3. *Haha ga/no suki na bijutsukan ga miemasu.* 4. *Nihonjin no isha desu.*
F. 1. *Shigoto ga owatte kara, eiga o mi ni ikimashita.* I went to see a movie after I finished my work. 2. *Uchi ni modottara, tomodachi ga matte imashita.* When I got home, my friend was waiting. 3. *Kuruma ga koshoo shite, sanji made ni ikemasen deshita.* My car broke down, so I was not able to go by three o'clock. 4. *Ane wa kangofu de, imooto wa jaanarisuto desu.* My older sister is a nurse, and my younger sister is a journalist.
G. 1. X 2. F 3. T 4. X 5. X 6. F
H. 1. 七時十五分 I was waiting until 7:15. 2. 本/六千三百 This book is 6,300 yen. 3. 二人/今/出 Both of them are out now. 4. 四日/行 I plan to go there on the fourth.

たしろさん、おげんきですか。

　シカゴは 今 とても あついです。とうきょうは どうですか。わたしは まい日 いそがしいですが、げんきで、がんばっています。

　なつやすみは らいしゅう はじまります[1]。ことしの なつは ホテルで はたらく つもりです。そのホテルは わたしの だいがく の そばに あって、うちから バスで 10分で 行く ことが できます。古いですが、おおきくて、りっぱな ホテルです。ともだちが まえ そこで はたらいたことが あるのですが、とても おもしろかった そうです。

　らいねんの なつ 日本に 行きたいと 思っています。日本の いろいろな ところを けんぶつしたいです。だから、今 日本ごを べんきょうしています。かんじを ならうのは たいへんですが、たのしいです。このあいだ[2]、かんじの さんこうしょ[3]を かいまし た。とても べんりで、いつも つかっています。テープも まいばん きいています。

　たしろさんの ごかぞくも みなさん おげんきですか。よろしく おつたえください[4]。では、また。　　　　　　　　　さようなら
5月20日

　　　　　　　　　　　　　　　　　　　　ジェーンハリス

たしろゆみこさま

TANGO TO HYOOGEN

1. はじまる		to begin
2. このあいだ		the other day
3. さんこうしょ		reference book
4. よろしくおつたえください。		Please say hello to them.

DAI NIJUU IKKA
Lesson 21
OSHOOGATSU.   New Year.

A. DAIAROOGU

Moo sugu oshoogatsu.

Ms. Tamura and Ms. Sagawa are colleagues taking calligraphy lessons
from Ueno *sensei*. They run into each other on the street.

TAMURA: Konnichi wá. Áme ga furisóo de, sámuku narimáshita
ne.

SAGAWA: Ée, démo gantan ní wa oténki ga yóku náru soo desu yo.

TAMURA: Sáa, dóo deshoo. Tenkiyóhoo wa yóku hazuremásu
kara ne.

SAGAWA: Oshoogatsu uchi ni irassháru n deshoo.

TAMURA: Iie, kono oshoogatsu wa uchi ni inái n desu. Gantan ni
Yokohama no áni no uchí ni ikú n desu. Shinseki ga takusan
atsumáru hazu désu kara, nigíyaka na oshoogatsu ni náru to
omoimásu.

SAGAWA: Íi desu née.

TAMURA: Sore kara, Kamakura no otto no ryóoshin no uchí e mo
itte, soko ni mikka máde iru tsumori ná n desu.

SAGAWA: Jáa, yokka góro Úeno senséi no otaku ni onénshi ni ikimasén ka.

TAMURA: Sóo desu ne. Úeno senséi no otaku wa Ikebúkuro
desu ne.

SAGAWA: Iie, Ogikubo deshóo. Tashikámete mimásu kedo.

TAMURA: Sóo desu ka. Jáa, mata nochihodo.

SAGAWA: Ée. Yoi otoshi o.

TAMURA: Hái, dóomo. Yoi otoshi o.

THE NEW YEAR IS COMING.

TAMURA: Hi. It looks like it will rain and has gotten cold.

SAGAWA: Yes. But I heard the weather will be [get] good on January first.

TAMURA: I wonder. Weather forecasts are often wrong.

SAGAWA: You're staying home for the New Year's holidays, aren't you?

TAMURA: No, we're going to my older brother's house in Yokohama on January first. Many of my relatives will be gathering there, so I think it will be a lively New Year.

SAGAWA: How nice!

TAMURA: Then we're going to my husband's parents' house, as well. We're planning to stay there until the third.

SAGAWA: Well then, why don't we go to Ueno *sensei*'s house around the fourth to make a New Year call?

TAMURA: Yes, I would like to. Ueno *sensei*'s house is in Ikebukuro, isn't it?

SAGAWA: No, I think it's in Ogikubo. I'll check her address.

TAMURA: Yes, please do. I'll talk to you later.

SAGAWA: Yes. Have a happy New Year.

TAMURA: Yes, thanks. Have a happy New Year.

B. BUNPOO TO YOOHOO

1. *NARU* "TO BECOME"

Naru "to become" is used in the following ways.

a. With an *i*-adjective

The KU form of an *i*-adjective precedes *naru*.

Samuku narimashita.
It has gotten cold.

Otenki ga yoku naru soo desu yo.
I heard the weather will get better [good].

Oshoogatsu ga chikazuite, isogashiku narimashita.
As the New Year has gotten closer, I have become busy.

b. With a noun or a *na*-adjective

The particle *ni* precedes *naru*.

*Shinseki ga takusan atsumaru hazu desu kara, nigiyaka na oshoogatsu ni
naru to omoimasu.*
　　Many of my relatives will gather there, so I think it will be [become] a
　　lively New Year.

Shodoo no sensei ni naritai n desu.
　　I want to become a calligraphy teacher.

Otona ni natte kara, osechi ryoori ga suki ni narimashita.
　　Once I became an adult, I came to like [became fond of] the type of
　　food served at New Year's.

2. *DESU* WITH LOCATION

Recall that the verbs *aru* and *iru*, which mean "to exist," are used with
a location noun followed by the particle *ni* (see Lesson 8, C1).

Gakkoo wa Koobe ni arimasu.
　　The school is in Kobe.

Fujii san wa ima toshokan ni imasu.
　　Mr. Fujii is at the library now.

Ni arimasu and *ni imasu* can be replaced by *desu*. Therefore, the sentences above can be changed to:

Gakkoo wa Koobe desu.
　　The school is in Kobe.

Fujii san wa ima toshokan desu.
　　Mr. Fujii is in the library now.

Here are more examples.

Ueno sensei no otaku wa Ogikubo ni arimasu.
Ueno sensei no otaku wa Ogikubo desu.
　　Ueno *sensei*'s house is in Ogikubo.

Ryooshin wa ima Yokohama ni imasu.
Ryooshin wa ima Yokohama desu.
　　My parents are in Yokohama.

3. DESHOO

Deshoo, derived from *desu*, means "probably" and is also used to form a tag question similar to *ne*. Usually the context decides its meaning.

Note that the form used immediately before *deshoo* is always a plain form, except in highly polite speech.

Imooto wa ashita kuru deshoo.
My younger sister will probably come tomorrow.

Ano hito wa ima paatii no junbi de isogashii deshoo.
He is probably busy now with preparations for the party.

Kyonen no gantan wa nichiyoobi datta deshoo.
The first of January was Sunday last year, wasn't it?

With a *na*-adjective and a noun in the present affirmative, the plain form of the copula *da* is deleted.

Ryooshin no uchi wa ima shizuka deshoo.
My parents' house is probably quiet now.

Kyoo wa imootosan no otanjoobi deshoo.
Today is your younger sister's birthday, isn't it?

Desu in the explanatory predicate (*n/no desu*) can be changed to *deshoo*.

Oshoogatsu uchi ni irassharu n deshoo.
You are going to be home for the New Year, aren't you?

Koobe Daigaku no natsuyasumi wa moo hajimatta n deshoo.
The summer break at Kobe University already started, didn't it?

Otaku wa itsumo shizuka na n deshoo.
Your house is always quiet, isn't it?

When *deshoo* is used with a question word, the sentence implies "I/we wonder." The sentence particle *ka* is optional.

Otenki ga yoku naru soo desu yo.
I heard the weather will get better.

Saa, doo deshoo.
Well, I wonder how it will be.

Moo omochi ga zenzen arimasen.
There are no rice cakes anymore.

Dare ga tabeta n deshoo.
    I wonder who ate them.

    Since *deshoo* is more indirect than *desu*, use *deshoo* when asking a more
    polite question. Compare:

Ima nanji desu ka.
    What time is it now?

Ima nanji deshoo ka.
    What time is it now? (I wonder what time it is now.)

4. SUMMARY OF *NA*-ADJECTIVES AND NOUNS IN THE PRESENT AFFIRMATIVE

When used with a *na*-adjective or a noun, the present affirmative
copula behaves in four different ways depending on the different sentence structures, while the other forms (e.g., present negative) behave
regularly. The following shows the four different ways (types), using
examples whose structures you have learned already.

TYPE I:

Both *na*-adjectives and nouns are followed by *da*.

    Before *soo desu* "hearsay":

Ano e wa yuumei da soo desu.
    I heard that picture is famous.

Yamada san no oneesan wa shodoo no sensei da soo desu.
    I heard Mr. Yamada's older sister is a calligraphy teacher.

    Before *to* with *omou* "to think," "to say," etc.:

Buraun san mo ozooni ga suki da to omoimasu.
    I think Ms. Brown also likes *ozooni* [soup with rice cakes].

Kore wa omoshiroi eiga da to itte imashita yo.
    She said that this is an interesting movie.

Na-adjectives are followed by *na* and nouns are followed by *no* in relative clauses.

Kore wa chichi no suki na okashi desu.
These are the sweets which my father likes.

Bengoshi no Nakamura san ga soo itte imashita.
Ms. Nakamura, who is a lawyer, said so.

TYPE III:

Both *na*-adjectives and nouns are followed by *na*.

In an explanatory predicate *(n desu/no desu):*

Maeda san wa osechi ryoori o tsukuru no ga joozu na n desu.
Ms. Maeda is good at making the foods served at New Year.

Kore wa sobo ga kureta kimono na n desu.
This is the kimono my grandmother gave me.

TYPE IV:

Neither *na*-adjectives nor nouns are followed by the copula. The copula is deleted.

Before *deshoo*:

Suzuki san wa ima hima deshoo.
Ms. Suzuki is not busy now, right?

Kore wa Suzuki san no kaban deshoo.
This is Ms. Suzuki's bag, isn't it?

Of course there are more examples of each of these four types, which will be discussed in later lessons. Whenever they are, please consult this section for reference.

5. SUMMARY OF PLAIN FORM STRUCTURES

You have seen sentence structures where plain forms of verbs, *i*-adjectives, the copula with *na*-adjectives, and the copula with nouns are used. Let's use *deshoo* in the summary of plain forms.

	PRESENT AFF.	PRESENT NEG.	PAST AFF.	PAST NEG.
VERB	*Iku deshoo.* He probably will go.	*Ikanai deshoo.* He probably will not go.	*Itta deshoo.* He probably went.	*Ikanakatta deshoo.* He probably did not go.
I-ADJECTIVE	*Oishi i deshoo.* It probably is tasty.	*Oishi kunai deshoo.* It probably is not tasty.	*Oishi katta deshoo.* It probably was tasty.	*Oishi kunakatta deshoo.* It probably was not tasty.
NA-ADJECTIVE PLUS COPULA	*Shizuka ø deshoo.* It probably is quiet.	*Shizuka ja/de (wa) nai deshoo.* It probably is not quiet.	*Shizuka datta deshoo.* It probably was quiet.	*Shizuka ja/de (wa) nakatta deshoo.* It probably was not quiet.
NOUN PLUS COPULA	*Ii otenki ø deshoo.* It probably is good weather.	*Ii otenki ja/de (wa) nai deshoo.* It probably is not good weather.	*Ii otenki datta deshoo.* It probably was good weather.	*Ii otenki ja/de (wa) nakatta deshoo.* It probably was not good weather.

As shown in B4 of this lesson, there are four types of present affirmative copula with *na*-adjectives and nouns. *Deshoo* is Type IV.

6. MULTIPLE PARTICLES

There are cases where more than one particle can be used.* The cases with *mo* and with *wa* are introduced here. Both of them function as the second element of multiple particle structures.

a. With *mo* "also"

First, review the usage of *mo* as a single particle.

   Mo replaces *wa* or *ga*.

Yamada san wa/ga kimashita.
   Mr. Yamada came.

Yamada san mo kimashita.
   Mr. Yamada came, also.

   Mo replaces *o*.

Yamada san wa omochi o tabemashita.
   Mr. Yamada ate rice cakes.

Yamada san wa omochi mo tabemashita.
   Mr. Yamada ate rice cakes, also [as well as something else].

   Mo is added. (*Mo* replaces ø [= no particle].)

Ashita ø samui deshoo. (no particle after *Ashita*)
   It probably will be cold tomorrow.

Ashita mo samui deshoo.
   It probably will be cold tomorrow, also.

Thus, *mo* replaces the particles *wa, ga, o*, or is used where no particles were used before. However, *mo* forms a multiple particle with other particles, such as *e, ni,* or *kara: e mo, ni mo, kara mo*. Compare:

Otto no ryooshin no uchi e itte, mikka made iru tsumori desu.
   We are planning to go to my parents-in-law's house and stay there until the third.

Otto no ryooshin no uchi e mo itte, mikka made iru tsumori desu.
   We are planning to go to my parents-in-law's house, also, [as well as somewhere else] and stay there until the third.

---

* Although there are cases where three particles are clustered, we will discuss only double particles.

257

Tanaka san ni mo iimashita.
I talked to Ms. Tanaka, as well [in addition to someone else].

Fukuyama san kara mo nengajoo o moraimashita.
I received a New Year card from Mr. Fukuyama, as well [as well as from someone else].

b. With *wa*

Just like *mo, wa* can replace *ga, o,* or no particle. *Wa* is used as a topic marker or to imply contrast on top of the meaning of topic (see Lesson 13, B7).

Hashimoto san ga uchi e kaerimashita.
Ms. Hashimoto went home. (*Hashimoto san* is emphasized.)

Hashimoto san wa uchi e kaerimashita.
Ms. Hashimoto went home. (*Hashimoto san* is not emphasized.)

Nengajoo o moo kakimashita ka.
Did you write your New Year cards already?

Nengajoo wa moo kakimashita ka.
Regarding New Year cards, did you write them already?

Kyoo atatakakatta desu. (no particle after *Kyoo*)
It was warm today.

Kyoo wa atatakakatta desu.
[Regarding] today, it was warm.

However, with other particles, *wa* forms a multiple particle translated as "as for/regarding." In addition, it can imply contrast. Compare:

Oomisoka ni otenki ga yoku naru soo desu yo.
I heard the weather will get better on December thirty-first.

Oomisoka ni wa otenki ga yoku naru soo desu yo.
[As for] on December thirty-first, I heard the weather will get better.

Takashi chan ni wa tako o agemashita ga, Haruo chan ni wa karuta o age-mashita.
I gave a kite to Takashi, but I gave a set of *karuta* [Japanese playing cards] to Haruo.

Tanaka san no otaku de wa oshoogatsu ni itsumo karutakai o suru soo desu.
I heard that in Ms. Tanaka's house they always have a *karuta* party for the New Year.

Ikebukuro e wa basu de ikimashita.
I went to Ikebukuro by bus.

C. MOJI

From now on, the dialogue in the beginning of each lesson will be reprinted in Japanese characters in the MOJI section so you can practice *kana* and *kanji*. Note that quotation marks in Japanese are written 「　。」.

1. DIALOGUE

たむら　　「今日は。雨が ふりそうで、さむく なりましたね。」

さがわ　　「ええ、でも がんたんには　お天気が よくなる
　　　　　　そうですよ。」

たむら　　「さあ、どうでしょう。天気よほうは よく はずれます
　　　　　　からね。」

さがわ　　「お正月 うちに いらっしゃるんでしょう。」

たむら　　「いいえ、この お正月は うちに いないんです。
　　　　　　がんたんに よこはまの あにの うちに 行くんです。
　　　　　　しんせきが たくさん あつまる はずですから、
　　　　　　にぎやかな お正月に なると 思います。」

さがわ　　「いいですねえ。」

たむら　　「それから、かまくらの おっとの りょうしんの うちへ
　　　　　　も 行って、そこに 三日まで いるつもりなんです。」

さがわ　　「じゃあ、四日ごろ うえの先生の おたくに おねんしに
　　　　　　行きませんか。」

たむら　　「そうですね。うえの先生の おたくは いけぶくろですね。」

さがわ　　「いいえ、おぎくぼでしょう。たしかめて みますけど。」

たむら　　「そうですか。じゃあ、また のちほど。」

さがわ　　「ええ、よい おとしを。」

たむら　　「はい、どうも。よい おとしを。」

2. *HIRAGANA*

As mentioned in Lesson 6, the second *o* of *oo*, usually written as *u* う, is written as *o* お in some words. In addition to the words listed in Lesson 6, *oomisoka* is written this way.

oomisoka	December 31st	おおみそか

3. NEW *KANJI*

The new *kanji* characters in this lesson are:

[30]	雨	*ame*	rain
[31]	天	*TEN*	heaven, sky
[32]	気	*KI*	spirit, energy
[33]	先	*SEN*	previous, ahead
[34]	生	*SEI*	life, birth, person
[35]	正	*SHOO*	right, correct e.g. お正月

STROKE ORDER

[30]	一 厂 冂 币 雨 雨
[31]	一 二 チ 天
[32]	ノ 𠂉 ⺈ 气 気 気
[33]	ノ ⺈ 㐄 生 先 先
[34]	ノ ⺈ 㐄 牛 生
[35]	一 丅 下 正 正

D. TANGO TO HYOOGEN

(o)shoogatsu	New Year
gantan/ganjitsu	January first
oomisoka	December thirty-first
(o)nenshi	New Year visit
(o)nenshi ni iku	to make a New Year visit

nengajoo	New Year card
(o)toshi	year
Yoi otoshi o.	Have a happy New Year (used before January first).
Akemashite omedetoo gozaimasu.	Happy New Year (used from January 1 through January 15).
osechi ryoori	New Year dishes
(o)mochi	rice cake
(o)zooni	soup with rice cakes
tako	kite
karuta	Japanese cards
karutakai	*karuta** party
junbi	preparation
shinseki	relatives
ryooshin	parents
otona	adult
bengoshi	lawyer
tenkiyohoo	weather forecast
shodoo	calligraphy
naru	to become
hazureru	not to come true
atsumaru	to gather
chikazuku	to approach
hajimaru	to begin
tashikameru	to check, make sure
hima	not busy, free
sore kara	and then
saa	well (I wonder)

RENSHUU

A. Answer the following questions based on the dialogue.

1. *Tamura san wa oniisan no uchi ni itsu ikimasu ka.*
2. *Tamura san no shinseki no hitotachi wa oniisan no uchi ni itsu atsumarimasu ka.*
3. *Sagawa san to Tamura san wa doko ni onenshi ni ikimasu ka.*
4. *Soko ni itsu iku tsumori desu ka.*

---

* *Karuta* is a traditional Japanese card game.

B. The following are weather forecasts on the radio. Make the appropriate choice from the lists below, and fill in the blanks.

1. *Ashita wa* _____ *narisoo desu. Yamazoi* (mountain areas) _____
   yuki ga sukoshi _____ *deshoo.*
   a. *samui*   b. *samuku*   c. *de wa*   d. *e wa*   e. *furimasu*   f. *furu*

2. *Oomisoka ni wa ame ga furimasu* _____, *gantan ni wa ii tenki*
   _____ *naru* _____.
   a. *ga*   b. *ewa*   c. *tsumori desu*   d. *ni*   e. *de*   f. *deshoo*

C. Fill in the blanks with *da, na,* or *no.* If nothing should be inserted, write X.

1. *Sagawa san wa e ga joozu* _____ *soo desu.*
2. *Kono hen wa yoru shizuka* _____ *deshoo.*
3. *Isha* _____ *Hayashi san ni mo kiite mimashoo.*
4. *Ozooni no oishii* _____ *mise o shitte iru n desu.*
5. *Niwa no rippa* _____ *uchi desu.*

D. Translate the following:

Taitei juunigatsu nijuu kunichi goro ni kaisha nado ("etc.") *de wa oshoogatsu yasumi ga hajimarimasu. Soshite uchi no naka de oshoogatsu no junbi o oomisoka made shimasu. Ichigatsu mikka made kaisha no shigoto wa yasumi desu. Yokka ka itsuka ni taitei shigoto ga hajimarimasu.*

E. Rewrite the following using *kanji.*

1. てんきよほう   weather forecast

2. きょう あめは ふらないでしょう。It will probably not rain today.

3. おしょうがつ せんせいの   I visited my teacher's house
   おたくに うかがいました。   on New Year's Day.

F. Rewrite the following sentences and say "I heard that _____."

Example: *ano e wa totemo yuumei <u>desu</u>.* → *ano e wa totemo yuumei <u>da soo desu</u>.*

1. *Nakayama san wa nihongo no <u>sensei</u> desu.*
2. *ano eiga wa <u>omoshiroi</u> desu.*
3. *Jon san no uchi wa totemo <u>kirei</u> desu.*
4. *Jon san wa kyoo wa <u>hima</u> desu.*

KARUCHAA NOOTO

The New Year is the most important time of the year in Japan. From the first through the third of January, many businesses are closed. Family members who are living far away from each other try to celebrate these holidays together. On these three days, usually in the mornings, people have New Year feasts. They eat *oshirako*, also called *zenzai*, a red bean soup with rice cakes, and *osechi ryoori*, which is a collective name for various dishes eaten during the New Year holidays, such as cooked carrots, *goboo* "burdock root," *konnyaku* "yam cake," and *shiitake* mushrooms.

Temples and shrines are crowded with people who pray for happiness throughout the year. The visit to a shrine or a temple during the New Year festivities is called *hatsumoode*. People visit their friends and relatives to exchange New Year greetings. A typical greeting is:

Akemashite omedetoo gozaimasu. Kyuunenchuu wa iroiro osewa ni narimashite arigatoo gozaimashita. Kotoshi mo doozo yoroshiku.
Happy New Year. I appreciate the kindness you showed me last year. Please let me ask you for your kindness this year also.

You can extend this greeting from January first through January fifteenth.

KOTAE

A. 1. *Gantan ni ikimasu.* 2. *Gantan ni atsumarimasu.* 3. *Ueno sensei no uchi ni onenshi ni ikimasu.* 4. *Yokka ni iku tsumori desu.*
B. 1. b, c, f   2. a, d, f
C. 1. *da*   2. X   3. *no*   4. X   5. *na*
D. Generally around December twenty-ninth, the New Year vacation starts in companies, [etc.]. Then you prepare for the New Year celebration until December thirty-first. Work in companies stops until January third. Generally on the fourth or fifth, work resumes [starts].
E. 1. 天気よほう 2. 今日 雨は ふらないでしょう。 3. お正月 先生の おたくに うかがいました。
F. 1. *Nakayama san wa nihongo no sensei <u>da soo desu</u>.* 2. *ano eiga wa omoshiroi <u>soo desu</u>.* 3. *Jon san no uchi wa totemo kirei <u>da soo desu</u>.* 4. *Jon san wa kyoo wa hima <u>da soo desu</u>.*

DAI NIJUU NIKA
Lesson 22
YUUBINKYOKU.   The Post Office.

A. DAIAROOGU

YUUBINKYOKU NO MADOGUCHI DE.

Mr. Miller, a student from the United States, goes to the post office to send a package home.

MIRAA: **Kono kozútsumi o Amerika máde okuritái n desu ga, kookuubin de dásu to nannichi gúrai de tsukimásu ka.**

KYOKUIN: **Isshuukan gúrai desu ne.**

MIRAA: **Jáa, funabin dá to dono gurai kakarimásu ka.**

KYOKUIN: **Sóo desu ne. Yonjuunichi gúrai kakáru deshoo ne.**

MIRAA: **Jáa, funabin de íi desu. Chótto omói n desu kedo, omókute mo okuremásu ka.**

KYOKUIN: **Kono hakari no ué ni nosete kudasái. . . . Hái, daijóobu desu. Yonsén nanáhyaku gojúuen desu.**

MIRAA: **Sore kara, kokusai yúubin no hagaki o sánmai kudasái.**

KYOKUIN: **Zénbu de yonsén kyúuhyaku rokujúuen desu.**

MIRAA: **Gaikoku yúubin mo pósuto ni ireté mo íi desu ka.**

KYOKUIN: **Ée, kamaimasén yo.**

MIRAA: **Jáa, genkin kákitome wa dóo desu ka.**

KYOKUIN: **Áa, genkin kákitome wa zettai ni pósuto ni irenái de kudasai.**

MIRAA: **Hái, wakarimáshita.**

AT THE WINDOW OF THE POST OFFICE.

MILLER: I want to send this package to the United States. Approximately how long will it take to get there if I send it via airmail?

CLERK: It will take about one week.

MILLER: Well then, how long will it take by surface mail?

264

CLERK: Let's see. It will probably take about forty days.

MILLER: Well then, surface mail will be all right. It's a little heavy, but can I send it anyway [even though it is heavy]?

CLERK: Put it on this scale. . . . Okay, it will be all right. It's 4,750 yen.

MILLER: And three international postcards, please.

CLERK: Your total is 4,960 yen.

MILLER: Can I put foreign mail into the mailbox, as well?

CLERK: Yes, that will be fine.

MILLER: And how about cash registered mail?

CLERK: Oh, please don't put cash registered mail in the mailbox, absolutely not.

MILLER: I see.

B. BUNPOO TO YOOHOO

1. "EVEN IF/EVEN THOUGH/MAY"

The TE form of a verb, an *i*-adjective, or the copula is used with *mo* to express "even if" or "even though." When *ii desu* "good" or *kamaimasen* "I don't mind" follows TE *mo*, the sentence expresses permission. The English equivalent would be "may." When *ii desu* is used, *mo* can be deleted after the TE form.

a. Verbs

Genkin o okutte mo ii desu ka.
May I [Is it all right even if I] send cash?

Tsuuchi o hagaki de dashite mo kamaimasen.
You may [I don't mind even if you] send the notice on a postcard.

Tegami de tazunete mo henji ga kimasen deshita.
Even though I asked about it in a letter, no reply came.

b. *I*-adjectives

Omokute mo okuremasu ka.
Can I send it even though it is heavy?

Ano yuubinkyoku wa, asa hayakute mo, konde imasu.
That post office is crowded [even] early in the morning.

Takakute ii desu kara, kookuubin de okutte kudasai.
Please send it by airmail even if it is expensive.

   c. The copula

Funabin de, ii desu.
It may go surface mail. [Even if it is surface mail it is all right.]

Genkin de mo ii desu ka.
Can I pay cash? [Is it all right even it is cash?]

Hima de mo tegami o amari kakanai n desu.
Although she is not busy, she does not write letters often.

2. NEGATIVE TE FORMS AND "NEED NOT" AND "DON'T HAVE TO"

The negative TE forms of verbs, *i*-adjectives, and the copula are formed just like the TE form of an *i*-adjective in the affirmative. That is, the final *-i* of the plain present negative is replaced by *-kute*.

VERB:	*ikanai*	→ *ikanakute*	not to go
I-ADJECTIVE:	*oishiku nai*	→ *oishiku nakute*	not to be tasty
NA-ADJECTIVE PLUS	*shizuka ja/de*	→ *shizuka ja/de*	not to be quiet
THE COPULA:	*(wa) nai*	*(wa) nakute*	
NOUN PLUS	*gakusei ja/de*	→ *gakusei ja/de*	not to be a student
THE COPULA:	*(wa) nai*	→ *(wa) nakute*	

When the negative TE form is followed by *(mo) ii desu* or *mo ka-maimasen*, the English equivalent is "need not" or "don't have to."

Kitte o haranakute ii desu.
You don't have to use [paste on] stamps.

Heya wa ookiku nakute mo ii desu.
The room does not have to be big.

Sokutatsu ja nakute mo ii desu.
It does not have to be special delivery.

3. NEGATIVE REQUESTS

To express "Please don't . . . ," use the following pattern.

plain present negative of a verb + *de* + *kudasai*

266

Kono kozutsumi wa mada akenai de kudasai.
Please don't open this package yet.

Yuubin bangoo o kaku no o wasurenai de kudasai.
Please don't forget to use [write] your Zip code.

4. PARTICLES

a. *To* "if/when"

Like TARA (see Lesson 17, B1) the clause particle *to* expresses
"if . . ." or "when. . . ." Before *to*, a plain present form is usually used.

Kookuubin de dashitara, nannichi gurai de tsukimasu ka. (TARA)
Kookuubin de dasu to, nannichi gurai de tsukimasu ka. (to)
If I mail it by airmail, [about] how long will it take to get there?

Omoi to, motenai deshoo.
If it is heavy, you can't carry it, can you?

Funabin da to, dono gurai kakarimasu ka.
If it is [sent by] surface mail, how long will it take?

Moo osoi desu kara, sokutatsu ja nai to, maniawanai deshoo.
Since it is late, if it is not [sent by] special delivery, it will probably not
arrive in time.

As with other subordinate clauses, *wa* cannot be used in a *to* clause.

Yuubinkyoku ga chikaku nai to, fuben desu nee.
If the post office is not close, it is inconvenient, isn't it?

Note that when the final clause expresses a request or suggestion, *to*
cannot be used, whereas TARA can.

Juusho ga kawattara, shirasete kudasai.
When your address changes, please let me know.

Karui kozutsumi dattara, yuubinkyoku made aruite ikimashoo ka.
If they are light packages, shall we walk to the post office?

b. *De* (after a quantity noun)

De is used after a quantity noun to express "total."

Zenbu de gosen hyaku juuen desu.
Your total is 5,110 yen. [It is 5,110 yen for all.]

Fuutoo wa juumai de nihyakuen desu.
Ten envelopes are two hundred yen.

Kozutsumi wa mittsu de gosen happyaku gojuuen desu.
The three packages are 5,850 yen.

c. *Ni* "into," "in"

With the verb *ireru* "to put . . . in(to)," *ni* is used after the noun referring to the location into which something is put.

Fuutoo o kono hako ni irete kudasai.
Please put the envelopes into this box.

Gaikoku yuubin mo posuto ni irete mo ii desu ka.
May I put foreign mail into the mailbox, as well?

Nimotsu wa heya ni iremashita.
I put the baggage in your room.

C. MOJI

1. DIALOGUE

ミラー　　「このこづつみを アメリカまで 送りたいんですが、
　　　　　こうくうびんで 出すと 何日ぐらいで つきますか。」

きょくいん「一 週間ぐらいですね。」

ミラー　　「じゃあ、ふなびんだと どのくらい かかりますか。」

きょくいん「そうですね。四十日ぐらい かかるでしょうね。」

ミラー　　「じゃあ、ふなびんで いいです。ちょっと おもいん
　　　　　ですけど、おもくても 送れますか。」

きょくいん「このはかりの うえに のせてください。…… はい、
　　　　　だいじょうぶです。四千七百五十円です。」

ミラー　　「それから、こくさいゆうびんの はがきを 三まい
　　　　　ください。」

きょくいん「ぜんぶで 四千九百六十円です。」

ミラー　　「外国（がいこく）ゆうびんも ポストに 入（い）れても
　　　　　いいですか。」

きょくいん「ええ、かまいませんよ。」

ミラー　　「じゃあ、げんきんかきとめは どうですか。」

きょくいん「ああ、げんきんかきとめは ぜったいに ポストに
　　　　　入れないで ください。」

ミラー　　「はい、わかりました。」

2. *HIRAGANA* (*JI* AND *ZU*)

Ji ぢ and *zu* づ are used instead of *ji* じ and *zu* ず in some cases (see Lesson 4).

In a compound word, elements not in the first position often undergo sound changes. If one such element begins with *chi* ち or *tsu* つ, and it becomes *ji* or *zu*, write ぢ or づ instead of *ji* じ or *zu* ず.

| こ small + つつみ wrapping | こづつみ | package |
| はな nose + ち blood | はなぢ | bloody nose |

When *ji* follows *chi* or *zu* follows *tsu* in a word, ぢ and づ are used for *ji* and *zu*.

| ちぢむ | to shrink |
| つづく | to continue |

3. NEW *KANJI*

[36]	送	*oku(ru)*	to send
[37]	何	*nani, nan*	what
[38]	週	*SHUU*	week
[39]	間	*KAN*	space, time e.g., 一週間、時間
[40]	円	*EN*	yen

[41]	外	*GAI*	outside
[42]	国	*KOKU*	country
[43]	入	*i(reru)*	to put in

STROKE ORDER

[36]	` ` ` ゛ ゛ ゛ 关 送
[37]	ノ イ 仁 何 何
[38]	) 刀 月 円 門 周 週
[39]	l 冂 冂 冂 冂 門 門 門 間
[40]	l 冂 冂 円
[41]	ク タ 列 外
[42]	l 冂 冂 冂 用 国 国 国
[43]	ノ 入

4. NEW READING

The following *kanji* was introduced in Lesson 20. Another reading is:

[25]	出	*de(ru)*, *de(kakeru)* (Lesson 20)	to go out
		da(su)	to send out, to mail, to publish

D. TANGO TO HYOOGEN

yuubin	mail
(yuubin)kyokuin	post office clerk
gaikoku yuubin	foreign mail
kokusai yuubin	international mail
yuubin bangoo	Zip code
posuto	mailbox (for outgoing mail)
kozutsumi	package
hagaki	postcard
kitte	postage stamp
fuutoo	envelope

kakitome	registered mail
genkin	cash
genkin kakitome	cash registered mail
sokutatsu	special delivery
kookuubin	airmail
funabin	surface mail
juusho	address
tsuuchi	notification
hakari	scale
hako	box
nimotsu	baggage
henji	reply
zenbu	total, all
dasu	to mail
okuru	to send
haru	to affix
ireru	to put in
noseru	to put (something) on (something)
kawaru	to change
maniau	to be in time, make it
akeru	to open
shiraseru	to notify
tazuneru	to inquire
motsu	to carry, hold
omoi	heavy
karui	light
hayai	early
osoi	late
fuben	inconvenient
zettai (ni)	absolutely

RENSHUU

A. Mark the statements true or false on the basis of the dialogue.

1. *Kozutsumi o Amerika made kookuubin de okuru to nanoka gurai kakarimasu.*
2. *Genkin kakitome wa posuto ni wa ireraremasen.*
3. *Miraa san wa funabin de kozutsumi o okurimashita.*
4. *Miraa san wa kitte o sanmai kaimashita.*

B. Suppose today is your first day of work. Ask your colleague the following questions in Japanese.

1. May I drink coffee here?
2. May I open this window?
3. May I hang a picture on the wall?
4. May I use this computer?
5. May I close the door?

C. There are various signs in a temple you are visiting. Fill in the blanks according to the English equivalents.

1. *Shashin o* ―――.
   Please don't take photographs.
2. ――― *esa o* ―――.
   Please don't feed [give food] to the fish.
3. *Koko ni* ―――.
   Please don't sit here.
4. *Kono mado o* ―――.
   Please don't open this window.
5. *Kono mizu o* ―――.
   Please don't drink this water.

D. Transform the TARA clauses into clauses with *to*.

Example: *Ano hon o yondara, wakarimasu yo.*
   → *Ano hon o yomu to, wakarimasu yo.*

1. *Ame ga futtara, samuku narimasu yo.*
2. *Ano kissaten ni ittara, itsumo Yamada san ga kite imasu.*
3. *Yuubinkyoku ga chikakattara, ii n desu ga.*
4. *Uchi ga shizuka dattara, yoku benkyoo dekiru n desu ga.*

E. Rewrite the following using *kanji*.

1. なんえんですか。 — How much is it?

2. がいこくゆうびんを だしたいんです。 — I would like to send some foreign mail.

3. みずを いれてください。 — Please put in water.

4. このこつづみを おくりたいんですが、なんしゅうかんぐらい かかりますか。 — I would like to send this package. How many weeks will it take?

KARUCHAA NOOTO

Japanese post offices are marked with the symbol 〒. They provide various kinds of services in addition to sending letters, cards, and packages. If you need to send money, you can put the cash in a special envelope for cash registered mail called *genkin kakitome*. Other methods of sending money are money orders and postal transfers. The post office also offers savings accounts. You can make automatic payments for utilities and government bills through the post office, and you can join a life insurance or pension plan administered by the post office, as well.

The busiest time for the post office is around the New Year. Toward the end of the year, the post office sells New Year cards. If you take your cards to the post office by a certain date in December announced by the post office, they will hold your cards until January first, and then deliver them immediately. That way your New Year greetings will arrive at exactly the right time.

KOTAE

A. 1. T 2. T 3. T 4. F

B. 1. *Koko de koohii o nonde (mo) ii desu ka.* or ——*nonde mo kamaimasen ka.* 2. *Kono mado o akete (mo) ii desu ka.* or ——*akete mo kamaimasen ka.* 3. *Kabe ni e o kakete (mo) ii desu ka.* or ——*kakete mo kamaimasen ka.* 4. *Kono konpyuutaa o tsukatte (mo) ii desu ka.* or ——*tsukatte mo kamaimasen ka.* 5. *Kono doa o shimete (mo) ii desu ka.* or ——*kamaimasen ka.*

C. 1. *toranai de kudasai* 2. *Sakana ni, yaranai de kudasai* 3. *suwaranai de kudasai* 4. *akenai de kudasai* 5. *nomanai de kudasai*

D. 1. *Ame ga furu to—* 2. *Ano kissaten ni iku to—* 3. *Yuubinkyoku ga chikai to—* 4. *Uchi ga shizuka da to—*

E. 1. 何円ですか。 2. 外国ゆうびんを 出したいんです。 3. 水を 入れてください。 4. このこづつみを 送りたいんですが、何週間ぐらいかかりますか。

DAI NIJUU SANKA
Lesson 23
KONREI.   Weddings.

A. DAIAROOGU

OSHIEGO NO KEKKONSHIKI.

Ms. Kawada, a member of the neighborhood association, talks to Ms. Tamai, the president of the association.

KAWADA: **Ashita no kaigoo ni shusseki shinákute mo íi desu ka.**

TAMAI: **Dóo shite desu ka.**

KAWADA: **Chótto tsugoo ga warúi n desu. Oshiégo no kekkónshiki ga áru n desu.**

TAMAI: **Sóo desu ka. Dóko de áru n desu ka.**

KAWADA: **Tama Hóteru na n desu.**

TAMAI: **Chótto tooí desu ne.**

KAWADA: **Ée, juuniji hán ni shikí ga hajimarimásu kara, juuji góro ni uchi o déreba maniáu to omóu n desu. Hiróoen wa yoji han góro ni owaru rashíi n desu. Hóteru ga chikákereba, modótte kara kaigoo ní mo deraréru n desu kedo.**

TAMAI: **Shínzoku ja nákute mo, shikí ni mo déru n desu ka.**

KAWADA: **Ée, shinzen kékkon nara, shínzoku de nái monó wa futsuu demasén kedo, kirisutokyoo no shikí desu kara, shussékisha wa minna deru rashíi n desu.**

TAMAI: **Hóteru no náka ni cháperu ga áru n desu ka.**

KAWADA: **Ée. Rippa na cháperu rashíi desu yo.**

TAMAI: **Kono goro hiróoen de wa hanáyome san ga nidó mo oironáoshi o shite, hade rashíi desu ne.**

KAWADA: **Ée. Démo oshiégo ga itte irú n desu kedo, hadé ja nákute mo nagóyaka de tanoshíi hiróoen o shitai rashíi desu.**

TAMAI: **Sore wa íi desu ne. Jáa, mata nochihodo.**

THE WEDDING OF A FORMER STUDENT.

KAWADA: Is it all right if I don't attend tomorrow's meeting?

TAMAI: Well, why can't you make it?

KAWADA: It's a little inconvenient. I want to attend the wedding of a former student.

TAMAI: Is that right? Where will it be?

KAWADA: It's at the Tama Hotel.

TAMAI: That's quite far, isn't it?

KAWADA: Yes. The ceremony starts at twelve-thirty. I'll only make it if I leave home around ten. I believe the reception will end around four-thirty. If the hotel were closer, I could attend the meeting, as well, after I came back.

TAMAI: You're going to attend the ceremony, too, even though you're not a relative?

KAWADA: Yes. If it's a Shinto wedding, non-relatives usually don't attend. This is a Christian ceremony, and I understand that all the participants attend.

TAMAI: Is there a chapel in the hotel?

KAWADA: Yes. I heard it's [a] magnificent [chapel].

TAMAI: I hear that nowadays the bride changes her clothes as often as twice during the reception and that the reception is luxurious.

KAWADA: Yes. But my former student says that he wants to have a casual and enjoyable reception, rather than a showy one.

TAMAI: That's good. Well, I'll see you later.

B. BUNPOO TO YOOHOO

1. AFFIRMATIVE BA FORMS ("IF . . . / PROVIDED THAT . . .")

The BA form, used at the end of a subordinate clause, means "if . . ." or "provided that. . . ." Here are its forms, along with some sample sentences.

a. Verbs

CONSONANT VERBS: The final -*u* of the dictionary form is replaced by -*eba*.

```
iku       →       ikeba
yomu      →       yomeba
```

VOWEL VERBS: The final *-ru* of the dictionary form is replaced by *-reba*.

```
taberu    →       tabereba
miru      →       mireba
```

IRREGULAR VERBS:

```
suru      →       sureba
kuru      →       kureba
```

Juuji goro ni uchi o dereba, maniau to omou n desu.
I think I will make it if I leave home around ten.

As with other subordinate clauses, the subject of a BA clause is followed by *ga*, not *wa*.

Moshi ano hoteru ni chaperu ga areba, soko de shiki o agetai desu.
If there is a chapel in that hotel, I want to have the ceremony there.

b. *I*-adjectives

The final *-i* of the dictionary form is replaced by *-kereba*.

```
ookii     →       ookikereba
ii (yoi)  →       yokereba
```

Hoteru ga chikakereba, modotte kara kaigoo ni mo derareru n desu kedo.
If the hotel were close, I could attend the meeting also, after I returned.

Otenki ga yokereba, shashin wa soto de torimasu.
Provided that the weather is good, we will take pictures outdoors.

c. The copula:

```
da        →       nara*
```

* The original form was *-naraba*. Thus, it is a type of BA form.

276

Shizuka nara, itte mitai desu.
If it is quiet, I want to go.

Shinzen kekkon nara, shinzoku de nai hito wa futsuu demasen.
If it is a Shinto wedding, non-relatives do not usually attend.

2. NEGATIVE BA FORMS ("IF . . . / PROVIDED THAT . . .")

The BA form of a negative is derived from the plain present negative. As with an affirmative *i*-adjective, the final *-i* is replaced by *-kereba*.

a. Verbs:

ikanai	→	*ikanakereba*
tabenai	→	*tabenakereba*

b. *I*-adjectives:

ookiku nai	→	*ookiku nakereba*
yoku nai	→	*yoku nakereba*

c. The copula:

The copula drops the optional *wa* in the BA form.

shizuka ja/de (wa) nai	→	*shizuka ja/de nakereba*
gakusei ja/de (wa) nai	→	*gakusei ja/de nakereba*

Kawada san ga ikanakereba, watashi mo ikimasen.
If Ms. Kawada does not go, I will not go, either.

Otenki ga yoku nakereba, hoteru made takushii de ikimasu.
If the weather is not good, I will take a taxi to the hotel.

Uchi ga shizuka de nakereba, toshokan de benkyoo shimasu.
If my house is not quiet, I will study in the library.

The BA form can have almost the same meaning as a TARA clause (see Lesson 17, B1) or a *-to* clause (see Lesson 22, B4).

Ame ga fureba, ii n desu ga.
Ame ga futtara, ii n desu ga.
Ame ga furu to, ii n desu ga.
    I hope it will rain. (It will be good if it rains.)

One difference between the BA clause and both the TARA and the *-to* clauses is that BA is rarely used with a main clause in the past tense. Thus the following idea could not be expressed with a BA clause.

Hoteru ni tsuitara, moo shussekisha wa kite imashita.
Hoteru ni tsuku to, moo shussekisha wa kite imashita.
    When I arrived at the hotel, the participants were there already.

3. *RASHII* (HEARSAY/ASSUMPTION)

Like *soo desu*, *rashii* is used to express "hearsay." It is preceded by a plain form and followed by *(n) desu*.

Hirooen wa yoji han goro ni owaru rashii n desu.
    I understand that the reception will end around four-thirty.

Kono hoteru wa mukashi chiisakatta rashii desu.
    I understand that years ago this hotel was small.

Hanayome san wa totemo kirei datta rashii desu.
    I understand that the bride was very pretty.

Remember that there are four types for the copula in the present affirmative (see Lesson 21, B4). *Rashii* belongs to Type IV because the copula in the present affirmative is deleted.

Kono hoteru wa yuumei ø rashii desu.
    I understand that this hotel is famous.

Rippa na chaperu ø rashii desu yo.
    I understand that it is a magnificent chapel.

Kono goro hirooen wa hade ø rashii desu ne.
    I understand that nowadays, receptions are showy.

While both *rashii* and *soo desu* indicate hearsay, *soo desu* is based on objective information, whereas *rashii* may involve the speaker's subjective interpretation. In certain cases, *rashii* is used simply based on the speaker's judgment rather than on what he or she has heard or read. In those cases, the English equivalent is "I assume."

Shiki wa moo owatta rashii desu.
    I assume that the ceremony has already ended.

For example, here the speaker could be judging from the fact that people are coming out of the room where the ceremony was conducted, rather than on having heard an announcement.

4. QUESTION WORDS

For questions with "why," use *naze* or *dooshite*. *Dooshite* is less formal than *naze*.

Dooshite desu ka.
　　Why is it?

Dooshite uedingu doresu o kariru n desu ka.
　　Why are you going to rent a wedding dress?

Naze shusseki shinakatta n desu ka.
　　Why didn't you attend it?

However, *doo* "how" followed by *shite* "do" (the TE form of *suru*) means "how." Thus, ambiguity may occur. Compare:

Dooshite Oosaka e iku n desu ka.
　　Why are you going to Osaka?

Doo shite Oosaka e iku n desu ka.
　　How are you going to Osaka?

5. PARTICLES

a. *Mo* (after quantity expressions)

When *mo* is used after a quantity expression, it means "as much as," "as many as," "as long as."

Hanayome san wa nido mo oironaoshi o shita n desu.
　　The bride changed her clothes as often as two times.

Shinkon ryokoo de shigoto o isshuukan mo yasumimashita.
　　Because of my honeymoon, I didn't go to work for an entire week.

Tomodachi o nijuunin mo yobimashita.
　　I invited as many as twenty friends.

b. *De* "at/in"

You have learned that the particle *ni* "at/in" is used after a location with the verb *aru* "to exist" (see Lesson 8, C1).

Hoteru no naka ni chaperu ga aru n desu.
　　There is a chapel in the hotel.

279

However, if an activity takes place in a location, use *de* "at/in" when referring to the location, even in sentences with the verb *aru*.

Kekkonshiki wa doko de aru n desu ka.
Where will the wedding take place?

Paatii wa Koobe no hoteru de aru rashii desu.
I understand that the party will be at a hotel in Kobe.

Kaigoo wa Tani san no uchi de aru soo desu.
I understand that the meeting will be held at Ms. Tani's house.

As *desu* can replace *ni arimasu* (see Lesson 21, B2), *de arimasu* can also be replaced by the appropriate forms of *desu*.

Kaigoo wa doko desu ka. (Kaigoo wa doko de arimasu ka.)
Where will the meeting take place?

Doko de aru n desu ka.
Where will it be?

Tama Hoteru na n desu. (Tama Hoteru de aru n desu.)
It will be in the Tama Hotel.

c. *Ni* (with "attend")

With the verb *deru* "to attend" or *shusseki suru* "to attend," *ni* is used after the noun referring to the event.

Shiki ni mo deru n desu ka.
Are you going to attend the ceremony, too?

Ashita no kaigoo ni shusseki shinakute mo ii desu ka.
Is it all right if I don't attend tomorrow's meeting?

Isogashikute, tomodachi no hirooen ni deraremasen deshita.
Since I was busy, I could not attend my friend's wedding reception.

6. THE HONORIFIC *SAN* WITH A ROLE, RANK, OR OCCUPATION

The honorific *san* is used not only with names but also with certain expressions denoting role or rank.

Kirei na hanayome san deshita.
She was a pretty bride.

Donata ga nakoodo san desu ka.
Who is the go-between (ceremonial matchmaker)?

Tamura san wa ano kaisha no buchoo san desu.
  Mr. Tamura is a department head of that company.

The following occupational terms may use *san*, as well.

untenshu san	professional driver
biyooshi san	hairdresser, beautician
bokushi san	Protestant church minister
kannushi san	Shinto priest

Ano biyooshi san wa totemo joozu desu.
  That hairdresser is very good.

Ano jinja no kannushi san wa dare desu ka.
  Who is the priest of that shrine?

Some occupational terms stem from the businesses themselves. The terms can mean either the store or the person and can be used with *san*.

pan'ya san	bakery, baker
hanaya san	flower shop, florist
hon'ya san	bookstore, book dealer

Pan'ya san to hanaya san e ikimashita.
  I went to the bakery and the flower shop.

Pan'ya san to hanaya san mo kaigoo ni kimashita.
  The baker and the florist also came to the meeting.

Some terms should be used with the polite marker *o* if *san* is used.

oisha san	medical doctor
okyaku san	guest, visitor, customer

Women tend to use *san* more often than men.

7. *HITO/KATA/MONO* "PERSON"

While *hito, kata*, and *mono* all mean "person," there are differences in usage.

Ano hito wa raigetsu kekkon suru rashii desu.
  I understand that that person is getting married next month.

Hirooen de shikai o suru hito wa dare desu ka.
  Who is the person that presides at the reception?

Kata is more polite than *hito*.

Ano kata ga nakoodo san desu.
   That person is the go-between.

Kyoo shikai o nasaru kata desu ne.
   You are the person who will preside over today's meeting, aren't you?

   Mono is usually humble. It is used when the speaker talks about him or herself, about a group of people including the speaker, or about the speaker's in-group. For example, Ms. Kawada says in the dialogue:

Shinzen kekkon nara, shinzoku de nai mono wa futsuu demasen kedo . . .
   If it is a Shinto wedding, usually non-relatives (like myself) do not attend.

Nochihodo kaisha no mono ga ukagaimasu.
   A person from our company will visit you later.

   Kata and *mono* are dependent nouns, i.e., they cannot be used without another word preceding them. *Hito*, however, can be used independently.

Hoteru no iriguchi ni hito ga takusan imashita.
   There were many people at the entrance of the hotel.

   Unlike with *hito* and *kata, kono* "this," *sono* "that," *ano* "that," and *dono* "which" are rarely used before *mono* in modern Japanese.

C. MOJI

1. DIALOGUE

かわだ 「あしたの かいごうに しゅっせきしなくても
      いいですか。」

たまい 「どうしてですか。」

かわだ 「ちょっと つごうが わるいんです。おしえごの
      けっこんしきが あるんです。」

たまい 「そうですか。どこで あるんですか。」

かわだ　「たまホテル なんです。」

たまい　「ちょっと 遠いですね。」

かわだ　「ええ、十二時半に しきが はじまりますから、
　　　　十時ごろに うちを 出れば まにあうと 思うんです。
　　　　ひろうえんは 四時半ごろに おわるらしいんです。
　　　　ホテルが 近ければ、もどってから、かいごうにも
　　　　出られるんですけど。」

たまい　「しんぞくじゃなくても しきにも 出るんですか。」

かわだ　「ええ、しんぜんけっこんなら、しんぞくでない ものは
　　　　ふつう 出ませんけど、キリストきょうの しきですから、
　　　　しゅっせきしゃは みんな 出るらしいんです。」

たまい　「ホテルの 中に チャペルが あるんですか。」

かわだ　「ええ、りっぱな チャペルらしいですよ。」

たまい　「このごろ ひろうえんでは 花よめさんが 二どとも
　　　　おいろなおしを して、はでらしいですね。」

かわだ　「ええ、でも、おしえごが 言っているんですけど、
　　　　はでじゃなくても なごやかで、たのしい ひろうえんを
　　　　したいらしいです。」

たまい　「それは いいですね。じゃあ、また のちほど。」

2. NEW *KANJI*

[44]	半	*HAN*	half
[45]	遠	*too(i)*	far
[46]	近	*chika(i)*	near
[47]	花	*hana*	flower
[48]	言	*i(u)*	to say

STROKE ORDER

[44]	` ` ` ` ` 半
[45]	十 土 吉 歩 歩 袁 遠
[46]	ｆ ｆ 斤 近
[47]	一 十 ｻ 扩 扩 扮 花
[48]	` 二 三 言 言

出 is also used for "to attend."

[25] 出   *de(ru), de(kakeru)* (Lesson 20)   to go out
          da(su) (Lesson 22)   to send out, to mail, to publish

          de(ru)   to attend

D. TANGO TO HYOOGEN

shiki   ceremony
shinzen kekkon   wedding according to Shinto rites
kirisutokyoo   Christianity
chaperu   chapel
hirooen   wedding reception
uedingu doresu   wedding dress
oironaoshi   changing outfits at the wedding reception
shinkon ryokoo   honeymoon
hanayome   bride
shinpu   bride (formal)
hanamuko   bridegroom
shinroo   bridegroom (formal)
nakoodo   go-between
shinzoku   relatives (formal)
kannushi   Shinto priest
bokushi   Protestant church minister
hanaya   flower shop, florist
untenshu   professional driver
oshiego   a teacher's former student
shussekisha   participant

mono	person (dependent noun)
kata	person (dependent noun)
kaigoo	meeting
shikai suru	to preside
shusseki suru	to attend
deru	to attend
yobu	to invite
shiki o ageru	to hold a ceremony
hade	gorgeous, luxurious, showy
nagoyaka	congenial, friendly
futsuu	usually, generally
naze	why
dooshite	why
doo shite	how

RENSHUU

A. Answer the following questions based on the dialogue.

1. *Kawada san wa dare no kekkonshiki ni demasu ka.*
2. *Kekkonshiki wa doko de arimasu ka.*
3. *Sono kekkonshiki wa shinzen kekkon desu ka.*
4. *Sono kekkonshiki wa nanji ni hajimarimasu ka.*

B. Fill in the blanks with BA forms.

1. *Hoteru made nanpun gurai de ikemasu ka.*
   ———, *juppun de tsukimasu yo.*
   If (you) go by taxi, you will arrive there in ten minutes.
2. *Ashita kimono o kimasu ka.*
   ———, *kiru tsumori desu.*
   If it does not rain, I plan to wear one.
3. *Hashimoto san ga ofisu ni kuru soo desu.*
   Aa, ———, *yoku shitte imasu yo.*
   Oh, if (it) is Ms. Hashimoto, I know her well.
4. *Otera o mi ni ikimasen ka.*
   Ee, ———, *ikitai desu.*
   Yes, if the weather is good, I want to go.

C. Change a's speech to hearsay by using *rashii (n) desu.*

1. a: *Tamura san wa raigetsu kekkon shimasu yo.*
   b: *Aite* (the partner) *wa dare desu ka.*
   a: *Tomodachi no oneesan desu.*

2. a: *Suzuki san wa yoku ano hoteru ni ikimasu yo.*
   b: *Dooshite ano hoteru ga ii n desu ka.*
   a: *Benri de yasui n desu.*
3. a: *Kaigoo wa kinoo atta n desu.*
   b: *Kawada san mo deta n desu ka.*
   a: *Iie, Kawada san wa demasen deshita.*

D. Translate the following:

Tanaka san no kekkonshiki wa kyoo juuniji han ni hajimarimasu.
Tanaka san wa asa kuji ni hoteru ni ikimashita. Biyooshi san wa moo
kite imashita. Uedingu doresu o kite kara, ryooshin to issho ni chaperu
ni iku to, bokushi san ga matte imashita. Shinroo to shinroo no
ryooshin mo kimashita. Sore kara, nakoodo san mo kimashita. Shiki no
renshuu o minna de shimashita.

E. Rewrite the following using *kanji.*

1. さんじはんに うちを でれば、   I will be on time if I leave
   まにあいます。   home at 3:30.

2. せんせいの おたくは とおいですか。 Is the teacher's house far?

3. ちかければ、いきたいと   She was saying that if it
   いっていましたよ。   was close she would go.

4. さくらの はなが すきです。   I like cherry blossoms.

F. Translate the underlined sections into Japanese.

1. I won't buy it <u>if it's not cheap</u>.
2. I will go to the library <u>if it's not quiet here</u>.
3. I won't go to see it <u>if it's not interesting</u>.

KARUCHAA NOOTO

Traditionally, marriages in Japan were arranged, and the custom is still
practiced. Usually, the parents give their daughter's or son's picture
and résumé to someone who is willing to do the matchmaking. Also,
anyone who knows the prospective couple directly or indirectly can be
a matchmaker without being asked. The matchmaker arranges a first
meeting. Then, the couple may date several times. If the matchmaking
is successful, the couple gets formally engaged. Nowadays, however,
most people find their mates by themselves.

Whether or not the marriage is arranged, the procedure for the en-
gagement and the wedding is the same. The couple asks another couple
to become the go-between (*nakoodo*) at their wedding. The go-between

can be the matchmaker or someone else. In many cases, the go-between is either the bride's or the groom's boss or former teacher.

Many weddings are conducted according to the rites of Shinto, a native Japanese religion. Christian ceremonies, however, are becoming popular, too. Big hotels have a room for this kind of ceremony, and therefore, many people hold their marriage ceremony in a hotel rather than in a shrine or a church. At a typical reception, the guests sit in designated seats to have a formal meal. There are speeches and entertainment during dinner. The bride changes her clothes once, twice, or even three times. The bridegroom also may change his clothes. Currently, there is a trend for weddings to become showy. This is partly because businesses such as hotels and the costume industry are trying to generate more profit, and thus encourage couples to spend more money on their ceremony.

KOTAE

A. 1. *Oshiego no kekkonshiki ni demasu.* 2. *Tama Hoteru de arimasu.*
3. *Iie, Kirisutokyoo no shiki desu.* 4. *Juuniji han ni hajimarimasu.*
B. 1. *Takushii de ikeba* 2. *Ame ga furanakereba* 3. *Hashimoto san nara*
4. *otenki ga yokereba*
C. 1. ——*kekkon suru rashii desu yo.* ——*oneesan rashii desu.* 2. ——*iku rashii desu yo.* ——*yasui rashii n desu.* 3. ——*atta rashii n desu.* ——*denakatta rashii desu.*
D. Ms. Tanaka's wedding begins at twelve-thirty today. Ms. Tanaka went to the hotel at nine in the morning. The beautician was already there. After putting on the wedding dress, she went to the chapel with her parents, where the minister was waiting. Then the bridegroom and his parents arrived. Next, the go-between [also] came. They rehearsed the ceremony together.
E. 1. 三時半に うちを 出れば、まにあいます。 2. 先生の おたくは 遠いですか。 3. 近ければ、行きたいと 言っていましたよ。
4. さくらの 花が 好きです。
F. 1. *yasuku nakattara* 2. *koko ga shizuka de wa/ja nakattara* 3. *omoshiroku nakattara*

DAI NIJUU YONKA
Lesson 24
RESUTORAN. Restaurants.

A. DAIAROOGU

SEIYOORYOORITEN DE NO SHOKUJI.

Mr. Hamada and Ms. Imai, who are colleagues, are going to a public lecture together.

HAMADA: Íma rokúji juppún mae desu ne. Kooen ga hajimaru máe ni shokuji o shimasén ka.

IMAI: Ée, onaka ga sukimáshita ne. Dóko e ikimashóo ka.

HAMADA: Chigusaya wa dóo desu ka. Ni-sanshuukan máe ni kaiten shita misé desu.

IMAI: Asoko wa íi soo desu ne. Ikimashóo.

Chigusaya de.

UEETORESU: Omatase shimáshita.

HAMADA: Bóku wa sutéeki ni shimásu. Sore ni súupu o kudasái.

UEETORESU: Konsome to potáaju to dóchira no hóo ga íi desu ka.

HAMADA: Konsome no hóo ga íi desu.

IMAI: Watashi wa osakana ga hoshíi n desu kedo, náni ga ichiban oishíi desu ka.

UEETORESU: Sóo desu ne. Masú ga oishisóo desu ne.

IMAI: Jáa, masú ni shimásu. Sore kara, ráisu ga áreba, pán yori ráisu no hóo ga íi n desu kedo.

UEETORESU: Hái, gozaimásu. Hoka ni gochuumon wa.

IMAI: Iie, kékkoo desu.

DINING AT A WESTERN-STYLE RESTAURANT.

HAMADA: It's ten minutes to six now, isn't it? Should we get something to eat before the lecture begins?

IMAI: Yes, I'm hungry; aren't you? Where should we go?

HAMADA: How about Chigusaya? It's a restaurant that opened a few weeks ago.

IMAI: I heard that it's nice. Let's go.

At Chigusaya.

WAITRESS: Sorry to have kept you waiting.

HAMADA: I'll have the steak. And the soup, please.

WAITRESS: Which would you like, consommé or potage?

HAMADA: I'd prefer consommé.

IMAI: I'm thinking about fish. Which fish do you recommend? [Which fish is the best?]

WAITRESS: Well, the trout is [looks] delicious.

IMAI: Well then, I'll have the trout. And I'd rather have rice than bread, if you have it.

WAITRESS: We do. Anything else?

IMAI: No, that's fine.

B. BUNPOO TO YOOHOO

1. *MAE* "BEFORE"

When *mae* is used independently, it means "previously" or "before" (see Lesson 5).

Mae koko de hataraite imashita.
I used to work here. [I worked here before.]

Mae is also used as a dependent noun in the following cases:

a. After a specific point of time or event

ichiji mae
just before one o'clock

oshoogatsu mae
before the New Year

kekkon mae
before marriage

Ima rokuji juppun mae desu ne.
It is ten minutes before six now, isn't it?

When something takes place before a certain incident, the particle *ni* is used together with *mae* to focus on the incident. *Ni*, however, is optional. This is also true with a period of time and a subordinate clause, presented below.

If the noun describes an event, *no* sometimes has to be inserted before *mae*, and sometimes is optional. Compare:

Shokuji (no) mae ni te o aratte kudasai. (optional)
Please wash your hands before having a meal.

Dezaato no mae ni koohii ga kimasu. (mandatory)
Coffee will come before dessert.

Natsuyasumi (no) mae ni issho ni osake demo nomimashoo. (optional)
Let's drink sake [or something else] together before the summer vacation.

b. With a term for a period of time

Mae with a term of duration means ". . . ago."

Ni-sanshuukan mae ni kaiten shita n desu.
It opened two or three weeks ago.

Kono reizooko wa gonen mae ni kaimashita.
I bought this refrigerator five years ago.

c. In a subordinate clause

Before *mae*, the dictionary form of the verb is used whether it refers to the present or past. The clause ending with *mae* means "before. . . ."

Suupu o nomu mae ni sarada ga hoshii desu.
I want salad before I eat soup.

Kaigi ga hajimaru mae ni kachoo ni denwa o shimashita.
I called the section manager before the conference began.

Nodo ga kawakimashita ne. Eiga o miru mae ni ocha demo nomimasen ka.
I'm thirsty, aren't you? Why don't we have tea or something before we see the movie?

Just as in most other subordinate clauses, *ga* is used instead of *wa* after the subject of the clause in the *mae* clause. *Ga* can also be changed to *no,* just as in relative clauses (see Lesson 19, B1).

Kooen ga/no hajimaru mae ni shokuji o shimasen ka.
Why don't we have a meal before the lecture begins?

2. SUPERLATIVES WITH NOUNS *

Unlike the English "small→smallest," the adjective does not change its form in the superlative. Instead, use the noun *ichiban* "number one," which functions like English superlative "most" or "-est."

a. Statements

Kono gakkoo ga ichiban yuumei desu.
This school is the most famous.

Masako ga ichiban chiisai desu.
Masako is the smallest.

De "in" or the phrase *no naka de* "of, in, among" is used to express the scope of the superlative.

Kono gakkoo ga machi de ichiban yuumei desu.
This school is the most famous in town.

Masako ga kodomotachi no naka de ichiban chiisai desu.
Masako is the smallest of the children.

Ano depaato wa kono hen de ichiban takai desu.
That department store is the most expensive in this vicinity.

Nihonryoori no naka de chawanmushi ga ichiban suki desu.
Among Japanese dishes, I like *chawanmushi* [steamed egg custard] best.

b. Questions

The typical sentence pattern for questions with a superlative is the following.

> question word/phrase *ga ichiban . . . ka.*

Dono osakana ga ichiban oishii desu ka.
Which fish is the most delicious?

To indicate the scope, the following two patterns are usually used:

> noun 1 *to* noun 2 *to* noun 3 *to de wa,* question word/phrase *ga ichiban . . . ka.*

* In Lesson 25, you will learn superlatives with verbal phrases (actions), e.g., "Swimming is the most fun."

In superlative questions, at least three nouns have to be compared. Of course you can compare even more. When comparing two nouns, use the comparative (see B3 below).

To de wa can be reduced to *to de* or *de wa*.

Masu to maguro to unagi to de wa dono osakana ga ichiban oishii desu ka.
Which fish is the most delicious, trout, tuna, or eel?

Masu ga ichiban oishii desu.
Trout is the most delicious.

Suteeki to tonkatsu to hanbaagu de wa dore ga ichiban suki desu ka.
Which do you like best, steak, pork cutlet, or hamburger?

Tonkatsu ga ichiban suki desu.
I like pork cutlet best.

The other sentence pattern for superlative questions is:

> noun *no naka de*/noun *de* question word/phrase *ga ichiban . . . ka.*

Nihon de dono shima ga ichiban ookii desu ka.
Which island is the largest in Japan?

Honshuu ga ichiban ookii desu.
Honshu is the largest.

Kono kudamono no naka de dore ga ichiban amasoo desu ka.
Of these fruits, which one seems the sweetest?

3. COMPARATIVES WITH NOUNS

As with superlatives, the adjective does not change its form in comparatives, either. Instead the following sentence patterns are used:

a. Statements

There are two typical sentence patterns. The first is:

> noun 1 *wa* noun 2 *yori . . .*

Niku wa sakana yori takai desu.
Meat is more expensive than fish.

Kono shichuu yori karai desu.
It is more spicy than this stew.

292

The other sentence pattern is:

> noun 2 *yori* noun 1 *no hoo ga* . . .

Pan yori raisu no hoo ga ii desu.
Rice is better than bread.

Ano ueetoresu no hoo ga teinei desu.
That waitress is more polite.

b. Questions

The sentence pattern for comparatives in questions is:

> noun 1 *to* noun 2 *to (de wa) dochira (no hoo) ga* . . . *ka.*

Konsome to potaaju to dochira ga ii desu ka.
Which would you rather have [Which would be better], consommé or potage?

Konsome no hoo ga ii desu.
Consommé would be better.

Seiyooryoori to nihonryoori to dochira no hoo ga ii desu ka.
Which would be better, Western cuisine or Japanese cuisine?

Tookyoo no aji to Oosaka no aji to de wa dochira no hoo ga suki desu ka.
Which do you like better, the taste of food from Tokyo or the taste of food from Osaka?

4. THE HONORIFIC VERB *GOZAIMASU*

Gozaimasu is used as a humble honorific and for simple politeness. The non-honorific equivalent is *aru* "to have/exist." Only the normal forms are used. All other forms (plain, TE, TARA, and BA forms) are obsolete. Store clerks and restaurant personnel often use *gozaimasu* when addressing customers. Used in ordinary conversation, it is very polite. Women tend to use it more often than men.

Raisu mo arimasu ka.
Do you have rice, too?

Hai, gozaimasu.
Yes, we have it.

Yookan ga hoshii n desu kedo.
I would like *yookan* [red bean sweets].

Hai, asoko ni gozaimasu.
　　Yes, it's over there.

Ima jikan ga gozaimasen kedo, nochihodo ukagaimasu.
　　Now I don't have time, but later I will visit you.

C. MOJI

1. DIALOGUE

はまだ　　　　　「今 六時十分前ですね。こうえんが　はじまる
　　　　　　　　　前に　しょくじを　しませんか。」

いまい　　　　　「ええ、おなかが　すきましたね。どこへ
　　　　　　　　　行きましょうか。」

はまだ　　　　　「ちぐさやは　どうですか。二、三週間前に　かいてん
　　　　　　　　　した店です。」

いまい　　　　　「あそこは　いいそうですね。行きましょう。」

　　　　　　　　　　　　　　　ちぐさやで

ウエートレス　　「おまたせ　しました。」

はまだ　　　　　「ぼくは　ステーキに　します。それに　スープを
　　　　　　　　　ください。」

ウエートレス　　「コンソメと　ポタージュと　どちらの　ほうが
　　　　　　　　　いいですか。」

はまだ　　　　　「コンソメの　方がいいです。」

いまい　　　　　「私は　お 魚が　ほしいんですけど、
　　　　　　　　　何が　一番 おいしいですか。」

ウエートレス　　「そうですね。ますが　おいしそうですね。」

いまい 「じゃあ、ますに します。それから、パンより
ライスの ほうが いいんですけど、ライスも
ありますか。」

ウエートレス 「はい、ございます。ほかに ごちゅうもんは。」

いまい 「いいえ、けっこうです。」

2. NEW *KANJI*

[49]	前	*mae*	front, ago, before
[50]	店	*mise*	store
[51]	私	*watashi, watakushi*	I
[52]	魚	*sakana*	fish
[53]	番	*BAN*	number, order e.g., 一番

STROKE ORDER

[49]	丶 丷 艹 甶 前 前
[50]	丶 亠 广 广 庐 店
[51]	丿 二 千 千 禾 私 私
[52]	丿 ⺈ 甶 魚
[53]	丿 ⺈ 丷 平 平 乑 乑 番 番 番

D. TANGO TO HYOOGEN

(go)chuumon	order
ueetoresu	waitress
niku	meat
suteeki	steak
tonkatsu	pork cutlet
hanbaagu	hamburger
shichuu	stew
suupu	Western-style soup
konsome	consommé

potaaju	potage
(o)sake	sake
chawanmushi	steamed egg custard
masu	trout
raisu	cooked rice (usually served on a plate with Western food)
sarada	salad
kudamono	fruit
dezaato	dessert
yookan	red bean sweets
reizooko	refrigerator
aji	taste, flavor
seiyoo	Western
seiyooryoori	Western cuisine
kooen	lecture
kaigi	conference, meeting
te	hand
shima	island
nomu	to eat (soup)
amai	sweet
karai	spicy
onaka	stomach, abdomen
suku	to become empty
onaka ga suku	to get hungry
nodo	throat
kawaku	to get dry
nodo ga kawaku	to get thirsty
kaiten suru	to open a shop
gozaimasu	to have, be (honorific)
teinei	polite
kekkoo	satisfactory, fine, good
hoka ni	else, in addition

RENSHUU

A. Answer the following questions based on the dialogue.

1. *Imai san to Hamada san ga itta resutoran no namae wa nan desu ka.*
2. *Dare ga suteeki o tabemasu ka.*
3. *Imai san wa dono osakana ni shimashita ka.*
4. *Hamada san wa donna suupu o nomimasu ka.*

B. It is 5:00 P.M. now. What did Mr. Fujii do today?

7:55 A.M.	He left home.
8:59	He arrived at his company.
11:55	He called the department head.
12:00 P.M.	He had lunch.
3:00–4:58	meeting

1. *Asa _____ fun mae ni uchi o demashita* ("left home").
2. *_____ ji mae ni kaisha ni tsukimashita.*
3. *Hirugohan o _____ mae ni buchoo ni denwa o kakemashita.*
4. *_____ kan _____ ni, kaigi ni demashita.*
5. *Kaigi wa _____ ji mae ni owarimashita.*

C. The following is a restaurant menu. Fill in the blanks according to the menu.

suteeki	3,000 en
tonkatsu	1,500 en
hanbaagu	800 en
sarada	500 en
konsome	600 en
potaaju	700 en
pan	100 en
raisu	150 en

1. *Raisu wa _____ yori takai desu.*
2. *_____ ga ichiban takai desu.*
3. *Hanbaagu yori tonkatsu _____ hoo ga _____ desu.*
4. *Suupu wa sarada yori _____ desu.*

D. Fill in the blanks with particles according to the English equivalents.

1. *Pan wa mittsu _____ gohyakuen desu.*
   Bread is five hundred yen for three pieces.
2. *Ueetoresu _____ naka _____, ano hito ga ichiban teinei desu.*
   Among the waitresses, she is the most polite.
3. *Niku _____ osakana _____ hoo ga suki desu.*
   I like fish better than meat.
4. *Paatii wa ano resutoran _____ aru soo desu.*
   I understand that the party will be at that restaurant.

E. Read the following and write the English equivalents.

1. 店の前

2. 八日前

F. Rewrite the following using *kanji*.

1. あのみせには に、さんしゅう　　　　　I went to that store two
   かんまえに いったんです。　　　　　　or three weeks ago.

2. わたしは おさかなが いちばん　　　　I like fish best.
   すきなんです。

G. Answer the following questions about yourself.

1. *neru mae ni nani o shimasu ka.* (before you go to sleep)
2. *kaisha ni iku mae ni nani o shimasu ka.* (before you go to the office)
3. *hashiru mae ni nani o shimasu ka.* (before you run)
4. *taberu mae ni nani o shimasu ka.* (before you eat)

KARUCHAA · NOOTO

You will find various kinds of restaurants and coffee shops in Japan. In most restaurants, except for in the more fancy ones, you can usually find a showcase near the entrance displaying the dishes, usually made of wax or plastic, and their prices. These replicas actually look like the real food, so you can get some idea of what you will be served. When you are seated at a table, the waiter or waitress brings complimentary water or Japanese tea. Usually, you get an *oshibori*, a wet hand towel, to cleanse your hands, as well. The *oshibori* is cold in summer and hot in winter. In many restaurants, however, you do not get napkins. As mentioned before, tipping is not customary in Japan.

KOTAE

A. 1. *Chigusaya desu.* 2. *Hamada san ga tabemasu.* 3. *Masu ni shimashita.*
4. *Konsome o nomimasu.*
B. 1. *hachiji go* 2. *Ku* 3. *taberu* 4. *Niji, mae* 5. *go*
C. 1. *pan* 2. *Suteeki* 3. *no, takai* 4. *takai*
D. 1. *de* 2. *no, de* 3. *yori, no* 4. *de*
E. 1. みせの まえ　in front of the store 2. ようかまえ　eight days ago

F. 1. あの店には 二、三しゅう間前に 行ったんです。　2. 私は お魚が
一番 好きなんです。
G. 1. *neru mae ni ha o migakimasu.* (I brush my teeth before I go to bed.)
2. *kaisha ni iku mae ni gohan o tabemasu.* (I eat before I go to the office.)
3. *hashiru mae ni sutoretchi o shimasu.* (I stretch before I run.) 4. *taberu mae ni te o araimasu.* (I wash my hands before I eat.)

DAI NIJUU GOKA
Lesson 25
ONSEN.　Hot Springs.

A. DAIAROOGU

ONSEN RYOKOO NO KEIKAKU.

Mr. Ikawa and Mr. Carter, an American, are colleagues.

IKAWA: Kono renkyuu ni onsen ni iku tsumori ná n desu kedo, Káataa san mo yókattara, ikimasén ka. Onsen ni háiru no wa uchi de kutsurógu yori íi desu yo.

KAATAA: Bóku wa onsen ní wa itta kotó ga nái n desu. Zéhi, tsurete ítte kudasái. Démo, takái deshoo ne.

IKAWA: Sóo desu ne. Amari yuumei de nái onsen nára, shukuhákuhi wa minná ga iu hodo tákaku nái to omoimásu yo. Sore ni, yuumei de, kónde iru onsen ni iku yóri, hito no amari ikanai onsen de kutsurógu hóo ga tanoshíi to omóu n desu.

KAATAA: Dóko no onsen ga ichiban kónde imásu ka.

IKAWA: Sóo desu ne. Hónshuu de wa Átami nado ga kónde iru deshóo ne.

KAATAA: Kusátsu wa dóo desu ka.

IKAWA: Kusátsu wa Átami hodo óokiku nái to omoimásu kedo, yahári, yuumei na onsen désu kara hito mo oozei irú deshoo ne. Kono aida tomodachi kara kiitá n desu kedo, Kyúushuu no kitá ni áru Himeshima to iu shimá ni chíisakute, shízuka na onsen ga áru soo na n desu. Dóo omoimásu ka.

KAATAA: Íi desu née. Norimono wa nán ni shimásu ka.

IKAWA: Mochíron hikóoki de ikú no ga ichiban hayái desu kedo, Shinkánsen ni notté mo íi desu ne. Háyaku kimeta hóo ga íi desu kara, ashita onsen no hón to jikokuhyoo o motte kimasu.

PLANNING A TRIP TO A HOT SPRING.

IKAWA: I'm planning to go to a hot spring for the coming [consecutive] holidays. If you like, why don't you come along? Taking a hot spring bath is better than relaxing at home.

CARTER: I've never been to a hot spring. I'd love to go [Please take me along by all means]. But it will probably be expensive, right?

IKAWA: Well, if it's not one of those famous hot springs, the lodging cost is not as high as everybody says [I think]. And besides, I think that relaxing in a hot spring that isn't crowded is more enjoyable than going to a famous one anyway.

CARTER: Which hot spring is the most crowded?

IKAWA: Well, on Honshu, Atami, for example, probably is.

CARTER: How about Kusatsu?

IKAWA: I don't think Kusatsu is as big as Atami. But still, since it's a famous hot spring, it's probably also crowded. The other day, I got information from a friend of mine, and according to him, there's a small, quiet hot spring on an island called Himeshima to the north of Kyushuu. What do you think?

CARTER: That'll be great. How would we get there?

IKAWA: Of course, [going by] plane would be the fastest, but taking the Shinkansen would be fine, too. It's best [better] to make a decision early, so I'll bring the book on hot springs and the train schedule tomorrow.

B. BUNPOO TO YOOHOO

1. SUPERLATIVES WITH VERBAL PHRASES

The following rules apply to superlatives with verbal phrases.

a. Statements

For statements, use this sentence structure.

dictionary form *no wa/ga ichiban . . .*

Hikooki de iku no ga ichiban hayai desu.
Going by plane is the fastest.

Onsen ni hairu no wa ichiban tanoshii desu.
Bathing in a hot spring is the most enjoyable.

b. Questions

In questions with superlatives, the following two sentence patterns are typically used.

> dictionary form 1 *no to* dictionary form 2 *no to* dictionary form 3 *no to de wa dore ga ichiban . . . ka.*

To de wa can be reduced to *to de* or *de wa.*

Onsen ni hairu no to eiga o miru no to ongaku o kiku no to de wa dore ga ichiban suki desu ka.
   Which do you like best, bathing in a hot spring, watching a movie, or listening to music?

Onsen ni hairu no ga ichiban suki desu.
   I like bathing in a hot spring best.

Oyogu no to sukii o suru no to hashiru no de wa dore ga ichiban omoshiroi desu ka.
   Which is the most interesting, swimming, skiing, or running?

The second sentence pattern for superlative verbal phrases is:

> (noun *no naka de*/noun *de*) question word/phrase + particle . . . dictionary form *no ga ichiban . . . ka.*

Supootsu no naka de nani o suru no ga ichiban muzukashii desu ka.
   Among sports, which [to do what] is the most difficult?

Oyogu no ga ichiban muzukashii desu.
   Swimming is the most difficult.

Kono kurasu de dare ga nihongo o yomu no ga ichiban joozu desu ka.
   Who is the best at reading Japanese in this class?

2. COMPARATIVES WITH VERBAL PHRASES

The following rules apply for comparative expressions with verbal phrases.

a. Statements

The first of the two typical sentence patterns is:

> dictionary form 1 *no wa* . . . dictionary form 2 *(no) yori* . . .

Onsen ni hairu no wa uchi de kutsurogu yori ii desu yo.
   Taking a hot spring bath is better than relaxing at home.

Shinkansen de iku no wa hikooki de iku yori omoshiroi desu.
Going by the Shinkansen Line is more interesting than going by plane.

And here is the second sentence pattern:

> dictionary form 2 *(no) yori* . . . dictionary form 1 *hoo ga* . . .

Konde iru onsen ni iku yori, hito no amari ikanai onsen de kutsurogu hoo ga tanoshii desu.
Relaxing at a small, little-known hot spring is more enjoyable than going to a crowded hot spring.

Kusuri o nomu yori onsen ni hairu hoo ga kookateki desu.
Bathing in a hot spring is more effective than taking medicine.

The dictionary form directly before *hoo ga* can be replaced by the plain past form. If you use the past tense, the sentence becomes more emphatic. Therefore, the above sentence can be changed to:

Kusuri o nomu yori onsen ni haitta hoo ga kookateki desu. (*haitta* past form)
Bathing in a hot spring is more effective than taking medicine.

Sekken de aratta hoo ga ii desu yo. (*aratta* past form)
It's better to wash with soap.

Basu de itta hoo ga hayai desu. (*itta* past form)
It's faster to go by bus.

b. Questions

The structure of comparatives in questions is:

> dictionary form 1 *no to* . . . dictionary form 2 *no to (de wa) dochira (no hoo) ga . . . ka.*

Hon o yomu no to ongaku o kiku no to de wa dochira no hoo ga suki desu ka.
Which do you like better, reading books or listening to music?

Oshieru no to narau no to dochira ga omoshiroi desu ka.
Which is more interesting, teaching or learning?

3. NEGATIVE COMPARISON

There are three kinds of negative comparisons. Their English equivalent is "not as . . . as."

a. Negative comparisons with nouns

> noun 1 *wa* noun 2 *hodo* ... negative

Kusatsu wa Atami hodo ookiku nai desu.
    Kusatsu is not as big as Atami.

Shikoku wa Hokkaidoo hodo samuku arimasen.
    Shikoku is not as cold as Hokkaido.

b. Comparisons with verbal phrases:

> dictionary form 1 *no wa* ... dictionary form 2 *hodo* ... negative

Nihongo o hanasu no wa kaku hodo muzukashiku nai desu.
    Speaking Japanese is not as hard as writing it.

Uchi de ofuro ni hairu no wa onsen ni hairu hodo tanoshiku arimasen.
    Taking a bath at home is not as much fun as taking a bath at a hot
    spring.

c. With verbs such as *omou* "to think" or *iu* "to say"

> noun *wa*/dictionary form *no wa* ... a person/persons *ga omou,*
> *iu*, etc., *hodo* ... negative

Takushii de iku no wa minna ga omou hodo takaku nakatta desu.
    Going by taxi was not as expensive as everybody thinks.

Shukuhakuhi wa minna ga iu hodo takaku nai desu.
    The cost of lodging is not as high as everybody says.

*Eki kara ryokan made aruku no wa Yamada san ga iu hodo raku ja
arimasen deshita.*
    Walking to the inn from the station was not as easy as Mr. Yamada
    says.

4. *TSURETE* AND *MOTTE*

Both *tsurete*, the TE form of *tsureru* "to accompany," and *motte*, the TE
form of *motsu* "to hold" followed by *iku* "to go," *kuru* "to come," or
kaeru "to return" mean "to take along," "to bring along," or "to take
back/to bring back." The destination is followed by *ni* or *e*, just as it is
with other motion verbs.

a. *Tsurete*

Tsurete is used to refer to a person, a large animal, such as a horse, or an animal closely associated with people, such as a dog.

tsurete iku	to take along
tsurete kuru	to bring along
tsurete kaeru	to take back, to bring back

Tomodachi o onsen ni tsurete ikimashita.
I took my friend along to the hot spring.

Inu o tsurete kite mo ii desu ka.
May I bring the dog along?

Zehi tsurete itte kudasai.
By all means, please take me along.

b. *Motte*

Motte is used to refer to an inanimate being, a small animal, or one not closely associated with people.

motte iku	to take along
motte kuru	to bring along
motte kaeru	to take back, to bring back

Ashita onsen no hon to jikokuhyoo o motte kimasu.
I will bring along the book on hot springs and the timetable tomorrow.

Ryokan ni nemaki o motte ikanakute mo ii desu.
You don't have to take nightclothes to the inn.

Onsen no omiyage o motte kaerimashita.
I brought back a souvenir from the hot spring.

5. THE KU FORM OF *I*-ADJECTIVES AS ADVERBS

The KU form (derived by replacing the final *-i* with *-ku*) is used like an adverb.

enjoyable	*tanoshii*	→	*tanoshiku*	enjoyably
tight	*kitsui*	→	*kitsuku*	tightly
fast/early	*hayai*	→	*hayaku*	fast/early
slow/late	*osoi*	→	*osoku*	slowly/late
long	*nagai*	→	*nagaku*	for a long time

Hayaku kimeta hoo ga ii desu.
    It is better to decide early.

Onsen de mikkakan tanoshiku sugoshimashita.
    We spent three days having fun (enjoyably) at the hot spring.

Yoru osoku tomodachi ga kimashita.
    A friend of mine came late at night.

6. PARTICLES

a. *Ni* (with *hairu*)

With the motion verb *hairu* "to enter," the particle *ni* is used after the noun referring to the destination or goal (i.e., what you enter), just as it is with other verbs of motion.

Kissaten ni hairimashita.
    I entered the coffee shop.

Onsen ni hairu no wa uchi de kutsurogu yori ii desu yo.
    Bathing in [entering] a hot spring is better than relaxing at home.

Neru mae ni ofuro ni hairimashita.
    I took [entered] a bath before going to bed.

The particle *e* can also be used, but *ni* is preferred.

b. *Nado* "etc."

Nado means "etc." or "and so forth." It can also be used as "for example." It is often used with another particle, as part of a multiple particle (see Lesson 21, B6).

Atami nado ga konde iru deshoo ne.
    Atami, for example, is probably crowded.

Nani o tsukurimashoo ka.
    What should we cook [make]?

Gyooza nado wa doo desu ka.
    How about *gyooza*, for example?

7. THE PARTICLE-LIKE PHRASE *TO IU*

Some phrases consisting of a particle and a verb function like particles. One of them is *to iu* "called."

Himeshima to iu shima ni chiisai onsen ga aru soo desu.
    I heard that there is a small hot spring on the island of [called] Himeshima.

Tomoda san to iu hito o shitte imasu ka.
    Do you know a person called Tomoda?

Kawabata Yasunari no Yukiguni no hiroin wa Komako to iu geisha desu.
    The heroine in Kawabata Yasunari's *Snow Country* is a geisha called
    Komako.

C. MOJI

1. DIALOGUE

いかわ   「このれんきゅうに おんせんに 行く つもりなんです
         けど、カーターさんも よかったら、行きませんか。
         おんせんに 入るのは うちで くつろぐのより
         いいですよ。」

カーター 「ぼくは おんせんには 行ったことが ないんです。ぜひ
         つれてい*ってください。でも、高いでしょうね。」

いかわ   「そうですね。あまり ゆうめいでない おんせんなら、
         しゅくはくひは みんなが 言うほど 高くないと
         思いますよ。それに ゆうめいで、こんでいる おんせんに
         行くより 人の あまり 行かない おんせんで くつろぐ
         ほうが たのしいと 思うんです。」

カーター 「どこの おんせんが 一番 こんでいますか。」

いかわ   「そうですね。本州では あたみなどが こんでいる
         でしょうね。」

カーター 「くさつは どうですか。」

いかわ   「くさつは あたみほど 大きくないと 思いますけど、
         やはり ゆうめいな おんせんですから、人も 大ぜい
         いるでしょうね。このあいだ 友だちから、
         きいたんですけど、九州の きたにある ひめしまという
         しまに 小さくて、しずかな おんせんが あるそう
         なんです。どう 思いますか。」

* The word following a TE form is written in *hiragana*.

306

カーター　「いいですねえ。のりものは　何に　しますか。」

いかわ　　「もちろん、ひこうきで　行くのが　一番　はやいですけど、
　　　　　　しんかんせんに　のっても　いいですね。はやく　きめた
　　　　　　ほうが　いいですから、あした　おんせんの　本と
　　　　　　時こくひょうを　持ってきます。」

2. *HIRAGANA*

In the following word, the second *o* of *oo* is written as お.

oozei	おおぜい	many (people)

3. NEW *KANJI*

[54]	高	*taka(i)*	expensive, high, tall
[55]	州	*SHUU*	province, state e.g.,　本州、九州、 　　コロラド州
[56]	大	*oo(kii)*	big
[57]	友	*tomo*	friend e.g., 友だち
[58]	小	*chii(sai)*	small
[59]	持	*mo(tsu)*	to hold e.g., 持ってくる

STROKE ORDER

[54]	一　亠　宁　高　高
[55]	丶　丿　刎　州　卅　州
[56]	一　ナ　大
[57]	一　ナ　方　友
[58]	亅　小　小
[59]	一　扌　扌　扌　扩　扗　拝　持　持

4. NEW READING

[43]	入	*i (reru)* (Lesson 22)	to put in
		hai (ru)	to enter, to take (a bath)

D. TANGO TO HYOOGEN

shukuhaku	lodging
shukuhakuhi	cost of lodging
nemaki	nightclothes (traditional)
sekken	soap
(o)furo	bath
geisha	geisha (traditional female entertainer)
jikokuhyoo	schedule (of transportation)
renkyuu	consecutive holidays, two or more days off in a row
ongaku	music
kurasu	class
sukii o suru	to ski
kutsurogu	to relax
kimeru	to decide
sugosu	to spend
tsureru	to accompany
kookateki	effective
raku	comfortable, easy
oozei	many (people)
zehi	by all means
yahari	still, after all, as expected
mochiron	of course

RENSHUU

A. Answer the following questions based on the dialogue.

1. *Ikawa san to Kaataa san wa itsu onsen ni iku tsumori desu ka.*
2. *Kaataa san wa onsen ni itta koto ga arimasu ka.*
3. *Atami no onsen to Himeshima no onsen to de wa dochira no hoo ga nigiyaka desu ka.*
4. *Ikawa san wa ashita nani o motte kimasu ka.*

B. Fill in the blanks with words from the list below.
ichiban, no, suru, iku, hoo

1. *Koko kara shiyakusho made basu de iku _____[1] to jitensha de iku _____[2] to dochira no _____[3] ga hayai desu ka.*
   Jitensha de _____[4] hoo ga hayai desu yo.
2. *Kono byooki o naoshitai n desu. Nani o _____[5] _____[6] ga ichiban ii deshoo ka.*
   Onsen ni _____[7] _____[8] ga _____[9] ii to omoimasu.

C. Transform the following into negative comparisons.

Example: *Densha wa basu yori takakatta desu.*
  → *Basu wa densha hodo takaku nakatta desu.*

1. *Kono sekken wa watashi no sekken yori ii desu.*
2. *Hokkaidoo yori Shikoku no hoo ga atatakai desu.*
3. *Basu ni noru yori aruite iku hoo ga omoshiroi desu.*
4. *Yoru osoku hataraku no wa asa hayaku hataraku no yori iya desu.*

D. Fill in the blanks according to the English equivalents.

Ano onsen ni kodomotachi mo _____¹ _____² tai n desu. Okane o ikura _____³ _____⁴ ba ii desu ka.
I want to take along my children to that hot spring also. How much money should we take?
Juuman'en gurai _____⁵ _____⁶ ra doo desu ka.
How about taking about 100,000 yen?

E. Read the following and write the English equivalents.

1. 八時前に 入ってください。

2. はこの 中に お魚を 入れてください。

F. Rewrite the following using *kanji*.

1. きょう ともだちが
   チケットを もってくるんです。

   A friend of mine will bring me a ticket today.

2. コロラドしゅうは ちいさいですか。

   Is the state of Colorado small?

   いいえ、おおきいですよ。

   No, it's big.

3. あのみせの まえに ひとが
   おおぜい いましたよ。

   There were many people in front of that store.

4. このほんは たかかったです。

   This book was expensive.

G. Answer the following questions about yourself.

1. *onsen ni hairu no to sukii o suru no to dochira ga suki desu ka.*
2. *hon o yomu no to eiga o miru no to dochira ga tanoshii desu ka.*
3. *terebi o miru no to shinbun o yomu no to dochira ga suki desu ka.*

KARUCHAA NOOTO

Because of its many volcanoes, Japan has many hot springs emerging naturally from the earth, and a large number of resorts taking advantage of them. There are more than 2,300 hot spring resorts in Japan—from small, rustic ones with just one inn to lavish and huge ones with various entertainment centers, and everything in between. Many people go to these hot springs not only to escape from their hectic city lives but also for medicinal reasons. The water contains various minerals, said to be good for ailments such as skin troubles or neuralgia. Different hot springs may treat different ailments.

The procedure for taking a hot spring bath is identical to that for taking a bath in a Japanese home. No soap can be used in the tub. You wash and rinse yourself outside of the tub, which is only for warming your body. Some people enjoy drinking sake on a tray floating on the hot spring water.

Hot springs are especially crowded during holidays, such as around New Year and *renkyuu* "consecutive holidays." *Renkyuu* usually refers to the three national holidays that come within short intervals of one another—Greenery Day (April 29), Constitution Day (May 3), and Children's Day (May 5). Also called "Golden Week," this is one of the most popular vacation periods.

KOTAE

A. 1. *Renkyuu ni iku tsumori desu.* 2. *Iie, arimasen.* 3. *Atami no onsen no hoo ga nigiyaka desu.* 4. *Onsen no hon to jikokuhyoo o motte kimasu.*

B. 1. *no* 2. *no* 3. *hoo* 4. *iku* 5. *suru* 6. *no* 7. *iku* 8. *no* 9. *ichiban*

C. 1. *Watashi no sekken wa kono sekken hodo yoku nai desu.* 2. *Hokkaidoo wa Shikoku hodo atatakaku nai desu.* 3. *Basu ni noru no wa aruite iku hodo omoshiroku nai desu.* 4. *Asa hayaku hataraku no wa yoru osoku hataraku hodo iya ja/de (wa) nai desu.*

D. 1. *tsurete* 2. *iki* 3. *motte* 4. *ike* 5. *motte* 6. *itta*

E. 1. はちじまえに はいってください。 Please enter before eight o'clock. 2. はこの なかに おさかなを いれてください。 Please put the fish into the box.

F. 1. 今日 友だちが チケットを 持ってくるんです。 2. コロラド州は 小さいですか。いいえ、大きいですよ。 3. あの店の 前に 人が 大ぜい いましたよ。 4. この本は 高かったです。

G. 1. *onsen ni hairu hoo ga suki desu.*
2. *hon o yomu hoo ga tanoshii desu.*
3. *shinbun o yomu hoo ga suki desu.*

FUKUSHUU 5

A. Who am I? *(Watashi wa dare deshoo*.)*

1. *Watashi wa shoosetsu o takusan kakimashita. Watashi no kaita shoosetsu no naka de Yukiguni* "Snow Country" *ga ichiban yuumei da to omoimasu.*
2. *Watashi wa eiga o takusan tsukurimashita. Ran ya Kagemusha wa Amerikajin mo oozei mimashita. Tabun nihonjin no eiga kantoku* "movie director" *no naka de watashi ga ichiban yuumei deshoo.*

B. Fill in the blanks.

Examples: *Itte mo ii desu ka.*   *Ee, doozo.*
              Itte mo ii desu ka.   *Iie, ikanai de kudasai.*
              Ikanakute mo ii desu ka.   *Ee, ii desu.*
              Ikanakute mo ii desu ka.   *Iie, itte kudasai.*

1. *Kippu o kawanakute mo ii desu ka.*
   Ee, _____.
2. *Ashita konakute mo ii desu ka.*
   Iie, _____.
3. *Enpitsu de kaite mo ii desu ka.*
   Iie, enpitsu de _____.
4. *Kono jikokuhyoo o karite mo ii desu ka.*
   Ee, _____.

C. Fill in the blanks with particles according to the English equivalents.

1. *Kekkonshiki ni iku _____, Tanaka san mo kite imashita.*
   When I went to the wedding, Ms. Tanaka was there also.
2. *Kyonen wa onsen ni sando _____ itta n desu.*
   Last year I went to hot spring resorts as often as three times.
3. *Seiyooryoori _____ chuugokuryoori _____ hoo ga suki desu.*
   I like Chinese cuisine better than Western cuisine.
4. *Konpyuutaa o narau no wa anata ga omou _____ muzukashiku nai desu yo.*
   Learning to use a computer is not as hard as you think.

---

* This is the title of a game show that used to be popular on Japanese radio.

D. Let's compare Tokyo and Kyoto. Fill in the blanks according to the chart below.

Tokyo	Kyoto
	older
	more quiet
bigger	
more lively	

1. *Tookyoo wa Kyooto hodo* ———— *ku nai desu.*
2. *Kyooto wa Tookyoo hodo* ———— *ku nai desu.*
3. ———— *wa* ———— *yori shizuka desu.*
4. ———— *yori* ———— *no hoo ga nigiyaka desu.*

E. Choose the appropriate word from the left-hand side for each of the definitions on the right-hand side.

1. *kakitome*   a. *nihonfuu no hoteru*
2. *ozooni*   b. *hikooki de okuru yuubin*
3. *kitte*   c. *ichigatsu tsuitachi*
4. *nakoodo*   d. *omochi ga haitte iru nihonfuu no suupu*
5. *ryokan*
6. *gantan*
7. *hagaki*
8. *kookuubin*

F. Answer the following questions.

1. *Nihon de dono yama ga ichiban takai desu ka.*
2. *Nihon de dono shima ga ichiban ookii desu ka.*
3. *Kyuushuu to Hokkaidoo to de wa dochira no hoo ga ookii desu ka.*
4. *Atami to Himeshima de wa dochira no onsen no hoo ga yuumei desu ka.*

G. Write the following sentences in Japanese using *kanji* for the underlined parts.

1. The <u>weather</u> will probably get better [become good].
2. Please do not <u>put big fish</u> <u>into the water</u>.
3. A <u>friend brought</u> pretty <u>flowers</u>.

H. Read the following letter, and then mark the statements below
T (true), F (false), or X (cannot tell).

ブラウンさん、

さむく なりましたが、おげん気ですか。この お正月 何を
なさいますか。私は お正月 りょうしんの いる なごやに かえる
つもりですが、ブラウンさんも よかったら、いらっしゃいません
か。おおみそかの あさ はやく 行く つもりですが、ブラウンさ
んの つごうが わるければ、おそくてもかまいません。四日の
しごとが はじまる前に もどりたいと 思っています。私は よる
たいてい うちに います。おでんわを まっています。

１２月１５日

まつなが ひさこ

1. __ Ms. Matsunaga has to leave for her parents' home early in the
   morning on December 31.

2. __ Ms. Matsunaga is planning to resume her work on the fifth of
   January.

3. __ Ms. Brown is going to spend the New Year with Ms. Matsunaga.

4. __ Ms. Matsunaga wants Ms. Brown to call her.

KOTAE

A. 1. *Kawabata Yasunari* 2. *Kurosawa Akira*
B. 1. *ii desu* 2. *kite kudasai* 3. *kakanai de kudasai* 4. *doozo*
C. 1. *to* 2. *mo* 3. *yori, no* 4. *hodo*
D. 1. *furuku* 2. *ookiku* 3. *Kyooto, Tookyoo* 4. *Kyooto, Tookyoo*
E. 2-d, 5-a, 6-c, 8-b
F. 1. *Fujisan ga ichiban takai desu.* 2. *Honshuu ga ichiban ookii desu.*
3. *Hokkaidoo no hoo ga ookii desu.* 4. *Atami no hoo ga yuumei desu.*
G. 1. （お）天気は／が よく なるでしょう。 2. 大きい （お）魚を
水 （の中）に 入れないで ください。 3. 友だちは／が きれいな 花を
持ってきました。
H. 1. F 2. F 3. X 4. T

DAI NIJUU ROKKA
Lesson 26
RYOKAN.   A Japanese Inn.

A. DAIAROOGU

RYOKAN NI TSUITE.

Mr. Wagner, an American tourist, is traveling alone in Japan. He arrives at a Japanese inn in Takamatsu, Shikoku.

WAGUNAA: **Wágunaa to mooshimásu. Kinoo denwa de yoyaku shimáshita ga.**

UKETSUKE: **Áa, Wágunaa sama desu ne. Irasshaimáse.**

Chekkuin shite.

ANNAI GAKARI: **Dóozo kochira e. Onímotsu o omochi shimásu.**

Heya no naka de.

ANNAI GAKARI: **Súgu kákari no monó ga mairimásu kara, shóoshoo omachi kudasái.**

Shibaraku shite.

HEYA GAKARI: **Irasshaimáse.**

WAGUNAA: **Kono heyá wa nagamé ga íi desu ne.**

HEYA GAKARI: **Ée, kyóo wa íi oténki desu kara, shimá ga kukkíri to míete, kírei desu ne. Kore wa kochira no méibutsu no okáshi de gozaimásu. Dóozo.**

WAGUNAA: **Áa, dóomo.**

HEYA GAKARI: **Oshokuji no máe ni, ofúro ni ohairi ni narimásu ka.**

WAGUNAA: **Ée, soo shimásu. Ofúro wa dóko desu ka.**

HEYA GAKARI: **Ofúro wa rooka no tsukiatari ni gozaimásu. Kono yukata to tenugui o otsukai ni nátte kudasai. Jáa, mata nochi-hodo. Dóozo goyukkúri.**

ARRIVING AT THE INN.

WAGNER: I am [Mr.] Wagner. I made reservations by phone yesterday.

RECEPTIONIST: Oh, you are Mr. Wagner. Welcome.

After checking in.

USHER: This way, please. Let me carry your baggage.

In the room.

USHER: The person in charge is coming soon, so please wait a moment.

A little later.

MAID: Welcome.

WAGNER: This room has a fine view. [As for this room, the view (from it) is good.]

MAID: Yes. We have nice weather today, so you can see the islands clearly. The scenery is pretty, isn't it? Here are some sweets, our local specialty. Please have some.

WAGNER: Oh, thanks.

MAID: Will you take a bath before the meal?

WAGNER: Yes. I will. Where is the bathroom?

MAID: The bathroom is at the end of the corridor. You can use this *yukata* and towel. Well, we shall see you later. Please make yourself at home.

B. BUNPOO TO YOOHOO

1. A *WA* B *GA* PREDICATE

The structure A *wa* B *ga* predicate is used to describe a person or thing by mentioning individual features. A is a topic, and B is an attribute or subset of A. B *ga* is followed by a predicate that is an adjective or, less frequently, a verb. The clause (B *ga* and the predicate) describes A.

A   B

Tanaka san wa kami ga nagai desu.
    Ms. Tanaka's hair is long. [As for Ms. Tanaka, her hair is long.]

The following sentence expresses a similar meaning.

Tanaka san no kami wa nagai desu.
    Ms. Tanaka's hair is long.

The first sentence places more emphasis on Ms. Tanaka as the topic.

Kono heya wa nagame ga ii desu ne.
    The view from this room is nice. [As for this room, the view (from it) is good.]

Watashi ga tomatta heya wa mado to tenjoo ga rippa deshita.
    The windows and ceiling of the room where I stayed were magnificent. [As for the room where I stayed, its windows and ceiling were magnificent.]

Wagunaa san wa uchi ga Tekisasu ni arimasu.
    Mr. Wagner's house is in Texas. [As for Mr. Wagner, his house is in Texas.]

2. THE TERM OF RESPECT *SAMA*

Sama is a term of respect for addressing people. It can be attached to the family name, the given name, or the full name. It is more polite than *san*, and it is rarely used in casual conversation. It is used with the name of the addressee on a letter and also when referring to or addressing a customer.

Aa, Wagunaa sama desu ne. Irasshaimase.
    Oh, you are Mr. Wagner. Welcome.

Sama can replace *san* in roles or occupations (see Lesson 23, B6). For example, an employee who is in charge of a wedding at a hotel may say:

Shinpu sama no oseki wa kochira desu.
    The bride's seat is this way.

Sama is quite common with kinship terms.

Okaasama mo ogenki desu ka.
    Is your mother also well?

3. HONORIFIC COPULA

De gozaimasu is the honorific equivalent of *desu*. It is used as a humble honorific, or for simple politeness, or for a combination of the two.

Kore wa kochira no meibutsu no okashi de gozaimasu.
Here are some sweets, our local specialty.

Oikura desu ka.
How much is it?

Nisen'en de gozaimasu.
It is two thousand yen.

As with *gozaimasu* "to have/exist" (see Lesson 24, B4), only the normal forms are used in modern Japanese. Other forms (such as the plain forms, the TE form, and so forth) are obsolete.

4. HUMBLE HONORIFIC VERBS

Mairu and *moosu* are commonly used humble honorifics.

a. *Mairu*

The non-honorific equivalents are *iku* "to go" and *kuru* "to come."

Sugu kakari no mono ga mairimasu kara, shooshoo omachi kudasai.
The person in charge is coming soon, so please wait a moment.

Another humble honorific equivalent of *iku* "to go" or *kuru* "to come" is, as mentioned before, *ukagau* (see Lesson 20, B6). *Ukagau* implies first that the person visiting, most likely the speaker, is humbled, and second that the person visited is elevated. With *mairu*, however, the person visiting is humbled, but the person visited is not necessarily elevated. *Mairu* therefore can be used when visiting a place belonging to nobody or to your in-group. In the sentences below, *ukagau* cannot be used.

Kinoo kaigan e mairimashita.
I went to the seashore yesterday.

Musume no uchi e mairimashita.
I went to my daughter's house.

b. *Moosu*

The non-honorific equivalent is *iu* "to say." *Moosu* is often used in a formal setting or with a stranger.

Watashi mo soo mooshimashita.
I said so, too.

When you say your name, use . . . *to mooshimasu* "to be called."

317

Wagunaa to mooshimasu.
I am [called] Wagner.

Hajimemashite. Abe to mooshimasu. Doozo yoroshiku.
How do you do. My name is Abe. Nice to meet you.

5. REGULAR HUMBLE HONORIFICS

All honorific verbs so far have been irregular. However, there are humble honorific expressions that are derived regularly from non-honorific verbs. The pattern is:

> *o* + pre-*masu* form of the verb + *suru*

matsu	→	*omachi suru*	to wait
yobu	→	*oyobi suru*	to invite

This particular humble honorific pattern is used when you do something for someone else.

Onimotsu o omochi shimasu.
I will carry your baggage.

Sugu futon o oshiki shimasu.
I will make the bed [spread the futon] for you.

The same pattern is used when someone in addition to the speaker is involved in the action. In the following sentence, "your father" and the speaker are both involved in the action of talking.

Kinoo otoosama to ohanashi shimashita.
I talked with your father yesterday.

This pattern cannot be used with verbs whose pre-*masu* form has only one syllable, like, for example, *suru* "to do," *kuru* "to come," *kiru* "to wear," or *miru* "to see."

6. REGULAR RESPECT HONORIFICS

All respect verbs so far have been irregular. However, there is a regular structure for respect honorifics similar to the one for humble honorifics.

> *o* + pre-*masu* form of the verb + *ni naru*

yomu	→	*oyomi ni naru*	to read
dekakeru	→	*odekake ni naru*	to go out

Oshokuji no mae ni ofuro ni ohairi ni narimasu ka.
    Do you want to take a bath before the meal?

Ano okyaku sama wa ototoi kara otomari ni natte imasu.
    That guest has been staying here since the day before yesterday.

Kono yukata to tenugui o otsukai ni natte kudasai.
    You can use [please use] this *yukata* and towel.

As with regular humble honorifics, verbs with one-syllable pre-*masu*
forms cannot take this pattern.

C. MOJI

1. DIALOGUE

ワグナー　　　　「ワグナーと申します。きのう でんわで
　　　　　　　　　よやくしましたが。」

うけつけ　　　　「ああ、ワグナー様ですね。
　　　　　　　　　いらっしゃいませ。」

―――――――――――――――――――

あんないがかり「どうぞ こちらへ。おにもつを お持ちします。」

　　　　　　　　　へやの中で

あんないがかり「すぐ かかりまの者が まいりますから、
　　　　　　　　　しょうしょう お待ちください。」

―――――――――――――――――――

へやがかり　　　「いらっしゃいませ。」

ワグナー　　　　「このへやは ながめが いいですね。」

へやがかり　　　「ええ、今日は いいお天気ですから、島が
　　　　　　　　　くっきりと 見えて、きれいですね。これは
　　　　　　　　　こちらの めいぶつの おかしでございます。どうぞ。」

ワグナー	「ああ、どうも。」
へやがかり	「おしょくじの前に、おふろに お入りに なりますか。」
ワグナー	「ええ、そうします。おふろは どこですか。」
へやがかり	「おふろは ろうかの つきあたりに ございます。 この ゆかたと てぬぐいを お使いに なって ください。じゃあ、また、のちほど。どうぞ、 ごゆっくり。」

2. NEW *KANJI*

[60]	申	*moo(su)*	to say (humble)
[61]	様	*sama*	term of respect
[62]	者	*mono*	person (humble)
[63]	待	*ma(tsu)*	to wait
[64]	島	*shima*	island
[65]	見	*mi(ru), mi(eru)*	to see
[66]	使	*tsuka(u)*	to use

STROKE ORDER

[60]	丨 冂 冂 日 申
[61]	木 木 栏 栏 栏 栟 様 様
[62]	土 尹 者
[63]	彳 彳 待 待 待
[64]	丨 冂 冂 臼 臼 島 島
[65]	丨 冂 冂 月 目 貝 見
[66]	亻 亻 佢 伊 使

D. TANGO TO HYOOGEN

rooka	corridor
tenjoo	ceiling
futon	futon mattress
yukata	cotton kimono
tenugui	towel
kakari	person in charge
meibutsu	local specialty
kaigan	seashore
nagame	view
tsukiatari	end (of a corridor, street, etc.)
sama	Mr., Mrs., Ms.
yoyaku suru	to make a reservation
tomaru	to stay overnight
shiku	to spread
mairu	to go, come, visit (honorific)
moosu	to say (honorific)
de gozaimasu	the copula (honorific)
kukkiri (to)	clearly
Doozo yoroshiku.	Nice to meet you.
Doozo goyukkuri.	Make yourself at home.

RENSHUU

A. Answer the following questions based on the dialogue.

1. *Wagunaa san wa ryokan ni iku mae ni yoyaku shimashita ka.*
2. *Wagunaa san no heya kara nani ga miemasu ka.*
3. *Wagunaa san wa shokuji o itsu suru tsumori desu ka.*
4. *Ofuro wa doko ni arimasu ka.*

B. Make comments about the Japanese hotels in town following the example.

Example: *Kikuya*   service   good
    → *Kikuya wa saabisu ga ii desu.*

ryokan no namae

1. *Kameya*	bath	magnificent
2. *Tsubakisoo*	fish	delicious
3. *Matsukazesoo*	entrance	dark
4. *Shiraki Ryokan*	*tatami* mats	old

C. Make the appropriate choice from the list below, and fill in the blanks with its proper form.

ukagaimasu, nasaimasu, mooshimasu, orimasu, irasshaimasu, shimasu, imasu, mairimasu

Tanaka: *Tanaka to _____¹. Doozo yoroshiku.*
Sawada: *Tanaka san wa itsu kono machi ni _____² n desu ka.*
Tanaka: *Ototoi _____³. Ima tomodachi no uchi ni _____⁴ n desu kedo, apaato o sagashite _____⁵ n desu.*

D. Fill in the blanks with the appropriate form of *o——ni naru* or *o——suru.*

a: *Moo repooto o _____¹ mashita ka.*
   Have you written the report yet?
b: *Iie, osoku natte sumimasen. Yuubin de _____² masu.*
   No, I am sorry for being late. I will mail it [send it by mail].
a: *Jaa, _____³ te imasu.*
   Well then, I will be waiting.

E. Read the following, and write the English equivalents.

a. まゆみさんの おかあ様ですか。島中と 申します。

b. ああ、まゆみは しんせきの者たちと いっしょに えいがを 見に 行ったんです。すぐもどりますから、よかったら、お待ちに なってください。

a. いいえ、また のちほどまいります。

b. あ、雨が ふっていますね。このかさを どうぞ。

a. いいんですか。

b. ええ、今 使っていませんから。

KARUCHAA NOOTO

There are many kinds of accommodations in Japan. In big cities, there are plenty of Western hotels, some of which are as luxurious as their American counterparts. The less expensive *bijinesu hoteru* "business hotels" are popular with business people for short stays. Rooms in these hotels are small and simple, but clean.

If you want to experience an authentic Japanese atmosphere, go to a Japanese inn, or *ryokan*. The rooms there are *tatami* rooms (see Lesson 18). Dinner and breakfast are included in the price, and the maid in charge of your room brings your meals to you. Normally, you are given no choices and are expected to eat what is served. After dinner, the maid makes your bed by spreading a *futon* on the *tatami* floor. Not all rooms have a private bath. However, there may be personal baths called *kazokuburo* "family baths," and public baths somewhere in the building. If the hotel is in a hot spring resort, the baths in the *ryokan* are most likely hot spring baths. Remember that tipping is not customary in Japan, although it is more common in inns than it is in restaurants and coffee shops.

KOTAE

A. 1. *Hai, shimashita.* 2. *Shima ga miemasu.* 3. *Ofuro ni haitte kara, suru tsumori desu.* 4. *Rooka no tsukiatari ni arimasu.*
B. 1. *Kameya wa (o)furo ga rippa desu.* 2. *Tsubakisoo wa (o)sakana ga oishii desu.* 3. *Matsukazesoo wa iriguchi ga kurai desu.* 4. *Shiraki Ryokan wa tatami ga furui desu.*
C. 1. *mooshimasu* 2. *irasshatta* 3. *mairimashita* 4. *iru* 5. *iru*
D. 1. *okaki ni nari* 2. *ookuri shi* 3. *omachi shi*
E. a.—— 様 (*sama*)—— 島中 (*shimanaka*)—— 申 (*moo*)

  b.—— 者 (*mono*)—— 見 (*mi*)—— 行 (*i*)—— 待 (*ma*)

  b.—— 雨 (*ame*)

  b.—— 今 (*ima*)—— 使 (*tsuka*)

a. Are you Mayumi's mother? I am called Shimanaka.

b. Mayumi went to see a movie with our relatives. She'll be back soon. If you would like to, please wait here.

a. No, I'll come back later.

b. Oh, it's raining. You may take this umbrella.

a. Is it all right?

b. Yes, we don't need it [aren't using it] now.

DAI NIJUU NANAKA
Lesson 27
REKISHI NO FURUI MACHI. Historical Towns.

A. DAIAROOGU

KYOOTO TO NARA.

Ms. Kaneko and Ms. Ford are colleagues at a company.

FOODO: **Kyóo Nyuuyóoku kara ryóoshin ga asobi ni kúru node, kono shuumatsu issho ni Kyóoto to Nára e ikú n desu.**

KANEKO: **Sóo desu ka. Dónna tokoró o kenbutsu surú n desu ka.**

FOODO: **Máda kimete inái n desu. Dóko ka íi tokoró o shirimasén ka.**

KANEKO: **Sóo desu ne. Watashi wa gakusei no tokí ni Kyóoto ni itte, iroiro na otera ya jínja o kenbutsu shitá n desu kedo, yahári ichiban yókatta no wa Ryóoanji desu ne. Watashi ga itta tóki wa juugatsú de kónde itá n desu kedo, sore démo, ano subarashíi niwa o míte, náni ka kuchi de wa ienai monó o kanjimáshita ne.**

FOODO: **Nára wa dóo desu ka.**

KANEKO: **Nára e wa kodomo no kóro ni itta kotó ga áru n desu kedo, amari shiranái n desu. Gakusei no tokí, sekkaku Kyóoto made ittá noni, zannen nágara, Nára e wa iku jikan ga nákatta n desu. Démo, kodomo no tokí ni míta Toodáiji no Daibutsu no migotósa wa íma de mo obóete imasu yo.**

FOODO: **Áa, ano Daibutsu wa watashi mo ítsu ka mitái to omótte itá n desu. Dóomo arígatoo. Jáa, mata raishuu oai shimásu.**

KANEKO: **Ée, ki o tsúkete.**

KYOTO AND NARA.

FORD: My parents are coming from New York today, and we're going to Kyoto and Nara this weekend.

KANEKO: Really? What are you going to see there?

324

FORD: We haven't decided yet. Do you have any suggestions? [Don't you know any nice places?]

KANEKO: Well, when I was a student, I went to Kyoto. I visited various temples and shrines, and the one I liked best [after all] was [is] Ryoanji. I went there in October [When I went there, it was in October], and it was crowded. But still, looking at that wonderful garden, I felt something I can't express in words [say with my mouth].

FORD: How about Nara?

KANEKO: I went to Nara [around the time] when I was a child, but I don't know much about it. Although I went all the way to Kyoto when I was a student, unfortunately, I did not have the time to go to Nara. But the splendor of the Great Buddha of Todaiji I saw when I was a child is something I remember even now.

FORD: Oh, yes, I wanted to see that Great Buddha someday, too. Thank you. See you next week.

KANEKO: Yes. Enjoy your trip.

B. BUNPOO TO YOOHOO

1. *TOKI* "WHEN"

Toki "time" is used with *ano* "that," *kono* "this," and similar words, or after a subordinate clause meaning "(the time) when."

Ano toki watashi wa mada gakusei deshita.
At that time I was still a student.

Tootoo ano mura e kaeru toki ga kimashita.
Finally, the time came for me to return to that village.

A *toki* clause used adverbially means "when. . . ." *Toki* can be followed by *ni* "at" to emphasize the time. *Wa* "as for" can also be used either after *ni* or directly after *toki* (if used without *ni*). With *wa*, the *toki* clause becomes a topic.

Watashi ga itta toki wa, konde ita n desu.
When I went there, it was crowded.

Ryooshin ga kita toki ni, kono omiyage o kuremashita.
When my parents came, they gave me this souvenir.

Kyooto o kenbutsu suru toki, chizu o motte ikimashoo.
When we visit Kyoto, let's take the map.

Like other subordinate clauses with negative, stative, or ongoing meanings, the *toki* clause can be in the present-tense <u>form</u> even if it conveys a past meaning.

Gakusei <u>no</u> toki, Kyooto ni itte, iroiro na otera ya jinja o kenbutsu shita n desu. (*No* before *toki* is a present-tense form.)
  When I was [am] a student, I went to Kyoto and visited various temples and shrines.

Hima ga <u>aru</u> toki, Nara Kooen o sanpo shimashita. (*Aru* before *toki* is a present-tense form.)
  When I had [have] free time, I took a walk in Nara Park.

When the clause has an action verb in the affirmative, the distinction between present and past becomes clear. The tense distinction, however, is different from that in English. Compare:

Nara ni <u>iku</u> toki, kamera o kaimasu.
  When I go [am going] to Nara, I will buy a camera.

Nara ni <u>itta</u> toki, shashin o torimasu.
  When I go to Nara, I will take pictures.

Both of the English "when" clauses above are in the present tense "(go)." In the Japanese sentences, however, the first example uses *iku* (present), whereas the second uses *itta* (past). The second sentence makes it clear that you will take pictures after the action of going to Nara has been completed, or, in other words, while you are in Nara.

Nara ni <u>iku</u> toki, kamera o kaimashita.
  When I <u>went</u> [was going] to Nara, I bought a camera.

Nara ni <u>itta</u> toki, shashin o torimashita.
  When I <u>went</u> to Nara, I took pictures.

Both of the English "when" clauses are in the past tense ("went"). However, in the Japanese sentences, the first *toki* clause is in the present tense *(iku),* while the second one is in the past tense *(itta).* This means that regardless of whether the final clause is in the present or past, the *toki* clause takes the present tense if its action has not been completed before the action in the final clause. If, however, the action in the *toki* clause has been completed before the action in the final clause, the *toki* clause takes the past tense.

Koro "(approximate) time" is used in a way similar to *toki.*

ano koro
  around that time

Nara e wa kodomo no koro ni itta koto ga aru n desu.
  I went [have been] to Nara during [around the time of] my childhood.

Gakkoo kara kaetta koro ni, denwa shimasu.
  I will call you around the time when I return from school.

2. THE CLAUSE PARTICLE *NODE* "BECAUSE"

Node is a clause particle that means "because," "since," "so," or "therefore." Like *kara*, it is used at the end of a causal clause (see Lesson 9, C5). A plain form usually precedes *node*, although a normal form is possible in polite speech.

Nyuuyooku kara ryooshin ga asobi ni kuru node, issho ni Kyooto to Nara e iku n desu.
  Since my parents are coming from New York to visit, we are going to Kyoto and Nara.

Ano otera wa konde ita node, hairanakatta n desu.
  Since that temple was crowded, we didn't go in.

Kyooto wa Oosaka kara chikai node, gogo iku tsumori desu.
  Kyoto is near Osaka, so I plan to go there in the afternoon.

The copula *da* turns into *na* in the present affirmative with *na*-adjectives and nouns. Therefore, *node* belongs to Type III (see Lesson 21, B4).

Kono jinja wa yuumei na node, hito ga takusan mi ni kimasu.
  Since this shrine is famous, many people come to see it.

Ashita wa doyoobi na node, uchi ni iru tsumori desu.
  Tomorrow is Saturday, so I plan to stay home.

3. COMPARISON OF *NODE* AND *KARA*

Both *node* and *kara* mean "because," but there are some differences between them. *Node* is sometimes considered more formal and polite. Although both *node* and *kara* can follow a plain form, *kara* follows the copula *da* in the present affirmative (Type I; see Lesson 21, B4), while *node* follows *na*.

Ano kooen wa shizuka da kara, yoku iku n desu.
Ano kooen wa shizuka na node, yoku iku n desu.
  Since that park is quiet, I often go there.

Furui machi da kara, furui tatemono ga takusan arimasu.
Furui machi na node, furui tatemono ga takusan arimasu.
  Since it's an old town, there are many old buildings.

4. *NONI* "ALTHOUGH"

Noni is a clause particle that means "although" or "but." Usually, a plain form precedes *noni,* although a normal form is possible in polite conversation.

Kyooto made itta noni, Nara e wa iku jikan ga nakatta n desu.
Although I went to Kyoto, I did not have the time to go to Nara.

Ano otera wa eki kara tooi noni, itsumo konde imasu.
Although that temple is far from the station, it is always crowded.

With *na*-adjectives and nouns, the copula *da* changes to *na* in the present affirmative. *Noni,* like *node,* belongs to Type III (see Lesson 21, B4).

Ryokoo ga suki na noni, iku jikan ga nai n desu.
I like traveling, but I don't have the time.

Asai ike na noni, sakana ga takusan imasu.
Even though it is a shallow pond, there are many fish.

5. COMPARISON OF *NONI* AND *KEDO*

Kedo "although, but" and its variants, *keredo* and *keredomo,* are similar to *noni* "although, but," but there are some differences between them. *Noni* implies a stronger sense of reversal or contrast than *kedo* (*keredo, keredomo*). Like *noni, kedo* can follow a plain form, but, with the copula in the present affirmative, *kedo* follows *da* (Type I; see Lesson 21, B4), while *noni* follows *na.*

Yamada san wa furansugo ga joozu da kedo, amari hanashimasen.
Yamada san wa furansugo ga joozu na noni, amari hanashimasen.
Although Mr. Yamada is good at French, he doesn't speak it much.

Kyoo wa nichiyoobi da keredo, otera wa konde imasen ne.
Kyoo wa nichiyoobi na noni, otera wa konde imasen ne.
Today is Sunday, but the temples are not crowded.

When the main clause expresses a request or suggestion, *kedo* and its variants can be used, but *noni* cannot.

Otenki ga warui keredo, shashin o totte kudasai.
The weather is bad, but please take pictures.

Ano bijutsukan wa tooi keredo, mi ni ikimashoo ka.
Although that museum is far, should we go to see it (anyway)?

6. QUESTION WORDS WITH *KA*

The combination of a question word such as *dare* "who" and *ka* means "some–" in a statement and "any/some–" in a question.

Dare ka (ga) soo itte ita n desu.
Someone was saying so.

Asoko ni nani ka (ga) arimasu ka.
Is there anything over there?

Dare ka (o) erande kudasai.
Please choose someone.

As seen above, the particles *ga* or *o* can be deleted. However, other particles should not be deleted.

Doko ka de shokuji shimasen ka.
Why don't we eat somewhere?

Kyooto e dare ka to issho ni itta n desu ka.
Did you go to Kyoto with someone?

With *itsuka* "sometime" or a quantity expression, such as *nanmai ka* "some (tickets)," no particle is used.

Itsuka mitai to omotte ita n desu.
I was thinking I wanted to see it sometime.

Chiketto o nanmai ka kaimashita.
I bought a certain number of tickets.

The question word plus *ka* can be followed by a noun phrase.

Doko ka ii tokoro o shitte imasu ka.
Do you know any place that is nice?

Dare ka rekishi no suki na hito ni kikimashoo.
Let's ask someone who likes history.

Ano subarashii niwa o mite, nani ka kuchi de wa ienai mono o kanjimashita.
Looking at that wonderful garden, I felt something that I couldn't express in words.

7. *NO* "ONE"

No is a dependent noun whose English equivalent is "one." It always follows its modifier.

A: *Dono otera ga yokatta desu ka.*
   Which temple was nice?

B: *Ichiban yokatta no wa Ryooanji desu.*
   The [one which was the] best one is Ryoanji.

A: *Donna kuruma ga ii desu ka.*
   What kind of car would you like?

B: *Ookii no ga hoshii desu.*
   I want a big one.

C: *Watashi wa chiisakute, benri na no ga hoshii desu.*
   I want a small and convenient one.

A: *Kore wa Nara de totta shashin desu.*
   These are the pictures I took in Nara.

B: *Kyooto de totta no mo arimasu ka.*
   Do you also have the ones you took in Kyoto?

8. *-SA*

If the suffix *-sa* is attached to an adjective, it becomes a noun.

a. *I*-adjectives

The final *-i* is replaced by *-sa*.

ookii	big	→	*ookisa*	size
nagai	long	→	*nagasa*	length

Ike no fukasa wa dono gurai desu ka.
   What is the depth of the pond?

Samusa de karada ga furuemashita.
   My body shivered with the cold.

b. *Na*-adjectives

The suffix *-sa* is attached directly to *na*-adjectives.

nigiyaka	lively	→	*nigiyakasa*	liveliness
soogon	solemn	→	*soogonsa*	solemnness

330

Toodaiji no Daibutsu no migotosa wa ima de mo oboete imasu.
　　Even now I remember the splendor of the Great Buddha of Todaiji.

Ano machi no nodokasa ga suki desu.
　　I like the tranquillity of that town.

C. MOJI

1. DIALOGUE

フォード 「今日 ニューヨークから りょうしんが あそびに 来る
　　　　 ので、このしゅうまつ いっしょに きょうとと ならへ
　　　　 行くんです。」

かねこ 「そうですか。どんな 所を けんぶつするんですか。」

フォード 「まだ きめていないんです。どこか いい所を
　　　　 しりませんか。」

かねこ 「私は 学生の 時に きょうとに 行って、いろいろな
　　　　 お寺や じんじゃを けんぶつしたんですけど、やはり、
　　　　 一番 よかったのは りょうあん寺ですね。 私が 行った
　　　　 時は 十月で、こんでいたんですけど、それでも、
　　　　 あのすばらしい 庭を 見て、なにか 口では
　　　　 言えないものを かんじましたね。」

フォード 「ならは どうですか。」

かねこ 「ならへは こどもの 時に 行ったことが あるんですけど、
　　　　 あまり しらないんです。せっかく きょうとまで 行った
　　　　 のに、ざんねんながら、ならへは 行く時間が なかったん
　　　　 です。でも、こどもの 時に 見た とうだい寺の だいぶつ
　　　　 の 見ごときは 今でも おぼえていますよ。」

フォード 「ああ、あのだいぶつは 私も いつか 見たいと 思って
　　　　 いたんです。どうも ありがとう。じゃあ、また
　　　　 らいしゅう お会いします。」

かねこ 「ええ、気をつけて。」

2. NEW *KANJI*

[67]	来	*ku(ru), ki(masu), ko(nai)*	to come
[68]	所	*tokoro*	place
[69]	学	*GAKU*	studying e.g., 学生
[70]	寺	*tera, JI*	temple
[71]	庭	*niwa*	garden
[72]	口	*kuchi*	mouth
[73]	会	*a(u)*	to meet

STROKE ORDER

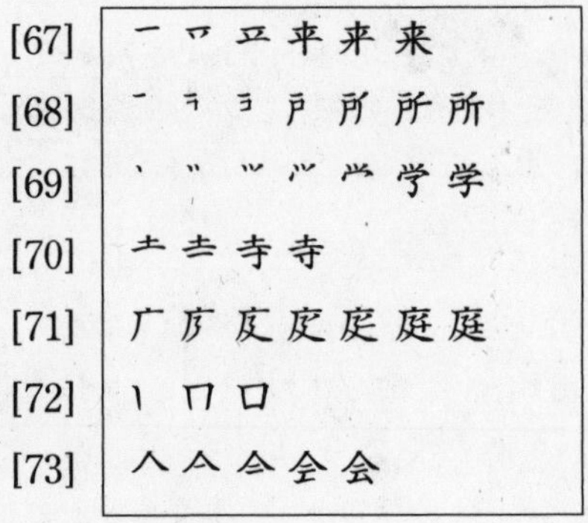

3. NEW READING

[28]	時	*JI* (Lesson 20)	time, o'clock
		toki	time

D. TANGO TO HYOOGEN

rekishi	history
mura	village
ike	pond
kuchi	mouth
shuumatsu	weekend
gogo	afternoon
toki	time, when . . .

koro	around the time of (dependent noun)
no	one (dependent noun)
sanpo suru	to take a walk
kanjiru	to feel
erabu	to select
furueru	to shiver
migoto	splendid
asai	shallow
fukai	deep
soogon	solemn
sekkaku	with trouble, by taking time
tootoo	finally
mada	yet (in a negative sentence)
zannen nagara	unfortunately
Ki o tsukete.	Good luck./Have a nice time.

RENSHUU

A. Answer the following questions based on the dialogue.

1. *Foodo san wa dare to Kyooto to Nara e iku tsumori desu ka.*
2. *Ryooanji wa doko ni arimasu ka.*
3. *Kaneko san wa itsu Nara e ikimashita ka.*
4. *Nara no Daibutsu wa dono otera ni arimasu ka.*

B. When do you use the following greetings? Fill in the blanks.

Example: *Oyasumi nasai.* <u>*neru*</u> toki

1. *Ohayoo gozaimasu.*   *asa* _____ *toki* ("when you get up")
2. *Gochisoosama.*   *gohan o* _____ *toki*
3. *Itadakimasu.*   *gohan o* _____ *toki*
4. *Doo itashimashite.*   *dare ka ga orei o* _____ *toki*

C. Fill in the blanks with *node* or *noni*.

a: *Sekkaku Nara no Daibutsu o mi ni itta* _____[1], *otenki ga waruku natta* _____[2], *iku no o yameta n desu.*

b: *Sugu okaeri ni natta n desu ka.*

a: *Iie, onaka ga suita* _____[3], *resutoran ni haitta n desu. Sono resutoran wa chiisai* _____[4], *iroiro na mono ga atte, sore ni aji mo ii* _____[5], *mata ikitai to omotte iru n desu.*

D. Fill in the blanks with question words.

a: *Ashita* _____¹ *ka e asobi ni ikimasen ka.*

b: _____² *ka ga itte ita n da kedo, Nara no Wakakusayama ga ii soo desu yo.*

a: *Aa, Wakakusayama e wa watashi mo* _____³ *ka ikitai to omotte ita n desu.* _____⁴ *ka taberu mono o motte ikimashoo ka.*

b: *Nara ni tsuite kara,* _____⁵ *ka de kaimasen ka.*

E. Read the following, and write the English equivalents.

きょうとに すんでいる 友だちの うちに 行きました。私たちが 学生の 時に よく 行った 所を けんぶつしました。でも、時間が なかったので、りょうあん寺の 庭は 見られませんでした。

F. Write characters in the boxes.

かたかな   かんじ

1. *ro*	2. "mouth"
3. *ni*	4. "two"
5. *ha*	6. "eight"

G. Answer the following questions about yourself using NODE.

Example: *Shinkansen ni noru toki, nani o motte ikimasu ka.*
→ *hima na node hon o motte ikimasu.*

1. *nihon ni iku toki, nani o motte ikimasu ka.*
2. *kaisha ni iku toki, nani o kite ikimasu ka.*
3. *tomodachi no uchi ni iku toki, nani o motte ikimasu ka.*

H. Answer the following questions.

Example: *Donna booshi ga hoshii desu ka. (guree no booshi)*
→ *Guree no ga hoshii desu.*

1. *donna baggu ga hoshii desu ka. (kurokute chiisai baggu)*
2. *donna kuruma ga ii desu ka. (akakute ookii kuruma)*
3. *kore wa dare no konpyuutaa desu ka? (Jon san no konpyuutaa)*

KARUCHAA NOOTO

The historical cities of Kyoto and Nara attract many foreign and Japanese tourists. Nara was the capital of Japan in the eighth century, and Kyoto was the capital from the eighth century to the nineteenth century. Tokyo only became the capital in 1868. Since the two co-existing religions, Shinto and Buddhism, were closely related to the daily life of the Japanese people, Buddhist temples and Shinto shrines were built, and priceless works of religious art were made and maintained. The Great Buddha in the Todaiji Temple in Nara, which is the largest wooden building in the world, is made of bronze and is 53.18 feet tall. The Ryoanji Temple in Kyoto is famous for its stone garden.

Besides Kyoto and Nara, other historical places include Kamakura and Nikko. Kamakura, west of Tokyo, was the political center controlled by samurai families from the twelfth to the fourteenth century, although Kyoto was still the capital where the emperors lived. Nikko, located north of Tokyo, is famous for the Toshogu Shrine built in honor of Tokugawa Ieyasu, who was a *shoogun*, or supreme military commander, in the early seventeenth century.

KOTAE

A. 1. *Ryooshin to iku tsumori desu.* 2. *Kyooto ni arimasu.* 3. *Kodomo no toki/koro (ni), ikimashita.* 4. *Toodaiji ni arimasu.*
B. 1. *okita* 2. *tabeta* 3. *taberu* 4. *itta*
C. 1. *noni* 2. *node* 3. *node* 4. *noni* 5. *node*
D. 1. *doko* 2. *Dare* 3. *itsu* 4. *Nani* 5. *doko*
E. __ 友(tomo) __ 行(i) __ 私(wata(ku)shi) __ 学生(gakusei) __ 時(toki) __ 行(i) __ 所(tokoro) __ 時間(jikan) __ 寺(ji) __ 庭(niwa) __ 見(mi)

I visited my friend who lives in Kyoto. We went to the places that we saw as [when we were] students. But since we did not have time, we were not able to see the garden of Ryoanji.

F. 1. ロ 2. 口 3. ニ 4. 二 5. ハ 6. 八
G. 1. *nihon o zenzen <u>shiranai node</u>, gaidobukku o motte ikimasu.* (I take a guidebook because I don't know anything about Japan.) 2. *ruuru <u>na node</u> suutsu o kite ikimasu.* (I wear a suit because it's a rule.) 3. *wain ga suki <u>na node</u> wain o motte ikimasu.* (I bring wine because he likes it.)
H. 1. *kurokute chiisai <u>no</u> ga hoshii desu.* 2. *akakute ookii <u>no</u> ga ii desu.*
3. *Jon san <u>no</u> desu.*

DAI NIJUU HACHIKA
Lesson 28
TENSAI. Natural Disasters.

A. DAIAROOGU

TAIFUU.

Ms. Obata and Mr. Imada are conversing in their office in Nagoya.

OBATA: **Ashita taifúu ga kúru soo desu ne.**

IMADA: **Ée, ookii no rashíi desu ne. Bókutachi no kodomo no kóro ni átta sugói taifúu o obóete imásu ka.**

OBATA: **Áa, Isewan Táifuu desu ne. Ano tóki wa, Sapporo no sofúbo no uchí ni asobi ni itte itá node watashi wa nani mo shiranái n desu kedo, are wa súgokatta sóo desu ne.**

IMADA: **Ée, bóku wa ano tóki, taifúu ga kúru kara, sóto ni asobi ni itté wa ikenái to iwarete itá noni, otootó to chikáku no yamá made asobi ni ittá n desu. Ténki ga ayashiku nátta to omóttara, totsuzen tsuyói kaze ni fukárete, sore ni áme mo furidáshita n desu. Kówakute, hisshi de hashítta n da kedo, háyaku hashirénakute, tochuu horaana ga átta node, soko ni háitta n desu. Náka wa kurákute, obáke ga desóo de, futaritomo furuete itá n desu. Yatto, kaze ga shizumátta node, isóide, uchi ni káetta n desu.**

OBATA: **Otóosan mo okáasan mo shinpai nasátte itá deshoo.**

IMADA: **Ée, bókutachi no kao o míte, anshin shitára, kóndo wa okoridáshita n desu.**

OBATA: **Shikararetá n desu ne.**

IMADA: **Ée, koppídoku.**

TYPHOON.

OBATA: I heard a typhoon is supposed to come tomorrow.

IMADA: Yes, I heard it's a big one. Do you remember the horrible typhoon that struck during our childhood?

OBATA: Oh, the Isewan Typhoon. I was visiting my grandparents' house in Sapporo at that time, so I don't know anything about it. But I heard it was horrible.

IMADA: Yes, it was. My younger brother and I went to a nearby mountain to play, even though I had been told not to go outside to play because the typhoon was approaching. When we noticed that the weather was starting to get threatening, a strong wind suddenly blew against us, and it began to rain. We got scared and ran as fast as we could. But we couldn't run fast enough. There was a cave on the way, and we went in. It was dark inside, and we thought it was haunted by ghosts, so both of us were shivering. When the wind finally calmed down, we went home as fast as we could.

OBATA: Your father and mother must have been worried.

IMADA: Yes. They were relieved to see our faces at first. But then they began to get angry.

OBATA: You got scolded, didn't you?

IMADA: Yes, severely.

B. BUNPOO TO YOOHOO

1. PASSIVE VERBS

Compare the following sentences.

Ryooshin wa Imada san o shikarimashita. (active voice)
His parents scolded Mr. Imada.

Imada san wa ryooshin ni shikararemashita. (passive voice)
Mr. Imada was scolded by his parents.

While in English the passive voice of a verb is formed with the verb "to be" and the past participle of the main verb, Japanese uses passive verbs, which are formed according to the following patterns.

VOWEL VERBS: The final *-ru* is replaced by *-rareru.*

taberu	→	*taberareru*
miru	→	*mirareru*

CONSONANT VERBS: The final *-u* is replaced by *-areru*.

kaku	→	*kakareru*
yobu	→	*yobareru*

When the dictionary form of a consonant verb ends in *-u* as a syllable, *-w* is inserted before *-areru*.

kau	→	*kawareru*
iu	→	*iwareru*

IRREGULAR VERBS:

suru	→	*sareru*
kuru	→	*korareru*

Passive verbs are vowel verbs and conjugate like other vowel verbs. The verb *shikaru* and its passive forms may serve as an example.

shikaru	(dictionary form)	to scold
shikarareru	(passive verb)	to be scolded
shikararemasu	(*masu* form of the passive form)	
shikararemashita	(past form of *shikararemasu*)	

2. PASSIVE SENTENCES

There are two kinds of passive sentence structures in Japanese.

a. Pure passives

In a pure passive construction, the direct object of the active sentence becomes the subject of the passive counterpart, and the subject in the active sentence (actor) is typically followed by *ni* "by." Note that this is exactly how it works in English.

SUBJECT (ACTOR)	DIRECT OBJECT	ACTIVE VERB
Ryooshin wa	*Imada san o*	*shikarimashita.*

The parents scolded Mr. Imada.

SUBJECT	ACTOR	PASSIVE VERB
Imada san wa	*ryooshin ni*	*shikararemashita.*

Mr. Imada was scolded by his parents.

SUBJECT (ACTOR)	DIRECT OBJECT	ACTIVE VERB
Shachoo wa	*buchoo o*	*yobimashita.*

The company president called the department head.

SUBJECT	ACTOR	PASSIVE VERB
Buchoo wa	*shachoo ni*	*yobaremashita.*

The department head was called by the company president.

There are also pure passives whose subjects were indirect objects in their active counterparts.

SUBJECT (ACTOR)	INDIRECT OBJECT	VERB PHRASE (ACTIVE)
Sensei wa	*kodomo ni*	*namae o kiita n desu.*

The teacher asked the child her name.

SUBJECT	ACTOR	VERB PHRASE (PASSIVE)
Kodomo wa	*sensei ni*	*namae o kikareta n desu.*

The child was asked her name by the teacher.

SUBJECT (ACTOR)	INDIRECT OBJECT	VERB PHRASE (ACTIVE)
Haha wa	*otooto ni*	*te ga kitanai to itta n desu.*

Mother told my younger brother that his hands were dirty.

SUBJECT	ACTOR	VERB PHRASE (PASSIVE)
Otooto wa	*haha ni*	*te ga kitanai to iwareta n desu.*

My younger brother was told by Mother that his hands were dirty.

b. Affective passives

While the English passive is equivalent to the Japanese pure passive, the second Japanese passive, the affective passive, has no English equivalent. The subject in the affective passive does not originate in the active counterpart as the direct or indirect object. Instead, the person affected by the event described is placed in the subject position. The actor is followed by *ni* as in the pure passives. Consider the following case.

EVENT:
Doroboo ga Yamada san no saifu o nusunda n desu.
A thief stole Mr. Yamada's wallet.

THE AFFECTEE:
Mr. Yamada

AFFECTIVE PASSIVE:
SUBJECT
Yamada san wa doroboo ni saifu o nusumareta n desu.
A thief stole Mr. Yamada's wallet [and he was affected by it].

The verb used in the affective passive can be either transitive (a verb that can take a direct object) or intransitive (a verb that cannot take a direct object).

Kodomo no toki, watashitachi wa haha ni shinareta n desu.
When we were children, our mother died. [Our mother died, and we were affected by it.]

Imada san wa totsuzen tsuyoi kaze ni fukarete, arukenakatta soo desu.
I heard that Mr. Imada could not walk because a strong wind blew at him. [A strong wind blew, and he was affected by it.]

3. MORE ABOUT THE PASSIVE

The following explanations are true for both pure and affective passives unless otherwise noted.
When the verb of the active sentence is a combination of a TE form and another element such as TE *iru* or TE *iku*, which element of the verb (the TE or the non-TE element) becomes passive depends on the kind of TE structure involved. For example, with TE *iru*, it is usually the TE form (and not *iru*) that becomes passive.

Chichi wa otooto o shikatte ita n desu.
My father was scolding my younger brother.

Otooto wa chichi ni shikararete ita n desu.
My younger brother was being scolded by my father.

With *motte iku* "to take" or *tsurete iku* "to take," *iku* usually becomes passive.

Doroboo ni okane o takusan motte ikareta n desu.
I had a lot of money taken from me by the thief.

Ryooshin ni byooin e tsurete ikaremashita.
I was taken to the hospital by my parents.

When *tsurete* instead of *iku* becomes passive, a slight shift in meaning occurs.

Kodomo wa gakkoo e ryooshin ni tsurete ikaremashita. (*iku* is passive)
Kodomo wa gakkoo e ryooshin ni tsurerarete ikimashita. (*tsurete* is passive)
The child was taken to school by her parents.

While both sentences mean the same thing, the first implies more coercion.

Usually, the subjects in passive sentences are animate. Inanimate subjects are possible in pure passives, but such sentences are often unnatural, especially when a *ni* phrase (the actor plus *ni*) is included. In some limited cases, however, they are well formed.

Kono uta wa minna ni utawarete imasu.
This song is sung by everyone.

Kono shoosetsu wa amerikajin ni yoku shirarete imasu.
This novel is well-known to Americans.

You have seen that the subject of the affective passive is affected by the event. This is also true of the subject of the pure passive. It is in the nature of passive sentences that the referent of the subject is affected. Furthermore, Japanese passives usually imply that the referent of the subject is affected negatively, although they may describe positive or neutral events.

Yamada san ni kuruma o arawareta n desu yo.
Mr. Yamada washed the car [and I am unhappy about it].

Usually the actor followed by *ni* is animate. It can also be a weather term.

Ame ni furareta n desu ka.
It rained on you?

Taifuu ni osowareta n desu.
We were hit [attacked] by a typhoon.

4. PROHIBITION

To prohibit someone from doing something, use the following pattern.

> TE form + *wa* + *ikemasen (ikenai)* / *dame desu (dame da)*.

This expression is much stronger and harsher than *-nai de kudasai* "Please don't—" (see Lesson 22, B3), so you should be careful about using it.

With TE verb forms:

Itte wa ikemasen.
Don't go./You must not go.

Taifuu ga kuru kara, soto ni asobi ni itte wa ikenai to iwarete ita n desu.
I had been told not to go outside to play because the typhoon was
approaching.

Jishin no toki, hi o tsukatte wa dame desu yo.
During an earthquake, you must not light any flames [use fire].

Koko de asonde wa ikenai soo desu.
I heard that we are not allowed to play here.

With TE forms of *i*-adjectives:

*Shooboosha ga hairenai node, michi ga semakute wa dame da to iwareta n
desu.*
We were told that since a fire engine couldn't enter, the road should
not be narrow.

Kore o niru toki, hi wa tsuyokute wa ikenai soo desu.
I understand that while cooking this, the flame [fire] should not be on
high [strong].

With the TE form of the copula (*de*):

Furui chizu de wa dame desu ne.
An old map won't do, will it?

5. QUESTION WORDS WITH *MO*

A question word with *mo* used in a negative sentence means "no . . ."
or "not any. . ." The particle *ga, wa,* or *o* cannot be used with *mo,* although other particles may occur before it.

Watashi wa nani mo shiranai n desu.
I don't know anything.

Kaji no toki, dare mo uchi ni inakatta n desu.
At the time of the fire, nobody was at home.

Taifuu ga kite, doko e mo ikemasen deshita.
The typhoon came, and I couldn't go anywhere.

A question word plus *mo* can be followed by a noun phrase.

Dare mo <u>koozui de shinda hito wa</u> imasen deshita.
No one [there was no one who] died because of the flood.

Kaminari ga ochita n desu ga, nani mo higai wa nakatta desu.
The lightning struck [the thunderbolt fell], but there was no damage.

Taifuu ga kuru node, doko mo <u>aite iru mise wa</u> arimasen.
Since a typhoon is coming, no stores are open.

6. COMPOUND WORDS WITH A PRE-*MASU* FORM

A pre-*masu* form and *-dasu* are used to mean "start/begin to . . . ."

Sore ni ame mo furidashita n desu.
And then it started to rain.

Bokutachi no kao o mite, anshin shitara, kondo wa okoridashita n desu.
They were relieved to see our faces, but then they began to get angry.

Kaze ga fukidashite, samuku narimashita.
The wind started blowing, and it became cold.

7. *I*-ADJECTIVES USED AS NOUNS

The KU form of a small number of *i*-adjectives can be used as nouns.

chikaku	vicinity
tooku	far place
hayaku	early time
osoku	late time
ooku	large amount

Chikaku no yama made asobi ni itta n desu.
I went to the mountains in the vicinity to play.

Tooku de kaminari ga naridashimashita.
It began to thunder in the distance.

Mainichi asa hayaku kara yoru osoku made benkyoo shita n desu.
I studied every day from early morning till late at night.

C. MOJI

1. DIALOGUE

おばた　　「あした　たいふうが　来るそうですね。」

いまだ　　「ええ、大きいのらしいですね。ぼくたちの　子どもの
　　　　　　ころに　あった　すごい　たいふうを　おぼえていますか。」

おばた 「ああ、いせわんたいふうですね。あの時は さっぽろの
そふぼの うちに あそびに 行っていたので、私は 何も
しらないんですけど、あれは すごかったそうですね。」

いまだ 「ええ、ぼくは あの時、たいふうが 来るから、外に
あそびに 行っては いけないと 言われていたのに、
おとうとと 近くの 山まで あそびに 行ったんです。
天気が あやしく なったと 思ったら、とつぜん つよい
かぜに ふかれて、それに、 雨も ふりだしたんです。
こわくて、ひっしで 走ったんですけど、はやく
走れなくて、とちゅう ほらあなが あったので、そこに
入ったんです。中は くらくて、おばけが 出そうで、
二人とも ふるえていたんです。やっと、かぜが
しずまったので、急いで、うちに かえったんです。」

おばた 「お父さんも お母さんも しんぱいなさって
いたでしょう。」

いまだ 「ええ、ぼくたちの かおを 見て、あんしんしたら、
今度は おこりだしたんです。」

おばた 「しかられたんですね。」

いまだ 「ええ、こっぴどく。」

2. NEW *KANJI*

[74]	子	*ko*	child e.g., 子ども
[75]	走	*hashi(ru)*	to run
[76]	急	*iso(gu)*	to hurry
[77]	父	*(o)too(san)*	father
[78]	母	*(o)kaa(san)*	mother
[79]	度	*DO*	time, degree

[74]	⁊ 了 子
[75]	土 キ キ 走 走
[76]	⁊ ⁊ ⁊ ⁊ 刍 急 急
[77]	⁊ ハ ク 父
[78]	し 乜 母 母 母
[79]	广 广 产 产 庐 庍 度

3. NEW READING

[40]　外　*GAI* (Lesson 22)　　　　　　　　　　　outside

　　　　soto　　　　　　　　　　　outside

D. TANGO TO HYOOGEN

kaze	wind
taifuu	typhoon
jishin	earthquake
kaminari	thunder, thunderbolt
koozui	flood
kaji	fire (incident)
hi	fire (substance)
higai	damage
shooboosha	fire engine
obake	ghost
horaana	cave
kao	face
sofubo	grandparents
shachoo	company president
doroboo	thief
uta	song
tochuu	midway
shinpai suru	to worry
anshin suru	to feel relieved
naru	to sound
fuku	to blow
osou	to attack

shizumaru	to calm down
shikaru	to scold
okoru	to get angry
nusumu	to steal
yobu	to call
utau	to sing
niru	to cook in liquid
sugoi	terrible, horrible
ayashii	threatening
totsuzen	suddenly
hisshi de	frantically
yatto	finally
kondo wa	then
koppidoku	scathingly, severely

RENSHUU

A. Mark each sentence T (true) or F (false) on the basis of the dialogue.

1. *Obata san ga kodomo no toki, ojiisan to obaasan no uchi wa Hokkaidoo ni arimashita.*
2. *Imada san wa taifuu no toki, horaana no naka ni imashita.*
3. *Imada san wa taifuu ga kuru noni, soto ni asobi ni itta node, ryooshin ni shikararemashita.*

B. Fill in the blanks to make passive sentences according to the statements in English.

1. A thief stole a computer.
   Doroboo ni _____ o _____ n desu.
2. I was cold because it rained on me.
   _____ ni _____ te, samukatta desu.
3. The teacher scolded the student.
   Gakusei wa _____ n desu.
4. The cat ate the fish.
   Neko ni _____ o _____ n desu.

C. When you are teaching children how to behave, what do you say? Fill in the blanks.

1. *_____ ga natte iru toki, ki no _____ ku ni _____ ikemasen yo.*
   You must not go near a tree when you hear thunder.
2. *_____ ga kuru kara, soto de _____ ikemasen yo.*
   Since a typhoon is coming, you must not play outside.
3. *Yoru _____ ku made terebi o mite i _____ dame desu yo.*
   You must not watch [be watching] TV till late at night.

346

D. When you are sick, what do you say? Fill in the blanks with question words.

1. _____ *mo tabetaku arimasen.*
2. _____ *e mo ikitaku arimasen.*
3. _____ *to mo hanashitaku arimasen.*

E. Fill in the blanks with *kanji* indicated by the *hiragana* under the lines.

1. a. きのう だれが＿＿＿＿なかったんですか。
　　　　　　　　　　こ

　 b. 私の＿＿＿＿どもが＿＿＿＿ませんでした。
　　　　　　こ　　　　　　き

2. a. お＿＿＿＿さんに いくつ あげたんですか。
　　　　とう

　 b. ＿＿＿＿あげたんです。
　　　とお

F. Match each *kanji* in Group I with the *kanji* in Group II that have a complementary or opposite meaning.

I		II	
1.	外	a.	子
2.	父	b.	近
3.	入	c.	走
4.	遠	d.	度
		e.	母
		f.	出
		g.	中

G. Explain the following rules to the children in Japanese.

Example: You should not eat too fast.
　　　　　→ *hayaku tabete wa ikemasen yo.*

1. You should not stay up late at night.
2. You should not talk to your friends over the phone for a long time.
3. You should not go out late at night by yourself.

KARUCHAA NOOTO

Japan is often affected by serious natural disasters, the two most frequent being typhoons and earthquakes. Typhoons produced in the Pacific Ocean often hit Japan from late August to the middle of September. The Isewan Typhoon, which hit around Nagoya in 1959, was one of the biggest in modern history. In addition, Japan is one of the most seismologically active areas in the world. A particularly severe earthquake devastated the Tokyo area in 1923. In 1995, an earthquake referred to as the *Hanshin Awaji Daishinsai* hit Awaji Island, Kobe, Ashiya, and Nishinomiya, one of the most heavily populated and economically vital areas in Japan. More than 6,000 people were killed, and many were left homeless. On top of typhoons and earthquakes, eruptions of volcanoes cause serious problems, too. Not only are human lives in danger, but crops can also be damaged by ash falls and lava flows.

Various efforts are being made to minimize the damaging effects of natural disasters. People are learning to take protective measures, and the construction of resistant buildings is being researched. However, the earthquake of 1995 reminded everyone that present protective measures are not yet good enough.

KOTAE

A. 1. T   2. T   3. T
B. 1. *konpyuutaa, nusumareta*   2. *Ame, furare*   3. *sensei ni shikarareta*
4. *sakana, taberareta*
C. 1. *Kaminari, chika, itte wa*   2. *Taifuu, asonde wa*   3. *oso, te wa*
D. 1. *Nani*   2. *Doko*   3. *Dare*
E. 1. 来子来 2. 父十
F. 1g,   2a,   2e,   3f,   4b
G. 1. *yoru <u>osoku</u> made okite ite wa ikemasen yo.* 2. *tomodachi to <u>nagaku</u> denwa o <u>shite wa</u> ikemasen yo.* 3. *yoru <u>osoku</u>, hitoride <u>dekakete wa</u> ikemasen yo.*

DAI NIJUU KYUUKA
Lesson 29
BOONENKAI.   A Year-end Party.

A. DAIAROOGU

KAISHA NO BOONENKAI.

Mr. Mikami and Mr. Carson, an American, work for the same department (section) in a company.

KAASON: **Míkami san mo boonénkai no kánji desu ne.**

MIKAMI: **Ée, sóo desu.**

KAASON: **Boonénkai wa ítsu áru n desu ka.**

MIKAMI: **Hoka no kánji no hitótachi wa níjuu rokunichi góro ga íitte iú n desu kedo, máda hakkíri kimete nái n desu. Káason san wa ítsu ga íi desu ka.**

KAASON: **Bóku wa níjuu sannichi ígo nara, ítsu de mo íi desu.**

MIKAMI: **Sukiyaki ga íi desu ka.**

KAASON: **Ée, sukiyaki dé mo, nán de mo íi desu. Sore ni amari tooku nákereba, dóko de mo íi desu yo.**

MIKAMI: **Minná ni hitorizútsu nán de mo sukí na utá o utatte morau tsumori ná n desu. Kachoo mo náni ka utatte kureru rashíi desu yo.**

KAASON: **Bóku wa utá wa nani mo shiranái n desu.**

MIKAMI: **Fookusóngu nara, takusan shittemásu kara, oshiete agemásu yo.**

KAASON: **Bóku wa ónchi na n desu yo. Komarimáshita née.**

MIKAMI: **Shinpai shinákute mo íi desu yo. Betsu ni joozú ni utaenákute mo íi n desu.**

A YEAR-END PARTY FOR EMPLOYEES.

CARSON: You're one of the people organizing the year-end party, too, aren't you?

MIKAMI: Yes, I am.

CARSON: When will it be?

MIKAMI: The other organizers suggested around the twenty-sixth, but we haven't made a definite decision yet. When would be good for you?

CARSON: Any time after the twenty-third is fine.

MIKAMI: Would you like to have sukiyaki?

CARSON: Yes, I love sukiyaki [or whatever], and if the restaurant is not too far, anywhere would be all right.

MIKAMI: We're planning to have everyone sing a [any] favorite song. I heard that our section manager will also sing something for us.

CARSON: I don't know any songs.

MIKAMI: When it comes to folk songs, I know a lot, so I will teach them to you.

CARSON: I'm tone-deaf. What shall I do?

MIKAMI: Don't worry, you don't have to be able to sing particularly well.

B. BUNPOO TO YOOHOO

1. GIVING OR RECEIVING A FAVOR

Here is a brief review of verbs for giving and receiving objects.

HUMBLING THE RECIPIENT	NEUTRAL	HONORIFIC
(1) *yaru* to give	*ageru* to give	*sashiageru* to give (humble)
(2) _____	*kureru* to give	*kudasaru* to give (respect)
(3) _____	*morau* to receive	*itadaku* to receive (humble)

(1) AGERU: Yamada san wa Suzuki san ni osake o agemashita.
　　　Mr. Yamada gave Ms. Suzuki some sake.

SASHIAGERU: Watashi wa sensei ni shootaijoo o sashiagemashita.
　　　I gave the teacher an invitation.

YARU: Haha wa inu ni mizu o yarimashita.
　　　My mother gave the dog water.

(2) KURERU: Yamada san wa watashi ni shashin o kuremashita.
　　　Mr. Yamada gave me the photographs.

KUDASARU: Tanaka san ga watashi no kodomo ni jisho o kudasaimashita.
　　　Ms. Tanaka gave my child a dictionary.

(3) *MORAU*: *Tachibana san wa Shinoda san kara/ni tegami o moraimashita.*
　　　　Ms. Tachibana received a letter from Ms. Shinoda.

ITADAKU: *Haha wa Yamamoto san kara/ni nengajoo o itadakimashita.*
　　　　My mother got a New Year card from Ms. Yamamoto.

The verbs above describe giving and receiving physical objects. If, however, you give or receive a favor, you must use different patterns. In these cases, the action is expressed with the TE form and is followed by one of the verbs of giving or receiving. The distinction among the verbs is the same as for giving or receiving physical objects.

a. TE *ageru*, TE *sashiageru*, TE *yaru*

The referent of the subject, followed by *wa* or *ga*, gives the favor. In many cases, the noun designating the recipient of the favor is followed by *ni*.

Watashi wa Kaason san ni uta o utatte agemashita.
　　I sang a song for Mr. Carson.

Otooto wa sensei ni chizu o kaite sashiageta soo desu.
　　I understand that my younger brother drew a map for the teacher.

Watashi wa neko ni sakana o katte yarimashita.
　　I bought a fish for my cat.

Tanaka san ni fookusongu o takusan oshiete agemashita.
　　I taught Ms. Tanaka many folk songs.

When the noun designating the recipient of the favor is originally the direct object, *o* follows it. Compare:

Watashi wa Yamada san o paatii ni tsurete ikimashita.
　　I took Mr. Yamada along to the party. (without implying a favor)

Watashi wa Yamada san o paatii ni tsurete itte agemashita.
　　I took Mr. Yamada along to the party. [I did the favor of taking Mr. Yamada to the party.]

Sometimes, the noun designating the recipient of the favor cannot be followed by *ni* or *o*. This is especially true of intransitive verbs.

Eki made itte agemashita.
　　I went as far as the station [for someone].

If you want to specify the recipient, *no tame ni* "for" can be used.

Eki made Mikami san no tame ni itte agemashita.
　　I went as far as the station for Mr. Mikami.

b. TE *kureru*, TE *kudasaru*

Kachoo mo nani ka utatte kureru rashii desu yo.
   I understand that the section manager will also sing something
   [for us].

The same items used to designate the recipient of the favor with TE
ageru can be used with TE *kureru* or TE *kudasaru*.

Sawada san ga bokutachi ni keeki o yaite kuremashita.
   Mr. Sawada baked a cake for us.

Maeda san wa imooto o bijutsukan ni tsurete itte kudasaimashita.
   Ms. Maeda took my younger sister to the museum.

Haha wa watashi no tame ni asa hayaku okite kuremashita.
   My mother got up early in the morning for me.

c. TE *morau*, TE *itadaku*

The recipient of the favor is placed in the subject position. The noun
designating the giver of the favor is followed by *ni*.

Watashitachi wa Tsuchiya san ni kangeikai no kanji ni natte moraimashita.
   We had Mr. Tsuchiya become an organizer of the welcome party.

Minna ni uta o utatte morau tsumori na n desu.
   We're planning to have everyone sing a song.

Haha wa Matsumoto san ni fookusongu o oshiete itadaita soo desu.
   I understand that my mother was taught folk songs by Ms.
   Matsumoto.

2. QUESTION WORD PLUS *DE MO*

When a question word is used with *de mo*, the combination means
"any . . ." or "without exception." *De* is the TE form of the copula *da*,
and *mo* is a particle. The particle *ga*, *wa*, or *o* is never used with *de mo*,
but other particles such as *ni* may precede it.

Nan de mo ii desu.
   Anything is all right.

Nijuu sannichi igo nara, itsu de mo ii desu.
   If it is after the twenty-third, anytime is fine.

Amari tooku nakereba, doko de mo ii desu.
   If it is not very far, anywhere is all right.

Chiketto wa nanmai de mo kaemasu.
   You can buy any number of tickets.

352

Fookusongu nara, dare ni de mo oshiete agemasu yo.
If they are folk songs, I will teach them to anybody.

The question word plus *de mo* can be followed by a noun phrase.

Dare de mo uta no suki na hito o yobimashoo.
Let's invite anyone who likes singing.

Ima doko de mo depaato wa konde imasu.
Any department store is crowded now.

Tooka izen nara, itsu de mo tsugoo no ii toki ni kite kudasai.
If it is before the tenth, please come anytime it is convenient.

3. *NA*-ADJECTIVES AS ADVERBS

Na-adjectives followed by *ni* are used adverbially (see Lesson 25, B5, for the adverbial use of *i*-adjectives).

shizuka ni   quietly
rippa ni   magnificently

Joozu ni utaenakute mo ii n desu.
You need not be able to sing well.

Teeburu no ue o kirei ni fukimashita.
I wiped the top of the table clean.

Yamada san ga shinsetsu ni iroiro na uta o oshiete kudasaimashita.
Mr. Yamada kindly taught me various songs.

4. CONTRACTIONS

In English "can't" and "isn't" are contractions of "cannot" and "is not." Japanese has contractions, too, which are used mostly in spoken Japanese. *Ja nai* (negative form of *da*), for example, is a contraction of *de wa nai*.

Kore wa Nihon no uta ja (← de wa) nai soo desu.
I understand that this is not a Japanese song.

Here are some more examples.

a. TE *ru* ← TE *iru*

Drop the *i-* of *iru* and its conjugated forms (TE *imasu*, TE *inai*, etc.).

Fookusongu nara, takusan shittemasu (← shitte imasu) kara, oshiete agemasu yo.
When it comes to folk songs, I know a lot, so I will teach them to you.

Mada hakkiri kimetenai (← kimete inai) n desu.
We haven't made a definite decision yet.

Donna kurasu o totteru (← totte iru)n desu ka.
What kind of class are you taking?

b. *Tte ← to*

The quotation *to* becomes -*tte*. What follows *to* is usually *iu* "to say" or its honorific form.

Hoka no kanji no hitotachi wa nijuu rokunichi goro ga iitte (← ii to) iu n desu.
The other organizers say that around the twenty-sixth would be fine.

Abe san no soobetsukai wa asoko no resutoran de surutte (← suru to) osshattemashita yo.
They were saying we will have Ms. Abe's farewell party at that restaurant over there.

To iu "called" can be contracted in the same way. It becomes -*tte iu.*

Karatachitte (← Karatachi to) iu kissaten ni itta n desu.
We went to the coffee shop called Karatachi.

Besides the verb "to say," verbs such as *kiku* "to hear, ask," *naku* "to cry," and *yorokobu* "to be delighted" can be used with the contraction -*tte.*

Kono ryokan wa yasuitte kikimashita yo.
I heard that this hotel is inexpensive.

Tomodachi ni damasaretatte naiteru n desu.
He is saying [crying] that he was cheated by his friend.

Musume wa omiyage o morattatte yorokonde imashita.
My daughter was delighted to have been given a souvenir.

C. MOJI

1. DIALOGUE

カーソン 「みかみさんも ぼうねん会の かんじですね。」

みかみ 「ええ、そうです。」

カーソン 「ぼうねん会は いつ あるんですか。」

みかみ 「ほかの かんじの 人たちは 26日ごろが いいって
言うんですけど、まだ はっきり きめてないんです。
カーソンさんは いつが いいですか。」

カーソン 「ぼくは 23日いごなら、いつでも いいです。」

みかみ 「すきやきが いいですか。」

カーソン 「ええ、すきやきでも、なんでも いいです。それに、
あまり 遠くなければ、どこでも いいですよ。」

みかみ 「みんなに 一人ずつ 何でも 好きな歌を 歌って
もらう つもりなんです。かちょうも 何か 歌って
くれるらしいですよ。」

カーソン 「ぼくは 歌は 何も 知らないんです。」

みかみ 「フォークソングなら、たくさん 知ってますから、
教えてあげますよ。」

カーソン 「ぼくは おんちなんですよ。困りましたねえ。」

みかみ 「しんぱい しなくても いいですよ。べつに じょうずに
歌えなくても いいんです。」

2. NEW *KANJI*

[80]	歌	*uta, uta(u)*	song, to sing
[81]	知	*shi(ru)*	to know
[82]	教	*oshi(eru)*	to teach
[83]	困	*koma(ru)*	to be troubled

STROKE ORDER

[80]	⸀ ⸀ ⸀ ⸀ ⸀ ⸀ ⸀ 歌
[81]	⸀ ⸀ ⸀ ⸀ ⸀ 知
[82]	⸀ ⸀ ⸀ ⸀ ⸀ ⸀ 教
[83]	⸀ ⸀ 困

3. NEW READING

[73]	会	*a(u)* (Lesson 27)	to meet
		KAI	meeting

D. TANGO TO HYOOGEN

boonenkai	year-end party
kangeikai	welcome party
soobetsukai	farewell party
sukiyaki	sukiyaki
keeki	cake
teeburu	table
fookusongu	folk song
onchi	tone-deafness
kanji	organizer
jisho	dictionary
fuku	to wipe
kaku	to draw, paint
naku	to cry
damasu	to cheat
yorokobu	to be delighted
komaru	to be troubled, be upset
shinsetsu	kind, nice

356

izen	prior to
igo	after
hakkiri	definitely
betsu ni	(not) particularly
no tame ni	for

RENSHUU

A. On the basis of the dialogue, mark each sentence T (true), F (false), or X (cannot tell).

1. *Boonenkai no kanji wa futari imasu.*
2. *Kaason san wa boonenkai no kanji desu.*
3. *Mikami san wa Kaason san ni uta o oshiete agetai to omotte imasu.*
4. *Boonenkai ni kachoo mo kimasu.*

B. Fill in the blanks with appropriate forms of *ageru, kureru,* or *morau.*

a: *Dare ni sono uta o oshiete _____ ¹ ta n desu ka.*
b: *Ane ga oshiete _____ ² ta n desu. Ane wa Tanaka san ni mo oshiete _____ ³ ta rashii desu.*
c: *Kore wa chichi ga katte _____ ⁴ ta jisho na n desu.*
d: *Watashi mo ii no o motte iru n desu kedo, tomodachi ni kashite _____ ⁵ te, ima nai n desu. Anata ga tsukatte inai toki ni, kashite _____ ⁶ tai n desu kedo.*
c: *Ee, ii desu yo.*

C. In a Japanese language class, a composition was assigned with the following instructions. Fill in the blanks according to what you think the teacher's instructions were.

dai "title"	any title
nagasa	any number of sheets of paper
teishutsu "submission"	anytime before the twenty-first
Do not write in pencil.	
You do not have to use a computer.	

1. *Dai wa _____ de mo ii desu.*
2. *Nagasa wa _____ mai de mo ii desu.*
3. *Teishutsu wa _____ de mo ii desu ga, nijuu ichinichi izen ni dashite kudasai.*
4. *Enpitsu de _____ ikemasen.*
5. *Konpyuutaa o _____ mo kamaimasen.*

D. In the following conversation, form contractions wherever possible.

a: *Mainichi gakkoo ni itte iru n desu ka.*

b. *Ee, itte imasu yo. Ima rekishi no kurasu no repooto o kaite iru n desu kedo, muzukashikute, komatte iru n desu.*

a: *Shibata san mo ima shukudai ga takusan atte, taihen da to itte imashita yo.*

b: *Shibata san wa donna kurasu o totte iru n desu ka.*

a: *Furansugo no kurasu da to omoimasu.*

E. Read the following, and write the English equivalents.

a. 外国の 歌を たくさん 知ってますか。

b. いいえ、知らないから、困ってるんです。
何か 教えてください、。

F. The following words all contain かい. For which かい can you write 会?

1. そうべつかい

2. ほっかいどう

3. かいごう

4. かいがん

5. かんげいかい

6. あたたかい

G. Ask someone to do the following using *na*-adjectives as adverbs.

Example: to wipe the table clean.
→ *teeburu o <u>kirei ni</u> fuite kudasai.*

1. to study quietly
2. to give directions *(michijun)* kindly
3. to treat *(toriatsukau)* carefully *(teinei)*

H. Rewrite the following sentences using <u>*te morau*</u>, <u>*te ageru*</u> or <u>*te kureru*</u>.

Example: *eki made tsurete <u>ikimashita</u>.*
→ *eki made tsurete itte agemashita.*

1. *Buraun san ga watashi ni eigo o <u>oshiemashita</u>.*
2. *Jon san ni gohan o <u>tsukurimashita</u>.*
3. *Yooko san ga watashi o paatii ni <u>tsurete ikimashita</u>.*

KARUCHAA NOOTO

The literal meaning of *boonenkai* is "forget-year-party," and it is held in late December. There are also other kinds of parties such as New Year parties, welcome parties, farewell parties, and just parties to get together for no particular reason. Whatever the occasion, traditional Japanese parties usually follow a typical pattern. They are usually held in restaurants rather than in private homes. Unlike cocktail parties in the United States, guests at Japanese parties sit down to eat. Sukiyaki, a dish of beef and vegetables served in a pot, is one of the most popular dishes for these parties. People drink sake or beer with the food. The party goes on with the guests providing the entertainment. They share talents such as singing songs and dancing.

KOTAE

A. 1. X   2. F   3. T   4. T

B. 1. *morat*   2. *kure*   3. *age*   4. *kure*   5. *age*   6. *morai*

C. 1. *nan*   2. *nan*   3. *itsu*   4. *kaite wa*   5. *tsukawanakute*

D. a: ——*itteru n desu ka*. b: ——*ittemasu yo*. ——*kaiteru n desu kedo* ——*komatteru n desu*. a: ——*taihen datte ittemashita yo*. b: ——*totteru n desu ka*. a: ø

E. a. 外国 (*gaikoku*) —— 歌 (*uta*) —— 知 (*shi*)

   b. 知 (*shi*) —— 困って (*koma*) —— 何 (*nani*) —— 教えて (*oshi*)

   a. Do you know many foreign songs?

   b. No, since I don't know many, I'm upset.
      Please teach me some (songs).

F. 1, 3, 5

G. 1. *shizuka ni benkyoo shite kudasai.* 2. *shinsetsu ni michijun o oshiete kudasai.* 3. *teinei ni toriatsukatte kudasai.*

H. 1. *oshiete kuremashita.* 2. *tsukutte agemashita.* 3. *tsurete itte kuremashita.*

DAI SANJUKKA
Lesson 30

INTAANETTO.　The Internet.

A. DAIAROOGU

INTAANETTO DE KAIMONO.

A conversation between Ms. Nagano and Mr. Chiba.

CHIBA: Áa, sore wa íma Amérika de wadai no hon desu né. Watashi mo yomítai to omótte ita n desuga, hón'ya de wa mitsukaranakatta n desu. Dóko de katta n desu ká.

NAGANO: Kono hon wa intaanetto de katta n desu. Hón'ya no hoomupeeji ni iku to, dónna hon de mo kaemasu yo. Hón'ya nado de chuumon suru yori hayái desu yo. Saikin watashi wa yóku onrain de kaimono o suru yoo ni natta n desu.

CHIBA: Dóo yatte shiharau n desu ka.

NAGANO: Nétto ni kurejitto kaado no bangoo o taipu suru n desu.

CHIBA: Kurejitto kaado no bangoo o taipu suru no wa abunaku kikoemasu ga, daijóobu desu ká.

NAGANO: Ée, daijoobu desu yo. Kono tebukuro mo webu de katta n desu. Íma depáato no hoomupeeji ni wa kurisumasu purezento ga takusan arimasu yo. Dono shoohin no shashin o mite mo honmono mitai ni kirei ni miemasu.

CHIBA: Sóo desu ka. Watashi mo korekara intaanetto o tsukau yoo ni shimasu yo. Uchi ni ite onrain de kaimono suru koto ga dekirunante bénri ni narimashita ne.

ONLINE SHOPPING.

CHIBA: Oh, that must be the book that is being talked about in the U.S. I wanted to read it, but I couldn't find it at any bookstore. Where did you buy it?

NAGANO: I bought this book on the Internet. If you go to the home page of any bookstore, you can get any book you want. It's also faster than ordering the book at the bookstore. Recently, I have begun to buy a lot of stuff online.

CHIBA: How do you pay?

NAGANO: You can type in your credit card number on the net.

CHIBA: It sounds dangerous to type in the credit card number on the net.
Is it safe?

NAGANO: Yes, it's fine. I bought these gloves on the web as well. There
are so many Christmas gifts on the home page of department stores
now. All the pictures of the products look as pretty as they do in real
life.

CHIBA: Really? I will try to use the Internet from now on. Isn't it convenient that we can shop online without leaving home?

B. BUNPOO TO YOOHOO

1. INTRANSITIVE AND TRANSITIVE VERBS

While transitive verbs are used with a direct object, intransitive verbs
are not. The English verbs "to rise" and "to lie," for example, are intransitive, whereas their counterparts "to raise" and "to lay" are transitive. While these transitive/intransitive pairs have different forms,
there are many that have the same form.

	INTRANSITIVE	TRANSITIVE
to begin	The game began.	We began the game.
to gather	The students gathered.	We gathered the students.
to open	The door opened.	I opened the door.

Japanese intransitive and transitive verb pairs usually have different
yet similar forms, much like "rise/raise" or "lie/lay" in English.

Kurasu wa itsu hajimatta n desu ka. (*hajimaru* to begin—intransitive)
When did the class begin?

Karaoke no renshuu o hajimeta n desu. (*hajimeru* to begin—transitive)
He began to do [began the practice of] karaoke.

Kazoku no mono ga minna atsumarimashita. (*atsumaru* to gather—intransitive)
All the family members gathered.

Deeta o atsumemashita. (*atsumeru* to gather—transitive)
I gathered the data.

Ano baa wa nanji ni aku n desu ka. (*aku* to open—intransitive)
What time does that bar open?

Mise o nanji ni akeru n desu ka. (*akeru* to open—transitive)
　　What time do you open the store?

　　Other pairs include:

INTRANSITIVE		TRANSITIVE	
ataru	to hit	*ateru*	to hit (something)
atatamaru	to get warm	*atatameru*	to warm (something)
	to warm oneself		
butsukaru	to bump	*butsukeru*	to bump (something)
chikazuku	to approach	*chikazukeru*	to bring (something) near
deru	to go out	*dasu*	to put (something) out
hairu	to go in	*ireru*	to put (something) in
kakaru	to take	*kakeru*	to take (time) . . . ,
			to apply (something)
kimaru	to be decided	*kimeru*	to decide (something)
kowareru	to break	*kowasu*	to break (something)
	(to be damaged)		
mitsukaru	to be found	*mitsukeru*	to find (something)
modoru	to return	*modosu*	to return (something)
naoru	to heal,	*naosu*	to heal (something)
	to be repaired		to repair (something)
ochiru	to fall	*otosu*	to drop
oreru	to break (in half)	*oru*	to break (something)
shimaru	to close	*shimeru*	to close (something)
tsunagaru	to be connected	*tsunagu*	to connect
yakeru	to be baked,	*yaku*	to bake (something)
	to burn		to burn (something)

2. *MIERU/KIKOERU* "LOOKS (LIKE)/SOUNDS (LIKE)"

The potential verbs *mieru* "to be visible," and *kikoeru* "to be audible,"
stand for "looks (like)" and "sounds (like)," respectively.

a. With *i*-adjectives

Mieru and *kikoeru* follow the KU form of an *i*-adjective.

Kono megane o kakeru to, ji ga ookiku miemasu.
　　When I wear these glasses, characters look big.

Kono heya de utau to, koe ga utsukushiku kikoemasu.
　　When you sing in this room, your voice sounds beautiful.

b. With *na*-adjectives or nouns

Mieru and *kikoeru* follow *ni* preceded by a *na*-adjective or a noun.

Otooto wa ookii kara, daigakusei ni mieru n desu.
Since my younger brother is big, he looks like a university student.

Karaoke de utau to joozu ni kikoeru n desu.
When you sing karaoke, it sounds good.

3. QUESTION WORDS WITH TE *MO*

To express "no matter . . ." or "-ever," such as "whatever (no matter what)," or "whoever (no matter who)," a question word is used with the TE form plus *mo*.

Ookesutora to issho ni utau n desu kara, nani o utatte mo joozu ni kikoeru n desu yo.
Since you sing with an orchestra, whatever you sing sounds good.

Dare ga bansoo shite kurete mo, ii desu.
It's all right with me no matter who accompanies me.

Donna kurashikku o kiite mo, tanoshiku narimasu.
No matter what kind of classical music I hear, it's enjoyable.

4. . . . *YOO NI NARU* "TO COME TO"/"TO BECOME"

Naru "to become," which can be used with an *i*-adjective, a *na*-adjective, and a noun (see Lesson 21, B1), may also be used with a verb. In this case, *yoo ni* stands between the plain present form (affirmative or negative) of the verb and *naru*.

Karaoke baa ni kayoidashite kara, iroiro na uta o utaeru yoo ni natta n desu.
Since he began to visit a karaoke bar regularly, he has learned [become able] to sing several songs.

Otona ni natte kara, kashu ni naritai to omou yoo ni narimashita.
After becoming an adult, I came to believe I wanted to become a singer.

Ani wa baa ni amari ikanai yoo ni narimashita.
Over time, my older brother came to go to bars less frequently [came not to go to bars often].

It has been mentioned that the verbs *dekiru* "to be able to" and *wakaru* "to understand" should not be used with *-tai* "to want to . . ." (see Lesson 6, C8). To express "to want to be able to," or "to want to understand," use . . . *yoo ni naru.*

Karate ga dekiru yoo ni naritai desu.
I want to be able to do karate.

Nihon no furui ongaku ga wakaru yoo ni naritai desu.
I want to understand old Japanese music.

5. ...*YOO NI SURU* "TO TRY TO..."

When you make an effort to do something, use .... *yoo ni suru* following the plain present form (affirmative or negative).

Otsukiai suru yoo ni shiteru n desu.
We try to spend time with him.

Ashita narubeku iku yoo ni shimasu.
If possible, I will try to go tomorrow.

Nihongo no kurasu de eigo o tsukawanai yoo ni shite kudasai.
In Japanese class, please try not to use English.

6. PARTICLES

a. *Nado* (emphasis)

Nado is used to mean "anything/anyone like" when emphasizing humbleness or impossibility. The original particle *wa, ga,* or *o* can follow *nado*.

Uta nado (wa/o) utatta koto wa nakatta n desu.
He had never sung [anything like] songs. (impossibility)

Watashi nado (wa/ga) dame na n desu.
Anyone like me is no good. (humbleness)

All particles other than *wa, ga*, or *o* remain and follow or precede *nado*.

Ongakkai nado ni/ni nado ikitaku nai desu.
I don't want to go to [anything like] a concert.

b. *Ni* (with *au*)

With the verb *au* "to meet/see (someone)," the noun denoting the person met is followed by *ni*.

Kinoo eki de tomodachi ni aimashita.
I met a friend of mine at the station yesterday.

Chiba san ni ai ni iku n desu.
I am going to see Mr. Chiba.

Otoosan ni wa shibaraku oai shitemasen.
I haven't seen your father for a long time.

c. Omission of particles

In spoken Japanese, the particle *wa* can be omitted. Less frequently, *o* and *e/ni* "to" can be omitted, too.

Otoosan (wa) ogenki desu ka.
   Is your father well?

Karaoke baa (wa) chikaku ni aru n desu ka.
   Is the karaoke bar nearby?

Kono aida karaoke (o) katta n desu.
   He bought karaoke equipment the other day.

Ashita ongakkai (e/ni) ikimasu ka.
   Are you going to the concert tomorrow?

In some cases, the speech sounds much more natural without a particle.

Moshi moshi, watakushi (wa) Suzuki desu ga.
   Hello, this is [I am] Suzuki.

In a classroom, the teacher says:

Nani ka shitsumon (wa) arimasu ka.
   Do you have any questions?

The fact that you can omit particles does not mean that you can do so whenever you feel like it. Instead, listen closely to the usage of native speakers.

C. MOJI

1. DIALOGUE

ちば   ああ、それは いま アメリカで わだいの 本 ですね。私も 読みたいと 思っていたんですが、本屋では 見つからなかったんです。どこで 買ったんですか。

ながの   この本は インターネットで 買ったんです。本屋の ホームページに 行くと、どんな本でも 買えますよ。本屋などで ちゅうもんするより 早いですよ。最近、私は よく オンラインで 買い物する ようになったんです。

ちば	どうやって しはらうんですか。
ながの	ネットに クレジットカードの ばんごうを タイプするんです。
ちば	クレジットカードの ばんごうを タイプするのは あぶなく聞こえますが、だいじょうぶですか。
ながの	ええ、だいじょうぶですよ。この てぶくろも ウェブで 買ったんです。今、デパートのホームページにはクリスマスプレゼントが たくさんありますよ。どのしょうひんの しゃしんを 見ても、本物みたいに きれいに 見えます。
ちば	そうですか。私も これから インターネットを つかうように しますよ。うちにいて オンラインで 買い物することが できるなんて べんりに なりましたね。

2. NEW *KANJI*

[84]	読	*yo(mu)*	to read, 読む
[85]	屋	*YA*	shop e.g., 本屋
[86]	物	*MONO*	things 買い物
[87]	買	*ka(u)*	to buy 買う
[88]	聞	*ki(ku)*	to hear 聞く

STROKE ORDER

[84]	` 丶 亠 亠 言 言 言 訂 訂 詰 詰 誌 読 読
[85]	一 コ 尸 尸 屄 居 居 屋 屋
[86]	ノ 一 ヒ 牛 牛 物 物 物
[87]	丶 一 罒 罒 罒 罒 尸 買 買 買 冒 買 買
[88]	一 一 ヨ 尸 尸' 門 門 門 門 門 閂 閂 閂 閏 聞

3. NEW READING

[77]	父	*(o)too(san)* (Lesson 28)	father
		chichi	father
[78]	母	*(o)kaa(san)* (Lesson 28)	mother
		haha	mother
[80]	歌	*uta, uta(u)* (Lesson 29)	song, to sing
		KA	song e.g., りゅうこう歌

D. TANGO TO HYOOGEN

wadai	something which is talked about
intaanetto	Internet
hoomupeeji	home page
chuumon suru	to order
onrain	online
saikin	recently
shiharau	to pay
honmono	real thing
tebukuro	gloves
webu	Web site
kurejitto kaado	credit card
koe	voice
baa	bar
ji	character, letter
megane	glasses
daigakusei	university student
shitsumon	question
otsukiai suru	to be in someone's company
taishoku suru	to retire
ateru	to hit (transitive)
atatameru	to warm (transitive)
atsumeru	to gather, collect (transitive)
butsukaru	to bump (intransitive)
chikazukeru	to bring (something) near
hajimeru	to begin (transitive)
kakeru	to take (time) (transitive), to wear (glasses)
kayou	to visit regularly, commute
kimaru	to be decided (intransitive)
kowareru	to break (intransitive)

kowasu	to break (transitive)
modosu	to return (transitive)
naosu	to heal, repair (transitive)
oru	to break (transitive)
otosu	to drop (transitive)
yakeru	to be baked, burn (intransitive)
utsukushii	beautiful
hitori de	alone
shibaraku	for a while
narubeku	if possible
kono aida	the other day

RENSHUU

A. Based on the above dialogue, mark each sentence true or false.

1. *Nagano san wa yoku intaanetto de kaimono o shimasu.* (   )
2. *Chiba san wa intaanetto de kaimono o shita koto ga arimasu.* (   )
3. *Hon'ya de hon o chuumon suru yori intaanetto de hon o kau hoo ga' osoi desu.* (   )
4. *Chiba san wa korekara intaanetto o tsukatte miyoo to omotte imasu.* (   )

B. Choose the correct verbs in the parentheses.

1. a: *Samui desu ne. Mado ga (aite/akete) iru n desu ka.*
   b: *Ee, (shimari/shime)mashoo ka.*
2. a: *Konpyuutaa ga (kowareta/kowashita) rashii n desu. Dare ka (naoru/naosu) koto ga dekimasu ka.*
   b: *Jikan o (kakareba/kakereba) dekiru to omoimasu kedo.*
3. a: *Saikin, kono hon o onrain de (mitsukatta/mitsuketa) n desu.*
   b: *Watashi mo tebukuro o onrain de (mitsuke/mitsukari) mashita.*

C. Ms. Suzuki is a popular person. The following statements are what her friends say about her. Fill in the blanks.

1. _____ o _____ mo, kirei _____ miemasu.
   Whatever she wears, she looks pretty.
2. _____ to _____ mo, teinei _____ hanashimasu.
   Whomever she talks with, she speaks politely.
3. _____ uta o _____ mo, joozu _____ utaimasu.
   Whatever kind of songs she sings, she sings them well.

D. Ms. King said the following about researching on the Internet. Fill in the blanks.

1. *amari konpyuutaa o* ———— *yoo ni* ———— *imasu.*
   (keep using = *tsukaisugiru*)
   I try not to keep using the computer for a long time.
2. *nandemo onrain de mitsuketa mono o* ———— *yoo ni* ———— *imasu.*
   I try not to buy everything I find online.
3. *intaanetto de* ———— *yoo ni* ———— *mashita.*
   I have begun to shop on the Internet
4. *intaanetto de shinbun o* ———— *yoo ni* ———— *mashita.*
   I have begun to read the newspaper on the Internet.

E. Write *kanji* in the blanks, based on the *hiragana* under the blanks.

a. きょう、やっと _____ でさがしていた ___を ___つけました。
　　　　　　　　　ほんや　　　　　　　　　　ほん　　み

b. ___を ___む のが すきですあか。
　ほん　　よ

c. _____は よく インターネットで ___い___ します。
　わたし　　　　　　　　　　　　　　か　もの

KARUCHAA NOOTO

There is a vast variety of popular music in Japan, ranging from traditional Japanese songs to those with Western elements. On December thirty-first, the singers who have been the most active professionally during the year are chosen to participate in a big concert shown on TV. Singers are adored and treated as stars.

Aside from professional singers, many amateurs enjoy singing as well, and karaoke has become popular. The word *karaoke* is a combination of *kara* "empty" and *oke* "orchestra," which refers to "an orchestra without its song (empty)." You sing the song with the orchestra, and you feel as if you were singing like a professional. There are many karaoke bars, and many people even own karaoke machines to enjoy doing karaoke at home.

A. 1. T 2. F 3. F 4. T
B. 1. *aite, shime* 2. *kowareta, naosu* 3. *mitsuketa, mitsuke*
C. 1. *Nani, kite, ni* 2. *Dare, hanashite, ni* 3. *Donna, utatte, ni*
D. 1. *tsukaisuginai, shite* 2. *kawanai, shite* 3. *kaimono suru, nari*
4. *yomu, nari*
E. a. 本屋、本、見

  b. 本、読

  c. 私、買（い）物

FUKUSHUU 6

A. Choose the words from the following list to match the definitions
given in items 1 through 5.

*jishin, ryokan, tenjoo, sekken, sofubo, rooka, ryooshin, toshokan, taifuu,
tenugui, kaminari*

Example: *hon o kariru tokoro*   (*toshokan*)

  1. *chichi to haha*   (   )
  2. *sugoi kaze to ame*   (   )
  3. *sora de naru mono*   (   )
  4. *te o aratta toki, tsukau mono* (   )
  5. *tomareru tokoro*   (   )

B. Choose from the words below, and fill in the blanks.

aite, akete, shimatta, shimeta, nani mo, nani ka, dare de mo

A thief got in Ms. Mori's house, and now she is talking to a police
officer.

M: Ms. Mori   P: police officer

P: _____¹ *toraremashita ka.*
M: *Iie,* _____² *torarenakatta to omoimasu.*
P: *Dono mado ga* _____³ *ita n desu ka.*
M: *Kono mado desu. Dekakeru toki, otto to watashi ga* _____⁴ *n desu
kedo.*
P: *Kono mado nara,* _____⁵ *akeraremasu yo.*

C. Translate the following:

Misora Hibari wa totemo yuumei na kashu deshita ga, gojuu nisai no *toki ni nakunarimashita.* * *Kodomo no toki ni, kashu ni natte kara, ooku no uta o utaimashita. Zannen nagara, amerikajin ni wa shirarete imasen.*

D. Fill in the blanks.

Sensei ni nan to iwareta n desu ka.
1. *Enpitsu de _____ wa ikenai to iwareta n desu.*
   (Don't write in pencil.)
2. *_____ ni mo tetsudatte _____ wa ikenai to iwareta n desu.*
   (Don't have anybody help you.)
3. *Kanji o _____ mo ii to iwareta n desu.*
   (You need not use kanji.)

E. Fill in the blanks according to the English equivalents. Use *agemasu, kuremasu,* or *moraimasu* in each sentence.

1. Mr. Yamada is going to teach me Japanese.
2. I am going to teach Mr. Yamada French.
3. Mr. Yamada is going to teach my son calligraphy.
4. Mr. Ueda is going to teach Mr. Yamada and me songs.

1. *Yamada san wa _____.*
2. *Watashi wa _____.*
3. *Musuko wa _____.*
4. *Ueda san wa _____.*

F. Fill in the blanks.

a: *Suzuki _____¹ mooshimasu.*
b: *Noda Masako no haha _____² gozaimasu.*
a: *Ano hon o moo _____³ yomi _____⁴ narimashita ka.*
b: *Ee, yomimashita.*
a: *Jaa, okari _____⁵ mo ii desu ka.*
b: *Ee, doozo.*
a: *Akachan wa moo arukemasu ka.*
b: *Ee, joozu _____⁶ arukeru _____⁷ narimashita.*

G. 1. Make as many *kanji* compound words as you can using the following *kanji.*

2. Write the reading of the compound words.

3. Write their English equivalents.

日　天　時　学　度　元　四　生　月

　　Example:　天気　　weather

* *nakunaru* "to die"

371

KOTAE

A. 1. *ryooshin* 2. *taifuu* 3. *kaminari* 4. *tenugui* 5. *ryokan*
B. 1. *Nani ka* 2. *nani mo* 3. *aite* 4. *shimeta* 5. *dare de mo*
C. Misora Hibari was a very famous singer, and she died at the age of fifty-two. Since becoming a singer as a child, she had sung many songs. Unfortunately, she is not known to Americans.
D. 1. *kaite* 2. *Dare, moratte* 3. *tsukawanakute*
E. 1. *watashi ni nihongo o oshiete kuremasu* 2. *Yamada san ni furansugo o oshiete agemasu* 3. *Yamada san ni shodoo o oshiete moraimasu*
4. *Yamada san to watashi ni uta o oshiete kuremasu*
F. 1. *to* 2. *de* 3. *o* 4. *ni* 5. *shite* 6. *ni* 7. *yoo ni*
G.

学生	がくせい	student
元気	げんき	healthy
四日	よっか	the fourth of the month, four days
四時	よじ	four o'clock
四度	よんど	four times
四月	しがつ	April

YOMU RENSHUU

ねこと十二し[1]*

　　十二しの どうぶつ[2] の なまえを 知っていますか。ねずみ[3]、うし[4]、とら[5]、うさぎ[6]、たつ[7]、へび[8]、うま[9]、ひつじ[10]、さる[11]、とり[12]、いぬ、いのしし[13]です。この中に ねこが 入っていません。どうしてでしょう。つぎ[14]が そのりゆう[15]です。

　　むかし、おう様[16]が どうぶつたちを よんで、パーティーを すると つたえました[17]。どうぶつたちは よろこんで、その日が 来るのを 待っていました。ねこは その日を わすれたので、ねずみに 聞きに 行くと、ねずみは わざと[18]、その日の あくる日[19]に あると 言ったのです。パーティーの 日、ねずみは 一ばんさきに[20] おう様の おしろに つきました。それから、うしが 来ました。どうぶつたちは せんちゃくじゅんに[21] すわって、おいしい ごちそう[22]を たべました。ねこは そのあくる日 おしろに 行ったのですが、もんばん[23]に パーティーは きのう あったと 言われたのです。ねこは すごく おこりました。それで、今も ねこと ねずみは なか[24]が わるいのです。ねこは パーティーに 行かなかったから、十二しに 入っていないのです。

　　* Adapted from "*Neko to juunishi*" (The cat and the twelve signs of zodiac) in *Nihon no Mukashibanashi I* (Japanese Old Tales I), ed. by Seki, Keigo. Tokyo: Iwanami, 1956.

TANGO TO HYOOGEN

1. 十二し　　　　　　12 signs of the zodiac
2. どうぶつ　　　　　animal
3. ねずみ　　　　　　rat
4. うし　　　　　　　ox/cow
5. とら　　　　　　　tiger
6. うさぎ　　　　　　rabbit
7. たつ　　　　　　　dragon
8. へび　　　　　　　snake
9. うま　　　　　　　horse
10. ひつじ　　　　　　sheep
11. さる　　　　　　　monkey
12. とり　　　　　　　rooster
13. いのしし　　　　　boar
14. つぎ　　　　　　　following
15. りゆう　　　　　　reason
16. おう様　　　　　　king
17. つたえる　　　　　to announce
18. わざと　　　　　　deliberately
19. あくる日　　　　　following day
20. 一ばんさきに　　　earliest of all
21. せんちゃくじゅん　in the order of arrival
22. ごちそう　　　　　feast
23. もんばん　　　　　gatekeeper
24. なか　　　　　　　relationship/inside

DAI SANJUU IKKA
Lesson 31
SHUUSHOKU NO MENSETSU.   A Job Interview.

A. DAIAROOGU

GANGU NO KAISHA DE NO MENSETSU.

Mr. Ooki is looking for a job. The department head is interviewing him in his office.

BUCHOO: Kono kaisha no seihin o gozónji desu ka.

OOKI: Hái, yoochíen ni itte iru oi ga iroiro na monó o mótte irú node, yóku shitte imásu.

BUCHOO: Daigaku de shinrígaku o senkoo saretá n desu ne.

OOKI: Hái, watashi no sotsuron wa jidoo shínri ni kansúru monó de, gángu ni tsúite mo iroiro benkyoo shimáshita.

BUCHOO: Máe no kaisha wa dóoshite yameraretá n desu ka.

OOKI: Hoken no shigoto wa kekkyoku watashi no shóogai no shigoto dé wa nái to omótta n desu. Sore ni kaisha ga toosúgite, taihen dátta n desu ga, totsuzen tsúma ga Amerika ni tenkin suru kotó ni nátta node, watashi mo yamete, issho ni iku kotó ni shitá n desu.

BUCHOO: Ítsu Nihón ni modoráreta n desu ka.

OOKI: Séngetsu no owari désu.

BUCHOO: Sóo desu ka. Jáa, raishuu no getsuyoobi góro ni renraku shimásu.

OOKI: Dóomo arígatoo gozaimashita.

INTERVIEW AT A TOY COMPANY.

DEPT. HEAD: Are you familiar with our company's products?

OOKI: Yes, my nephew, who is in kindergarten, has many of your toys, so I know your products well.

DEPT. HEAD: You majored in psychology at the university, right?

OOKI: Yes, my thesis was on child psychology, and I did a lot of research on toys as well.

DEPT. HEAD: May I ask why you left your previous job?

OOKI: In the long run, I didn't see myself in the insurance business. Besides, my office was too far away [to cope with it]. And when [suddenly it was decided that] my wife was transferred to America, [so] I decided to quit my job and go along with her.

DEPT. HEAD: When did you come back to Japan?

OOKI: At the end of last month.

DEPT. HEAD: I see. Well, we'll get back to [contact] you around Monday of next week.

OOKI: Thank you very much.

B. BUNPOO TO YOOHOO

1. REGULAR HONORIFIC VERBS (RESPECT)

Respect can be expressed using the pattern *o* + pre-*masu* + *ni naru* (see Lesson 26, B6). Another kind of regular respect honorific is expressed with a verb form identical to the passive verb. For example, both the passive and the honorific verb forms of *yomu* "to read" are *yomareru*. Since the passive and the honorific verbs are identical, refer back to the explanation about passive verbs (see Lesson 28, B1).

Daigaku de shinrigaku o senkoo sareta n desu ne.
You majored in psychology at the university, right?

Moo rirekisho o okuraremashita ka.
Did you send your résumé yet?

Abe san wa kinoo korarenakatta soo desu.
I heard Ms. Abe didn't come yesterday.

The *rare* honorific expresses a lesser degree of respect than the *o* pre-*masu ni naru* and irregular honorific verbs (e.g., *ossharu* "to say"). Thus you use the *rare* honorific when you do not want to be overly polite.

A small number of verbs such as *kureru* "to give," *aru* "to have," or potential verbs (e.g., *yomeru* "can read") cannot be changed into either the honorific form or the passive form. The passive verb can be formed from *iru* "to exist" (i.e., *irareru*), but you should use the irregular honorific form *irassharu*.

Since the passive verb and the honorific verb are identical, ambiguity may occur. For example:

Yamada san ga shikarareta n desu.
    Mr. Yamada was scolded. (passive)
    Mr. Yamada scolded someone. (honorific)

Usually the context or other elements in the sentence will clarify the meaning. Compare:

Yamada san ga Toda san ni shikarareta n desu.
    Mr. Yamada was scolded by Mr. Toda. (passive)

Yamada san ga Toda san o shikarareta n desu.
    Mr. Yamada scolded Mr. Toda. (honorific)

2. COMPOUND VERBS WITH *-SUGIRU*

The verb *sugiru* "to exceed" can be attached to another element to form a compound that means "too . . ."

a. With verbs

-sugiru is attached to the pre-*masu* form.

tabesugiru
    to eat too much

Paatii de tabesugimashita.
    I ate too much at the party.

Hatarakisugite, byooki ni narimashita.
    I worked too much and got sick.

Osake o nomisuginai yoo ni shite kudasai.
    Please try not to drink too much sake.

b. With *i*-adjectives

When *-sugiru* forms a compound with an *i*-adjective, the final *-i* is dropped.

toosugiru
    to be too far (verb)

Kaisha ga toosugite, taihen datta n desu.
    My office was too far away to cope with it.

Ano mensetsu wa nagasugimashita.
    That interview was too long.

Oobo suru no ga ososugite, dame deshita.
I was too late in applying, so it didn't work out.

c. With *na*-adjectives

-sugiru can also be attached to a *na*-adjective.

kantansugiru
to be too easy (verb)

Kono shigoto wa kantansugimasu.
This job is too easy.

Kono biru wa shizukasugite, kowai desu.
This building is too quiet, and it is scary.

Himasugite, taikutsu shite imasu.
I'm at loose ends, and I'm bored.

3. ...*KOTO NI SURU* "TO DECIDE..."

To express a decision to do something, use the following pattern.

> plain present form of the verb + *koto ni suru*

Watashi mo issho ni iku koto ni shita n desu.
I decided to go along.

Itoko wa daigaku de shakaigaku o senkoo suru koto ni shita rashii desu.
I understand that my cousin decided to major in sociology at the university.

Yoru osoku made hatarakanai koto ni shimashita.
I decided not to work until late at night.

4. ...*KOTO NI NARU* "TO BE DECIDED..."

Like ...*koto ni suru* "to decide ...," ...*koto ni naru* follows the plain present verb form and expresses a decision. However, unlike ...*koto ni suru*, a sentence with ...*koto ni naru* does not specify the decision maker.

Abe san wa Hiroshima de hataraku koto ni narimashita.
It was decided that Ms. Abe will work in Hiroshima.

Atarashii konpyuntaa o kau koto ni natta n desu.
It was decided that we will buy a new computer.

Kotoshi wa dare mo atarashii hito o yatowanai koto ni narimashita.
It was decided that we will not hire a new employee this year.

5. TO HAVE

Like *aru* "to have," *motte iru* also means "to have." It consists of the TE form of *motsu* "to hold" and *iru*. One use of TE *iru* is stative (see Lesson 15, B1). Once you acquire, i.e., hold something, you have it.

Oi wa iroiro na omocha o motte imasu.
My nephew has various kinds of toys.

Mukashi kimono o takusan motte imashita.
I had many kimonos years ago.

Ima meishi o motte inai n desu.
I don't have my business card now.

6. THE PARTICLE *NI* "TO"

With motion verbs—*tenkin suru* "to be transferred," *shutchoo suru* "to travel on business," and *hikkosu* "to move (change residence)"—the noun referring to the destination or goal is followed by *ni* or *e*.

Tsuma ga Amerika ni tenkin suru koto ni narimashita.
It was decided that my wife will be transferred to America.

Mei wa raigetsu Doitsu e shutchoo suru koto ni natta soo desu.
I heard it was decided that my niece will go to Germany next month on business.

Kyonen Hiroshima ni hikkoshita n desu.
We moved to Hiroshima last year.

7. PARTICLE-LIKE PHRASES

There are phrases consisting of a particle and a verb that function like particles (see Lesson 25, B7).

a. *Ni tsuite* "about"

Tsuite is the TE form of *tsuku* "to attach."

Gangu ni tsuite benkyoo shimashita.
I studied [about] toys.

Ano kaisha ni tsuite nani ka shitte imasu ka.
Do you know anything about that company?

b. *Ni kansuru* "related to," "on"

The verb *kansuru* means "to relate" and is rarely used by itself.

Watashi no sotsuron wa jidoo shinri ni kansuru mono desu.
My thesis is on child psychology. [My thesis is something on child psychology.]

Shuushoku ni kansuru joohoo ga hoshii desu.
I want information on employment.

8. *IROIRO* AS ADVERB

Iroiro "various" has been introduced as a *na*-adjective.

Mago wa iroiro na omocha o katte moratte, yorokonde imasu.
My grandchild is delighted to have received various toys as presents.

Iroiro can also be used as an adverb without a noun following it. In this case, *to* follows optionally.

Gangu ni tsuite mo iroiro (to) benkyoo shimashita.
I studied a lot about toys, as well.

Wakai koro, shigoto o iroiro (to) kaemashita.
I changed jobs frequently when I was young.

C. MOJI

1. DIALOGUE

ぶちょう　「この会社の せいひんを ごぞんじですか。」

大木　　　「はい、ようちえんに 行っている おいが いろいろな
　　　　　物を 持っているので、よく 知っています。」

ぶちょう　「大学で しんり学を せんこうされたんですね。」

大木　　　「はい、私の そつろんは じどうしんりに かんする物で、
　　　　　がんぐについても いろいろ べんきょうしました。」

ぶちょう　「前の 会社は どうして やめられたんですか。」

大木　「ほけんの しごとは けっきょく 私の しょうがいの
　　　　しごとではないと おもったんです。それに、会社が
　　　　遠すぎて、たいへんだったんですが、とつぜん つまが
　　　　アメリカに てんきんする ことに なったので、私もやめて、
　　　　いっしょに 行くことに したんです。」

ぶちょう　「いつ 日本に もどられたんですか。」

大木　「先月の 終りです。」

ぶちょう　「そうですか。じゃあ、来週の 月曜日ごろに れんらく
　　　　します。」

大木　「どうも ありがとう ございました。」

2. NEW *KANJI*

[89]	社	*SHA*	company
[90]	物	*mono*	thing
[91]	終	*owa(ri), owa(ru)*	end, to end
[92]	曜	*YOO*	shining

STROKE ORDER

[89]	ネ ネ 社 社
[90]	ノ ヒ 牛 牜 物 物
[91]	く 幺 幺 幺 糸 糸 糸 紀 紙 終 終
[92]	日 日¹ 日³ 日³ 旺 曜 曜 曜 曜

3. NEW READING

[56]	大	*oo(kii)* (Lesson 20)	big
		DAI	big e.g., 大学、大好き
[27]	月	*GATSU* (Lesson 27)	month
		GETSU	month, Monday e.g., 先月、月曜日

| [59] | 来 | *ku(ru)*, etc. (Lesson 25) | to come |
| | | *RAI* | coming e.g., 来週 |

4. DAYS OF THE WEEK

The following are the *kanji* for the days of week.

ようび　　　Days of the Week

[23]	日	*NICHI*	sun	日曜日	Sunday
[71]	月	*GETSU*	moon	月曜日	Monday
[93]	火	*KA* (new)	fire	火曜日	Tuesday
[4]	水	*SUI*	water	水曜日	Wednesday
[1]	木	*MOKU*	tree	木曜日	Thursday
[94]	金	*KIN* (new)	gold	金曜日	Friday
[95]	土	*DO* (new)	soil	土曜日	Saturday

STROKE ORDER

[93]	丶 丷 少 火
[94]	ノ 人 入 全 全 余 金 金
[95]	一 十 土

D. TANGO TO HYOOGEN

mensetsu	interview
rirekisho	résumé
shuushoku	employment
seihin	product
meishi	business card
biru	building (Western-style, big)
joohoo	information
hoken	insurance
sotsuron	thesis (for a bachelor's degree)
shakaigaku	sociology
shinrigaku	psychology
jidoo	child (more formal than *kodomo*)
jidoo shinri(gaku)	child psychology
omocha	toy
gangu	toy (more formal than *omocha*)
yoochien	kindergarten
mago	grandchild
omagosan	grandchild (somebody else's)
oi	nephew
oigosan	nephew (somebody else's)
mei	niece
meigosan	niece (somebody else's)
itoko	cousin
itokosan/itoko no kata	cousin (somebody else's)
hajime	beginning
owari	end
shoogai	lifetime
oobo suru	to apply
tenkin suru	to be transferred
shutchoo suru	to take a business trip
renraku suru	to contact
senkoo suru	to major
taikutsu suru	to get bored
yatou	to hire
kaeru	to change (transitive)
hikkosu	to move (changing residence)
motte iru	to have
wakai	young
kantan	simple, easy
kekkyoku	in the long run
Gozonji desu.	(Somebody) knows. (respect)

RENSHUU

A. Make appropriate choices from the words below based on the dialogue, and fill in the blanks.

omocha, shakaigaku, shinrigaku, hoken, oi, mago, sotsuron

1. *Ooki san wa daigaku de ——— o senkoo shimashita.*
2. *Ooki san wa ——— no kaisha no buchoo to hanashite imasu.*
3. *Ooki san wa mae ——— no kaisha ni tsutomete imashita.*
4. *Ooki san no ——— wa ima yoochien ni itte imasu.*

B. Is the underlined word potential, passive, or honorific?

1. a. *Nakagawa: Miyashita san, ashita ofisu ni <u>koraremasu</u> ka.*
   b. *Ee, <u>korareru</u> to omoimasu kedo.*
2. a. *Paatii ni kamera o <u>motte ikaremasu</u> ka.*
   b. *Iie, kinoo otooto ni <u>motte ikarete</u>, ima nai n desu.*

C. Translate the following using *-sugimasu*.

1. A student is complaining about her homework.
   a. It is too complicated.
   b. It is too long.
   c. It takes too much time.
2. Someone is giving the reasons why she does not want to buy certain confectionery products.
   a. They are too expensive.
   b. They are too sweet.
   c. The advertisement is too showy.

D. Translate the following:

Raigetsu Nagoya ni tenkin suru koto ni narimashita. Kazoku no mono wa tsugoo ga warui to iu node, watashi ga hitori de Nagoya ni hikkosu koto ni shimashita.

E. Fill in the blanks below based on the following sentence.

来週の 月曜日は 四月二日です。

1. _____ 週の _____ 曜日は 三月三十一日です。

2. _____ 週の _____ 曜日は 四月四日です。

3. _____ 週の _____ 曜日は 三月二十三日でした。

383

F. Rewrite the following sentences using the regular honorific form of the verb.

Example: *daigaku de shinrigaku o benkyooshita n desu ne.*
  → *daigaku de shinrigaku o benkyoosareta n desu ne.*

1. *Kinoo nani o <u>tabemashita ka</u>.*
2. *koohii o <u>nomimasu ka</u>.*
3. *yoku gorufu o <u>shimasu ka</u>.*

KARUCHAA NOOTO

Japanese companies have traditionally tried to guarantee lifetime employment for their (male) employees. While many people in the United States change their jobs and move from company to company frequently, Japanese employees tend to be loyal to one company until they retire. This loyalty is mutual: a Japanese company will try to keep its employees under any circumstances, even during an economic crisis, and an employee will stay with his company, even if it means taking a salary cut or performing a lesser duty. Therefore, changing companies during one's career may carry a bit of a stigma in Japan. However, lifetime employment is now becoming less common, and the prejudice toward changing jobs is gradually fading.

When you go to job interviews, you usually use a ready-made résumé form. Add a photo of the applicant, and information on the applicant's gender, age, and family. The age factor is especially important, as many classified advertisements will specify the age group desired for the position. Such specifications are not considered discriminatory in Japan, a fact that reflects the age-consciousness of Japanese society.

KOTAE

A. 1. *shinrigaku* 2. *omocha* 3. *hoken* 4. *oi*
B. 1. a: potential or honorific b: potential 2. a: honorific (It is possible to interpret it as potential, but it is not the standard potential form. *Motte ikeru* is the standard potential form.) b: passive
C. 1. a. *Fukuzatsusugimasu.* b. *Nagasugimasu.* c. *Jikan ga kakarisugimasu.* 2. a. *Takasugimasu.* b. *Amasugimasu.* c. *Kookoku ga hadesugimasu.*
D. It has been/was decided that I will be transferred to Nagoya next month. Since my family members say it is inconvenient, I have decided to move to Nagoya alone.
E. 1. 今、土 2. 来、水 3. 先、金
F. 1. *taberaremashita ka* 2. *nomaremasu ka* 3. *saremasu ka.*

DAI SANJUU NIKA
Lesson 32
KAISHAIN.   Company Employees.

A. DAIAROOGU

SHUKKIN DAI ICHINICHIME.

The section manager introduces Mr. Ooki to the group of people in his department.

KACHOO: **Kyóo kara koko de hataraite morau kotó ni nátta Ooki Tomóichi kun desu.**

OOKI: **Dóozo yoroshiku.**

KACHOO: **Nakayama kun, chótto kíte kuremasu ka.**

NAKAYAMA: **Hái.**

Kachoo no seki de.

KACHOO: **Ooki kun ni maaketingu risáachi ni tsúite iroiro oshiete agete hoshíi n desu yo.**

NAKAYAMA: **Hái, wakarimáshita.**

OOKI: **Oséwa ni narimásu.**

Shibaraku shite.

NAKAYAMA: **Kyóo hónsha ni kono shíryoo o okuranákute wa ikenái n desu. Fákkusu de okutte kuremasén ka.**

OOKI: **Hái. Anoo, fákkusu no bangóo o oshiete itadakemasén ka.**

NAKAYAMA: **Fákkusu no bangóo wa koko ni káite arimasu.**

OOKI: **A, sumimasén. Wakarimáshita.**

THE FIRST DAY OF WORK.

MANAGER: This is Mr. Tomoichi Ooki. He'll start working here today.

OOKI: Nice to meet you.

MANAGER: Mr. Nakayama, would you come over here for a moment?

NAKAYAMA: Sure.

At the manager's desk.

MANAGER: I would like you to introduce Mr. Ooki to our marketing research and train him.

NAKAYAMA: Yes, I will. [I understood.]

OOKI: Thank you. [I am going to receive your assistance.]

A little later.

NAKAYAMA: We have to send this material to the main office today. Would you send it by fax, please?

OOKI: Yes. Uhh, may I ask you to tell me the fax number?

NAKAYAMA: The fax number is written here.

OOKI: Oh, thanks, I see.

B. BUNPOO TO YOOHOO

1. TE *ARU*

TE *aru* is used to express the result of something that has been done for a certain purpose. Consider the following sentences.

Mado o shimemashita. (action)
[Someone] closed the window.

Mado wa/ga shimete arimasu. (state)
The window is closed.

In English the direct object of the first sentence becomes the subject in the second. In Japanese, the result of an action rather than the action itself is expressed with the TE form of the verb followed by *aru*. The actor does not appear in the sentence.

Fakkusu no bangoo wa koko ni kaite arimasu.
The fax number is written here.

Ryooshuusho wa hikidashi no naka ni irete arimasen deshita.
The receipt wasn't [put] in the drawer.

Tsukue no ue ni shorui ga oite arimasu.
The documents are [placed] on the desk.

2. OBLIGATION

There are various expressions for obligation, i.e., for the English "must," "should," or "have to." Prohibition is a related construction: TE *wa ikemasen (ikenai)/dame desu (dame da)* (see Lesson 28, B4).

Itte wa ikemasen/dame desu.
You must/should not go. [It won't do if you go.]

For obligation, the TE form of the negative is used.

Ikanakute wa ikemasen/dame desu.
You must/should/have to go. [It won't do if you don't go.]

The following is a summary of negative TE forms.

	NEGATIVE	NEGATIVE TE
VERB	*ikanai* to not go	*ikanakute*
I-ADJECTIVE	*oishiku nai* to not be tasty	*oishiku nakute*
NA-ADJECTIVE + COPULA	*shizuka ja/de (wa) nai* to not be quiet	*shizuka ja/de nakute*
NOUN + COPULA	*kaishain ja/de (wa) nai* to not be a company employee	*kaishain ja/de nakute*

Kyoo honsha ni kono shiryoo o okuranakute wa ikenai n desu.
We have to send this material to the main office today.

Kore mo kopii shinakute wa ikemasen ka.
Do I have to copy this, too?

Repooto wa kuwashiku nakute wa dame desu yo.
The report has to be detailed.

Menbaa wa kaishain ja nakute wa ikenai soo desu.
I understand that members must be company employees.

3. TE *HOSHII* "TO WANT SOMEONE TO . . ."

Compare the following sentences:

Watashi wa kono shigoto ga hoshii n desu.
I want this job.

Watashi wa kono shigoto o tsuzuketai n desu.
I want to continue [having] this job.

Watashi wa Hara san ni kono shigoto o tsuzukete hoshii n desu.
I want Ms. Hara to continue this job.

Unlike "to want" plus noun (see Lesson 7, C1) and unlike "to want to" plus verb (see Lesson 6, C8), "to want someone to" plus verb is expressed as follows:

> person who wants (=the subject) *wa/ga* + another person *ni* . . . TE *hoshii*

Watanabe san ni shisha made itte hoshikatta n desu.
(I) wanted Ms. Watanabe to go to the branch office.

Musuko ni wa sarariiman ni natte hoshiku nakatta n desu.
(I) did not want my son to become a white-collar worker (salaried man).

Ooki kun ni iroiro oshiete agete hoshii n desu.
(I) want (you) to train [teach various things to] Mr. Ooki.

Moraitai "want to receive the favor of . . ." can be used to express a similar meaning.

Abe san ni kite moraitai n desu.
(I) want Ms. Abe to come. [(I) want to receive the favor of Ms. Abe's coming.]

To be more polite, use *itadakitai.*

Sasaki san ni waapuro o kashite itadakitakatta n desu.
(I) wanted Ms. Sasaki to lend (me) a word processor.

4. VARIOUS REQUEST EXPRESSIONS

Japanese offers various ways to make requests.* Let's review them. An example of a possible speaker and addressee is given in parentheses after each sentence.

a. TE *kudasai*

Senmu ni denwa shite kudasai. (colleague → colleague)
Please call the executive director.

---

* The Japanese is only approximately matched with its English equivalent, since they do not parallel each other exactly.

b. *O* pre-*masu kudasai*

Uketsuke de omachi kudasai. (employee → visitor)
Please wait at the reception desk.

c. TE *hoshii n desu*

Kyoo zangyoo shite hoshii n desu. (boss → subordinate)
I want you to work overtime today.

d. TE *moraitai n desu*

Ashita doyoobi da kedo, shukkin shite moraitai n desu. (boss → subordinate)
Even though tomorrow is Saturday, I want you to come to work.

e. TE *itadakitai n desu*

Kono shorui o mite itadakitai n desu kedo. (subordinate → boss, colleague → colleague)
I would like you to look at this document.

The following are new forms of request expressions.

f. TE *kuremasu ka*

Chotto kite kuremasu ka. (boss → subordinate)
Could you come over here for a moment?

g. TE *kuremasen ka*

Fakkusu de okutte kuremasen ka. (senior member → junior member, colleague → colleague)
Would you send it by fax, please?

h. TE *itadakemasu ka*

Kono memo o mite itadakemasu ka. (junior member → senior member, subordinate → boss)
May I ask you to look at this memo?

i. TE *itadakemasen ka*

Fakkusu no bangoo o oshiete itadakemasen ka. (junior member → senior member, subordinate → boss)
May I ask you to tell me the fax number?

j. TE *kudasaimasu ka*

Boonenkai ni kite kudasaimasu ka. (junior member → senior member, subordinate → boss)
Will you please do us the honor of coming to the year-end party?

k. TE *kudasaimasen ka*

Denpyoo o misete kudasaimasen ka. (junior member → senior member, subordinate → boss)
Would you please show me the bill?

l. TE *moraemasu ka*

Kono shigoto o tetsudatte moraemasu ka. (colleague → colleague)
May I have you help me with this job?

m. TE *moraemasen ka*

Kore o taipu shite moraemasen ka. (junior member → senior member)
May I have you type this, please?

There are still more request expressions, but let's compare what we have seen so far in items a. through m. above. Some of these expressions are more polite than others. The following is a scale of these request patterns from the most polite to the least polite.

i	e	k	h	j	b	m	l	g	f	d	a	c

← more polite

The order of politeness is somewhat subjective. However, as a general guideline, this scale will be quite helpful.

5. THE HONORIFIC *KUN*

When speaking directly to or referring to a person, *kun* can be used instead of the honorific *san* in certain situations. It is an honorific that is less formal and polite. First, you cannot use it with your superior, since this would be considered very impolite. Second, people addressed as *kun* are usually male, although sometimes women may be called *kun*. For example, a high school teacher may call his female student *kun*. Third, people using *kun* are usually male as well, although in some cases, women use *kun*, too. For example, a young female student may use *kun* with her male classmate. Fourth, a woman never addresses another woman *kun*.

In the dialogue, the manager addresses Mr. Nakayama and Mr. Ooki as *kun*. They are all men. There are two additional factors. One is that the manager has a higher status in the hierarchy of the company. The other factor is age: that is, both Mr. Nakayama and Mr. Ooki are probably younger than the manager. If not, the manager would never use *kun*.

C. MOJI

1. DIALOGUE

かちょう 「今日から ここで 働いて もらうことに なった
大木くんです。」

大木 「どうぞよろしく。」

かちょう 「中山くん、ちょっと 来てくれますか。」

中山 「はい。」

　　　　　かちょうの せきで。

かちょう 「大木くんに マーケティングについて いろいろ 教え
て　　　　　　　あげてほしいんです。」

中山 「はい、わかりました。」

大木 「おせわに なります。」

─────────────────

中山 「今日 本社に このしりょうを 送らなくては
いけないんです。ファックスで 送ってくれませんか。」

大木 「はい、あのう、ファックスの 番号を 教えて
いただけませんか。」

中山 「ファックスの 番号は ここに 書いてあります。」

大木 「あ、すみません。わかりました。」

2. NEW *KANJI*

[96]	働	*hatara(ku)*	to work
[97]	号	*GOO*	number e.g., 番号
[98]	書	*ka(ku)*	to write

STROKE ORDER

[96]
[97]
[98]

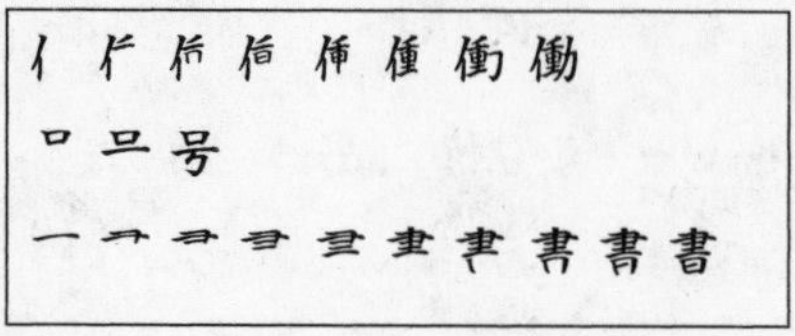

D. TANGO TO HYOOGEN

kaishain	company employee (general)
cf. **shain**	company employee (in a particular company)
sarariiman	white-collar worker (salaried man)
senmu	executive director
menbaa	member
shisha	branch office
fakkusu	fax
waapuro	word processor
hikidashi	drawer
shiryoo	materials (documents, records, etc.)
shorui	document
memo	memo
denpyoo	bill
ryooshuusho	receipt
tsukue	desk
maaketingu risaachi	marketing research
kun	Mr. (Ms.)
sewa	favor, assistance
sewa ni naru	to receive a favor
sewa o suru	to do a favor, to look after
shukkin suru	to go to work
zangyoo suru	to work overtime
kopii suru	to copy
taipu suru	to type

tsuzukeru	to continue (transitive)
tetsudau	to help
kuwashii	detailed

RENSHUU

A. Fill in each blank with one of the following on the basis of the dialogue.

kachoo, Nakayama san, Ooki san

1. _____ *wa* _____ *ni iroiro oshiete moratte imasu.*
2. _____ *wa* _____ *o minna ni shookai shimashita.*
3. _____ *wa* _____ *ni fakkusu no bangoo o kikimashita.*

B. Ms. Maeda is expecting guests and has made the following preparations. Write about the resulting situations.

Example: *Osara o araimashita.*
  → *Osara ga aratte arimasu.*

1. *Kabe ni e o kakemashita.*
2. *Mado o akemashita.*
3. *Omiyage o kaimashita.*
4. *Biiru o reizooko ni iremashita.*
5. *Teeburu no ue ni oodoburu (hors d'oeuvres) o okimashita.*

C. Fill in the blanks according to the English equivalents.

a: *Kyoo kaisha o yasumitai n desu ga, yasumenai n desu.*
b: *Dooshite desu ka.*
a: *Asa Sapporo no shisha ni* _____[1] *ikenai n desu.*
  I have to send a document to the branch office in Sapporo.
  Sore kara, kaigi ni _____[2] *ikenai n desu.*
  Then I have to attend a meeting.
  Sore kara, gogo senmu ni _____[3] *ikenai n desu.*
  Then I have to see the executive director in the afternoon.

D. Which word or phrase does not seem to fit in the group?

Example: *otooto, oi, musuko, oba*

1. *shorui, shiryoo, waapuro, memo*
2. *kachoo, shain, buchoo, senmu*
3. *shinpai suru, shukkin suru, zangyoo suru, taishoku suru*
4. *Itte hoshii n desu. Itte moraitai n desu. Itte itadakitai n desu. Itte agetai n desu.*

E. Write *kanji* in the blanks based on the *hiragana* written under the blanks.

ファックスの＿＿＿＿＿1. は ここに＿＿＿＿＿2. いてあります。
　　　　　　 ばんごう　　　　　　　　　　 か

＿＿＿＿＿3. の＿＿＿＿＿＿＿4. までに
 らいしゅう　　 もくようび

KARUCHAA NOOTO

In typical Japanese companies, there are different departments, and each department has subsections. The rankings from the top down are the president, executives, department heads, section managers, and ordinary employees. While merit certainly plays a role, in general the longer employees have been with a company, the higher their salary and position.

Sarariiman is a word used frequently, which was originally derived from the English "salaried man." Its original meaning, however, has been narrowed down to mean white-collar worker. The work ethic of a *sarariiman* is generally quite strong. He works hard for his company, often well beyond office hours, sacrificing his personal life. *Karooshi*, "death due to exhaustion," catches up with some of the *sarariiman*. The *sarariiman*'s hard work has contributed a lot to Japan's economic growth, but this attitude toward work has recently come under attack.

KOTAE

A. 1. *Ooki san, Nakayama san* 2. *Kachoo, Ooki san* 3. *Ooki san, Nakayama san*
B. 1. *Kabe ni e ga kakete arimasu.* 2. *Mado ga akete arimasu.* 3. *Omiyage ga katte arimasu.* 4. *Reizooko ni biiru ga irete arimasu.* 5. *Teeburu no ue ni oodoburu ga oite arimasu.*
C. 1. *shorui o okuranakute wa* 2. *denakute wa* or *shusseki shinakute wa*
3. *awanakute wa*
D. 1. *waapuro* 2. *shain* 3. *shinpai suru* 4. *Itte agetai n desu.*
E. 1. 番号 2. 書 3. 来週 4. 木曜

DAI SANJUU SANKA
Lesson 33
CHA NO YU.   The Tea Ceremony.

A. DAIAROOGU

MIZUKI SAN NO UCHI DE.

Ms. Hall, an American, is visiting Ms. Mizuki and her daughter, Hideko.
She sees a kimono hanging.

HOORU: **Kírei na kimono désu ne. Dóko ka ni irassháru n desu
ka.**

MIZUKI: **Ée, ashita ochakai ga áru node, kono kimono o kiyóo to
omótteru n desu.**

HOORU: **Ocha o nasátteru n desu ka.**

MIZUKI: **Mukashi sóbo ni narawasáreta n desu kedo, kono goro
mata hajimetá n desu.**

HOORU: **Ocha o nónda kotó wa nái n desu kedo, oishíi n desu ka.**

MIZUKI: **Watashi wa oishíi to omoimásu kedo. Jáa, kore kara
watashi ga ocha o tatemásu kara, nónde mite kudasai.**

HOORU: **Oisogashíi noni, íi n desu ka.**

MIZUKI: **Ée, daijóobu desu. Hídeko ni tetsudawasemásu kara.**

HOORU: **Jáa, gochisoo ni narimásu.**

MIZUKI: **Odoogu o kurá kara dáshite kimásu kara, chótto omachi
kudasái ne.**

HOORU: **Gomendoo kakemásu. Sumimasén.**

———————

AT MS. MIZUKI'S HOUSE.

HALL: This is a pretty kimono, isn't it? Are you going somewhere special?

MIZUKI: Yes, there's a tea ceremony party tomorrow, and I'm thinking of
wearing it there.

HALL: Do you perform the tea ceremony yourself?

MIZUKI: My grandmother made me learn it [I was made to learn it by my grandmother] years ago. Recently, I started doing it again.

HALL: I've never had powdered tea. Is it good?

MIZUKI: I myself think it's delicious. Well then, I'll make tea for you. Please have some and see how it is.

HALL: You seem too busy. Are you sure?

MIZUKI: Yes, it's no problem. I'll have Hideko help me.

HALL: Then I'll accept your offer.

MIZUKI: I'm going to get the utensils from the storage room. I'll be right back [Please wait].

HALL: I'm afraid I'm bothering you. But thank you.

B. BUNPOO TO YOOHOO

1. CAUSATIVE SENTENCES

a. Causative verbs.

Consider the following English sentences.

	CAUSATIVE SENTENCE
My friend went there.	I had my friend go there.
The baby walked.	Mr. Yamada made the baby walk.
My younger sister drank the tea.	My mother let my younger sister drink the tea.

In the above sentences, "I," "Mr. Yamada," and "my mother" are causers who made the events happen, and "my friend," "the baby," and "my younger sister" are causees, who were made to do the actions. While English uses several different causative verbs (to have, to let, to get, to cause, etc.) depending on the situation, Japanese forms causative verbs by adding a suffix -*(s)aseru* to express any causative meaning. Here is how they are formed.

VOWEL VERBS: The final -*ru* is replaced by -*saseru*.

taberu	→	*tabesaseru*
yameru	→	*yamesaseru*

396

CONSONANT VERBS: The final *-u* is replaced by *-aseru*.

yomu	→	*yomaseru*
hataraku	→	*hatarakaseru*

When the dictionary form of a consonant verb ends in vowel + *u*, *-w* is inserted before *-aseru* after the *-u* is dropped.

morau	→	*morawaseru*
kau	→	*kawaseru*

IRREGULAR VERBS:

suru	→	*saseru*
kuru	→	*kosaseru*

Like passive verbs, causative verbs are vowel verbs, and conjugate like other vowel verbs (see Lesson 28, B1).

b. Causative sentences

Sentences with causative verbs derived from intransitive verbs appear in the following pattern:

causer *wa/ga* + causee *o/ni* + . . . causative verb

Watashi wa tomodachi o/ni ikasemashita.
I had my friend go.

Kimura san wa Hayashi san o/ni yoru osoku made hatarakasemashita.
Mr. Kimura made Mr. Hayashi work until late at night.

Kodomo o/ni puuru de oyogasete yarimashita.
I let my child swim in the swimming pool.

The causee is followed by either *o* or *ni*. However, when the causee is inanimate, *ni* cannot be used.

Iroiro sewa o shite, kirei ni hana o sakasemashita.
I took good care of the plant, and the flowers bloomed [made the flowers bloom] beautifully.

Sentences with causative verbs derived from transitive verbs appear in the following pattern.

> causer *wa/ga* + causee *ni* + . . . causative verb

Haha wa imooto ni kusuri o nomasemashita.
My mother made my younger sister take medicine.

Kodomo ni oyu o wakasasemashita.
I had my child boil water.

c. More about causatives

The following points are generally true of causatives, regardless of whether they come from intransitive or transitive verbs.

Although the causer in causative sentences is usually animate, there are cases where it is inanimate.

Ochashitsu no fun'iki ga watashi no kimochi o nagomasete kureta.
The atmosphere of the room of the tea ceremony made me [my feelings] calm down.

Causative sentences should not be used when the causee is superior to the causer. Even when the two of them are of equal status, causative sentences are often inappropriate. In these cases, use TE *morau* or TE *itadaku*.

Haha ni cha no yu no hon o katte moraimashita.
I had my mother buy a book on the tea ceremony.

Otoosama ni ocha o tatete itadakimashita.
Your father made [I had your father make] tea [in the tea ceremony] for me.

Here are some examples of the causatives of phrases consisting of the TE form and another element. The causative form of *matte iru* "to be waiting" can be *matasete iru* or *matte isaseru*. The former, with the causative of the TE form, focuses on the progressive action of the causer, and the latter, with the causative of *iru*, on the progressive action of the causee.

Otooto o eki de matasete ita n desu.
I was having my younger brother wait at the station.

Otooto o eki de matte isaseta n desu.
I arranged for my younger brother to be waiting at the station.

With *motte iku* "to take" or *motte kuru* "to bring," *iku* and *kuru* become the causative forms: *motte ikaseru* and *motte kosaseru*.

Musuko ni okane o motte ikemashita.
    I had my son take money.

Kodomo ni zabuton o motte kosasemasu.
    I will have my child bring cushions.

2. CAUSATIVE PASSIVE SENTENCES

Causative sentences can be made passive: "to be made to . . ."

Mazui okashi o tabesaseraremashita.
    I was made to eat tasteless sweets.

The causative passive verb is derived from the causative verb. Since a causative verb is a vowel verb, the formation of its passive form is like that of any other vowel verb.

ORIGINAL VERB	CAUSATIVE VERB	CAUSATIVE PASSIVE VERB
taberu (vowel verb)	*tabesaseru* (vowel verb)	*tabesaserareru*
narau (consonant verb)	*narawaseru* (vowel verb)	*narawaserareru*

When the original verb is a consonant verb not ending with *-su* (e.g., not *hanasu* "to talk"), another, shorter causative passive can be formed. The suffix *-sera-* is shortened to *-sa-*. For example, the long form *narawaserareru* becomes *narawasareru*. In fact, the shorter causative passive forms are used much more often than their longer counterparts.

LONGER FORM	SHORTER FORM	
yomaserareru	*yomasareru*	to be caused to read
mataserareru	*matasareru*	to be caused to wait

Now let's see how a causative sentence is made passive.

Haha wa imooto ni osakana o tabesasemashita. (causative sentence)
    My mother made/let my younger sister eat the fish.

Imooto wa haha ni osakana o tabesaseraremashita. (passive causative sentence)
    My younger sister was made to eat the fish by my mother.

The causative sentence above could describe either coercion ("—make—") or permission ("—let—"). However, as the person in the subject position in passive sentences is usually affected negatively, a causative passive sentence implies that the person in the subject position, who is the causee in the causative sentence, is not necessarily happy about the caused event. Therefore, the causative passive describes coercion, and not permission.

Mukashi sobo ni narawasareta n desu.
My grandmother made me learn it [I was made to learn it by my grandmother] years ago.

Tomodachi ni nijikan mo matasareta n desu.
My friend made me wait [I was made to wait by my friend] for as long as two hours.

3. PLAIN FORM OF *-MASHOO*

You learned that *-mashoo* means "let's . . ." and *-mashoo ka* means "should (shall) we/I—?" The plain form of *-mashoo* is used in certain sentence structures. Here is how it is formed.

VOWEL VERBS: The final *-ru* is replaced by *-yoo*.

taberu	→	*tabeyoo*
miru	→	*miyoo*

CONSONANT VERBS: The final *-u* is replaced by *-oo*.

iku	→	*ikoo*
nomu	→	*nomoo*

IRREGULAR VERBS:

suru	→	*shiyoo*
kuru	→	*koyoo*

In this lesson you will learn how to express intention and suggestion using the plain form of *-mashoo*. To express intention, the plain form of *-mashoo* is followed by *to* and a verb such as *omou* "to think" or *kangaeru* "to think over/to consider."

Kono kimono o kiyoo to omotteru n desu.
I am thinking of wearing this kimono.

Obi to tabi o kaoo to omoimasu.
I think I will buy a kimono sash and split-toed socks.

Raigetsu ochakai o shiyoo to kangaete iru n desu.
I'm considering having a tea ceremony party next month.

To express suggestion, the plain form is followed by *to* and a verb such as *iu* "to say."

Atarashii yakan o kaoo to haha ni itta n desu.
I suggested to my mother that we buy a new teakettle.

The particle *ka* used after the plain form of *-mashoo* shows that the intention or suggestion is less strong.

Sadoo kyooshitsu ni ikoo ka to omou n desu.
I think I'll go to a class on the tea ceremony.

4. TE *KURU*

A TE form followed by *kuru* "to come" is used when the subject is about to leave his or her present location and then return.

Odoogu o kura kara dashite kimasu.
I am going to go get the utensils out of the storage room.

Okashi o katte kite kuremasen ka.
Will you go buy sweets?

Matsumoto san ni kiite kimasu.
I will go ask Ms. Matsumoto.

Itte kimasu.
See you later. [I will go and come.]

Itte kimasu is a fixed expression. You use it when you leave your house or a place where you belong and expect to come back.

5. THE PARTICLE *NE* AS SOFTENER

The particle *ne* after a request in expressions using TE *kudasai* or *o* pre-*masu kudasai* softens the tone of the request. However, it should be avoided when the addressee is superior to you.

Odoogu o kura kara dashite kimasu kara, chotto omachi kudasai ne.
I am going to get the utensils out of the storage room, so please wait.

Minna ni gochisoo shite agete kudasai ne.
Please prepare a feast for everybody.

C. MOJI

1. DIALOGUE

ホール 「きれいな 着物ですね。どこかに いらっしゃるん
ですか。」

水木 「ええ、あした お茶会が あるので、この着物を
着ようと 思ってるんです。」

ホール 「お茶を なさってるんですか。」

水木 「昔 そぼに 習わされたんですけど、このごろ
また 始めたんです。」

ホール 「おまっ茶は のんだことは ないんですけど、
おいしいんですか。」

水木 「私は おいしいと 思いますけど。じゃあ、これから
私が お茶を たてますから のんでみてください。」

ホール 「お忙しいのに、いいんですか。」

水木 「お道具を くらから 出してきますから、ちょっと
お待ちくださいね。」

ホール 「ごめんどう かけます。すみません。」

2. NEW *KANJI*

[99]	着	*ki(ru)*	to wear e.g., 着物
[100]	道	*DOO*	road, way
[101]	具	*GU*	tool e.g., 道具
[102]	茶	*CHA*	tea e.g., お茶
		SA	tea e.g., 茶道

[103]	昔	*mukashi*	years ago
[104]	習	*nara(u)*	to learn
[105]	忙	*isoga(shii)*	busy

STROKE ORDER

[99]	⸀ ⸀ ⸀ ⸀ 並 差 着 着
[100]	⸀ ⸀ ⸀ 首 首 道
[101]	冂 目 旦 具
[102]	一 艹 艹 犬 犬 茶 茶 茶
[103]	一 艹 艹 昔
[104]	⸀ 羽 羽 習 習 習
[105]	⸀ ⸀ 忄 忄 忙 忙

D. TANGO TO HYOOGEN

ocha	tea ceremony (informal term)
sadoo	tea ceremony (more formal than *ocha*)
cha no yu	tea ceremony (more formal than *ocha,* softer than *sadoo*)
sadoo kyooshitsu	tea ceremony class
(o)chakai	tea ceremony party
(o)chasitsu	room for the tea ceremony
(o)matcha	powdered tea
(o)yu	warm or hot water
cf. **mizu**	cold water
yakan	teakettle
(o)doogu	utensil, tool
kura	storage room
obi	sash
tabi	split-toed socks worn with kimono
fun'iki	atmosphere
kimochi	feelings
tateru	to make (tea during the tea ceremony)
wakasu	to boil (water)
dasu	to take out

403

kangaeru	to think over, consider
nagomu	to calm down
gochisoo	feast, treat
gochisoo ni naru	to receive a treat
gochisoo suru	to treat somebody, provide food for somebody
(go)mendoo	trouble
(go)mendoo o kakeru	to give someone trouble

RENSHUU

A. Fill in the blanks on the basis of the dialogue.

1. *Mizuki san no obaasan wa Mizuki san _____ ocha o _____ mashita.*
2. *Hooru san wa _____ o nonda koto ga arimasen.*
3. *Mizuki san wa Hideko san ni _____ yoo to omotte imasu.*
4. *Mizuki san wa ocha no doogu o _____ kara dashite _____ yoo to omotte imasu.*

B. Ms. Matsuyama has five children—Takeshi, Kazuko, Kenji, Yasuko, and Keiko—and she had them do chores. Each one had a task. Describe the tasks using causative verbs.

Example: *Takeshi wa keeki o yakimashita.*
     → *Takeshi ni keeki o yakasemashita.*

1. *Kazuko wa kuruma o araimashita.*
2. *Kenji wa ocha o kai ni ikimashita.*
3. *Yasuko wa sandoitchi o tsukurimashita.*
4. *Keiko wa shokki o kura kara dashimashita.*

C. Following your supervisor's instructions, you did the things listed below. Write down your activities using causative passive sentences.

Example: *Tooi tokoro made kaisha no seihin o motte ikimashita.*
     → *Tooi tokoro made kaisha no seihin o motte ikasaremashita.*

1. *Kuji made zangyoo shimashita.*
2. *Nagai repooto o kakimashita.*
3. *Doyoobi mo hatarakimashita.*
4. *Muzukashii shigoto o tetsudaimashita.*

D. People are describing what they are planning to do tomorrow. Fill in the blanks according to the English equivalents.

Example: *Ginza de kutsu o katte koyoo to omoimasu.*
      I think I will go buy shoes in Ginza.

1. *Kuruma o ——— omoimasu.*
I think I'll wash my car.
2. *Rirekisho o ——— omoimasu.*
I think I'll write my résumé.
3. *Uchi de terebi o ——— omoimasu.*
I think I'll watch TV at home.
4. *Puuru de ——— omoimasu.*
I think I'll swim in the swimming pool.

E. Read the following, and write the English equivalents.

昔 茶道を 習って いたので、お茶の 道具は たくさん 持っています。
来週 会社の 友だちが あそびに 来るので、お茶を たててみよう
と思っています。

F. Translate the following sentences into English.

1. *benkyoo o shiyoo to omotta noni haha ni kaimono ni ikasaremashita.*
2. *terebi o miyoo to omotta noni hatarakasaremashita.*
3. *neyoo to omotta noni chichi ni shigoto o tetsudawasaremashita.*

G. Offer to do the following things for your friends using "TE form of verbs + *kimasu.*"

Example: "I forgot to buy some meat. . . ."
      → *"watashi ga niku o katte kimasu yo."*
      (I'll go buy some meat for you.)

1. "I left my hat on the bus. . . ."

      ———————————————————
(I'll go look for it for you.) look for = *sagasu*
2. "I'm not sure how I should make this. . . .

      ———————————————————
(I'll go ask someone for you.) someone = *dareka*
3. "I need to go get the book from the storage. . . ."

      ———————————————————
(I'll go get it for you.)

KARUCHAA NOOTO

The tea ceremony, called *ocha, sadoo,* or *cha no yu,* has been popular in Japan for centuries. Tea was introduced from China in the ninth century, and gradually the tea ceremony developed. It was established in its present form in the sixteenth century by Sen no Rikyu, a tea master who was given an important position by the famous warlord Toyotomi Hideyoshi.

The tea used in the tea ceremony is green powdered tea. The host puts the powdered tea in a tea bowl, pours hot water over it, and mixes the two with a whisk called a *chasen*. The whole procedure for making, serving, and drinking the tea is strictly prescribed. Both host and guest follow the procedure meticulously. The purpose of the tea ceremony is to foster spiritual communion between the host and the guest(s).

It takes years of study to perfect the tea ceremony. Classes on the tea ceremony are offered by private teachers, in culture schools, or in tea ceremony clubs at schools and workplaces. These classes are particularly popular among women. One can perform the tea ceremony at home and some houses even have a special tea room. More formal tea parties are sometimes held at a teacher's home or in a public building. The New Year tea party is especially important.

KOTAE

A. 1. *ni, narawase*   2. *(o)matcha*   3. *tetsudawase*   4. *kura, ko*

B. 1. *Kazuko ni kuruma o arawasemashita.* 2. *Kenji ni ocha o kai ni ikasemashita.* 3. *Yasuko ni sandoitchi o tsukurasemashita.* 4. *Keiko ni shokki o kura kara dasasemashita.*

C. 1. *Kuji made zangyoo saseraremashita.* 2. *Nagai repooto o kakasaremashita.* 3. *Doyoobi mo hatarakasaremashita.* 4. *Muzukashii shigoto o tetsudawasaremashita.*

D. 1. *araoo to*   2. *kakoo to*   3. *miyoo to*   4. *oyogoo to*

E. 昔 *(mukashi)* 茶 *(sa)* 道 *(doo)* __ 習 *(nara)* __ 茶 *(cha)* __ 道 *(doo)* 具 *(gu)* __ 持 *(mo)* __ 来 *(rai)* 週 *(shuu)* 会 *(kai)* 社 *(sha)* __ 友 *(tomo)* __ 来 *(ku)* __ 茶 *(cha)* __ 思 *(omo)* __

Since I took lessons on the tea ceremony long ago, I have many utensils for it. Since my friends from work are coming to visit next week, I am thinking of making tea.

F. 1. Though I thought I would study, I was made to go shopping by my mother. (my mother made me go shopping.) 2. Though I thought I would watch TV, I was made to work. 3. Though I thought I would sleep, I was made to help my father by him. (my father made me help him.)

G. 1. *watashi ga sagashite kimasu yo.* 2. *watashi ga dare ka ni kiite kimasu yo.* 3. *watashi ga totte kimasu yo.*

DAI SANJUU YONKA
Lesson 34
SHITSUNAI GORAKU.   Indoor Entertainment.

A. DAIAROOGU

SHOOGI.

Gen'ichi and Tomoko are a young couple.

GEN'ICHI: **Kyóo náni ka yotei áru?**

TOMOKO: **Watashi wa nani mo nái kedo.**

GEN'ICHI: **Bóku wa kore kara yuubínkyoku de kozútsumi o dáshite koyóo to omóu n da kedo, sore ga owattára, hima dá kara, hisashiburi ni shoogi démo shiyóo ka.**

TOMOKO: **Shoogi wa nágaku yatte nái kara, yóku obóete nái wa yo.**

GEN'ICHI: **Súgu omoidásu yo.**

TOMOKO: **Shoogi dóko ni átta kashira.**

GEN'ICHI: **Dóko datta kana. Áa, séngetsu oosóoji shita tóki ni, génkan no oshiire ni iretá to omóu yo.**

TOMOKO: **Áa, sóo datta wa ne. Jáa, anáta ga káeru made ni shoogi dáshite oku wa. Itte okimásu kedo, watashi shoogi wa tsúyokatta n desu yo.**

GEN'ICHI: **Áa, tanoshími ni shitemásu yo.**

SHOGI: JAPANESE CHESS.

GEN'ICHI: Do you have any plans today?

TOMOKO: No, I don't.

GEN'ICHI: I think I'll mail a package at the post office now, but once that's done, I'll be free. Do you want to play shogi [which we haven't played in a long time] or something else?

TOMOKO: I haven't played shogi in a long time, so I don't remember it well.

GEN'ICHI: It'll all come back right away.

TOMOKO: I wonder where the shogi set is [was].

GEN'ICHI: So do I. Oh, I think we put it in the closet of the foyer when we were housecleaning last month.

TOMOKO: Oh, that's [was] right. Well then, I'll have the shogi set out [in advance] by the time you get back. Let me warn you [I'll say it in advance]. I was good [strong] at shogi.

GEN'ICHI: Oh, I look forward to seeing that.

B. BUNPOO TO YOOHOO

1. NORMAL STYLE AND PLAIN STYLE

All the sentences we have dealt with so far were in so-called normal style, i.e., their final predicates are in the normal form. Consider the following.

(1) *Joonzu san wa shoogi o suru koto ga dekimasu.*
Ms. Jones can play shogi.

(2) *Tanaka san ga itta pachinkoya wa tooi desu.*
The pinball parlor that Ms. Tanaka went to is far away.

(3) *Shimada san wa oyogu no ga joozu desu.*
Mr. Shimada is good at swimming.

(4) *Asoko ni iru otoko no hito wa Abe san no otoosan desu.*
The man who is over there is Ms. Abe's father.

(5) *Kinoo pachinko de sen'en maketa n desu.*
I lost one thousand yen at the pinball game yesterday.

The final predicates of these sentences can be put into the plain form.

(6) *Joonzu san wa shoogi o suru koto ga dekiru.*
(7) *Tanaka san ga itta pachinkoya wa tooi.*
(8) *Shimada san wa oyogu no ga joozu da.*
(9) *Asoko ni iru otoko no hito wa Abe san no otoosan da.*
(10) *Kinoo pachinko de sen'en maketa n da.*

While sentences (1) through (5) have the same meanings as sentences (6) through (10), they are stylistically different from each other.* The plain-style sentences [(6)–(10)] are used when talking to peers, some-

---

* The appropriateness of sentences (6) through (10) depends on the sex of the speaker and on whether they are spoken or written. For now, in studying these sentences, do not worry about such situational differences. They will be explained later in this and subsequent lessons.

one younger, or someone close, while the normal-style sentences [(1)–(5)] are used when talking to someone older, someone socially higher than you, or to someone not close. Children usually learn plain style first. Newspapers, magazines, and books are normally written in plain style, but some of them may be written in normal style. Letters are generally written in normal style.

Look at the above example sentences again. They have plain forms in the middle of the sentences: *suru* "do" in (1) and (6), *itta* "went" in (2) and (7), *oyogu* "swim" in (3) and (8), *iru* "is" in (4) and (9), and *maketa* "lost" in (5) and (10). These appear as plain forms regardless of whom you are talking to. A plain form in a non-final position is a grammatical plain form as opposed to a stylistic plain form, which occurs in the final position of a sentence.

Next consider the dialogue. In many cases, married couples use the plain style, although in some cases, especially among the older generation, wives use the normal style while husbands use the plain style. However, the styles are often mixed. For example, when trying to act aloof, either seriously or in jest, people may switch from plain to normal style, as is shown in the dialogue. You see the plain style all the way through except in the last two sentences.

Itte okimasu kedo, watashi shoogi wa tsuyokatta n desu yo.
Let me warn you. I was good at shogi.

Aa, tanoshimi ni shitemasu yo.
Oh, I look forward to seeing that.

The wife is bragging about herself and threatening her husband (perhaps jokingly), trying to be somewhat distant by speaking in normal style. In response to that, the husband switches to the normal style to be distant, too.

In speaking, you can sometimes switch between plain and normal styles, but in writing, you should not.

2. MALE AND FEMALE SPEECH

While the difference between male and female speech is not as strong as it was in the past, there are still several things to remember. One distinction we have already dealt with is *boku* "I," which is used by males, never by females. Other differences are:

a. *Kashira* and *kana*

Both *kashira* and *kana* "I wonder" are sentence particles. Normally they follow the plain style. They belong to Type IV (see Lesson 21, B4).

Kashira is used by females.

Shoogi doko ni atta kashira.
I wonder where the shogi set is [was].

Go wa muzukashii kashira.
I wonder whether *go* [a Japanese board game] is difficult.

Kana is normally used by males, although women sometimes use it, too.

Doko datta kana.
I wonder where it was.

A variant of *kana* is *kanaa*.

Are wa maajan'ya kanaa.
I wonder if that over there is a mah-jongg parlor.

b. *Yo* and *ne(e)*

The sentence particles *yo* and *ne(e)* after a sentence in normal style are used by both men and women. After a sentence in plain style, however, they are almost exclusively used by men.

Sugu omoidasu yo.
It'll come back to you right away.

Sengetsu oosooji shita toki ni, genkan no oshiire ni ireta to omou yo.
I think we put it in the closet of the foyer when we were housecleaning last month.

Ano karuta wa takakatta nee.
That set of (Japanese) cards was expensive, wasn't it?

When women use the plain style with *yo* or *ne(e)*, the sentence particle *wa* is inserted between the sentence and *yo* or *ne(e)*.

Shoogi wa nagaku yatte nai kara, yoku oboete nai wa yo.
I haven't played shogi in a long time, so I don't remember it well.

A, soo datta wa ne.
Oh, that's how it was.

Women also have the option of inserting *wa* between a normal-style sentence and *yo* or *ne(e)*, but men do not.

Watashi no chichi wa shoogi ga suki deshita wa yo.
My father liked shogi.

c. *Wa*

The sentence particle *wa* can end a sentence in either plain or normal style. It is used mostly by women. *Wa* has a meaning similar to that of *yo* or *ne(e)*.

Kodomo no toki, toranpu o yoku shita wa.
When I was a child, I often played (Western) cards.

Ano hito wa kakegoto ga suki desu wa.
He likes gambling.

Shoogi nara watashi ga oshiete ageru wa.
If it is shogi, I will teach you.

d. Questions

Usually the sentence particle *ka* follows a normal-style sentence. But even without *ka*, rising intonation indicates that the sentence is a question.

Nani ka yotei arimasu. (rising intonation)
You have plans?

In plain-style sentences, *ka* is usually not used.

Nani ka yotei aru. (rising intonation)
You have plans?

This is true for both men and women. However, in a very casual situation, men may use *ka*, although such a question sounds harsh. Women do not use *ka* in plain-style questions.

3. TE *OKU*

When the verb *oku* "to put" or "to place" is used with a TE form, the combination means "to do such and such in advance/for later and leave it that way."

Shoogi o dashite okimasu.
I will get the shogi set out [in advance].

Shoogi no koma o narabete okimashoo.
Let's arrange the shogi pieces [in advance].

Doogu wa oshiire ni irete okimashita.
I put the tools in the closet [for later].

Itte okimasu kedo, watashi shoogi wa tsuyokatta n desu yo.
I will say it in advance. I was good at shogi.

4. *MADE NI* OR *MADE* WITH A VERB

As mentioned before, the particles *made ni* "by" (see Lesson 14, B8) and *made* "until" (see Lesson 12, B6) follow time nouns.

Doyoobi made ni shimasu.
I will do it by Saturday.

Yoake made maajan o shite imashita.
We were playing mah-jongg until dawn.

Made ni and *made* can follow a verb in its dictionary form, too.

Anata ga kaeru made ni shoogi dashite oku wa.
I will get out the shogi set by the time you get back.

Nihon ni iku made ni Nihon bunka ni tsuite iroiro naraitai desu.
I want to learn various things about Japanese culture by the time I go to Japan.

Katsu made ganbarimasu.
I will keep trying until I win.

5. STATIVE VERBS AND THE COPULA IN THE PAST

When you are not sure if you remember something, a stative verb or the copula is used in the past tense.

Shoogi doko ni atta kashira. (*atta*—past tense)
I wonder where the shogi set is [was].

Yamada san deshita ne. (*deshita*—past tense)
You are Mr. Yamada, aren't you? [If I remember right.]

C. MOJI

1. DIALOGUE

元一　　「今日 何か よてい ある。」

友子　　「私は 何も ないけど。」

元一　　「ぼくは これから、ゆうびんきょくで、こづつみを
　　　　出して こようと 思うんだけど、それが 終ったら、
　　　　ひまだから、ひさしぶりに しょうぎでも しようか。」

412

友子　　　「しょうぎは、長く やってないから、よく 覚えて
　　　　　ないわよ。」

元一　　　「すぐ 思い出すよ。」

友子　　　「しょうぎ どこに あったかしら。」

元一　　　「どこだったかな。ああ、先月 大そうじした時に、
　　　　　げんかんの おし入れに 入れたと 思うよ。」

友子　　　「ああ、そうだったわね。じゃあ、あなたが 帰るまでに
　　　　　しょうぎ 出しておくわ。言っておきますけど、私
　　　　　しょうぎは 強かったんですよ。」

元一　　　「ああ、楽しみに してますよ。」

2. *HIRAGANA*

The feminine sentence particle *wa* is written as わ, not は.

3. NEW *KANJI*

[106]	長	*naga(i)*	long
[107]	覚	*obo(eru)*	to remember
[108]	帰	*kae(ru)*	to return
[109]	強	*tsuyo(i)*	strong
[110]	楽	*tano(shii), tano(shimi)*	enjoyable

STROKE ORDER

[106]	ノ 「 F F 三 토 長 長
[107]	⺌ ⺍ 凸 凸 覚
[108]	リ ⺹ ⺹ 尸 帰 帰
[109]	⁊ ⁊ ⁊ 弓 弘 弘 強 強 強
[110]	⺊ ⌒ 白 白 泊 泊 楽

413

D. TANGO TO HYOOGEN

shoogi	shogi (Japanese chess)
koma	shogi piece
go	go (a Japanese board game with black and white tiles)
toranpu	Western-style cards
pachinko	pinball game
pachinkoya	pinball parlor
maajan	mah-jongg
maajan'ya	mah-jongg parlor
kakegoto	gambling
genkan	foyer, entryway of a house
oshiire	closet
yoake	dawn
bunka	culture
yotei	plan, schedule
tanoshimi	expectation
tanoshimi ni suru	to look forward to
oosooji suru	to houseclean thoroughly
yaru	to do
omoidasu	to recall
naraberu	to arrange on a surface
hisashiburi ni	after a long absence

RENSHUU

A. On the basis of the dialogue, mark each sentence T (true), F (false), or X (cannot tell).

1. *Tomoko san to Gen'ichi san wa shoogi o mainichi shite imasu.*
2. *Tomoko san wa Gen'ichi san ga yuubinkyoku ni iku made ni shoogi o oshiire kara dasu tsumori desu.*
3. *Gen'ichi san wa shoogi ga joozu desu.*
4. *Gen'ichi san wa yuubinkyoku ni ikimasu ga, Tomoko san wa ikimasen.*

B. Transform the following sentences into normal-style sentences.

Kyoo Kanazawa no kaisha ni tsutomete iru itoko ga asobi ni kita. Moo sugu Ginza ni aru honsha ni tenkin suru rashii. Kare wa pachinko ga suki na node, issho ni chikaku ni aru pachinkoya ni itta. Hisashiburi ni pachinko o shite, tanoshikatta.

414

C. Among the following four phrases, which ones can you match with *Boku wa?*

Boku wa   1. *ikitaku nai yo.*
           2. *itsu de mo korareru wa yo.*
           3. *kaette wa ikenai kashira.*
           4. *ii to omou n da kedo.*

D. Imagine that tomorrow you are going on a trip by car. Describe what you did to prepare using *-te okimashita.*

1. I washed the car.
2. I put gas in it.
3. I made sandwiches.
4. I bought a map.

E. Rewrite the following using *kanji,* and then translate.

A daughter phones her mother.

むすめ　「おかあさん、わたし、らいしゅうの　かようびに
　　　　　かえるわ。」

はは　　「ながい　しゅっちょうだったわね。たのしみに
　　　　　してるわよ。」

F. Indicate male speech with an "M" and female speech with an "F" for the following sentences.

1. *kyoo nani o tabeyoo kashira.* ——
2. *ashita tenisu o suru tsumori da.* _____
3. *ano hito to doko de atta kashira.* _____

G. Correct the style of the verbs according to the situation.

1. (to a teacher); *sumimasen sensei, shukudai o wasureta yo.*
2. (to a neighbor); *Sato san, sumimasen ga, shizuka ni shite yo.*
3. (to a stranger); *sumimasen ga, ima nanji ka oshiete kureru.*

KARUCHAA NOOTO

Although computer games have become very popular among young Japanese, more traditional games are still played extensively.

Pachinko, for example, is an upright pinball machine. There are many *pachinko* parlors all over Japan. If you win, you get prizes, such as candy or cigarettes.

Mah-jongg, which originated in China, is a game played by four people with small tiles. Each player builds up various combinations of tiles to get points.

Shoogi is similar to Western chess. The player who checkmates the other player's king wins, but the procedure is more complicated than that of Western chess.

Go is also played by two people. One player has white pieces, and the other has black ones. Players take turns putting their pieces on a square board with a grid. The player who surrounds the largest territory is the winner.

There are various kinds of *karuta*, traditional Japanese cards, for children and adults. A typical game for adults is called *Hyakunin Isshu* and played in the following manner: The cards are placed on the *tatami* or a table. While the leader reads a poem, the players are supposed to find the card with the poem's second half as fast as possible, before the leader finishes reading.

Western-style cards are popular, too. A deck of cards is called a *toranpu*, derived from the English word "trump."

KOTAE

A. 1. F 2. F 3. X 4. T
B. *Kyoo Kanazawa no kaisha ni tsutomete iru itoko ga asobi ni kimashita. Moo sugu Ginza ni aru honsha ni tenkin suru rashii desu. Kare wa pachinko ga suki na node, issho ni chikaku ni aru pachinkoya ni ikimashita. Hisashiburi ni pachinko o shite, tanoshikatta desu.*
C. 1,4
D. 1. *Kuruma o aratte okimashita.* 2. *Gasorin o irete okimashita.*
3. *Sandoitchi o tsukutte okimashita.* 4. *Chizu o katte okimashita.*
E. むすめ 「お母さん、私、来週の 火曜日に 帰るわ。」

　母　　「長い しゅっちょうだったわね。楽しみに してるわよ。」

Daughter: Mother, I'll be back on Tuesday of next week.
Mother: It's been a long business trip, hasn't it? We look forward to your return.
F. 1. F 2. M 3. F
G. 1. *wasuremashita* 2. *shizuka ni shite kudasai* 3. *oshiete kudasaimasuka.*

DAI SANJUU GOKA
Lesson 35

SEIJI. Politics.

A. DAIAROOGU

SHICHOO SENKYO.

Mr. Terashima and Ms. Ooyama, who are classmates at their university, go to a political meeting to listen to a candidate's speech.

KOOHOSHA: **Kyóo wa óoku no katágata ni kíte itadaki, makoto ni kánsha shite orimásu. Watakushi wa wakái koró kara, gakkoo kyóoiku no bá de, iroiro keiken shite mairimáshita. Sono keiken o ikáshi, kyooiku no juujitsu o hakaritái to kangáete orimasu. Watakushi wa íma rokujuu gósai de arimásu ga, máda máda génki de, hataraite ikitái to omótte orimasu. . . .**

Enzetsu ga owatte.

TERASHIMA: **Enzetsu dóo omótta.**

OOYAMA: **Yuunoo na hitó daroo to omóu kedo, máda yóku wakará-nai wa.**

TERASHIMA: **Koohósha wa sannin irú kara, enzetsu o zénbu kiité kara, kuraberaréru yo. Toohyóobi made máda isshúukan áru kara ne.**

OOYAMA: **Ée, kono shichoosen omoshíroku nátte kitá wa ne.**

THE MAYORAL ELECTION.

CANDIDATE: I really appreciate so many people coming here today. Throughout my life [Since I was young], I have had varied experiences in the field of [school] education. I wish to utilize my experience, and I will work hard for the fulfillment of my goals in education. Although I am now sixty-five, I will still be working vigorously. . . .

After the speech.

TERASHIMA: What did you think of the speech?

OOYAMA: I guess he's a competent man, but I really don't know yet.

TERASHIMA: There are three candidates. After we've heard all the speeches, we'll be able to compare. We still have a week until election day.

OOYAMA: Yes. This mayoral election has gotten interesting, hasn't it?

B. BUNPOO TO YOOHOO

1. *DAROO*

The plain form *daroo* is derived from *da*, and its normal equivalent is *deshoo* (see Lesson 21, B3). *Daroo* can be used at the end of a sentence by both men and women in writing, but in speech, only men can use it at the end of a sentence.

Ano hito wa toosen suru daroo.
She will probably win the election.

Daroo is also used before the particle *to*, which is in turn used before verbs such as *omou* "to think," *iu* "to say," and *hanasu* "to talk" to imply speculation. Just like *deshoo*, it can follow a verb, an *i*-adjective, a *na*-adjective, a noun, or *n/no*. *Daroo* can be used by both men and women in speech and writing if it is not in the final position.

Watashi no haha wa rippa na seijika ni nareru daroo to omoimasu.
I think my mother will probably [be able to] become a great politician.

Otto ga kono uchi no zeikin wa takai daroo to ittemashita.
My husband was saying that the taxes on this house are probably high.

Yuunoo na hito daroo to omou kedo.
I guess he is a competent man.

Kare wa daigishi ni naru tsumori na n daroo to hanashiteta n desu.
We were saying that he probably plans to become a Diet member.

2. *DE ARIMASU* AND *DE ARU*

De arimasu and *de aru* are expository-style or audience-style equivalents of the copula.

a. *De arimasu*

De arimasu may replace the copula *desu*. It is used after a noun, a *na*-adjective, or *no* (or much less commonly *n*) without changing the meaning of the sentence. It is mainly used in public speech, not in daily conversation.

Watakushi wa rokujuu gosai desu/de arimasu.
   I am sixty-five.

Seiji no sekai wa fukuzatsu desu/de arimasu.
   The political world is complicated.

Wareware wa kirei na senkyo o yaritai no desu/de arimasu.
   We want to have a clean election.

   b. *De aru*

De aru is the plain equivalent of *de arimasu* and can also be used after a noun, a *na*-adjective, or *no* (not *n*) without changing the sentence's meaning. It is commonly used in writing, either in the middle or at the end of a sentence. In speech, *de aru* is not used at the end of a sentence, but it occasionally occurs in the middle of a sentence.

Nihon no shuto wa Tookyoo da/de aru ga, sono mae wa Kyooto ga shuto datta/de atta.
   The capital of Japan is Tokyo, but before that, Kyoto was the capital.

Ane de aru watashi de mo shiranai n desu.
   Even I, who am his older sister, don't know it.

De aroo "probably" is derived from *de aru* and can replace *daroo* (see B1). *De aroo*, unlike *daroo*, is mostly used in writing.

Nihon no seiji wa nagaku kawaranai daroo/de aroo.
   Politics in Japan will probably not change for a long time.

3. SEQUENTIAL, PARALLEL, AND CAUSAL RELATIONSHIPS

As already mentioned, TE forms are used to express sequential, parallel, and causal relationships (see Lesson 17, B2, and Lesson 18, B1–3).

Ane wa enzetsukai ni itte, imooto wa ongakkai ni ikimashita.
   My older sister went to a public speech, and my younger sister went to a concert.

There are other, more formal ways to express the same meanings. They are mainly used in public speech or writing. The TE form is replaced by:

a. The pre-*masu* form of verbs

Keiken o ikashi, kyooiku no juujitsu o hakaritai to omoimasu.
   I think I want to make use of my experience and work for the fulfillment of my goals in education.

Ooku no katagata ni kite itadaki, kansha shite imasu.
   Many people have come over, and I appreciate it.

419

With the verb *iru* "to exist," *ori* is used instead of *i*.

Uchi ni kodomo ga sannin ori, isogashii.
Since I have three children at home, I am busy.

   b. The KU form of *i*-adjectives

Ano daigishi wa isogashiku, hisho ni aimashita.
Since that Diet member was busy, I saw his secretary.

Otenki ga waruku, yasai no nedan ga agatta.
The weather was bad, so the prices of vegetables rose.

   c. *de ari* (pre-*masu* form of *de arimasu*) with *na*-adjectives and nouns

Ano daijin wa munoo de ari, monku o iu hito ga fuete iru.
That government minister is incompetent, and the number of people who are complaining is increasing.

Kore wa atarashii hooritsu de ari, mada amari shirarete inai.
This is a new law, and it is not yet well-known.

4. TE *KURU* AND TE *IKU*

To express that an action or a state continues over a period of time, use TE *kuru* or TE *iku*.

   a. TE *kuru*

TE *kuru* is used when something continues <u>toward</u> a certain point in time, whether it is in the present, the future, or the past. The speaker's focus is on that point in time.

Kyooiku no ba de iroiro keiken shite kimashita.
I have had varied experience in the field of education.

Kono shichoosen omoshiroku natte kita wa ne.
This mayoral election has gotten interesting, hasn't it?

Ashita wa dandan harete kuru deshoo. (weather forecast)
Tomorrow it will become clear gradually.

Kyonen no natsu made, furansugo o benkyoo shite kimashita.
I had been studying French until the summer of last year.

   b. TE *iku*

TE *iku* is used when something continues <u>starting from</u> a certain point in time. The speaker's focus is on that point in time.

Watashi wa ima nanajussai desu ga, mada mada genki de hataraite ikitai to omoimasu.
I think I want to still be working vigorously although I am seventy.

Chijisen wa dorojiai ni natte ikimashita.
The gubernatorial election was starting to become a mudslinging contest.

Seifu wa mada mada yosan o fuyashite iku deshoo.
Probably the government will still continue to increase the budget.

5. HONORIFICS

The following verbs are honorifics.

a. Humble

NEUTRAL EQUIVALENT	HONORIFIC
iru	*oru*
kuru	*mairu*
iku	*mairu*

b. Respect

NEUTRAL EQUIVALENT	HONORIFIC
iru	*irassharu*
kuru	*irassharu*
	korareru
iku	*irassharu*
	ikareru

These honorific verbs can be used with TE forms just as *iru, kuru,* and *iku* are.

Genki de hataraite ikitai to omotte orimasu.
I think I want to be working vigorously.

Wakai koro kara, kyooiku no ba de iroiro keiken shite mairimashita.
Throughout my life [Since I was young], I have had varied experiences in the field of education.

Gakusei no koro kara kono shigoto o shite korareta soo desu.
I understand she has had this job since she was a student.

6. PLURALS

Some plurals are expressed by repeating the word. A voiceless consonant starting the first word is voiced in the repetition.

kata	person(s)	*katagata*	people
hito	person(s)	*hitobito*	people
ware (obsolete)	I	*wareware*	we
yama	mountain(s)	*yamayama*	mountains
kuni	nation(s)	*kuniguni*	nations

Even without the repetition, *kata, hito, yama,* and *kuni* can be plural (see Lesson 10, C8). *Hitobito* is used for "people in general." For specific people, use *hitotachi* with a modifier, since *hitotachi* is a dependent noun: *ano hitotachi* "those people." The number of these plurals is limited.

C. MOJI

1. DIALOGUE

こうほしゃ 「今日は 多くの かたがたに 来ていただき、まことに かんしゃして おります。私は若いころから、教育の場で、いろいろ けいけんして まいりました。そのけいけんを いかし、学校教育の じゅうじつを はかりたいと 考えて おります。私は 今65才で ありますが、まだまだ 元気で 働いて 行きたいと 思っております…。」

えんぜつが 終わって

寺島 「えんぜつ どう 思った。」

大山 「ゆうのうな 人だろうと 思うけど、まだ よく わからないわ。」

寺島 「こうほしゃは 三人 いるから、えんぜつを ぜんぶ 聞いてから、比べられるよ。とうひょう日まで まだ 一週間 あるからね。」

大山 「ええ、この市長せん、おもしろく なって きたわね。」

2. NEW *KANJI*

[111]	多	*oo(i)*	many, much
[112]	若	*waka(i)*	young
[113]	育	*IKU*	growing
[114]	場	*ba*	place, area
[115]	校	*KOO*	school
[116]	考	*kanga(eru)*	to think, to consider
[117]	才	*SAI*	age
[118]	比	*kura(beru)*	to compare
[119]	市	*SHI*	city

STROKE ORDER

[111]	夕 多
[112]	一 サ 艹 芋 若
[113]	亠 𠫓 育
[114]	扌 圢 坦 垱 場
[115]	木 木 杧 栌 校
[116]	土 耂 考
[117]	一 十 才
[118]	一 𠂆 比
[119]	亠 亡 市 市

3. NEW READING

[82]	教	*oshi(eru)* (Lesson 29)	to teach
		KYOO	teaching e.g., 教育、キリスト教
[69]	学	*GAKU* (Lesson 27)	
		[*GAK-*]*	
[106]	長	*naga(i)* (Lesson 34)	long
		CHOO	chief, long e.g., 市長、学長、社長

* When a syllable starting with k follows *GAKU*, *GAKU* becomes *GAK*, e.g., 学校

D. TANGO TO HYOOGEN

seifu	government
seiji	politics
seijika	politician
daijin	government minister
daigishi	Diet member
chiji	governor
shichoo	mayor
koohosha	candidate
toohyoo	voting
toohyoobi	voting day
senkyo	election
chijisen(kyo)	gubernatorial election
shichoosen(kyo)	mayoral election
enzetsu	public speech
enzetsukai	public speech meeting
zeikin	tax
yosan	budget
nedan	price
hooritsu	law
kyooiku	education
dorojiai	mudslinging contest
sekai	world
ba	field, place, area
shuto	capital (of a nation)
juujitsu	fulfillment
monku	complaint
wareware	we
yasai	vegetable
keiken	experience
keiken suru	to experience
toosen suru	to win an election
kansha suru	to appreciate
hakaru	to work for
ikasu	to make use of
kuraberu	to compare
fueru	to increase (intransitive)
fuyasu	to increase (transitive)
hareru	to become clear
yuunoo	competent
munoo	incompetent
makoto ni	really, truly

mada mada   still more

dandan   gradually

RENSHUU

A. Mark the statements concerning the candidate who is giving the speech T (true), F (false), or X (cannot tell).

1. *Chijisen no koohosha de aru.*
2. *Kyooiku ni kansuru shigoto o shite kita.*
3. *Rokujussai ni naru made hatarakitai to omotte iru.*
4. *Hoka no koohosha yori wakai.*

B. Three people are making predictions for next year. Fill in the blanks.

1. *Ookii _____ ga _____ daroo to omoimasu.*
   I am guessing there will be a big earthquake.
2. *_____ wa _____ daroo to omoimasu.*
   I am guessing that taxes will not go up.
3. *_____ no _____ ga _____ daroo to omoimasu.*
   I am guessing that the budget for education will increase.

C. In the following sentences, replace words with *da* or one of its conjugated forms wherever possible.

Koohosha wa minna yuunoo na hitotachi de aru. Ashita chikaku no gakkoo de enzetsukai ga aru. Omoshiroi senkyo de aru kara, ooku no hito ga kiki ni iku de aroo.

D. Choose from the words provided for each dialogue, and fill in the blanks with the appropriate form.

1. *mairu, oru, irassharu*
   a: *Ojoosan moo kaette _____ masu ka.*
   b: *Iie. Demo, moo sugu kaette _____ masu.*
2. *mairu, korareru*
   a: *Daigaku de nani o oshiete _____ ta n desu ka.*
   b: *Shinrigaku o oshiete _____ mashita.*
3. *oru, irassharu*
   a: *Otooto san ima ryokoo shite _____ n desu ne.*
   b: *Iie, moo kaette _____ masu.*

E. Write *kanji* in the blanks based on the *hiragana* under the blanks.

a. あの＿＿＿＿＿＿の＿＿＿＿＿＿さんは いくつですか。

　　　かいしゃ　　しゃちょう

b. 45＿＿＿＿＿＿です。

　　　さい

a. ＿＿＿＿＿＿いですね。

　　わか

F. Match *kanji* in group I and group II to form compound words.

I	II
教	長
学	具
先	校
市	月
道	育

KARUCHAA NOOTO

Japan's political structure changed drastically after World War II. Under the new Constitution, the government is composed of three independent powers: the Diet, the Cabinet, and the courts. The Diet is the only legislative body. It consists of the House of Representatives and the House of Councillors. The administrative power lies with the Cabinet, which consists of the prime minister and his or her ministers. The judiciary power is vested in the court system, and ultimately in the Supreme Court.

People elect the members of the two Houses, the prefectural governors, the assembly members of prefectures, the mayors of cities, towns, and villages, and the assembly members of cities, towns, and villages in direct elections. Election campaigns are conducted through rallies, posters, speeches on the street, and so forth. Speeches on the street are especially common scenes during election times.

A. 1. F 2. T 3. F 4. X
B. 1. *jishin, aru* or *kuru* 2. *Zeikin, agaranai* 3. *Kyooiku, yosan, fueru*
C. —*hitotachi da.* —*Omoshiroi senkyo da kara,* —*kiki ni iku daroo.*
D. (1) a: *irasshai* b: *mairi* (2) a: *korare* b: *mairi* (3) a: *irassharu* b: *ori*
E. a. 会社、社長 b. 才 a. 若

F. 教育、学長、学校、先月、市長、道具

FUKUSHUU 7

A. Fill in the blanks with particles.

1. *Musuko ——— shodoo ——— narawasemashita.*
   I had my son learn calligraphy.
2. *Hayashi san ——— sewa ——— shite itadakitai n desu.*
   I would like Ms. Hayashi to take care of it.
3. *Sapporo ——— tenkin suru koto ——— narimashita.*
   It has been decided that I will be transferred to Sapporo.
4. *Boku mo ikanakute ——— ikenai ———.*
   I wonder if I have to go also.

B. Fill in the blanks with the appropriate form of *iru, aru,* or *kuru.*

a: *Samuku natte ———¹ mashita ne. Mado ga aite ———² n desu ka.*
b: *Iie, shimete ———³ masu yo.*
a: *Ashita no ochakai no junbi o shite ———⁴ n desu.*
b: *Moo okashi wa katte ———⁵ masu ka.*
a: *Iie, ato de katte ———⁶ yoo to omotte ———⁷ ru n desu.*

C. Make the correct choice from the words in parentheses.

1. *Ashita ame ga (furu daroo/furoo) to omoimasu.*
2. *Kono kutsu wa (ooki/ookii) sugimasu.*
3. *Chichi ni yoru osoku made benkyoo (saserareta/saresaseta) n desu.*
4. *Tanaka san wa ima shokuji o shite (iraremasu/irasshaimasu).*

D. The following is a Japanese translation of an entry in the diary of Ms. Campbell, whose son lives in Japan. Answer the questions.

Kyoo terebi de Koobe de ookii jishin ga atta to kiita. Maaku ga ima Koobe de hataraite iru node, denwa shite mita ga, denwa wa tsunagaranakatta. Daijoobu daroo ka. Ashita hayaku okinakute wa ikenai node, neru koto ni shita. Ashita no ban moo ichido denwa shite miyoo to omotte iru.

427

1. *Kyanberu san no musuko san wa ima doko de nani o shite imasu ka.*
2. *Kyoo doko de nani ga arimashita ka.*
3. *Kyanberu san wa neru mae ni nani o shimashita ka.*
4. *Kyanberu san wa itsu musuko san ni denwa suru tsumori desu ka.*

E. Match the phrases in Group I with the appropriate ones in Group II to form questions asked in an interview with a mayoral candidate.

I	II
1. *Itsu senkyo ni deru* ("run in the election") *koto ni*	a. *doo omowaremasu ka.*
2. *Kaisha de donna shigoto o shite*	b. *osshatte imasu ka.*
3. *Kono machi no gakkoo kyooiku ni tsuite*	c. *itadakitai n desu ka.*
4. *Gokazoku wa nan to*	d. *nasatta n desu ka.*
	e. *korareta n desu ka.*

F. Choose the correct responses for the following situations.

What do you say when:
1. you look forward to something?
2. you accept an offer of food or drink?
3. you are going to accept somebody's help?
4. you ask somebody to do something?

a. *Gochisoo shimasu.*
b. *Osewa shimasu.*
c. *Tanoshimi ni shite imasu.*
d. *Gochisoo ni narimasu.*
e. *Shite morawanai n desu.*
f. *Shite itadakitai n desu.*
g. *Osewa ni narimasu.*

G. Fill in the blanks in *kanji* based on the English equivalents.

1. a. どなたが あの＿＿＿＿＿の＿＿＿＿＿ですか。

                  university   president

   b. ＿＿＿＿＿です。

     Prof. Nagashima

2. a. どのりきしが＿＿＿＿＿いですか。

              the strongest

   b. ＿＿＿＿＿だろうと＿＿＿＿＿います。

     Hanawaka   think

3. a. かんじを いくつ＿＿＿＿＿いましたか。

           learn

b. 20 ぐらい＿＿＿＿＿っていましたが、もう ぜんぜん

     know

＿＿＿＿＿えていません。

  remember

H. You are working for a hotel in Tokyo. Describe to your boss what you
have done for a customer using "＿＿＿*TE okimashita.*"

1. I changed the sheets.
2. I cleaned the room.
3. I prepared *(junbi shimasu)* the meal.
4. I made coffee *(koohii o iremasu).*

KOTAE

A. 1. *ni, o* 2. *ni,* or *o* 3. *ni* or *e, ni* 4. *wa, kana*

B. 1. *ki* 2. *iru* 3. *ari* 4. *iru* 5. *ari* 6. *ko* 7. *i*

C. 1. *furu daroo* 2. *ooki* 3. *saserareta* 4. *irasshaimasu*

D. 1. *Koobe de hataraite imasu.* 2. *Koobe de jishin ga arimashita.*
3. *Musuko san ni denwa shite mimashita.* 4. *Ashita no ban suru tsumori
desu.*

E. 1. d 2. e 3. a 4. b

F. 1. c 2. d 3. g 4. f

G. 1. a. 大学、学長 b. 長島先生 2. a. 一番強 b. 花若、思 3. a. 習
b. 知、覚
H. 1. *shiitsu o kaete okimashita.* 2. *heya o sooji shite okimashita.* 3. *shokuji o
junbi shite okimashita.* 4. *koohii o irete okimashita.*

DAI SANJUU ROKKA
Lesson 36
KYOOIKU.   Education.

A. DAIAROOGU

HAHA TO MUSUKO.

Follow this conversation between a mother and her son, a junior high student.

HAHA: Chótto súupaa ni itte kitái no. Okáasan ga inai aida ni Séndai no obasan kara denwa ga áttara, kónban denwa surútte itte óite ne.

MUSUKO: Ún.

HAHA: Móo shukudai shitá no?

MUSUKO: Oyátsu tábete kara suru.

HAHA: Júku ni iku máde ni shite shimainasái yo.

Shibaraku shite.

HAHA: Tadaima.

MUSUKO: Okaeri. Denwa nákatta yo.

HAHA: Sóo. Áa, rájio kikinagara, benkyoo shiterú no?

MUSUKO: Kono bangumi owattára, yameru. Áto júppun de owarú kara.

HAHA: Áa, kono tokei kowárete shimattá wa. Kore furúi kedo, íi tokei ná no yo. Dóko de shúuri shite kurerú kashira.

MUSUKO: Bóku ga benkyoo shiteru aida, damáttete yo.

MOTHER AND SON.

MOTHER: I'm going to the supermarket for a while. If your aunt in Sendai calls while I'm gone, tell her that I'll call her back this evening.

SON: Okay.

MOTHER: Have you done your homework yet?

SON: I'll do it after I have a snack.

MOTHER: You have to be done by the time you go to *juku* [cram school], okay?

A little later.

MOTHER: I'm home.

SON: Hi [Welcome back]. There weren't any phone calls.

MOTHER: I see. You're studying while listening to the radio?

SON: I'll stop listening after this program. It'll be over in ten more minutes, so . . .

MOTHER: Oh, this watch is broken. It's old, but it's a good watch. I wonder where it can be fixed.

SON: Be quiet while I'm trying to study.

B. BUNPOO TO YOOHOO

1. TE *SHIMAU*

The verb *shimau* "to conclude" in combination with the TE form of a verb expresses a completed action.

Moo shukudai o shite shimaimashita.
I finished doing my homework already.

Hiragana wa isshuukan de oboete shimaimashita.
I completely memorized all the *hiragana* characters in one week.

In addition, TE *shimau* may express regret about an occurrence.

Kono tokei kowarete shimatta wa.
This watch broke (and I regret it).

Chuugakusei ni nattara, motto benkyoo shinai to, rakudai shite shimaimasu yo.
When you become a junior high student, you'll flunk if you don't study more (and you will regret it).

Since TE *shimau* can express completion as well as regret, the context has to determine the meaning; often the two meanings are combined.

Oyatsu wa tabete shimaimashita.
I ate all the refreshments.
I ate the refreshments, and I shouldn't have done that.
I ate all the refreshments, and I shouldn't have done that.

2. *AIDA* "WHILE"

Aida following a clause means "while. . . ." The clause ends in plain forms just like relative clauses. The subject in the modifying clause is followed by *ga* (not by *wa*), which can be changed to *no* optionally. The tense of the *aida* clause is often in present-tense form, even when the meaning is past.

When the *aida* clause ends in a *na*-adjective with the copula in the present affirmative, the copula becomes *na*. If it ends in a noun with the copula in the present affirmative, the copula becomes *no*, so *aida* belongs to Type II (see Lesson 21, B4).

Musuko ga benkyoo shite iru aida ni, suupaa ni ikimashita.
While my son was studying, I went to the supermarket.

Kookoosei no aida ni, Nihon e ikitai desu.
I want to go to Japan while I'm a high school student.

Ryooshin ga genki na aida ni, kisei suru tsumori desu.
I plan to go back to my hometown while my parents are healthy.

In the sentences above, *ni* follows *aida*. Cases where *ni* does not follow *aida* have slightly different meanings than those where it does. Compare:

Nihon ni iru aida, daigaku de benkyoo shimashita.
I studied at a university [the whole time] while I was in Japan.

Nihon ni iru aida ni, daigaku de benkyoo shimashita.
I studied at a university [part of the time] while I was in Japan.

With *aida ni*, the activity doesn't last the entire time span in question, but with *aida*, it does.

Watashi ga benkyoo shite iru aida, damatte ite kudasai.
Please be quiet while I am studying [during the whole time that I'm studying].

Watashi ga benkyoo shite iru aida ni, denwa shite kudasai.
Please call me while I am studying [during some part of the time span when I am studying].

3. -NAGARA "WHILE . . ."

-nagara attached to a pre-*masu* form also means "while."

Tomodachi o machinagara, hon o yomimashita.
I read a book while waiting for my friend.

Tomodachi o matte iru aida, hon o yomimashita.
I read a book while waiting for my friend.

Unlike *aida* "while," *-nagara* cannot be used when the two actions are performed by different people, only when the same person performs two actions simultaneously. The main action is described by the final verb.

Hatarakinagara, kookoo ni ikimashita.
I was working while I went to high school [I went to high school while working].

Jisho o hikinagara, nihongo no sakubun o kakimashita.
I wrote a Japanese composition with a dictionary [while consulting a dictionary].

4. COMMAND/INVITATION *(-NASAI)*

To command or invite someone to do something, a pre-*masu* form attached to *-nasai* may be used. This structure is used only by superiors giving orders, most typically by parents or teachers giving orders to children. Also, instructions on a test might use it. Never use *-nasai* toward a superior or even a peer.

Koko e kinasai.
Come here. [I order you to come/I invite you to come.]

Juku ni iku made ni shukudai o shite shimainasai.
Finish your homework before you go to *juku*.

Kanji o kakinasai.
Write *kanji*.

With certain honorific verbs, *-nasai* is dropped.

osshaimasu	→	*Osshai.*	Say it.
nasaimasu	→	*Nasai.*	Do it.
irasshaimasu	→	*Irasshai.**	Come. Go. Stay.

* The fixed expression *Irasshai* "welcome" originates from the command *irasshai*.

Although these respectful verbs soften the command or invitation, they still should not be used with your superiors or peers.

5. REQUEST (TE)

To make a casual request among friends and relatives, use a TE form.

Sono kyookasho misete.
Will you show me that textbook?

Damattete. * *(Damatte ite.)*
Please be quiet.

Suupaa de kaimono shite kite.
Please go do some shopping at the supermarket.

6. PARTICLES

a. *No* (sentence particle)

The sentence particle *no* used at the end of a sentence has the same meaning as the explanatory predicate *n/no desu*. It belongs to Type III (see Lesson 21, B4). Grown men do not use *no* in statements, but only in questions in plain style. On the other hand, women use *no* in statements and questions in both normal and plain style (plain style is more common in statements with *no*).

Chotto suupaa ni itte kitai no. (female speaker)
I want to go to the supermarket for a moment.

Kyoo wa shoogakkoo no undookai desu no. (female speaker)
Is today a sports day at the elementary school?

Moo shukudai shita no? (female or male speaker)
Did you do your homework yet?

Donna sankoosho katta no. (female or male speaker)
What kind of reference book did you buy?

b. *Ne/yo* (with a request, a command, or an invitation)

The sentence particle *ne* softens a request or an invitation (see Lesson 33, B5). It also does so in commands.

---

* For more on contractions, see Lesson 29, B4.

434

Daidokoro ni oyatsu ga aru kara, tabenasai ne.
There are refreshments in the kitchen, so help yourself [eat them].

Natsuyasumi ni uchi ni irasshai ne.
Come to my house during the summer vacation.

When the particle *yo* is used with a request, command, or invitation, it sounds more insistent.

Juku ni iku made ni shite shimainasai yo.
Finish doing it by the time you go to *juku*.

Boku ga benkyoo shiteru aida, damattete yo.
Be quiet while I'm studying.

7. NON-SPEAKER'S PERSPECTIVE

Often when speaking, you assume the perspective of the addressee. Often a father will say to his child, "Daddy [the child's father, i.e., I] will do it for you" and mean himself, or ask "Where is Grandpa?" and mean the child's grandfather. This kind of talk is rather common in English, and even more so in Japanese.

Okaasan ga inai aida ni Sendai no obasan kara denwa ga attara, konban denwa surutte itte oite ne.
If your aunt in Sendai calls while I am [mother is] gone, please tell her that I'll call her back this evening.

A wife may even refer to her husband as *otoosan* "daddy," regardless of whether the children are present or not.

Otoosan, denwa desu yo.
Dad, there's a phone call for you.

Often elementary school teachers call themselves *sensei* "teacher" when talking to their students.

Chuugakkoo ni itte mo, itsu de mo sensei ni ai ni kite kudasai.
Even after you go to junior high, you can come see me [the teacher] anytime.

C. MOJI

1. DIALOGUE

母 「ちょっと スーパーに 行ってきたいの。お母さんが
いない間に せんだいの おばさんから 電話が あったら、
今晩 電話するって 言っておいてね。」

むすこ 「うん。」

母 「もう しゅくだいしたの。」

むすこ 「おやつ 食べてから、する。」

母 「じゅくに 行くまでに してしまいなさいよ。」

─────────

母 「ただいま。」

むすこ 「お帰り。電話なかったよ。」

母 「そう。ああ、ラジオ 聞きながら、勉強してるの。」

むすこ 「この番ぐみ 終ったら、やめる。あと 十分で 終るから。」

母 「ああ、このとけい こわれてしまったわ。これ
古いけど、いい とけいなのよ。どこで しゅうりして
くれるかしら。」

むすこ 「ぼくが 勉強してる間、だまっててよ。」

2. NEW *KANJI*

[120]	電	*DEN*	electricity
[121]	話	*WA*	talking e.g., 電話
[122]	晩	*BAN*	evening e.g., 今晩

[123]	食	*ta(beru)*	to eat
[124]	勉	*BEN*	making efforts

STROKE ORDER

[120]
[121]
[122]
[123]
[124]

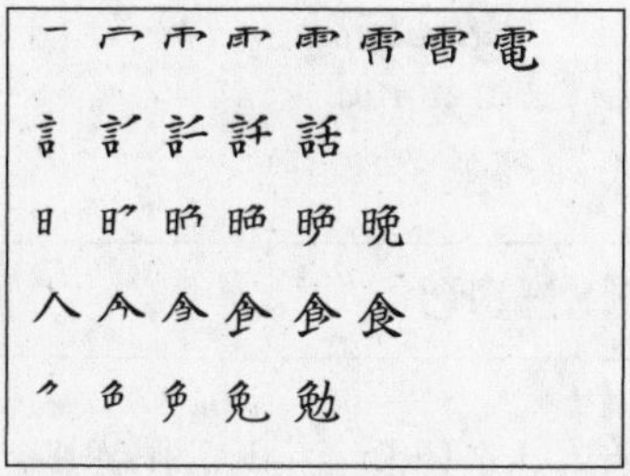

C. NEW READING

[35]	間	*KAN* (Lesson 22)	space, time
		aida	space, time, while
[109]	強	*tsuyo(i)* (Lesson 34)	strong
		KYOO	strong e.g., 勉強

D. TANGO TO HYOOGEN

shoogakkoo	elementary school
chuugakkoo	junior high school
juku	cram school
kyookasho	textbook
sankoosho	reference book
sakubun	composition
undookai	sports day
chuugakusei	junior high student
kookoosei	high school student
suupaa	supermarket
daidokoro	kitchen
oyatsu	refreshments, snack
rakudai suru	to flunk
shuuri suru	to repair
kaimono suru	to go shopping
kisei suru	to go back to one's hometown
damaru	to be quiet
hiku	to consult (a dictionary)

ato	the remainder
ato **juppun**	ten minutes from now
motto	more
un	OK. Yeah.
Soo.	I see. (casual equivalent of *Soo desu ka.*)
Tadaima.	I'm home.

RENSHUU

A. What did the mother and her son do? Indicate which of the statements are true, based on the dialogue.

haha:　　1. *Tokei o shuuri shimashita.*
　　　　　2. *Musuko ga juku ni itte iru aida ni, dekakemashita.*
　　　　　3. *Kaimono ni ikimashita.*
musuko:　1. *Juku ni iku mae ni suupaa ni ikimashita.*
　　　　　2. *Rajio o kikinagara, benkyoo shimashita.*
　　　　　3. *Sendai no oba to denwa de hanashimashita.*

B. Fill in the blanks with the appropriate form of the Japanese equivalents of the English words below.

to forget, to break, to eat too much, to lose

1. a: *Jishin wa doo deshita ka.*
   b: *Uchi ga _____ shimatta n desu.*
2. a: *Byooki desu ka.*
   b: *Ee, _____ shimatta n desu.*
3. a: *Shukudai o motte kimashita ka.*
   b: *Iie, _____ shimatta n desu.*
4. a: *Shiai wa doo deshita ka.*
   b: *_____ shimatta n desu.*

C. Four people answered the following question. Fill in the blanks.

Itsu Nihon no rekishi o benkyoo suru tsumori desu ka.
When do you plan to study Japanese history?

1. *Daigaku de nihongo o narai _____, benkyoo suru tsumori desu.*
   I plan to study it while I am learning Japanese at the university.
2. *Tookyoo no shisha ni tsutomete iru _____ ni, benkyoo suru tsumori desu.*
   I plan to study it while I am working for the branch office in Tokyo.
3. *Nihon ni _____ ni, benkyoo suru tsumori desu.*
   I plan to study it before I go to Japan.
4. *Daigakuin ni _____, benkyoo suru tsumori desu.*
   I plan to study it after I've started [entered] graduate school.

D. Choose the correct particles.

1. *otto*:   *Onaka ga suita (ne/wa). Nani ka tabeyoo (no/ka).*
2. *tsuma*: *Watashi wa nodo ga kawaita (no/yo). Nani ka nomitai (wa/yo).*
3. *otto*:   *Asoko ni resutoran ga aru (yo/wa).*

E. Write *kanji* in the blanks based on the *hiragana* written under the blanks.

1. a. _____ _____ しましたか。
      きょう　　べんきょう

  b. ええ、_____ にいる_____ に_____ しました。
        がっこう　　　　あいだ　　いちじかん

2. a. _____ あのレストランで_____ べませんか。
     こんばん　　　　　　　　　　た

  b. ええ、よやくしなくては いけないから、

   _____ しましょう。
   でんわ

F. Combine the following sentences, describing two things done at the same time.

Example: *uta o utaimasu + shawaa o abimasu*
      → *uta o utainagara shawaa o abimasu.*

1. *terebi o mimasu + benkyoo shimasu*
2. *rajio o kikimasu + hon o yomimasu*
3. *tabemasu + hanashimasu*
4. *denwashimasu + konpyuutaa o shimasu*
5. *sooda o nomimasu + arukimasu*
6. *tomodachi to hanashimasu + jogingu o shimasu*
7. *hon o yomimasu + nemasu*

G. Change verb form to command your students or children to perform the following actions.

1. *asobumae ni shukudai o <u>shite kudasai</u>.*
2. *shizuka ni <u>shite kudasai</u>.*
3. *nihongo o <u>hanashite kudasai</u>.*
4. *kaimono ni <u>itte kudasai</u>.*
5. *koko e <u>kite kudasai</u>.*
6. *kanji de <u>kaite kudasai</u>.*

KARUCHAA NOOTO

After World War II, the Japanese school system changed drastically. The present educational system is similar to that in the United States: six years of elementary school, three years of junior high school, three years of senior high school, and four years of college. In addition, there are kindergartens, junior colleges, graduate schools, and vocational schools.

In general, to get a job at a first-rate enterprise, you need to graduate from a first-rate university. Therefore, students work hard to get into top universities by preparing for and taking the difficult entrance exams given by individual schools in addition to general nationwide exams. Assuming that regular schools do not provide enough preparation for the entrance exams, many students go to *juku* "cram school" after regular school hours.

Entrance exams are given only once a year in February or March. If a student fails, he or she has to wait an entire year to retake them. High school graduates preparing for another try at the entrance exams are called *roonin*. Originally this meant "samurai without a master," but it has come to mean "student without a school."

In many Japanese families, mothers rather than fathers take care of the children's education, struggling to help their children succeed. The slang expression *kyooiku mama* "education mother" is often used facetiously to describe a mother who is obsessed with her children's studies.

KOTAE

A. *haha* 3   *musuko* 2
B. 1. *kowarete*   2. *tabesugite*   3. *wasurete*   4. *Makete*
C. *nagara*   2. *aida*   3. *iku mae*   4. *haitte kara*
D. 1. *ne, ka*   2. *no, wa*   3. *yo*
E. 1. a. 今日、勉強

    b. 学校、間、一時間

  2. a. 今晩、食

    b. 電話

F. 1. *terebi o minagara benkyoo shimasu.* 2. *rajio o kikinagara hon o yomimasu.* 3. *tabenagara hanashimasu.* 4. *denwashinagara konpyuutaa o shimasu.* 5. *soda o nominagara arukimasu.* 6. *tomodachi to hanashinagara jogingu o shimasu.* 7. *hon o yominagara nemasu.*

G. 1. *shukudai o shinasai.* 2. *shizuka ni shinasai.* 3. *nihongo o hanashinasai.* 4. *kaimono ni ikinasai.* 5. *koko e kinasai.* 6. *kanji de kakinasai.*

DAI SANJUU NANAKA
Lesson 37
DENTOO ENGEKI.   Traditional Theater.

A. DAIAROOGU

KABUKI.

Mr. Wakayama is showing his visiting friend Mr. Clark around Tokyo.

KURAAKU: **Ano tatémono wa nán desu ka.**

WAKAYAMA: **Are wa Kabukiza désu. Kabuki o míta kotó ga arimásu ka.**

KURAAKU: **Ée, Nyuuyóoku de ichido dake míta kotó ga áru n desu. Íshoo ga kírei da shi, odori mo subaráshikatta n desu kedo, kotobá ga yoku wakarimasén deshita.**

WAKAYAMA: **Ée, kabuki no nihongo wa fúrukute, wakarinikúi desu ne. Nihonjín de mo kúroo shimásu yo. Démo, hanashí wa mukashi kara áru monó de, hajime kara dónna sujigaki ka wakátteru kara, kékkoo tanoshimemásu kedo ne.**

KURAAKU: **Íma náni ka yatterú n desu ka.**

WAKAYAMA: **Kyóo yatterú ka dóo ka shirimasén kedo, chótto itte mimashóo ka. Íi no o miraréru ka mo shiremasén yo.**

KURAAKU: **Ée, Chuushingura tóka, bóku no shitteru hanashí nara, míte mitái desu.**

KABUKI.

CLARK: What's that building over there?

WAKAYAMA: That's the Kabuki Theater. Have you ever seen a kabuki performance?

CLARK: Yes, I saw one [only] once in New York. The costumes were [are] pretty, and the dances were wonderful. But I had trouble understanding the language.

WAKAYAMA: Yes, I know. The language used in kabuki is old and hard to understand. Even Japanese people have a hard time. But since the stories have been around since the old days and we know the plot beforehand, we can still really enjoy them.

CLARK: Are they performing anything now?

WAKAYAMA: I don't know if there is a performance today, but we can just go there to find out. We may be able to see a good one.

CLARK: Yes, if it is a story I know well, like *Chushingura*, I'd like to see it.

B. BUNPOO TO YOOHOO

1. *KA MO SHIRENAI* "MAY/MIGHT"

"May" or "might" is expressed by *ka mo shirenai* following a plain form. In the present affirmative, there is no copula. Thus, *ka mo shirenai* is Type IV (see Lesson 21, B4).

Ii dashimono o mirareru ka mo shiremasen yo.
We may be able to see a good performance.

Hooru san wa kabuki o mita koto ga nai ka mo shiremasen.
Ms. Hall may never have seen a kabuki performance.

Ano kabuki no hon wa takai ka mo shiremasen.
That book on kabuki might be expensive.

Kyoo no dashimono wa Chuushingura ka mo shirenai.
The performance announced for today may be *Chushingura*.

Tanaka san wa kyoo isogashii no ka mo shiremasen.
Ms. Tanaka may be busy today.

2. "WHETHER/IF"

In English, a yes-no question may be embedded in a sentence by using "whether" or "if." The Japanese equivalent is . . . *ka doo ka* or . . . *ka . . . ka* after a plain form. Both forms belong to Type IV (see Lesson 21, B4).

a. . . . *ka doo ka* "whether or not . . ./if . . ."

To express "whether (or not) . . ." or "if . . ." with only one item, use . . . *ka doo ka* after the plain form.

Kyoo yatteru ka doo ka shirimasen.
I don't know whether they are performing today.

442

Serifu o zenbu oboerareru ka doo ka shinpai shite iru n desu.
   I am worried about whether I can memorize all my lines.

Kuraaku san ni kabuki ga suki ka doo ka kikitakatta n desu.
   I wanted to ask Mr. Clark whether he likes kabuki.

   b. . . . *ka* . . . *ka* "whether/if . . . or . . ."

   To express "whether/if A or B (with two items)," use A *ka* B *ka*. Often
   A is in the affirmative and B is in the negative.

Wakayama san to Kuraaku san ga kabuki o mita ka minakatta ka shiri-masen.
   I don't know whether Mr. Wakayama and Mr. Clark saw kabuki [or
   didn't see it].

Ano geki wa kigeki ka higeki ka shirimasen.
   I don't know whether that play is a comedy or a tragedy.

Eiga no chiketto wa takakatta ka yasukatta ka oboete imasen.
   I don't remember whether the movie ticket was expensive or inexpensive.

3. QUESTION WORDS IN EMBEDDED SENTENCES

   Much as yes-no questions can be embedded in a sentence, so can
   questions requiring a question word. The embedded sentence with a
   question word ends in the question particle *ka*. The copula before *ka* is
   deleted, so this structure belongs to Type IV as well (see Lesson 21,
   B4).

Oosaka no doko de kabuki o mirareru ka shirimasen.
   I don't know where we can see kabuki in Osaka.

Chiketto o nanmai kattara ii no ka kiite kudasai.
   Please ask them how many tickets we should buy.

Dono yakusha ga joozu ka wakarimasen.
   I can't tell which of these actors is good.

4. PARTICLES

   a. *Shi* "and/therefore"

   Shi is a clause particle that normally follows a plain form. It has two
   meanings: "and furthermore," and "therefore." Usually, the meaning is
   determined by the context. Often the particle *mo* "also" is used in the
   sentence to emphasize *shi*.

Wakai toki, shamisen mo naratta shi, okoto mo naratta.
> When I was young, I learned how to play the *shamisen* (a three-stringed banjolike instrument), and also, I learned how to play the *koto* (a kind of harp with thirteen strings).

If the copula is in the present affirmative, use *da* before *shi*. *Shi* belongs to Type I (see Lesson 21, B4).

Kono yakusha wa hansamu da shi, gei mo tassha desu.
> This actor is handsome, and what's more, he is also good at his art.

If the verb used before *shi* expresses a state, a habit, or the continuity of an action, you can use the present tense, even if you are referring to the past.

Ishoo ga kirei da shi, odori mo subarashikatta n desu.
> Their costumes were [are] pretty, and the dances were wonderful.

Kinoo wa ame mo furu shi, dekakeru no o yamemashita.
> Yesterday, it rained [rains], and therefore, I didn't go out.

In polite speech, *shi* can follow a normal form if the final clause ends in a normal form (normal style).

Nihon e itta toki, kabuki mo mimashita shi, bunraku mo mimashita.
> When I went to Japan, I saw a kabuki performance, and I also saw a bunraku puppet performance.

b. *Toka* "such as/like"

Toka is used to introduce examples.

Chuushingura toka, boku no shitteru hanashi nara, mite mitai desu.
> If it is a story I know well, such as *Chushingura*, I want to see it.

Toka is repeated with each example.

Kabuki toka, noo toka, Nihon no dentooteki na engeki ga suki desu.
> I like traditional Japanese plays, such as kabuki and noh.

Suda san toka, Shimizu san toka, kabuki no suki na daigakusei wa takusan imasu.
> There are many college students, such as Ms. Suda and Ms. Shimizu, who like kabuki.

c. *Dake* "only"

The particles *ga, wa,* and *o* are optional after *dake*. Compare:

Yamada san ga/wa kimashita.
Mr. Yamada came.

Yamada san dake (ga) kimashita.
Only Mr. Yamada came.

Kabuki o mimashita.
I saw a kabuki performance.

Kabuki dake (o) mimashita.
I saw only kabuki.

When another particle (i.e., not *ga, wa,* or *o*) is used, *dake* stands either before or after it.

Tanaka san ni iimashita.
I said it to Ms. Tanaka.

Tanaka san ni dake/dake ni iimashita.
I said it only to Ms. Tanaka.

Often *dake* is used after quantity expressions.

Nyuuyooku de ichido dake mita koto ga aru n desu.
I have only seen it once [only once] in New York.

Chiketto o sanmai dake kaimashita.
I only bought three [only three] tickets.

5. COMPOUND WORDS

Pre-*masu* forms can form compound words with -*nikui* "hard to . . ." and -*yasui* "easy to. . . ." The compound words are *i*-adjectives.

Kabuki no nihongo wa wakarinikui desu.
The Japanese in kabuki is hard to understand.

Ano biru wa tatenikukatta soo desu.
I heard that building was difficult to construct.

Kyoogen no nihongo wa wakariyasui desu ka.
Is the Japanese used in kyogen [a type of comic play] easy to understand?

Kono kanji wa machigaeyasui desu.
It is easy to make a mistake with this *kanji*.

C. MOJI

1. DIALOGUE

クラーク 「あの建物は 何ですか。」

若山 「あれは かぶきざです。かぶきを 見たことが あります
か。」

クラーク 「ええ、ニューヨークで 一度だけ 見たことが
あるんです。いしょうが きれいだし、踊りも
すばらしかったんですけど、ことばが よく
わからなかったんです。」

若山 「かぶきの 日本語は 古くて わかりにくいですね。
日本人でも苦労しますよ。でも、話は 昔から ある物で、
始めから どんな すじがきか わかってるから、けっこう
楽しめますけどね。」

クラーク 「今 何か やってるんですか。」

若山 「今日 やってるか どうか、知らないですけど、
ちょっと 行って みましょうか。いいのを 見られるかも
しれませんよ。」

クラーク 「ええ、ちゅうしんぐらとか、ぼくの 知っている 話なら、
見てみたいです。」

2. NEW *KANJI*

[125]	建	*ta(teru)*	to build, to construct
		tate(mono)	building e.g., 建物
[126]	踊	*odo(ri)*	dance
[127]	語	*GO*	language e.g., 日本語、フランス語
[128]	苦	*KU*	suffering
[129]	労	*ROO*	labor, trouble e.g., 苦労

446

[125] ㄱ ㄱ ㅋ ㅌ 聿 肀 律 建

[126] ㅁ ㅁ ㅁ ㅁ ㅁ ㅁ ㅁ 踊 踊 踊

[127] ㅑ 誩 語 語

[128] 一 艹 艹 芢 苦

[129] ㅛ 庐 労

3. NEW READING

[121] 話   *WA* (Lesson 36)   talking

         hana(su)   to talk

         hanashi   story

D. TANGO TO HYOOGEN

kabuki	kabuki (traditional play)
bunraku	bunraku (traditional puppet play)
noo	noh or no (traditional play with masks)
kyoogen	kyogen (traditional comic play)
geki	drama, play
engeki	dramatic performance
kigeki	comedy
higeki	tragedy
hanashi	story
sujigaki	plot
odori	traditional dance
kotoba	language, speech
serifu	script, actors' lines
dashimono	what is scheduled to be performed
gei	art, artistic performance
yakusha	actor (usually for traditional dramas)
ishoo	costume
shamisen	shamisen or samisen (three-stringed banjo-like instrument)
(o)koto	a zither-like instrument
kuroo suru	to have a hard time
machigaeru	to make a mistake

hansamu	handsome
tassha	skillful
dentooteki	traditional

RENSHUU

A. Fill in the blanks on the basis of the dialogue.

1. *Kuraaku san wa Nyuuyooku de mita kabuki ni tsuite, doo omoimashita ka.*
   (1) _____ *ga* _____ *deshita.*
   (2) _____ *ga* _____ *desu.*
   (3) _____ *ga* _____ *nikukatta desu.*
2. *Wakayama san to Kuraaku san wa nani o shiritai to omotta n desu ka.*
   (1) *Kabukiza de kyoo yatte iru* _____ *shiritai to omotta n desu.*
   (2) *Moshi yatte ireba, donna dashimono* _____ *shiritai to omotta n desu.*   (particle)

B. Fill in the blanks according to the English equivalents.

1. a: *Mado ga aite imasu yo.*
   b: _____ *ga* _____ *ka mo shiremasen ne.*
   A thief might get in.
2. a: *Hanada san wa kyoo yasunderu n desu.*
   b: _____ *ka mo shiremasen ne.*
   She may be sick.
3. a: *Ashita otenki wa doo deshoo ka.*
   b: _____ *ga* _____ *ka mo shiremasen ne.*
   It might snow.
4. a: *Shimada san ga apaato o karita soo desu ne.*
   b: *Ee, amari* _____ *ka mo shiremasen kedo, ii apaato desu yo.*
   Yes, it may not be very big, but it's a good apartment.

C. Fill in the blanks according to the English equivalents.

1. a. *Moo sakubun o kakimashita ka.*
   b: *Iie,* _____ *ka mada kimetenai n desu.*
   No, I haven't decided what to write.
2. a: *Shichoosen wa doo deshita ka.*
   b: _____ *ka mada shiranai n desu.*
   I don't know who was elected yet.
3. a: *Kyuukoo wa moo demashita ka.*
   b: _____ *shiranai n desu kedo, hoomu ni amari hito ga inai kara, moo* _____ *no ka mo* _____ *masen ne.*
   I don't know whether or not it left, but since there are not many people on the platform, it might have left already.

448

D. Choose from the words below, and fill in the blanks.

shi, ka, node, dake, yo, toka

a: *Ashita Sakaiya to iu depaato ni ikitai n da kedo, doko ni aru _____*[1]
shittemasu ka.

b: *Eki no chikaku desu yo. Sono hen ni pachinkoya _____*[2] *iroiro na*
mise ga aru n da kedo Sakaiya wa ookii _____[3] *atarashii tatemono*
da kara, sugu wakarimasu yo. Ichido _____[4] *itta koto ga aru n da*
kedo, fun'iki no ii depaato desu yo.

E. Figure out what the following words mean.

1. 食べ物

2. 語学

3. 教育学

F. Match *kanji* in Group I and Group II to form words.

I	II
苦	物
電	晩
勉	強
今	労
建	月
	話
	週

G. Answer the following questions about yourself using "_____ *kamo*
shiremasen."

Example: Tookyoo e ittara _____
    → *Tookyoo e ittara kabuki o <u>miru kamo shiremasen</u>.*
        (If I go to Japan, I may see Kabuki.)

1. *shuumatsu tenki ga yokattara* _____
   (If it's nice weather on the weekend, _____)
2. *nyuuyooku e ittara* _____
   (If I go to New York, _____)
3. *sora o tobetara* _____
   (If I could fly in the sky, _____)

KARUCHAA NOOTO

Kabuki is a type of play that involves music and dancing. It is well known for its elaborate costumes and makeup. Some kabuki plays depict samurai warriors and others common people. For example, *Chuushingura*, one of the most popular kabuki plays, is the story of how forty-seven samurai avenged the death of their master.

Kabuki originated at the beginning of the seventeenth century. At first, women were the main performers, but today, only male performers are allowed, even in female roles. The majority of the main theaters that perform kabuki are in Tokyo. Kabuki troupes have also performed outside of Japan, including in the United States and Europe.

Besides kabuki, you can enjoy a variety of other traditional forms of theater in Japan such as bunraku, noh, and kyogen. Bunraku is a form of puppet theater in which the narrative and dialogue are chanted by a storyteller accompanied by *shamisens* (stringed instruments). Three people in black robes manipulate each puppet, allowing it to make complicated, lifelike motions. Noh is a form of dance drama accompanied by chants and a small group of instruments. The principal characters wear masks. Kyogen is a form of comic sketch often performed on the noh stage as an interlude between the more somber noh plays.

KOTAE

A. 1. (1) *Ishoo, kirei*   (2) *Odori, subarashikatta*   (3) *Kotoba, wakari*
2. (1) *ka doo ka*   (2) *ka*
B. 1. *Doroboo, hairu*   2. *Byooki*   3. *Yuki, furu*   4. *ookiku nai*
C. 1. *nani o kaku*   2. *Dare ga toosen shita*   3. *Deta ka doo ka, deta, shire*
D. 1. *ka*   2. *toka*   3. *shi*   4. *dake*
E. 1. food たべもの   2. language study ごがく   3. study of education きょういくがく

F. 苦労、電話、勉強、今晩、今月、今週、建物
G. 1. *gorufu o* <u>*suru ka mo shiremasen*</u>. 2. *myuujikaru o* <u>*miru ka mo*</u> <u>*shiremasen*</u>. (musical) 3. *nihon e* <u>*iku ka mo shiremasen*</u>.

DAI SANJUU HACHIKA
Lesson 38

BIJUTSU.　Fine Arts.

A. DAIAROOGU

UKIYOE.

Ms. Omae and Mr. Mizushima are taking an art history class together at a Japanese university.

OOMAE: **Dónna repóoto káku ka kimeta?**

MIZUSHIMA: **Bóku wa hanga ga sukí da kara, ukiyoe ni tsúite kakóo to omótteru n da kedo, shíryoo atsuméru noni kúroo shiteru n da yo.**

OOMAE: **Kono natsuyásumi ni Amerika ni itta tóki, Bósuton no bijutsúkan ni ittá no yo. Séiyoo no bijutsúhin o míru tamé ni ittá n da kedo, Nihon no ukiyoe ga takusan átte bikkúri shitá wa.**

MIZUSHIMA: **Bósuton no nihonbíjutsu no korékushon wa subarashii rashíi ne. Démo, zannen nágara, íma kara Bósuton made iku wáke ni wa ikanái shi, náni ka chikáku ni íi shíryoo nái kanáa.**

OOMAE: **Áa, sóo, soo. Iroiro na ukiyoe o shookai shiteru bídeo míta koto áru?**

MIZUSHIMA: **Sonna bídeo míta koto nái kedo.**

OOMAE: **Otootó ga nihon búnka ni kánsuru bídeo takusan mótte ite, watashi mo míru kotó ga árụ n da kedo, sono ukiyoe no bídeo mo míta kotó ga áru wa. Íma tsukatte inai yóo da kara, otootó kara karite agemashóo ka.**

MIZUSHIMA: **Ún, zéhi onegai surú yo. Arígatoo.**

UKIYOE.

OMAE: Have you decided what you're going to write about for your report?

MIZUSHIMA: Since I like woodblock prints, I'm thinking of writing about *ukiyoe*, but I am having a hard time finding [collecting] materials.

OMAE: I went to America during [this] summer vacation, and I visited the museum in Boston. I went there to see Western works of art, but I was surprised to see so many *ukiyoe.*

MIZUSHIMA: Yes, I've heard that the collection of Japanese art in Boston is wonderful, but unfortunately, I can't go as far as Boston now. I wonder if there are any good materials around here.

OMAE: Oh, now I remember. . . . Have you ever seen a videotape that introduces all kinds of *ukiyoe*?

MIZUSHIMA: No, I've never seen any such a videotape.

OMAE: My younger brother has several videotapes on Japanese culture, and I've seen [I sometimes see] some of them. I have seen the videotape on *ukiyoe* he has. I don't think [It seems that] he is [not] using it now, so I could borrow it from him for you. Should I?

MIZUSHIMA: Yes, please, by all means. That's really nice of you.

B. BUNPOO TO YOOHOO

1. PURPOSE *"TAME NI"*

One way to express purpose is a pre-*masu* form plus *ni* with a motion verb (see Lesson 11, B6).

Bijutsukan e seiyoo no bijutsu o mi ni ikimashita.
I went to the museum to see Western works of art.

Another expression of purpose is *tame ni.*

Bijutsukan e seiyoo no bijutsu o miru tame ni ikimashita.
I went to the museum to see Western works of art.

With *tame ni*, the purpose is emphasized more than with a pre-*masu* form plus *ni. Tame ni* follows a plain present verb or a noun plus *no.* While a negative purpose ("in order not to . . .") cannot be expressed with pre-*masu ni*, it is possible with *tame ni.* Also, while pre-*masu ni* can only be used with a motion verb such as *iku* "to go" in final position, *tame ni* can be used with other verbs as well.

Nihon bunka o benkyoo suru tame ni, bideo ya sankoosho o kaimashita.
I bought videotapes, a reference book, and more in order to study Japanese culture.

Rakudai shinai tame ni, donna benkyoo o shitara ii desu ka.
What should I do to study so that I don't flunk?

If *tame ni* is used following a noun plus *no*, the best translation is "for," "for the sake of," or "for the purpose of." *

Kore wa shoogakusei no tame ni kakareta sankoosho desu.
This is a reference book written for elementary school children.

Nihonga no kenkyuu no tame ni Nihon e ikimashita.
I went to Japan for the purpose of research on Japanese painting.

2. PURPOSE/PROCESS *"NONI"*

Noni is also used to express purpose "in order to. . . ." In contrast to *tame ni, noni* refers to a process. It cannot follow a negative form or a noun, only the plain present affirmative form (dictionary form) of a verb.

Shiryoo atsumeru noni, kuroo shiterun da yo.
I am having a hard time collecting materials.

Gaka ni naru noni donna benkyoo ga hitsuyoo desu ka.
In order to become a painter, what kind of studies are necessary?

Tenrankai ni iku noni, takushii ni norimashita.
I took a taxi to get to the exhibition.

3. *YOO* "TO SEEM"

Yoo following a plain form means "it seems that." When used with a *na*-adjective or a noun in the present affirmative, *yoo* belongs to Type III (see Lesson 21, B4).

Kono bideo wa ima tsukatte inai yoo desu.
It seems that he is not using this videotape now.

Ano toshokan ni wa hanga no hon ga takusan aru yoo desu.
It seems that there are many books on woodblock prints in that library.

Are wa Noguchi Isamu no chookoku no yoo desu.
That seems to be a sculpture by Noguchi Isamu.

4. OCCASIONAL ACTIONS OR SITUATIONS

. . . *koto ga aru* following a plain form in the present tense means "sometimes—."

---

* *No tame ni* "for" can also follow the recipient of the favor with a TE form plus *ageru, kureru*, etc. (see Lesson 29, B1).

Watashi mo otooto no bideo o miru koto ga aru n desu.
I, too, sometimes watch my younger brother's videotapes.

Nihonga o mi ni iku koto ga aru n desu.
I go to see Japanese paintings sometimes.

Kono hen wa samui koto mo arimasu kedo, taitei kikoo wa ii desu.
Sometimes it is cold in this area as well, but all in all, the climate is nice.

With *na*-adjectives, use the copula *na*; with nouns, use *no*.

Fude wa hitsuyoo na koto ga aru ka mo shirenai kara katte okimashoo ka.
We may need a brush [sometimes]. Should we buy one?

Ano tenrankai no sakuhin wa yooga no koto mo arimasu ga, maitoshi daitai nihonga ga ooi desu.
Some of the works in that exhibition are sometimes Western paintings as well, but generally most of them are Japanese every year.

5. *WAKE*

Wake itself means "reason," or "meaning." It is often used idiomatically in phrases.

a. *. . . wake ni (wa) ikanai*

. . . wake ni (wa) ikanai "can't . . . ," "to be not supposed to . . . ," or "the circumstances don't allow . . ." follows the dictionary form of a verb or words such as *sonna* "that kind of" and *soo iu* "such."

Ima kara Bosuton made iku wake ni wa ikanai.
I can't go to Boston now.

Kono e o uttara doo desu ka.
Why don't you sell this picture?

Kore wa chichi no katami da kara, soo iu wake ni wa ikanai n desu.
Since this is a memento of my late father, there's no way I could do such a thing.

b. *-nai wake ni (wa) ikanai*

When the plain present negative of a verb precedes *wake*, *-nai wake ni (wa) ikanai* means "to have to do . . . (even if one does not want to)."

Jugyoo ni detakute mo, yasumanai wake ni ikanakatta n desu.
Although I wanted to attend class, I had to skip it.

Tooi node, takushii ni noranai wake ni wa ikanakatta n desu.
Because it was far, I had to take a taxi.

C. MOJI

1. DIALOGUE

大前　　「どんな　レポートを　書くか　決めた？」

水島　　「ぼくは　はんがが　好きだから、うきよ絵について
　　　　書こうと　思ってるんだけど、しりょう　集めるのに、
　　　　苦労してるんだよ。」

大前　　「この夏休みに　アメリカに　行った時、ボストンの
　　　　びじゅつかんに　行ったのよ。せいようの　びじゅつを
　　　　見るために　行ったんだけど、日本の　うきよ絵が
　　　　たくさん　あって、びっくりしたわ。」

水島　　「ボストンの　日本びじゅつの　コレクションは
　　　　すばらしいからね。でも、ざんねんながら、今から
　　　　ボストンまで　行くわけには　いかないし、近くに　何か
　　　　いい　しりょうないかなあ。」

大前　　「ああ、そうそう、いろいろな　うきよ絵を　しょうかい
　　　　してる　ビデオ　見たこと　ある？」

水島　　「そんな　ビデオ　見たこと　ないけど。」

大前　　「おとうとが　日本ぶんかに　かんする　ビデオを　たくさん
　　　　持っていて、私も　見ることが　あるんだけど、その
　　　　うきよ絵の　ビデオも　見たことが　あるわ。今　使って
　　　　いないようだから、おとうとから　借りて
　　　　あげましょうか。」

水島　　「うん、ぜひ　おねがいするよ。」

2. NEW *KANJI*

[130]	決	*ki(meru)*	to decide
[131]	絵	*E*	picture, painting, drawing
[132]	集	*atsu(meru)*	to collect, gather (transitive verb)
		atsu(maru)	to gather (intransitive verb)
[133]	夏	*natsu*	summer
[134]	休	*yasu(mu)*	to rest, be absent e.g., 夏休み
[135]	借	*ka(riru)*	to borrow, rent

STROKE ORDER

[130]	氵 汀 沪 沪 決
[131]	糸 糹 絵
[132]	亻 亻 什 隹 隼 集
[133]	一 丆 百 百 夏 夏
[134]	亻 休
[135]	亻 伴 借

D. TANGO TO HYOOGEN

tenrankai	exhibition
bijutsuhin	works of art
sakuhin	piece of work
korekushon	collection
ukiyoe	*ukiyoe,* a kind of woodblock print produced in the seventeenth, eighteenth, and nineteenth centuries
hanga	woodblock print
chookoku	sculpture
nihonga	Japanese painting
yooga	Western painting
gaka	painter, artist
fude	brush for painting or calligraphy
bideo	videotape

456

katami	memento of the deceased
shoogakusei	elementary school student
jugyoo	class session
kenkyuu	research
kikoo	climate
uru	to sell
bikkuri suru	to be surprised
shookai suru	to introduce
hitsuyoo	necessary
daitai	generally
sonna	that kind of
soo iu	such

RENSHUU

A. Mark the statements T (true), F (false), or X (cannot tell) on the basis of the dialogue.

1. *Oomae san no repooto wa seiyoo no bijutsu ni kansuru mono desu.*
2. *Oomae san wa natsuyasumi ni Bosuton no bijutsukan ni ikimashita.*
3. *Mizushima san wa repooto no shiryoo o atsumeru tame ni Bosuton e iku tsumori desu.*
4. *Mizushima san wa Oomae san ni bideo o kashite moraoo to omotte imasu.*

B. Three people answered the following question. Fill in the blanks using *tame ni*.

Q: *Dooshite Nihon e iku n desu ka.*
A: 1. _____, *Nihon e iku n desu.*
  In order to study Japanese
 2. _____, *Nihon e iku n desu.*
  In order to teach English
 3. _____, *Nihon e iku n desu.*
  In order to see my friends

C. For each situation below, choose from among the following English phrases, and fill in the blanks with the appropriate form.

went back, is sick *(byooki)*, is too expensive, is free *(hima)*

situation
1. *Kyoo inu wa nani mo tabemasen deshita.*
   → *Inu wa* _____ *yoo desu ne.*
2. *Ane wa ima nani mo shite imasen.*
   → *Ane wa* _____ *yoo desu ne.*
3. *Dare mo ano e o kaimasen.*
   → *Ano e wa* _____ *yoo desu ne.*
4. *Abe san wa ofisu ni imasen deshita.*
   → *Abe san wa* _____ *yoo desu ne.*

D. Fill in the blanks.

1. a: *Tenrankai ni iku koto ga arimasu ka.*
   b: *Ee,* _____ *no benkyoo no* _____ *ni tokidoki iku n desu.*
   Yes, I sometimes go to [exhibitions] study fine art.
2. a: *Saikin kisei saremashita ka.*
   b: *Iie, isogashikute, kisei suru* _____ *ni wa* _____ *n desu.*
   No, I am too busy to go back to my hometown.
3. a: *Osokatta desu ne.*
   b: *Ee,* _____ *noni, sanjuppun mo matta n desu.*
   Yes, I waited as long as thirty minutes to get a taxi.

E. Fill in the blanks with *kanji* based on the *hiragana*.

1. a. うちを_____ったそうですね。

   　　　　　か

   b. いいえ、_____りたんです。

   　　　　　　か

2. a. _____いつ_____まるか_____めましょうか。

   　こんど　　　　　あつ　　　　　　　　き

   b. ええ、_____みはどうですか。

   　　なつやす

458

F. Rewrite the following sentences using "———— *koto ga arimasu.*"

Example: *tokidoki, nihongo no shinbun o yomimasu.*
→ *tokidoki, nihongo no shinbun o yomu koto ga arimasu.*

1. *yoku tomodachi to kabuki o <u>mimasu</u>.*
2. *tokidoki, eiga no nihongo ga <u>wakarimasu</u>.*
3. *tokidoki, Tookyoo no tomodachi no uchi e <u>ikimasu</u>.*

KARUCHAA NOOTO

Japan is rich in various kinds of works of fine arts. Japanese artists today follow either the Japanese or the Western tradition of painting. The Japanese tradition originated in China and was introduced to Japan many centuries ago. The Western tradition was introduced to Japan as late as the nineteenth century. Both traditions have produced prominent artists.

During the Edo era (seventeenth to nineteenth centuries), *ukiyoe* became popular. Literally *ukiyoe* means "picture of the floating world." They are mostly woodblock prints, many of them depicting beautiful women, kabuki actors, or scenery. The collected works on Mt. Fuji by Katsushika Hokusai, for example, are regarded as masterpieces. With the modern era in the nineteenth century came the trend to prefer Western art over Japanese art. At that time, *ukiyoe* were regarded as cheap works and sold accordingly. Now, however, they are highly regarded again.

KOTAE

A. 1. X 2. T 3. F 4. T
B. 1. *Nihongo o benkyoo suru tame ni* 2. *Eigo o oshieru tame ni*
3. *Tomodachi ni au tame ni*
C. 1. *byooki no* 2. *hima na* 3. *takasugiru* 4. *kaetta*
D. 1. *bijutsu, tame* 2. *wake, ikanai* 3. *takushii ni noru*
E. 1. a. 買

    b. 借

  2. a. 今度、集、決

    b. 夏休
F. 1. *yoku tomodachi to kabuki o miru koto ga arimasu.* 2. *tokidoki, eiga no nihongo ga wakaru koto ga arimasu.* 3. *tokidoki, Tookyoo no tomodachi no uchi e iku koto ga arimasu.*

DAI SANJUU KYUUKA
Lesson 39
HON'YA. Bookstores.

A. DAIAROOGU

KANDA NO FURUHON'YA DE.

The following is a conversation between an elderly store owner and one of her regular customers, a young man who teaches at a university.

SHIMA: **Konnichi wá.**

SHUJIN: **Ára, hisashiburi ne. Shibáraku miénai kara, dóo shitá no ka to omótteta n desu yo.**

SHIMA: **Kyóoto no daigaku de koogí o tanomáreta node, Tookyoo to Kyóoto no aida o ittári kítari shitetá n desu yo.**

SHUJIN: **Isogáshikute, taihen ne.**

SHIMA: **Ée . . . Kyóo wa imooto no tamé ni kíta n desu. Imootó ga *Hiratsuka Ráichoo Shuu* o katte kíte kurétte iú n da kedo, sonná no arimásu ka.**

SHUJIN: **Kono kóonaa ni joséigaku no hón takusan áru n desu kedo, Hiratsuka Ráichoo no wa nái yóo desu ne. Súgu hitsuyoo ná n desu ka.**

SHIMA: **Íma sotsuron o káiteru n da kedo, sore ga súgu iru rashíi n desu.**

SHUJIN: **Toriyoseraréru ka mo shirenái kara, áto de renraku shimásu.**

SHIMA: **Sóo desu ka. Onegai shimásu . . . Shibáraku kónai aida ni ironná no ga háitteru yóo desu ne.**

SHUJIN: **Ée, senséi no suki sóo na no ippai áru deshoo.**

SHIMA: **Sono uchi yukkúri mí ni kimásu.**

SHUJIN: **Sóo, jáa mata.**

AT A USED-BOOK STORE IN KANDA.

SHIMA: Hello.

OWNER: Oh, it's been a long time. I was wondering what had happened to you because you hadn't come in for a while.

SHIMA: I was asked to lecture at a university in Kyoto, and I've been traveling back and forth between Tokyo and Kyoto.

OWNER: You must be busy.

SHIMA: Yes, I guess I am. I came for my sister today. She asked [asks] me to go buy *A Collection of the Works of Hiratsuka Raicho.* Do you have that?

OWNER: There are many books on women's studies in this corner, but Hiratsuka Raicho's don't seem to be here. Does she need it right away?

SHIMA: She's writing her thesis, and I understand that she does [need it right away].

OWNER: I may be able to order it, so I'll let you know later.

SHIMA: Okay. Thank you . . . During the time I haven't been here, a lot of new books seem to have come in.

OWNER: Yes, I'm sure there are many that you'd like to read, aren't there?

SHIMA: One of these days, I'll be able to take some time to browse through them.

OWNER: Okay, see you later.

B. BUNPOO TO YOOHOO

1. PLAIN COMMANDS

Plain commands are formed as follows.

VOWEL VERBS: The final *-ru* is replaced by *-ro*.

taberu	→	*Tabero.*	Eat.
okiru	→	*Okiro.*	Get up.
kureru	→	*Kure.* (irregular)	Give it to me.

CONSONANT VERBS: The final *-u* is replaced by *-e*.

iku	→	*Ike.*	Go.
hashiru	→	*Hashire.*	Run.

IRREGULAR VERBS:

suru	→	*Shiro.*	Do it.
kuru	→	*Koi*	Come.

Negative plain commands add *na* to the dictionary form.

iku	→	*Iku na.*	Don't go.
makeru	→	*Makeru na.*	Don't be defeated.

These commands are harsh and are not commonly used, although men may use them in a casual situation or when they're trying to sound tough. Also, you may find them in a telegram, a proverb, a poem, directions on a test, or in other forms of impersonal communication.

Sugu kaere. (telegram)
Come back right away.

Tetsu wa atsui uchi ni ute. (proverb)
Strike while the iron is hot.

Kanji o kake. (test directions)
Write *kanji*.

Using a plain command form in the middle of a sentence is possible, too. This usage is more common than placing it at the end of a sentence, and both men and women do so, especially when quoting someone else's command or request.

Imooto ga Hiratsuka Raichoo Zenshuu o katte kite kurette (=kure to) iu n desu.
My younger sister asked me to go buy *A Collection of the Works of Hiratsuka Raicho*.

Chichi ga sankoosho wa furuhon'ya de kae to iu n desu.
My father tells me to buy reference books at used-book stores.

Kurai heya de hon o yomu natte (=na to) shikatta n desu.
I told [scolded] him not to read [books] in the dark [room].

2. ENUMERATION

To list more than one action or state, use TARI forms.

Tookyoo to Kyooto no aida o ittari, kitari shiteta n desu.
I was going [and coming] back and forth between Tokyo and Kyoto.

To generate a TARI form, attach *-ri* to the plain past form.

VERBS:

kaita	wrote	→	*kaitari*
nonda	drank	→	*nondari*

I-ADJECTIVES:

ookikatta	was big	→	*ookikattari*
takakatta	was expensive	→	*takakattari*

THE COPULA:

datta	→	*dattari*

Although most often two TARI forms are juxtaposed, it is possible to use just one to mean "or something." It is also possible to use more than two TARI forms. The last TARI form is usually followed by *suru*.

Kono hen no kikoo wa atsukattari, samukattari shite, yoku kawarimasu.
The climate in this area often changes between hot and cold.

Byooki dattari shite, korarenai toki wa renraku shite kudasai.
When you can't come because you're sick [or something], please tell me.

3. MALE AND FEMALE SPEECH

As discussed before, there are many differences between male and female speech. Further differences are:

a. The copula in the present affirmative

When the sentence particle *ne* or *yo* is used in a sentence in plain style, women drop the copula in the present affirmative (*da*), while men do not.

Hisashiburi ne. (female)
Hisashiburi da ne. (male)
　　I haven't seen you for a long time.

Ano hon wa besutoseraa yo. (female)
Ano hon wa besutoseraa da yo. (male)
　　That book is a best-seller.

　　b. Interjections

Ara, meaning "oh" or "my goodness," is used only by women.

Ara, hisashiburi ne.
　　Oh, I haven't seen you for a while.

The male equivalent is *yaa* or *are*. *Are* shows more surprise than *yaa*.

Yaa/Are, hisashiburi da ne. (male)
　　Oh, I haven't seen you for a while.

Are can be used by women, too.

Ara/Are kono hyooshi yabureteru wa. (female)
　　My goodness, this [book] cover is torn.

4. *IRU* "TO NEED"

With *iru* "to need" (as with *aru* "to have," *wakaru* "to understand," or *dekiru* "can do"), the Japanese noun whose English equivalent is the direct object is followed by *ga*, not by *o*.

Ima sotsuron o kaite iru n da kedo, sono hon ga iru rashii n desu.
　　She is writing her thesis, and I understand that she needs that book.

Hon ga takusan aru kara, honbako ga iru n desu.
　　Since I have so many books, I need a bookcase.

Kashihon'ya de hon o kariru noni, gakuseishoo ga irimasu ka.
　　In order to borrow books at the rental bookstore, do we need our student IDs?

5. COMPOUND NOUNS

Some *i*-adjectives and nouns can form compound nouns. The final *-i* of the adjective is dropped.

furui ido　　　　　　old well　　　　　*furuido*　　　　　　old well

Often the compound noun has a different meaning than the adjective and noun phrase.

furui hon	old book	*furuhon*	used book
yasui mono	inexpensive thing	*yasumono*	cheap [poorly made] thing

furuhon'ya de totemo furui hon o kaimashita.
I bought a very old book at a used-book store.

Bazaa de yasui mono o ippai kaimashita. Demo yasumono ja nai desu yo.
I bought many inexpensive things at the bazaar. But they are not cheap things.

C. MOJI

1. DIALOGUE

島 　　　「今日は。」

主人 　　「あら、ひさしぶりね。しばらく 見えないから、
　　　　　どうしたのかと 思ってたんですよ。」

島 　　　「京都の 大学で こうぎを 頼まれたので、東京と 京都の
　　　　　間を 行ったり 来たり してたんですよ。」

主人 　　「忙しくて、たいへんね。」

島 　　　「ええ、今日は いもうとの ために 来たんです。
　　　　　いもうとが 「ひらつからいちょうしゅう」を 買ってきて
　　　　　くれって 言うんだけど、そんなの ありますか。」

主人 　　「このコーナーに じょせい学の 本 たくさん
　　　　　あるんだけど、ひらつからいちょうのは ないようですね。
　　　　　すぐ ひつようなんですか。」

島 　　　「今 そつろんを 書いてるんだけど、それが すぐ いる
　　　　　らしいんです。」

主人 　　「とりよせられるかも しれないから、あとで れんらく
　　　　　します。」

島　　　　「そうですか。お願いします。」…

　　　　　「しばらく 来ない 間に、いろんなのが 入っているよう
　　　　　ですね。」

主人　　　「ええ、先生の 好きそうなの いっぱい あるでしょう。」

島　　　　「そのうち ゆっくり 見に 来ます。」

主人　　　「そう、じゃあ また。」

2. NEW *KANJI*

[136]	主	*SHU*	main e.g., 主人
[137]	京	*KYOO*	capital (of a nation)
[138]	都	*TO*	capital (of a nation) e.g., 京都
[139]	頼	*tano(mu)*	to request
[140]	東	*TOO*	east e.g., 東京
[141]	願	*nega(u)*	to wish

STROKE ORDER

[136]	丶 十 丰 主
[137]	亠 古 亨 亨 京
[138]	土 耂 者 者 都
[139]	一 口 市 束 束 軒 軒 軺 頼
[140]	一 冂 曰 車 東 東
[141]	厂 厂 厇 原 願 願 願

D. TANGO TO HYOOGEN

furuhon	used book
furuhon'ya	used-book store
kashihon'ya	rental bookstore
besutoseraa	best-seller
hyooshi	(book) cover
honbako	bookcase
joseigaku	women's studies
gakuseishoo	student ID
koogi	lecture
cf. **kooen**	public lecture
koonaa	corner (of a room or store)
tetsu	iron (metal)
ido	well (for water)
furuido	old well
bazaa	bazaar
yasumono	cheap (poorly made) thing
aida	distance, space
uchi ni	while, within
toriyoseru	to order/get merchandise
yabureru	to tear (intransitive)
utsu	to strike, to hit
mieru	to come (respect)
tanomu	to request, to order
iru	to need (consonant verb)
ironna	various (informal form of *iroiro na*)
ippai	a lot (more informal than *takusan*)
ara, are, yaa	oh
Hisashiburi desu ne.	I haven't seen you for a long time.

RENSHUU

A. Mark the statements T (true), F (false), or X (no way to know) on the basis of the dialogue.

  1. *Kono hon'ya wa Tookyoo ni aru.*
  2. *Shima sensei wa Tookyoo no daigaku de shinrigaku o oshiete iru.*
  3. *Shima sensei wa Hiratsuka Raichoo no hon o kai ni kita.*

B. Your doctor has given you some advice. Fill in the blanks according to the English statements, imagining that you are telling an acquaintance what the doctor said to you.

Examples: Come again tomorrow (also).
Ashita mo koi to iwareta n desu.
Don't take a bath today.
Kyoo ofuro ni hairu na to iwareta n desu.

1. Take this medicine.
_____ *to iwareta n desu.*
2. Don't eat meat.
_____ *to iwareta n desu.*
3. Go to bed early.
_____ *to iwareta n desu.*
4. Don't drink coffee.
_____ *to iwareta n desu.*

C. What do you do in the following situations? Fill in the blanks with TARI forms according to the English words in parentheses.

1. *boonenkai* (drink beer, sing songs)
_____ *shimasu.*
2. *oshoogatsu* (eat rice cakes, play *karuta*)
_____ *shimasu.*
3. *hirooen* (have a feast, take pictures)
_____ *shimasu.*

D. Mark the statements M, F, or X depending on whether the speaker is male, female, or either.

1. _____ a: *Ano biru rippa da ne.*
_____ b: *Subarashii desu nee.*
2. _____ a: *Kore omoshiroi hon ne.*
_____ b: *Demo, yomu noni jikan kakaru yo.*
3. _____ a: *Are, ame ga furisoo desu ne.*
_____ b: *Hayaku kaetta hoo ga ii ne.*
4. _____ a: *Biiru nomu?*
_____ b: *Ee, itadaku wa.*

E. Fill in the blanks with *kanji* based on the *hiragana* below.

1. あの_____の_____に_____んであげましょうか。

みせ　　　しゅじん　　　たの

2. ええ、お_____いします。

ねが

468

F. Describe what you will do over the weekend using the TARI form of the given verbs.

Example: eat, drink; *shuumatsu, watashi wa tabetari nondari shimasu.*

1. swim, run
2. see Kabuki, go to a concert
3. study, read books
4. play, meet my friends

KARUCHAA NOOTO

The Japanese enjoy reading books and magazines. Japanese newspapers have numerous book and magazine advertisements. Magazine advertisements are especially elaborate and include detailed tables of contents. There are a large number of bookstores in Japan, and many department stores and supermarkets also sell books and magazines. Not surprisingly, the relationship between the store owner and regular customers tends to be more personal in small stores than in big ones. Kanda, a part of Tokyo, contains many kinds of bookstores, including many used-book stores, where you may enjoy searching for valuable old books.

KOTAE

A. T 2. X 3. T
B. *Kono kusuri o nome* 2. *Niku o taberu na* 3. *Hayaku nero* 4. *Koohii o nomu na*
C. 1. *Biiru o nondari, uta o utattari* 2. *Omochi o tabetari, karuta o shitari* 3. *Gochisoo o tabetari, shashin o tottari*
D. 1. a: M b: X 2. a: F b: M 3. a: X b: M 4. a: X b: F
E. 1. 店、主人、頼

   2. 願

F. *shuumatsu, watashi wa* 1. *oyoidari hashittari shimasu.* 2. <u>*kabuki o mitari konsaato ni ittari*</u> *shimasu.* 3. *benkyoo shitari hon o yondari shimasu.* 4. <u>*asondari tomodachi ni attari*</u> *shimasu.*

DAI YONJUKKA
Lesson 40
SHIKA. Poetry.

A. SELECTED POETRY

HAIKU.

The following are two well-known *haiku* poems by Basho, a seventeenth-century *haiku* poet. *

Furuike ya kawazu tobikomu mizu no oto

Araumi ya Sado ni yokotau ama-no-gawa
　　　—Matsuo Bashoo

GENDAISHI.

The following poem is from the collection of poems *Arare* by Senke Motomaro, a twentieth-century poet.

　　　Ochiba
Yamaji o aruite yuku to
Ima ochita bakari no
Kiiroi hoo no ha ga go-rokumai
Shinagutsu no yoo ni sorikaette
Michi ni sanran shite ita
Aa kono adeyaka na iro no mezamashisa
Marude dare ka tootoi hitotachi ga
Kutsu o nugisutete
Suashi de satta
Yume no shiin no ato no yoo na shizukasa
　　　—Senke Motomaro

* You can find other translations of Basho's *haiku* in the following books: Aston, W. G. Aston. *A History of Japanese Literature*. Tokyo: Charles E. Tuttle Company, 1972; and Keene, Donald. *Anthology of Japanese Literature*. New York: Grove Weidenfeld, 1955.

HAIKU.

An old pond, a frog jumps in, the sound of the water.

What a rough sea, the Milky Way, which lies on Sado Island.
  —Matsuo Basho

MODERN POETRY.

    Fallen Leaves
When I went walking on the mountain road
Five or six yellow *hoo* leaves
That had just fallen
Bent like Chinese shoes
Were scattered about on the road.
Oh, how spectacular this fascinating color was!
How quiet it was as if it were a trace of a dream scene
From which some nobles kicking off their shoes
Had left barefoot!
  —Senke Motomaro

B. BUNPOO TO YOOHOO

1. CLASSICAL AND MODERN JAPANESE

While most prose is written in modern Japanese, poetry is often still written in classical Japanese. The two *haiku* poems introduced are written in classical Japanese, and the modern poem in modern Japanese. Since you do not need to learn about classical Japanese in detail at this stage, a few notes will suffice.

a. *Ya*

Ya is a particle expressing exclamation or excitement.

Furuike ya.
  What an old pond it is!

Araumi ya.
  What a rough sea it is!

b. *Yokotau*

Yokotau is a verb meaning "to lie." The modern equivalent is *yokotawaru*.

Sado ni yokotau ama-no-gawa
the Milky Way, which lies on Sado Island

2. PARTICLES

a. *Bakari* "just"

To express that an action has just occurred, use the particle *bakari* between the plain past affirmative of the verb and the copula.

Sado ryokoo kara kaetta bakari desu.
She has just returned from a trip to Sado.

Ano shijin wa ano koro, hajimete no shishuu o dashita bakari de, mada namae wa shirarete inakatta.
Around that time, that poet had just published his first collection of poems, and his name was not known yet.

Ochita bakari no ha ga michi ni sanran shite iru.
The leaves that have just fallen are scattered about on the road.

b. *De* (for circumstances)

De describes how or under what circumstances an action is performed.

Suashi de satta.
They left barefoot.

Hitori de kurai michi o arukimashita.
I walked along a dark road by myself.

Minna de tanka o benkyoo shimashita.
We studied *tanka* poems together.

c. *Ni* (with *yokotawaru*)

With the verb *yokotawaru* (*yokotau* in classical Japanese) "to lie (down)," the noun referring to location is followed by *ni*.

Sado ni yokotau ama-no-gawa
the Milky Way, which lies on Sado Island

Neko ga yuka ni yokotawatte, nete iru.
The cat is lying down on the floor sleeping.

3. *YOO* "AS IF"

Yoo "to seem" (see Lesson 38, B3) can also refer to what is contrary to the fact and mean "as if." *Yoo* "as if" follows a noun plus *no* or, less commonly, the plain form of a verb. *Yoo* operates like a *na*-adjective: it is followed by the copula, which changes its form as it does with a *na*-adjective. Compare (1) and (2).

(1) A: *Ongaku ga kikoemasu ne.*
   I hear music.

   B: *Nihon no ongaku no yoo desu ne.*
   It sounds like Japanese music. [It seems that it is Japanese music.]

(2) A: *Kore wa Tai no ongaku desu.*
   This is Thai music.

   B: *Nihon no ongaku no yoo desu ne.*
   It sounds as if it were Japanese music [but it's not].

Haiku no yoo na mijikai shi desu.
   It is a short poem like a haiku.

Kiiroi ha ga shinagutsu no yoo ni sorikaette, michi ni sanran shite ita.
   Yellow leaves, bent like Chinese shoes, were scattered about on the road.

The adverb *marude* "exactly like" is often used in a sentence with *yoo* for emphasis.

Marude otona ga kaita yoo na zuihitsu desu.
   It is an essay that looks as if an adult wrote it.

4. COMPOUND VERBS

a. *Suteru* "with"

In a limited number of cases, *suteru* "to throw away" is attached to the pre-*masu* form of a verb to form a compound meaning "to do such and such and not care what happens after that."

Dare ka tootoi hitotachi ga kutsu o nugisutete, suashi de satta.
   Some noble people left barefoot, having kicked off their shoes.

Doroboo wa kuruma o norisutete, nigete shimatta.
   The thief got out of the car [leaving it there], and fled.

b. *Komu* "with"

Komu, which is not used by itself any longer, originally meant "to hide." The combination of the pre-*masu* form of a verb and *komu* means "to immerse (oneself or something) in something completely."

Kaeru wa mizu ni tobikomimashita.
The frog jumped into the water.

Man'in no kyuukoo ni norikonda.
I struggled into the packed express train.

5. SOUND CHANGES IN COMPOUND WORDS

If the second element in a compound word starts with a voiceless consonant, it often becomes voiced.

shinagutsu	Chinese shoes	←	*Shina* *	China	+ *kutsu*	shoes
ama-no-gawa	the Milky Way	←	*ama* † *-no*	heaven's	+ *kawa*	river
ochiba	fallen leaf	←	*ochi-* (pre-*masu* form of *ochiru* "to fall")		+ *ha*	leaf
haizara	ash tray	←	*hai*	ash	+ *sara*	plate
hondana	bookshelf	←	*hon*	book	+ *tana*	shelf

C. MOJI

1. SELECTED POETRY‡

HAIKU

古池や、かわず　とびこむ　水の音

あらうみや、さどに　よこたう　あまのがわ

--まつお　ばしょう

---

* Now China is called *Chuugoku* instead of *Shina*, but the compound word *shinagutsu* is still used.

† *Ama*, which means "heaven" or "sky," is not used by itself in modern Japanese.

‡ The original works are written in the old writing system. Not all the *kanji* in the original works are used here.

山路を　歩いて　ゆくと

今　おちたばかりの　ほおの　はが　五、六枚

しなぐつのように　そりかえって

道に　さんらんしていた。

ああ、このあでやかな　いろの　めざましさ

まるで　だれか　とうとい人たちが

くつを　ぬぎすてて

すあしで　さった　夢の　シーンの　あとのような　しずかさ。

　　　　--せんけ　もとまろ

2. HIRAGANA

ほお (not ほう)　a kind of tree

3. NEW KANJI

[142]	池	*ike*	pond
[143]	音	*oto*	sound
[144]	路	*ji*	road e.g., 山路
[145]	歩	*aru(ku)*	to walk
[146]	枚	*MAI*	counter for flat things e.g., 一枚
[147]	夢	*yume*	dream

STROKE ORDER

[142]	氵 氵 汋 池
[143]	一 立 立 音
[144]	口 ߱ 묘 뫔 몯 趵 趵 路
[145]	ㅏ ㅓ 止 屮 ホ 歩
[146]	木 木 朾 杖 枚
[147]	艹 苧 苩 莔 夢 夢

4. NEW READING

[102] 道   *DOO* (Lesson 33)   road, way

      michi   road, way

D. TANGO TO HYOOGEN

haiku	haiku
tanka	tanka
zuihitsu	essay
shi	poem
shijin	poet
shishuu	collection of poems
yume	dream
yamaji	mountain road (poetic)
ama-no-gawa	the Milky Way
araumi	rough sea
shiin	scene
ha	leaf
ochiba	fallen leaf
hoo	a kind of tree
yuka	floor
furuike	old pond
kaeru	frog
kawazu	frog (poetic)
shinagutsu	Chinese shoes
hai	ash
haizara	ashtray
tana	shelf

hondana	bookshelf
suashi	barefoot
ato	trace
man'in	full of people, packed to capacity (noun)
Tai	Thailand
sanran suru	to be scattered about
saru	to leave
nigeru	to run away
suteru	to throw away
yuku	to go (more archaic than *iku*)
yokotawaru	to lie (down)
sorikaeru	to be bent
nugu	to take off (clothes or shoes)
tootoi	noble
mezamashii	fascinating
adeyaka	spectacular
marude	exactly like
hajimete no	first

RENSHUU

A. Answer the following questions based on the two *haiku* and the poem "Fallen Leaves."

Haiku
1. *Doko ni kaeru wa tobikonda n desu ka.*
2. *Ama-no-gawa wa doko ni yokotawatte iru n desu ka.*

Ochiba
3. *Ochiba wa nanmai gurai arimashita ka.*
4. *Ochiba no iro wa naniiro deshita ka.*
5. *Ochiba wa nan no yoo ni miemashita ka.*

B. Match each phrase in Group I with one in Group II to form a sentence.

I	II
1. *Haru no yoo ni*	a. *shiroi desu.*
2. *Kaeru no yoo ni*	b. *nihongo o hanashimasu.*
3. *Nihonjin no yoo ni*	c. *joozu ni oyogimasu.*
4. *Umi no yoo ni*	d. *aoi desu.*
5. *Yuki no yoo ni*	e. *nimotsu ga takusan arimasu.*
6. *Yama no yoo ni*	f. *atatakai desu.*

C. Choose from the words below, and fill in the blanks with the appropriate form.

shokuji suru, tsuku, okiru

1. a: *Moo asagohan o tabemashita ka.*
   b: *Iie, ima ———— bakari desu.*
2. *denwa de*
   a: *Ima doko ni iru n desu ka.*
   b: *Ima Aomori ni ———— bakari na n desu.*
3. a: *Onaka suitenai n desu ka.*
   b: *Ee, ima ———— bakari na n desu.*

D. Match the *kanji* in Group I with the associated word in Group II.

	I		II
1.	池	a.	きっぷ
2.	枚	b.	ねる
3.	歩	c.	水
4.	音	d.	行く
5.	夢	e.	聞く

E. Write the following dialogue using *kanji*.

a. きょう、きょうとえきから あるいて かえったんです。

b. みちは どうでしたか。

c. きや はなが おおくて、たのしかったですよ。

KARUCHAA NOOTO

The tradition of Japanese poetry reaches back to ancient times. Among the different kinds of poetry, *haiku* and *tanka* are still popular today. *Haiku* have seventeen syllables consisting of phrases of five, seven, and five syllables. Matsuo Basho is perhaps the best-known *haiku* poet. *Tanka* have thirty-one syllables consisting of phrases of five, seven, five, seven, and seven syllables. Even in contemporary *haiku* and *tanka*, classical Japanese is often used. Poetry in modern Japanese (such as *Ochiba* "Fallen Leaves" in the text) became popular in the early twentieth century. Famous poets include Takamura Kotaro, Muro Saisei, and Miyazawa Kenji. You can find many poetry clubs in Japan where amateur poets get together and enjoy reading and writing poetry.

A. 1. *Furuike ni tobikonda n desu.* 2. *Sado ni yokotawatte iru n desu.* 3. *Gorokumai arimashita.* 4. *Kiiro deshita.* 5. *Shinagutsu no yoo ni miemashita.*
B. 1. f   2. c   3. b   4. d   5. a   6. e
C. 1. *okita*   2. *tsuita*   3. *shokuji shita*
D. 1c, 2a, 3d, 4e, 5b

E. a. 今日、京都駅から 歩いて 帰ったんです。   b. 道は どうでしたか。
c. 木や 花が 多くて、楽しかったですよ。

FUKUSHUU 8

A.   Choose the correct word in parentheses.

1. a: *Ano hon'ya de nani ka (katta/kau) koto ga arimasu ka.*
      Have you ever bought anything at that bookstore?
   b: *Iie, otto wa (itta/iku) koto ga aru rashii n desu kedo.*
      No, [I understand that] my husband goes there sometimes.
2. a: *Ano kawa de (oyoida/oyogu) koto ga dekimasu ka.*
      Can we swim in that river?
   b: *Ee, Yamada san ga (oyogu/oyoida) koto ga arutte ittemashita yo.*
      Yes, Mr. Yamada said he has swum there.

B.   Figure out what the following compound words mean.
      (The second element has undergone a sound change.)

1. *hidokei*
2. *hokengaisha*
3. *yukigeshiki*
4. *koohiijawan*
5. *kodomobeya*

C.   What do you say in the following cases? Choose from among the expressions below.

What do you say when:
1. somebody comes home?
2. you remember something?
3. you return home?
4. you are surprised?

a. *Tadaima.*
b. *Aa, soo, soo.*
c. *Gomendo kakemasu.*
d. *Okaerinasai.*
e. *Bikkuri shimashita.*
f. *Hisashiburi desu ne.*

D. Fill in the blanks with particles. Do not use *wa*.

1. *Kamera wa katta _____ de, mada tsukatte imasen.*
   I just bought the camera, and I haven't used it yet.
2. *Shinrigaku no sankoosho _____ iru n desu kedo, doko _____ kaemasu ka.*
   I need a reference book on psychology, so where can I buy one?
3. *Hitori _____ kabuki _____ mi _____ itta n desu.*
   I went to see the kabuki performance alone.
4. *Ano resutoran wa udon mo aru _____, osushi mo aru shi, yoku iku n desu.*
   Since that restaurant has noodles, and what's more, it has sushi, I often go there.

E. Mark the statements T (true) or F (false) on the basis of the following:

Bashoo wa Edo jidai (Edo era) *no hito desu. Haiku o takusan tsukuri-mashita.* <u>*Oku no hosomichi*</u> *to iu tabinikki* (travelogue) *wa yuumei desu. Kono tabinikki ni haiku mo takusan kakimashita. Edo (Tookyoo) kara kita ni iki, Matsushima ya Hiraizumi o tootte, minami ni iki, Oogaki ga shuuten deshita.*

1. In his *Oku no Hosomichi*, Basho wrote many *haiku*.
2. His journey started in Kyoto.
3. He visited Matsushima.
4. His journey ended in Edo.

F. Fill in the blanks with *kanji* and *hiragana* according to the English equivalents.

1. a. _____に_____を する つもりですか。

   While you are in Tokyo, what do you plan to do?

   b. _____たり、_____の_____へ

   _____たり したいんです。

   I want to do things like studying Japanese and going to temples in Kyoto.

2. a. ＿＿＿＿＿＿＿＿＿をたくさん＿＿＿＿＿＿＿＿＿いるんですね。

You have many kimonos, don't you?

b. ええ、でも、＿＿＿＿＿＿＿のに＿＿＿＿＿＿＿するので、

いつも＿＿＿＿＿＿＿は いかないんです。

Yes, but since I have a hard time putting them on, I can't
always wear them.

G. Write *kanji* incorporating the following parts (=classifiers/radicals).
Write as many *kanji* as possible.

氵

辶

亻

艹

宀

KOTAE

A. 1. a: *katta*   b: *iku*   2. a: *oyogu*   b: *oyoida*
B. 1. sundial   2. insurance company   3. snowy scenery   4. coffee cup
5. children's room
C. 1d   2b   3a   4e
D. 1. *bakari*   2. *ga, de*   3. *de, o, ni*   4. *shi*
E. 1. T   2. F   3. T   4. F
F. 1. a. 東京にいる間、何

    b. 日本語を勉強し、京都、お寺、行っ

 2. a. 着物、持って

    b. 着る、苦労、着るわけに

G. 決、池

  遠、近、道

  何、使、休、借

  花、茶、若、苦、夢

  主、京

YOMU RENSHUU

サラリーマンの あさ

私は 東京の 会社に つとめている サラリーマンである。うちは JR[1]
のえきから 遠いので、毎日 えきまで じてんしゃに のって行き、
７時１５分の きゅうこうに のる。このきゅうこうは いつも
こんでいて、のるのに たいへんである。今日は あさねぼうして[2]、
あさごはんを 食べる 時間が なかったので、東京に ついてから、
えきの 中に ある きっさてんで トースト[3]を 食べた。きっさてんは
私のように しゅっきんの 前に あさごはんを 食べに 入った 人たち
で いっぱいだった。会社の しごとは おもしろいが、つうきん[4]の
ために 時間が かかるので、ほんとうに つかれてしまう。

はやくちことば[5]

なまむぎ[6]、なまごめ[7]、なまたまご[8]
ぼうず[9]が びょうぶ[10]に じょうずに ぼうずの 絵を かいた。

TANGO TO HYOOGEN

1.	J R	JR Line
2.	あさねぼうする	to oversleep
3.	トースト	toast
4.	つうきん	commuting to work
5.	はやくちことば	tongue twisters
6.	なまむぎ	raw wheat
7.	なまごめ	raw rice
8.	なまたまご	raw egg
9.	ぼうず	monk (archaic)
10.	びょうぶ	folding screen

APPENDICES

A. ACCENTS

Japanese accents words through pitch, while English does so through stress. An accented syllable is high pitched, and the syllable immediately next to it is low pitched. In the dialogues throughout this book, an accent mark (e.g., *á*) is used to denote a drop in the pitch directly after the accented syllable. This accent mark is not part of the regular Japanese spelling, but we use it to facilitate pronunciation. Here are some hints for understanding the pitch system in standard Japanese.

1. In an unaccented word of any given length, the pitch is held even, except on the first syllable, where it is lower.

		L	H	H	H	(H = high, L = low)
gakusei	student	ga-	ku-	se-	i	

2. In words that are accented on the first syllable, the pitch drops directly after the accented syllable and is then maintained for the rest of the word.

		H	L	L	L
dáijin	minister	da-	i-	ji-	n

3. On words that are accented on the second or any syllable thereafter, the high pitch starts immediately after the first syllable and ends only after the accented syllable. The low pitch is then maintained through the end of the word.

okáasan	mother	L	H	L	L	L
		o-	ka-	a-	sa-	n
reizóoko	refrigerator	L	H	H	L	L
		re-	i-	zo-	o-	ko
kawairashíi	cute	L	H	H	H	H	L
		ka-	wa-	i-	ra-	shi-	i

It is possible for the last syllable to be accented. In this case, particles following the word are pronounced with a low pitch. Compare:

UNACCENTED		ACCENTED	
hana	nose	*haná*	flower
hashi	end	*hashí*	bridge

Let's take the first pair above as an example. In both of the words, *ha* is low pitched and *na* is high pitched, so they cannot be distinguished when pronounced in isolation. However, when you use a particle such as *mo* "also" after the words, the accentual difference shows up. Compare:

L	H	H		L	H	L	
ha -	*na*	*mo*	nose also	*ha* -	*na*	*mo*	flower also

Note also that more than one word may form a cluster to become one accentual unit.

H	L	L		L	L	L	L	
ka	i	te		ku	da	sa	i	Please write it.
L	H	H		H	H	H	L	
a	ke	te		ku	da	sa	i	Please open it.

Note that the accentuation in this text doesn't illustrate this phenomenon. Standard Japanese originated in a dialect spoken in uptown Tokyo. Since being designated as standard Japanese in the nineteenth century, it has become widespread through the mass media and compulsory education. While standard Japanese is understood by everyone, many regional dialects are still spoken in Japan. Although the different dialects have different accentual systems, these differences do not cause serious communication problems among speakers of different dialects.

B. PARTICLES

The numbers in brackets refer to the lesson in which the particle is introduced.

bakari "has just ..." [40]

dake "only" [39]

de "at/in" [2,23]; "among/in" (in superlatives) [24,25]; "because of" [6]; "totalizing" [22]; (for circumstances) [40]; duration *de* "within/in" [19]; means of an action *de* [4]; plain present negative *de* "Please don't ..." [22]

demo "or something/for example/perhaps" [16]

e destination *e* "to" [1]

ga subject *ga* [4]; (double noun phrase construction) [4,26]; direct object *ga* (with most of potential verbs optionally replacing *o*) [20]; "but/and," (softener) [20]; with the following words:
... *ga aru* "to have ..." [6]; ... *koto ga aru* (experience) [16]; ... *koto ga aru* (occasional actions or situations) [38]; ... *ga dekiru* "can do ..." [6]; ... *ga hoshii* "want ..." [7]; ... *ga iru* "need ..." [39]; ... *ga kikoeru* "can hear ..." [20]; ... *ga mieru* "can see ..." [20]; ... *ga wakaru* "understand ..." [6];

hodo "to the extent that ..." [25]

ka A *ka* B "A *or* B" [7]; A *ka* B *ka* "whether A or B ..." [37]; question word *ka* [27]; (question marker) [1, 34]; question word ... *ka* [37]; ... *ka mo shirenai* [37]

kana "I wonder ..." [34]

kara location and point of time *kara* "from" [12]; giver *kara* "from" [11]; "because ..." [9, 10]; "after ..." [16]

kashira "I wonder ..." [34]

kedo, keredo, keredomo "but/and" (softener) [3, 4, 27]

made "as far as ..." [12]; "until" [12, 34]

made ni "by" [14]; "by the time when ..." [34]

mo "also/either" [1, 6, 7, 21]; "as many as/as much as/as long as" [23]; even if .../even though ..." [22]; question word *mo* [28]; question word *de mo* [29]; question word TE *mo* [30]; ... *ka mo shirenai* [37]; A *mo* B *mo* "both A and B/neither A nor B" [10]

nado "etc." [25]; "anything like ..." [30]

nagara "while ..." [36]

ne (tag question marker, judgment, opinion) [4, 34]; (softener) [33, 36]

ni	point of time *ni* "at/on/in/during" [9]; "to" (destination/goal *ni*) [15]; *o* pre-*masu* form *ni naru*: (respect) [26]; ... *mae ni* [24]; ... *toki ni* [27]; ... *aida ni* [36];"per" [19]; actor in a passive sentence *ni* "by" [28]; causee in a causative sentence *ni* [33]; receiver *ni* "to" [11, 29]; giver *ni* "from" [11, 29]; pre-*masu* form *ni*: purpose [11]; *tame ni* "for" [29, 38]; with the following words: ... *ni aru* "exist in ..." [8]; ... *ni au* "meet ..." [30]; ... *ni butsukeru* "hit something against ..." [19]; ... *ni denwa suru/denwa o kakeru* ("make a phone call to ..." [20]; ... *ni deru/shusseki suru* "attend ..." [21]; ... *ni hanasu* "talk to ..." [14]; ... *ni hikkosu* "move to ..." [31]; ... *ni ii/warui* "for ..." [16]; ... *ni ireru* "put something into/in ..." [22]; ... *ni iru* "exist in ..."[8]; ... *ni kaku* "write on ..." [14]; ... *ni kaku* "write to ..." [15]; ... *ni mieru/kikoeru* "looks/sounds ..." [30]; ... *ni miseru* "show something to ..." [15]; ... *ni naru* "become ..." [21]; ... *ni noru* "ride ..." [16]; ... *ni oku* "put something on ..." [14]; ... *ni shutchoo suru* "go on a business trip to ..."[31]; ... *ni sumu* "live in ..." [9]; ... *ni suru* "choose ..." [14]; ... *ni suwaru* "sit on ..." [14]; ... *ni tenkin suru* "be transferred to ..." [31]; ... *ni tsuku* "arrive at ..." [20]; ... *ni tsutomeru* "work for ..." [15]; ... *ni yokotawaru* "lie on ..." [40]; someone *ni* TE *hoshii* "want someone to" [32]; ... *koto ni naru* "be decided to ..." [31]; ... *koto ni suru* "decide to ..." [31]; ... *wake ni (wa) ikanai* (negative potential) [38]; ... *nai wake ni (wa) ikanai* (obligation) [38]
no	A *no* B (possession, relation, location) [1, 5, 6, 8]; *no* in a phone number [20]; ... *no hoo ga* (comparatives) [24]; *no* replacing *ga* optionally in a subordinate clause such as a relative clause [19, 24]; ... *no mae* "before ..." [24]; (question marker) [36]; *no* used by women (softener) [36]
node	"because ..." [27]
noni	"although ..." [27]; "in order to ..." [38]
o	direct object [1,7]; "through/ along/at" [17]; causee in a causative sentence *o* [33]; ... *o oriru* "get off ..." [16]
shi	"and what's more" [37]; reason *shi* [37]
to	A *to* B "A and B" [2]; someone *to* "with" [13]; ... *to omou/iu/kiku*, etc. (e.g., "I think ...") [19]; "when/if" [22]
toka	"such as/like" [37]

wa	(topic) [1, 5, 7, 13, 21]; (contrast) [13, 21]; (used by women) [34]; TE *wa ikenai* (prohibition) [28]; ... *nakute wa ikenai* (obligation) [31]; ... *wake ni (wa) ikanai* (negative potential) [38]; ... *nai wake ni (wa) ikanai* (obligation) [38]
ya	A *ya* B "A and B, and the like" [6]; (explanation, excitement) [40]
yo	(emphasis) [3, 34, 36]
yori	"than ..." [24, 25]
particle-like phrases	
	... *to iu* "called ..." [25]; ... *ni tsuite* "about ..." [31]; ... *ni kansuru* "related to ..." [31]

GLOSSARY

JAPANESE-ENGLISH

1. Verbs that are introduced up to Lesson 11 are listed in both dictionary form and *masu*-form. *Masu*-forms are in parentheses.
2. The symbols *c* and *v* refer to consonant verbs and vowel verbs, respectively. For definitions of these terms, see Lesson 12.
3. The abbreviations *intr* and *tr* refer to intransitive verbs and transitive verbs, respectively.
4. The symbols *i* and *na* represent *i*-adjectives and *na*-adjectives, respectively.
5. The numbers to the right refer to the lesson in which the word is introduced.

A

a(a) *oh*	1
abunai *(i) dangerous*	19
achira *that way*	14
adeyaka *(na) spectacular*	40
agaru *(c) to step up, rise, go up*	18
ageru (agemasu) *(v) to give*	11
aida *while, interval, space*	36, 39
ainiku *unfortunately*	7
aji *taste*	24
aka *red*	7
akai *(i) red*	7
akachan *baby*	10
akarui *(i) bright*	3
Akemashite omedetoo gozaimasu	
Happy New Year	21
akeru *(v) (tr) to open*	22
aki *fall, autumn*	6
akkenai *(i) short and simple*	4
aku (akimasu) *(c) (intr) to open, be vacated*	9
ama-no-gawa *the Milky Way*	40
amai *(i) sweet*	24
amari *(not) very*	5
ame *rain*	6
Amerika *USA*	2
amerikajin *American person*	2
amerikaryoori *American cuisine*	2
amu *(c) to knit*	13
anata *you (sg)*	1
anatatachi *you (pl)*	1
anatagata *you (pl)*	1
ane *older sister*	10
ani *older brother*	10
ano *that*	5
anoo *um, uh*	8
anshin (suru) *relief (to be relieved)*	28
ao *blue*	7
aoi *(i) blue*	7
apaato *apartment*	6
ara *oh*	39
arasu *(c) to damage*	19
arau *(c) to wash*	14
araumi *rough sea*	40
are *that one*	5

are *oh*	39
(Doomo) arigatoo *Thank you.*	1
(Doomo) arigatoo gozaimasu.	
Thank you very much.	1
(Doomo) arigatoo gozaimashita.	
Thank you very much (for what	
you've done).	19
Doomo *Thank you.*	1
aru (arimasu) *(c) to have, exist*	6, 8
aruku *(c) to walk*	14
asa *morning*	6
asagohan *breakfast*	3
asai *(i) shallow*	27
asatte *the day after tomorrow*	2
ashi *foot, leg*	16
ashita *tomorrow*	1
asobu *(c) to play, enjoy oneself*	13
asoko *that place*	8
atarashii *(i) new*	5
ataru *(c) to get hit*	18
atatakai *(i) warm*	6
atatamaru (atatamarimasu) *(c) (intr)*	
to warm oneself	6
atatameru *(v) (tr) to warm*	30
ateru *(v) (tr) to hit*	30
ato *remainder*	36
ato *trace*	40
atsui *(i) hot*	6
atsumaru *(c) (intr) to gather*	21
atsumeru *(v) (tr) to gather, collect*	30
au *(c) to meet*	9
ayashii *(i) threatening*	28

B

ba *field, area*	35
baa *bar*	30
ban *evening*	6
bangohan *evening meal*	2
bangoo *number*	20
bangumi *program*	13
bansoo (suru) *musical accompaniment*	
(to accompany)	30
bara *rose*	3
basu *bus*	16
basutei *bus stop*	16

489

490

sain (suru) *signature (to write a*
   signature)   11
sainoo *talent*   38
saiwai *fortunately*   16
saizu *size*   7
sakana *fish*   3
(o)sake *sake (rice wine)*   24
sakkaa *soccer*   13
sakki *a little while ago*   20
saku *(c) to bloom*   13
sakubun *composition*   36
sakuhin *piece of work*   38
sakura *cherry blossom, cherry tree*   9
sama *(suffix attached to a person's*
   name; honorific)   26
samui *(i) cold*   6
san *(suffix attached to a person's name)*   1
san *three*   3
   sangatsu *March*   9
sandoitchi *sandwich*   14
sankoosho *reference book*   36
sanpo (suru) *stroll (to take a walk)*   27
sanran suru *to be scattered about*   40
(o)sara *plate*   11
sarariiman *salaried man*   32
saru *(c) to leave*   40
sashiageru (sashiagemasu) *(v) to give*
   (humble honorific)   11
Sayonara *Good-bye*   1
seetaa *sweater*   7
seifu *government*   35
seihin *product*   31
seiji *politics*   35
   seijika *politician*   35
seikoo (suru) *success (to succeed)*   19
seiyoo *Western country*   24
   seiyooryoori *Western cuisine*   24
sekai *world*   35
seki *seat*   13
sekkaku *by making efforts*   27
sekken *soap*   25
semai(i) *narrow, not spacious*   18
sen *one thousand*   3
-senchi *centimeter* (counter)   14
sendenbu *publicity department*   15
sengetsu *last month*   6
senkoo (suru) *major (to major in)*   31
senkyo *election*   35
senmu *managing director*   32
sensei *teacher*   1
senshuu *last week*   6
sentaku (suru) (shimasu) *laundry*
   (to do laundry)   7
serifu *script, actors' lines*   37
setto *set*   11
sewa (suru) *favor (to do a favor)*   32
   (o) sewa ni naru *(c) to receive a favor*   32
   (o) sewa (o) suru *to do a favor*   32
shachoo *company president*   28
shain *company employee*   20
shakaigaku *sociology*   31
shamisen *a banjo-like musical instrument*   37
shanpuu *shampoo*   14
shashin *photograph*   4
shashoo *conductor of a train or a bus*   16
shatsu *shirt*   11

shi *four*   3
   shigatsu *April*   9
shi *poem*   40
   shijin *poet*   40
   shishuu *collection of poems*   40
shiai *tournament*   4
shibaraku *for a while*   30
   Shibaraku desu ne. *I haven't seen you for*
   a long time.   1
shichaku (suru) *trying something on*
   (to try something on)   7
   shichakushitsu *dressing room*   7
shichi *seven*   3
   shichigatsu *July*   9
shichoo *mayor*   35
   shichoosen(kyo) *mayoral election*   35
shichuu *stew*   24
shigoto *job*   10
shiharau *to pay*   30
shiin *scene*   40
shikai (suru) *chairpersonship (to preside)*   23
shikaru *(c) to scold*   28
shiken *test*   19
shiki *ceremony*   23
   shiki o ageru *(v) to hold a ceremony*   23
shikikin *deposit money*   9
shiku *(c) to spread*   26
shima *island*   24
shimaru *(c) (intr) to close*   17
shimeru *(v) (tr) to close*   7
Shina *(old name for China)*   40
   shinagutsu *Chinese shoes*   40
shinbun *newspaper*   15
shingoo *traffic lights*   17
Shinkansen *Shinkansen Line*   16
shinkon ryokoo *honeymoon*   23
shinpai (suru) *anxiety (to be worried)*   28
shinpu *bride*   23
shinrigaku *psychology*   31
shinroo *bridegroom*   23
shinseki *relatives*   21
shinsetsu *(na) kind, nice*   29
shinshitsu *bedroom*   18
shinu *(c) to die*   13
shinzen kekkon *wedding according*
   to Shinto rites   23
shinzoku *relatives*   23
shiraberu *(v) to investigate*   25
shiraseru *(v) to inform*   22
(o)shiro *castle*   16
shiro *white color*   7
   shiroi *(i) white*   7
shiru *(c) to know*   15
shiryoo *materials* (documents, records, etc.)   32
shisha *branch office*   32
shita *below*   8
shiyakusho *city hall*   17
shizuka *(na) quiet*   4
shizumaru *(c) to become quiet*   28
shodoo *calligraphy*   21
shokki *dishes*   11
shokubutsuen *botanical garden*   6
shokudoo *cafeteria*   1
shokugo *after a meal*   19
shokuji (suru) *meal (to have a meal)*   8
shooboosha *fire engine*   28

shoobu *iris* 6
shoogai *lifetime* 31
shoogakkoo *elementary school* 36
shoogakusei *elementary school child* 38
shoogi *shogi* 34
shookai (suru) *introduction (to introduce)* 38
shoosetsu *novel* 4
shooshoo *a little, for a while* 20
shootaijoo *letter of invitation* 11
shorui *document* 32
shujin *husband, master* 10
shujutsu *surgery* 19
shukkin (suru) *going to work (to go to work)* 32
shukudai *homework* 16
shukuhaku (suru) *lodging (to stay overnight)* 25
shukuhakuhi *cost of lodging* 25
shusseki (suru) *attendance (to attend)* 23
shussekisha *participant* 23
shusshinchi *hometown* 16
shutchoo (suru) *business trip (to take a business trip)* 31
shutchoo ryokoo *business trip* 2
shuto *capital* 35
-shuukan *week* (counter) 12
shuumatsu *weekend* 27
shuuri (suru) *repair (to repair)* 36
shuushoku (suru) *getting a job (to get a job)* 31
shuuten *terminal* 16
soba *vicinity* 8
sobo *grandmother* 10
sochira *there* 14
sofu *grandfather* 10
sofubo *grandparents* 28
sokkusu *socks* 11
soko *there* 8
sokutatsu *express mail* 22
sono *that* 5
soo *so* 8
(Aa) soo. *I see.* 36
(Aa) soo desu ka. *I see.* 1
(Aa) soo soo. *(oh), that's right* 12
Soo desu ne. *Let me see, well* 4
Soo desu ne. *I agree.* 11
soo iu *that kind of* 38
. . . soo desu (hearsay) 15
-soo *to look, seem* 19
soobetsukai *farewell party* 29
soogon *(na) solemn* 27
sora *sky* 7
sore *that one* 5
sore demo *still, nevertheless* 6
sore ni *besides* 16
sore ni shite mo *nevertheless, however* 6
sorikaeru *(v) to bend* 40
soroeru *(v) to trim* 14
soshite *and* 19
soto *outside* 8
sotsugyoosei *alumna, alumnus* 1
sotsuron *graduation thesis* 31
suashi *barefoot* 40
subarashii *(i) wonderful* 6
sugiru *(v) to exceed* 31

sugoi *(i) horrible* 28
sugosu *(c) to spend (time)* 25
sugu *right away* 8
sugu *easily* 18
suiyoobi *Wednesday* 9
sujigaki *plot* 37
sukaafu *scarf* 7
sukaato *skirt* 7
suki *(na) to like* 4
sukii (suru) *skiing (to ski)* 25
sukiyaki *sukiyaki* 29
sukoshi *a few, a little, for a moment* 6, 7
suku *(c) to become empty* 24
Sumimasen. *Thank you. I am sorry. Excuse me.* 1
sumu (sumimasu) *(c) to finish* 8
sumu (sumimasu) *(c) to live* 9
sumoo *sumo wrestling* 4
supootsu *sports* 13
supootsu bangumi *sports program* 13
suru (shimasu) *to do, play, make* 3, 13, 14
suru to *then* 17
(o)sushi *sushi* 2
sutairu *style* 7
suteki *(na) chic* 7
suteru *(v) to throw away* 40
sutoobu *stove* 6
suupaa *supermarket* 36
suupu *soup* 24
suutsu *suits* 7
suwaru *(c) to sit* 18
suzushii *(i) cool* 6

T

taberu *(v) to eat* 1
tabi (Japanese) *socks* 33
tabun *perhaps* 2
-tachi *(plural form for people)* 1
Tadaima. *I'm home.* 36
Tai *Thailand* 40
-tai(i) *to want to* 6
taifuu *typhoon* 28
Taiheiyoo *the Pacific Ocean* 12
taihen *hard* 16
taiin (suru) *release from hospital (to leave a hospital)* 19
taikutsu (suru) *boredom (to get bored)* 31
taipu suru *to type* 31
taitei *generally* 16
takai *(i) expensive* 3
tako *kite* 21
takusan *many, much* 6
takushii *taxi* 12
tama ni *occasionally* 16
tame ni *for, in order to* 29, 38
tanbo *rice field* 18
tanjoobi *birthday* 9
tanka *tanka poem* 40
tanomu *to request* 39
tanoshii *(i) enjoyable* 6
tanoshimi *enjoyment* 34
tanoshimi ni suru *to look forward to* 34
tashikameru *(v) to confirm* 21
tassha *(na) skillful* 37
tatami *tatami mat* 18
tatemono *building* 5

500

ENGLISH–JAPANESE

A

a little *chotto, sukoshi*
abdomen *onaka*
about *gurai, goro, ni tsuite*
absent (to be) *yasumu*
accompaniment (musical) *bansoo*
   to accompany *bansoo suru*
   accompanied (to be) *tsureru*
actor *yakusha*
address *juusho*
advertisement *kookoku*
after *igo*
afternoon *gogo*
again *mata*
ago *mae*
airmail *kookuubin*
America *Amerika*
American *amerikajin*
   American cuisine *amerikaryoori*
all right *daijoobu*
all together *minna de*
already *moo*
alumna *sotsugyoosei*
alumnus *sotsugyoosei*
always *itsumo*
and *soshite* (after verbs, adjectives, and copula),
   to (between nouns)
angry (to get) *okoru*
anxiety *shinpai*
apartment *apaato*
apparel *yoofuku*
apple *ringo*
application *oobo*
   to apply for *oobo suru*
approach (to) *chikazuku*
appropriate *tekitoo*
approximately *gurai, goro*
April *shigatsu*
area *ba, hen*
arrange on the surface (to) *naraberu*
arrive (to) *tsuku*
artistic performance *gei*
as much as possible *narubeku*
ask (to) *kiku* (a question), *tazuneru*
   (a question), *tanomu* (a request)
associate (to) *otsukiai suru*
at all *zenzen*
at first *hajime (wa)*
atmosphere *fun'iki*
attendance *shusseki*
   to attend *shusseki suru*
audible (to be) *kikoeru*
August *hachigatsu*
aunt *oba, obasan*
awful *hidoi*

B

baby *akachan*
back *ushiro*
bad *warui*
bag *kaban*

baggage *nimotsu*
bake (to) *yaku, yakeru*
baker *pan'ya*
bakery *pan'ya*
bandage *hootai*
bangs *maegami*
bank *ginkoo*
bar *baa*
barefoot *hadashi, suashi*
be (to) *da, de aru*
beauty parlor *biyooin*
become (to) *naru*
   become empty (to) *suku*
   become quiet (to) *shizumaru*
bedroom *shinshitsu*
beer *biiru*
before *izen, mae*
begin *hajimaru, hajimeru*
behind *ushiro*
bell *beru*
below *shita*
bend (to) *sorikaeru*
besides *sore ni*
best-seller *besutoseraa*
bicycle *jitensha*
big *ookii*
bill *denpyoo*
birthday *tanjoobi*
black *kuro, kuroi*
blackboard *kokuban*
blanket *moofu*
bloom (to) *saku*
blouse *burausu*
blow (to) *fuku*
blue *ao, aoi, buruu*
body *karada*
boil (to) *wakasu*
bone *hone*
book *hon*
   bookcase *honbako*
   bookshelf *hondana*
   bookstore *hon'ya*
bored (to get) *taikutsu suru*
boredom *taikutsu*
borrow (to) *kariru*
boss *jooshi*
botanical garden *shokubutsuen*
bowl *owan*
branch office *shisha*
bread *pan*
break (to) *kowasu, kowareru, oru, oreru,*
   koshoo suru
breakfast *asagohan*
bride *hanayome, shinpu*
bridegroom *hanamuko, shinroo*
bright *akarui*
brown *chairo, chairoi*
brush *fude*
budget *yosan*
build (to) *tateru*
building *biru, tatemono*
bunraku *bunraku*

bus *basu*
  bus stop *basutei*
business trip *shutchoo*
busy *isogashii*
but *demo, ga, kedo, keredo, keredomo*
button *botan*
buy (to) *kau*
by *soba, chikaku*
  by all means *zehi*
  by oneself *hitori de*
  by the way *tokoro de*

C

cafeteria *shokudoo*
call (to) *yobu*
calligraphy *shodoo*
calling card *meishi*
calm down (to) *nagomu*
camera *kamera*
can do *dekiru*
Canada *Kanada*
Canadian *kanadajin*
candidate *koohosha*
cap *booshi*
capital *shuto*
car *kuruma*
card *karuta, toranpu*
cash *genkin*
  cash registered mail *genkin kakitome*
castle *(o)shiro*
cat *neko*
cave *horaana*
ceiling *tenjoo*
centimeter *-senchi*
ceremony *shiki*
chair *isu*
chairpersonship *shikai*
change *(o)tsuri* (money)
change (to) *kaeru, kawaru*
chapel *chaperu*
charge *kakari*
cheap thing *yasumono*
cheat (to) *damasu*
cherry blossom *sakura, sakura no hana*
cherry tree *sakura, sakura no ki*
chic *suteki*
child *kodomo*
  child psychology *jidoo shinri (gaku)*
China *Chuugoku*
  Chinese *chuugokujin*
  Chinese cuisine *chuugokuryoori,*
    chuukaryoori
  Chinese shoes *shinagutsu*
choose (to) *erabu*
Christianity *kirisutokyoo*
church *kyookai*
  church minister *bokushi*
city hall *shiyakusho*
class *jugyoo, kurasu*
classical music *kurashikku*
clearly *kukkiri*
climate *kikoo*
close (to) *shimeru, shimaru*
closet *oshiire*
clothes *fuku*
coffee *koohii*

coffee shop *kissaten*
cold *samui, tsumetai*
collect (to) *atsumeru*
collection *korekushon*
  collection of poems *shishuu*
college *daigaku*
color *iro*
comb *kushi*
come (to) *kuru*
  come back (to) *kaeru, modoru*
comedy *kigeki*
commute (to) *kayou*
commuting hell *tsuukin jigoku*
company *kaisha*
  company employee *kaishain*
  company president *shachoo*
compare (to) *kuraberu*
competent *yuunoo*
complaint *monku*
complicated *fukuzatsu*
computer *konpyuutaa*
concert *ongakkai*
conditioner *rinsu, kondishonaa*
conductor *shashoo*
conference *kaigi*
confirm (to) *kakunin suru*
confirmation *kakunin*
congenial *nagoyaka*
connect (to) *tsunagaru, tsunagu*
consecutive holidays *renkyuu*
consommé *konsome*
consult a dictionary (to) *hiku*
contact (to) *renraku suru*
continue (to) *tsuzukeru, tsuzuku*
continuously *zutto*
convenience *tsugoo*
convenient *benri*
cool *suzushii*
copy *kopii*
  copy (to) *kopii suru*
corner *kado, koonaa*
costume *ishoo*
country *kuni*
  countries *kuniguni*
coupon *kuupon*
cousin *itoko*
cover *hyooshi* (book)
cram school *juku*
credit card *kurejitto kaado*
cross (to) *wataru*
crowded (to get) *komu*
cry (to) *naku*
cultivated field *hatake*
culture *bunka*
customarily *fudan*
cut (to) *kiru*
cute *kawaii*

D

damage *higai*
damage (to) *arasu*
dangerous *abunai, kiken*
dark *kurai*
data *deeta*
daughter *musume, ojoosan*
dawn *yoake*

day *hi*
the day before yesterday *ototoi*
the day after tomorrow *asatte*
the other day *kono aida*
deceive (to) *damasu*
December *juunigatsu*
deep *fukai*
decide (to) *kimeru*
definitely *hakkiri*
delighted (to be) *yorokobu*
department store *depaato*
deposit money *shikikin*
design *dezain*
desk *tsukue*
dessert *dezaato*
detailed *kuwashii*
development *hattatsu*
diary *nikki*
dictionary *jisho*
die (to) *shinu*
Diet member *daigishi*
difficult *muzukashii*
dine-in kitchen *dainingu kitchin*
dinner *bangohan*
dirty *kitanai*
dish *ryoori, shokki*
dislike (to) *kirai*
dislike very much (to) *daikirai*
division director *buchoo*
do (to) *suru, yaru*
do research (to) *kenkyuu suru*
do sight-seeing (to) *kenbutsu suru*
document *shorui*
dog *inu*
doll *ningyoo*
door *doa*
drama *engeki, geki*
draw (to) *kaku*
drawer *hikidashi*
dream *yume*
dressing room *shichakushitsu*
drink (to) *nomu*
drive *unten*
drive (to) *unten suru*
driver *untenshu*
dry (to) *kawaku*
dryer *doraiaa*

E

each *zutsu*
ear *mimi*
early *hayai*
early hour *hayaku*
earthquake *jishin*
easily *nakanaka* (in a negative sentence)
east *higashi*
easy *yasashii*
eat (to) *taberu*
education *kyooiku*
eel *unagi*
effect *kooka*
effective *kookateki*
egg custard dish *chawanmushi*
eight *hachi, yattsu*
elapse (to) *tatsu*
elect (to) *erabu*

election *senkyo*
elementary school *shoogakkoo*
elementary school child *shoogakusei*
eleven *juuichi*
end *owari, tsukiatari*
end (to) *owaru*
engine *enjin*
enjoy oneself (to) *asobu*
enjoyable *tanoshii*
enjoyment *tanoshimi*
enter (to) *hairu*
entrance *iriguchi*
envelope *fuutoo*
envious *urayamashii*
eraser *keshigomu*
essay *zuihitsu*
evening *ban*
every *mai-*
every day *mainichi*
every month *maigetsu, maitsuki*
every week *maishuu*
every year *mainen, maitoshi*
exceed (to) *sugiru*
Excuse me. Sumimasen.
exhibition *tenrankai*
exist (to) *aru, iru*
expensive *takai*
experience *keiken*
express *kyuukoo*
express mail *sokutatsu*
eye *me*

F

face *kao*
fall *aki*
fall (to) *ochiru, furu* (rain, snow)
fallen leaf *ochiba*
family *kazoku*
famous *yuumei*
far *tooi*
far place *tooku*
farewell party *soobetsukai*
fascinating *mezamashii*
father *chichi, otoosan*
favor *sewa*
do a favor *sewa o suru*
receive a favor *sewa ni naru*
fax *fakkusu*
feast *gochisoo*
February *nigatsu*
feel (to) *kanjiru*
feelings *kimochi*
fellowship *(o)tsukiai*
female sibling *onna (no) kyoodai*
fence *hei*
fever *netsu*
few (a) *chotto, sukoshi*
field *ba, tanbo* (rice field)
finally *tootoo, yatto*
find (to) *mitsukeru*
fine art *bijutsu*
finish (to) *owaru, sumu*
fire *hi*
fish *sakana*
five *go, itsutsu*
flood *koozui*

floor *yuka*
floor cushion *zabuton*
folk song *fookusongu*
foot *ashi*
for all the world *zettai (ni)*
for a while *chotto*
forget (to) *wasureru*
foreign language *gaikokugo*
foreign mail *gaikoku yuubin*
foreigner *gaikokujin*
fortunately *saiwai*
fountain *funsui*
four *shi, yon, yottsu*
foyer *genkan*
France *Furansu*
frantically *hisshi de*
free *hima*
French *furansujin*
  French cuisine *furansuryoori*
  French language *furansugo*
Friday *kin'yoobi*
friend *tomodachi*
frog *kaeru*
front *mae*
fruit *kudamono*
futon mattress *futon*

G

garden *niwa*
gas station *gasorin sutando*
gasoline *gasorin*
gather (to) *atsumaru, atsumeru*
generally *daitai, taitei*
Germany *Doitsu*
  German *doitsujin*
  German cuisine *doitsuryoori*
get (to) *morau, toru*
  get off (to) *oriru*
  get on (to) *noru*
  get up (to) *okiru*
  get used to (to) *nareru*
ghost *obake*
give (to) *ageru, kureru, yaru, sashiageru,*
  kudasaru
glasses *megane*
gloves *tebukuro*
go (to) *iku*
  go back (to) *kaeru*
  go back to one's hometown (to)
    kisei suru
  go out (to) *dekakeru, deru*
  go regularly (to) *kayou*
  go to work (to) *shukkin suru*
  going back to one's hometown *kisei*
go-between *nakoodo*
golf *gorufu*
good *ii, yoi*
  good at *joozu, tassha*
Good-bye. *Sayoonara.*
gorgeous *hade*
government *seifu*
governor *chiji*
gradually *dandan*
graduate school *daigakuin*
graduation thesis *sotsuron*
grandchild *mago*

grandfather *sofu, ojiisan*
grandmother *sobo, obaasan*
grandparents *sofubo*
gratitude *kansha, (o)rei*
gray *guree, haiiro, nezumiiro*
green *guriin, midori*
growth *hattatsu*
gubernatorial election *chijisen(kyo)*

H

haiku poem *haiku*
hair *kami*
haircut *(hea)katto*
hairdresser *biyooshi*
half *han*
hallway *rooka*
hamburger *hanbaagu*
hand *te*
handbag *handobaggu*
handkerchief *hankachi*
handsome *hansamu*
handy *benri*
hard *muzukashii, taihen*
hardship *kuroo*
  to have a hard time *kuroo suru*
harmony *choowa*
hat *booshi*
have (to) *aru, motte iru*
he *kare*
heal (to) *naoru, naosu*
healthy *genki*
hear (to) *kiku*
heaven *ten*
heavy *omoi*
hell *jigoku*
help (to) *tetsudau*
hire (to) *yatou*
history *rekishi*
hit (to) *butsukeru*
hit (to be) *ataru, butsukaru*
hold (to) *motsu*
  hold a ceremony *shiki o ageru*
home page *hoomupeeji*
hometown *shusshinchi, kuni*
homework *shukudai*
honeymoon *shinkon ryokoo*
horrible *sugoi*
hospital *byooin*
hospitalization *nyuuin*
hot *atsui*
  hot spring *onsen*
  hot water *(o)yu*
hotel *hotel, ryokan*
house *uchi, otaku*
how *doo, doo shite*
  how many, much, long, far *dono gurai/dono*
    kurai
however *sore demo, sore ni shite mo*
hungry (to get) *onaka ga suku*
hurry (to) *isogu*
husband *goshujin, shujin, otto*

I

I *boku, watakushi, watashi*
I agree. *Soo desu ne.*
I see. *(Aa) soo desu ka.*

if *moshi*
illness *byooki*
in fact *jitsu wa*
in order to *noni, tame ni*
incompetent *munoo*
inexpensive *yasui*
increase (to) *fueru, fuyasu*
inform (to) *shiraseru*
information *joohoo*
injury *kega*
insect *mushi*
inside *naka*
insurance *hoken*
interesting *omoshiroi*
international call *kokusai denwa*
international mail *kokusai yuubin*
Internet *intaanetto*
interval *aida*
interview *mensetsu*
 interview (to) *mensetsu suru*
introduce (to) *shookai suru*
introduction *shookai*
investigate (to) *shiraberu*
invite (to) *yobu*
invitation letter *shootaijoo*
iris *shoobu*
iron *tetsu*
island *shima*

J

jam *jamu*
Japan *Nihon*
 Japanese cuisine *nihonryoori*
 Japanese language *nihongo*
 Japanese person *nihonjin*
 Japanese socks *tabi*
 Japanese-style *nihonfuu*
 Japanese-style inn *ryokan*
 Japanese-style room *nihonma*
ji *character*
job *shigoto*
 get a job (to) *shuushoku suru*
joke *joodan*
journalism *jaanarizumu*
journalist *jaanarisuto*
July *shichigatsu*
jump (to) *tobu*
June *rokugatsu*
junior high school *chuugakkoo*
 junior high student *chuugakusei*
just *choodo*
juusu *juice*

K

kabuki *kabuki*
kanji *kanji character*
karaoke *karaoke*
 karaoke bar *karaoke baa*
kilometer *kiro (meetoru)*
kimono *kimono*
kind *shinsetsu*
kindergarten *yoochien*
kitchen *daidokoro*
kite *tako*
knit (to) *amu*
knock *nokku*

know (to) *shiru*
koto *koto* (musical instrument)
kyogen *kyoogen*

L

lab *rabo*
labor for (to) *hakaru*
language *kotoba*
last month *sengetsu*
last week *senshuu*
late *osoi*
 late time *osoku*
later *ato de, nochi hodo*
lately *kono goro*
laundry *sentaku*
 do laundry *sentaku suru*
law *hooritsu*
lawyer *bengoshi*
leaf *ha*
learn (to) *narau, oboeru*
leave (to) *dekakeru, deru, saru*
lecture *koogi, kooen*
left-hand side *hidari*
leg *ashi*
leisurely *nonbiri (to)*
lend (to) *kasu*
let's see *eetto, Soo desu ne.*
letter *tegami*
library *toshokan*
lie (to) *yokotawaru*
lifetime *shoogai*
like (to) *suki*
 like very much (to) *daisuki*
listen (to) *kiku*
little (a) *chotto, sukoshi*
live (to) *sumu*
living room *ima*
lively *nigiyaka*
local specialty *meibutsu*
local train *futsuu densha*
lodging *shukuhaku*
long *nagai*
look for (to) *sagasu*
look forward to (to) *tanoshimi ni suru*
lose (to) *makeru* (in games and tournaments)
lunch *hirugohan*

M

magazine *zasshi*
 magazine-publishing company *zasshisha*
magnificent *rippa*
mah-jongg *maajan*
 mah-jongg parlor *maajan'ya*
mail *yuubin*
 mail (to) *dasu*
 mailbox *posuto*
main office *honsha* (company)
mainly *omo ni*
make (to) *tsukuru*
 make a mistake (to) *hazureru, machigaeru*
 make efforts (to) *ganbaru*
 make tea (to) *ocha o tateru (during the tea ceremony)*
 make use of (to) *ikasu*
male sibling *otoko (no) kyoodai*
man *otoko no hito*

managing director *senmu*
many *ippai, ooku, takusan*
map *chizu*
March *sangatsu*
marketing research *maaketingu risaachi*
marriage *kekkon*
master *shujin*
material *shiryoo*
matter *koto*
May *gogatsu*
mayor *shichoo*
  mayoral election *shichoosen-(kyo)*
meal *gohan, shokuji*
meat *niku*
medical cost *iryoohi*
medical doctor *isha*
medicine *kusuri*
meet (to) *au*
meeting *kaigi, kaigoo*
memento *katami*
member *menbaa*
memo *memo*
memorize (to) *oboeru*
meter *meetoru*
method *hoohoo*
Milky Way (the) *ama-no-gawa*
minister *daijin*
minute *-fun(kan)* (counter)
Monday *getsuyoobi*
money *okane*
month *-gatsu* (counter)
more *moo, motto*
morning *asa*
mother *haha, okaasan*
mountain *yama*
  mountains *yamayama*
mouth *kuchi*
move (to) *hikkosu suru*
movie *eiga*
  movie theater *eigakan*
much *ippai, ooku, takusan*
mudslinging *dorojiai*
museum *bijutsukan*

N

name *namae*
namely *tsumari*
narrow *semai*
nationality *kokuseki*
near *chikai*
necessary *hitsuyoo*
need (to) *iru*
nephew *oi*
nevertheless *sore demo, sore ni shite mo*
new *atarashii*
New Year *(o)shoogatsu*
  New Year card *nengajoo*
  New Year dish *osechiryoori*
  New Year visit *(o)nenshi*
newspaper *shinbun*
next *tsugi, tonari*
  next month *raigetsu*
  next week *raishuu*
  next year *rainen*
nice *shinsetsu, ii*
niece *mei*

night *yoru*
  nightwear *nemaki*
nine *ku, kyuu, kokonotsu*
no *iie*
noble *tootoi*
noh/no *noo*
noon *hiru*
north *kita*
nothing *nani mo*
  nothing particular *betsu ni*
notification *tsuuchi*
novel *shoosetsu*
November *juuichigatsu*
now *ima*
number *bangoo*
  number one *ichiban*
nurse *kangofu*

O

obtain (to) *toriyoseru*
occasionally *tama ni*
October *juugatsu*
office *ofisu*
oh *a(a)*
old *furui*
  old well *furuido*
older brother *ani, oniisan*
older sister *ane, oneesan*
one *ichi, hitotsu*
one hundred *hyaku*
  one person *hitori*
  one-piece dress *wanpiisu*
  one thousand *sen, issen*
  one week *isshuukan*
online *onrain*
only *dake, tatta*
  only child *hitorigo, hitorikko*
open (to) *aku, akeru*
oppose (to) *hantai suru*
opposition *hantai*
orchestra *ookesutora*
order *chuumon*
order (to) *toriyoseru, chuumon suru*
ordinarily *fudan*
organizer *kanji*
other *hoka no*
  the other day *kono aida*
  the other side *mukai*
outside *soto*
oven *oobun*
overcoat *kooto*
overtime work *zangyoo*
  work overtime (to) *zangyoo suru*

P

package *kozutsumi*
painful *itai*
painkiller *itamidome*
painter *gaka*
paper *kami*
parents *ryooshin*
park *kooen*
party *paatii*
pass (to) *tooru*
pay (to) *harau*
peaceful *nodoka*

pen *pen*
pencil *enpitsu*
people *hito, hitobito*
perhaps *tabun*
person *hito, kata, mono*
personnel section *jinjika*
pharmacy *yakkyoku*
phone *denwa*
  phone number *denwa bangoo*
  phone (to) *denwa suru*
photograph *shashin*
picture *e*
pinball game *pachinko*
  pinball game parlor *pachinkoya*
pine *matsu*
pink *pinku*
place *tokoro*
plan *yotei*
plane *hikooki*
plate *(o)sara*
platform *(puratto)hoomu*
play (to) *asobu, suru* (sports), *hiku*
  (instruments)
  play tennis (to) *tenisu suru*
please *doozo*
poem *shi*
poet *shijin*
pond *ike*
poor at *heta, nigate*
polite *teinei*
political rally *enzetsukai*
politician *seijika*
politics *seiji*
popular song *ryuukooka*
pork cutlet *tonkatsu*
post office *yuubinkyoku*
post office clerk *(yuubin)*
  kyokuin
postage stamp *kitte*
postcard *hagaki*
potage *potaaju*
powdered tea *matcha*
practice *renshuu*
  practice (to) *renshuu suru*
preparation *junbi*
present *purezento*
pretty *kirei*
previously *mae*
price *nedan*
product *seihin*
program *bangumi, dashimono*
psychology *shinrigaku*
public lecture *kooen*
public phone *kooshuu denwa*
public speech *enzetsu*
publicity department *sendenbu*
publish (to) *dasu*
purple *murasaki*
put (to) *oku*
  put in (to) *ireru*
  put on top (to) *noseru*
physical exercise *undoo*

Q

quality goods *kookyuuhin*
quiet *shizuka*

quit (to) *yameru*
quite *kekkoo*

R

racket *raketto*
radio *rajio*
rain *ame*
rapidly *dondon*
read (to) *yomu*
real estate agent *fudoosan'ya*
real thing *honmono*
recall (to) *omoidasu*
receipt *ryooshuusho*
receive (to) *morau, itadaku*
recently *saikin*
reception desk *uketsuke*
receptionist *uketsuke*
recruit (to) *boshuu suru*
recruitment *boshuu*
red *aka, akai*
reference book *sankoosho*
refreshment *oyatsu*
refrigerator *reizooko*
registered mail *kakitome*
related to *ni kansuru*
relative *shinseki, shinzoku*
relatively *wari to*
relax (to) *kutsurogu*
relief *anshin*
relieved (to be) *anshin suru*
remainder *ato*
remember (to) *oboete iru*
rental bookstore *kashihon'ya*
repair (to) *naosu, shuuri suru*
reply *henji*
report *repooto*
request (to) *tanomu*
research *kenkyuu*
  do research (to)
    kenkyuu suru
reservation *yoyaku*
  make a reservation (to) *yoyaku suru*
residence *juutaku*
residential area *juutakuchi*
rest (to) *yasumu*
résumé *rirekisho*
rice *gohan, raisu*
  rice bowl *(o)chawan*
  rice cake *(o)mochi*
  rice field *tanbo*
ride (to) *noru*
right away *sugu*
right-hand side *migi*
rise (to) *agaru*
river *kawa*
road *michi*
rock *iwa*
room *heya*
rose *bara*
rural area *inaka*
run (to) *hashiru*

S

sake *sake*
salary *(o)kyuuryoo*
  salaried man *sarariiman*

salty *karai*
sandwich *sandoitchi*
sash *obi*
Saturday *doyoobi*
say (to) *iu*
scale *hakari*
scarf *sukaafu*
scathingly *koppidoku*
scattered (to be) *sanran suru*
scenery *keshiki*
school *gakkoo*
scissors *hasami*
scold (to) *shikaru*
script *serifu*
sculpture *chookoku*
sea *umi*
seamail *funabin*
season *kisetsu*
seat *seki*
secretary *hisho*
section chief *kachoo*
see (to) *miru*
sell (to) *uru*
send (to) *okuru*
senior high school *kookoo*
  senior high school student
    kookoosei
September *kugatsu*
set *setto*
seven *nana, shichi*
severely *koppidoku*
shallow *asai*
shampoo *shanpuu*
she *kanojo*
Shinkansen Line *Shinkansen*
Shinto priest *kannushi*
ship *fune*
shirt *shatsu*
shoes *kutsu*
shogi *shoogi*
  shogi piece *koma*
shopping *kaimono*
short *mijikai*
show (to) *miseru*
shrine *jinja*
sibling *kyoodai*
sight-seeing *kenbutsu*
  sight-seeing trip *kankoo ryokoo*
silent (to be) *damaru*
simple *kantan, namayasashii*
sing (to) *utau*
singer *kashu*
sit (to) *suwaru, kakeru*
six *roku, muttsu*
skiing (to ski) *sukii (suru)*
skillful *joozu, tassha*
skirt *sukaato*
sky *sora*
sleep (to) *neru*
sleepy *nemui*
sleeve *sode*
slow *osoi*
slowly *yukkuri*
small *chiisai*
snack *oyatsu*
snow *yuki*

so *soo*
so-so *maa maa*
soap *sekken*
sociology *shakaigaku*
socks *sokkusu*
solemn *soogon*
some *ikutsu ka*
  someday *itsuka*
  sometime *itsuka, kondo*
something that is talked about *wadai*
sometimes *tokidoki*
son *botchan, musuko*
song *uta*
soon *sugu, moo sugu*
sound *oto*
  sound (to) *naru*
soup *suupu*
souvenir *(o)miyage*
spacious *hiroi*
spectacular *adeyaka*
speech *kotoba*
spend (to) *sugosu*
spicy *karai*
splendid *migoto*
sports *supootsu*
  sports program *supootsu bangumi*
spread (to) *shiku*
spring *haru*
stage *butai*
station *eki*
stay (to) *iru*
  stay overnight *tomaru*
steak *suteeki*
step up (to) *agaru*
stew *shichuu*
still *mada (mada), sore demo,*
    yahari
stomach *onaka, i*
storage room *kura*
store *mise*
  store clerk *ten'in*
story *hanashi*
stove *sutoobu*
straight *massugu*
stream *ogawa*
street *toori*
strike (to) *utsu*
stroll *sanpo*
  stroll (to) *sanpo suru*
strong *tsuyoi*
student *gakusei*
  student ID *gakuseishoo*
study (to) *benkyoo suru*
studying *benkyoo*
style *sutairu*
subway *chikatetsu*
succeed *seikoo suru*
success *seikoo*
such *soo iu*
suddenly *totsuzen*
suits *suutsu*
sukiyaki *sukiyaki*
summer *natsu*
  summer vacation *natsuyasumi*
sumo *sumoo*
  sumo wrestler *rikishi*

sun *hi*
Sunday *nichiyoobi*
supermarket *suupaa*
surgery *shujutsu*
surprised (to be) *bikkuri suru*
sushi *(o)sushi*
sweater *seetaa*
sweet *amai*
sweets *okashi*
swim (to) *oyogu*
swimming pool *puuru*

T

Tadaima. *I'm home.*
take (to) *toru, tsurete iku, kakaru, nomu* (medicine)
  take a walk (to) *sanpo suru*
  take along (to) *motte iku, tsurete iku*
  take off (to) *nugu* (clothes, shoes)
  take out (to) *dasu*
talent *sainoo*
talk (to) *hanasu*
tanka poem *tanka*
tape *teepu*
taste *aji*
tasteless *mazui*
tasty *oishii*
tatami mat *tatami*
tax *zeikin*
taxi *takushii*
tea *ocha*
  tea ceremony *ocha, cha no yu, sadoo*
  tea ceremony class *sadoo kyooshitsu*
  tea ceremony party *(o)chakai*
  tea ceremony room *(o)chashitsu*
teach (to) *oshieru*
teacher *sensei*
team *chiimu*
tear (to) *yabureru*
telephone *denwa*
  telephone card *terehon kaado*
television *terebi*
temple *(o)tera*
tempura *tenpura*
ten *juu, too*
tennis *tenisu*
  tennis court *tenisu kooto*
terminal *shuuten*
terrace *engawa* (Japanese)
test *shiken*
Thailand *Tai*
Thank you. *Arigatoo gozaimasu.*
that *sono, ano*
  that is *tsumari*
  that one *sore, are*
  that way *sochira, achira*
then *soshite, kondo wa, suruto*
there *asoko, soko*
therefore *dakara*
they *karera, karetachi, kanojotachi*
thing *koto, mono*
think (to) *omou, kangaeru*
thirsty (to get) *nodo ga kawaku*
this *kono*
  this month *kongetsu*
  this one *kore*

this place *koko*
this way *kochira*
this week *konshuu*
this year *kotoshi*
threatening *ayashii*
three *san, mittsu*
throat *nodo*
throw away *suteru*
thunder *kaminari*
Thursday *mokuyoobi*
ticket *kippu, chiketto*
tight *kitsui*
time *jikan, toki*
  be on time (to) *maniau*
timetable *jikokuhyoo*
  (for transportation)
today *kyoo*
together *issho ni*
tomorrow *ashita*
tone deafness *onchi*
too bad *zannen*
tool *doogu*
top *ue*
tournament *shiai*
towel *taoru, tenugui*
town *machi*
toy *gangu, omocha*
trace *ato*
traditional *dentooteki*
traffic lights *shingoo*
tragedy *higeki*
transfer *tenkin*
transferred (to be) *tenkin suru*
translation *hon'yaku*
travel *ryokoo*
  travel (to) *ryokoo suru*
  travel agency *ryokoosha*
treat *gochisoo*
treat (to) *gochisoo suru*
treated (to be) *gochisoo ni naru*
tree *ki*
trim (to) *soroeru*
trouble *mendoo*
  get in trouble (to) *komaru*
truly *makoto ni*
Tuesday *kayoobi*
tuna *maguro*
twelve *juuni*
twenty *nijuu*
two *ni, futatsu*
  two hundred *nihyaku*
  two thousand *nisen*
type (to) *taipu suru*
typhoon *taifuu*

U

uh *anoo*
ukiyoe *ukiyoe*
umbrella *kasa*
uncle *oji, ojisan*
understand (to) *wakaru*
undesirable *iya*
unfortunately *zannen nagara, ainiku*
university *daigaku*
  university president *gakuchoo*
  university student *daigakusei*

unskillful *heta*
use (to) *tsukau*
used book *furuhon*
  used-book store *furuhon'ya*
usually *futsuu*
utensil *doogu*

V

vacated (to be) *aku*
vacation *kyuuka, yasumi*
various *iroiro*
very *amari* (in a negative sentence),
  totemo
vicinity *chikaku, mawari, soba*
videotape *bideo*
vigor *genki*
village *mura*
visible (to be) *mieru*
visit (to) *kenbutsu suru, ukagau*
voice *koe*
vote (to) *toohyoo suru*
voting *toohyoo*
  voting day *toohyoobi*

W

walk (to) *aruku*
wall *kabe*
wallet *saifu*
wait (to) *matsu*
want (to) *hoshii*
warm *atatakai*
  warm oneself (to) *atatamaru*
wash (to) *arau*
watch *tokei*
water *mizu, (o)yu*
we *watakushitachi, watashitachi,*
  wareware
wear (to) *kakeru* (glasses), *haku, kiru*
weather *(o)tenki*
  weather forecast *tenki yohoo*
Web site *webu*
wedding (ceremony) *kekkonshiki*
  wedding dress *uedingu doresu*
  wedding reception *hirooen*
  wedding according to Shinto rites *shinzen*
    kekkon
Wednesday *suiyoobi*
week *-shuukan* (counter)
  weekend *shuumatsu*
welcome party *kangeikai*
well *ido*
well *yoku*
well *eetto, saa*
well then *dewa, jaa*

west *nishi*
  Western country *seiyoo*
  Western cuisine *seiyooryoori*
  Western picture *yooga*
  Western-style *yoofuu*
  Western-style room *yooma*
what *nani*
  what kind of *donna*
when *itsu*
where *doko*
which *dono, dochira no*
  which one *dore, dochira*
while *aida, -nagara*
  a little while ago *sakki*
white *shiro, shiroi*
who *dare, donata*
why *dooshite, naze*
wife *kanai, tsuma*
win (to) *katsu, toosen suru* (election)
wind *kaze*
window *mado*
winter *fuyu*
wipe (to) *fuku*
woman *onna no hito*
women's studies *joseigaku*
wonderful *subarashii*
woodblock print *hanga*
word processor *waapuro*
work *shigoto*
world *sekai*
work (to) *hataraku, tsutomeru, shigoto suru*
work(s) *bijutsuhin* (art), *sakuhin*
wound *kizu*
write (to) *kaku*

X

X ray *rentogen*

Y

year *toshi*
year-end party *boonenkai*
yellow *kiiro, kiiroi*
yen *en*
yes *ee, hai, un*
yesterday *kinoo*
yet *mada*
you *anata, anatagata, anatatachi*
young *wakai*
younger brother *otooto, otootosan*
younger sister *imooto, imootosan*

Z

zero *rei, zero*
zip code *yuubin bangoo*

INDEX